OCLC

Plate I. Courtesy of OCLC
The bas-relief cast in bronze was presented to Frederick G. Kilgour at the dedication of the current OCLC installation in Dublin, Ohio, on September 21, 1981. It is the work of Gary W. Ross (Capital University, Columbus, Ohio) and is on permanent display in the atrium of the new Center.

OCLC
A Decade
of Development,
1967-1977

KATHLEEN L. MACIUSZKO
Baldwin-Wallace College
Berea, Ohio

Foreword by
ROBERT F. CAYTON

Epilogue by
PHILIP SCHIEBER

LIBRARIES UNLIMITED, INC.

Littleton, Colorado
1984

LIBRARIES UNLIMITED, INC.
P.O. Box 263
Littleton, Colorado 80160-0263

Permission to reprint from the following source is acknowledged.

Donald D. Spencer, Excerpts from *Computer Dictionary for Everyone*. Copyright © 1977, 1979 Camelot Publishing Company, Inc. Reprinted with the permission of Charles Scribner's Sons.

Library of Congress Cataloging in Publication Data

Maciuszko, Kathleen L. (Kathleen Lynn), 1947-
 OCLC, a decade of development, 1967-1977.

  Bibliography: p. 343
  Includes indexes.
  1. OCLC--History. 2. Library information networks--United States--History. 3. Library cooperation--United States--History. 4. Libraries--United States--Automation --History. I. Title. II. Title: O.C.L.C., a decade of development, 1967-1977.
Z674.82.015M33 1984   027.7'09771   84-3894
ISBN 0-87287-407-9

Libraries Unlimited books are bound with Type II nonwoven material that meets and exceeds National Association of State Textbook Administrators' Type II nonwoven material specifications Class A through E.

To my husband,
Jerzy (George),
without whom this book could
never have been written

TABLE OF
CONTENTS

CHRONOLOGY OF SIGNIFICANT EVENTS (cont'd)

LIST OF
ILLUSTRATIONS

Tables (cont'd)

Plates

FOREWORD
By Robert F. Cayton

It is one of the paradoxes of the library world that a profession charged with the collecting, cataloging, and servicing of information fails to record with any regularity its own history. Fortunately, Kathleen L. Maciuszko acted on her notion that the history of the first years of OCLC must not be lost. In this book she has detailed with clarity the complexities of OCLC's founding and early growth, recalled some of the people involved in its work, and provided the basic plot of the drama of the first decade of its existence.

The importance of the conception and development of OCLC to the world of librarianship, to the world of scholarship, and ultimately to the world at large should never be minimized. In the second half of the twentieth century librarians began to realize with some degree of alarm that they — and scholars and lay people as well — must have quick and ready access to the rapidly burgeoning mass of information in order to survive. Ohio academic librarians early set out in the wake of this realization to find ways of logically controlling access to information. Their explorations led them slowly but surely to founding a great servant of librarians, OCLC.

Henry James once observed that it took "a great deal of history to produce a little literature," and so it took a great deal of planning, maneuvering, and above all, imagination to conceive a vision of automated library service in the state of Ohio. Even more of these same elements were needed to evolve from this vision a tangible producer of the products and services that librarians and scholars were demanding in order to make information easily accessible.

The conception and development of OCLC were at once dramatic and complex. The drama of OCLC's birth was played on a small stage of committee meetings in Lewis Branscomb's office at The Ohio State University Library. The heat of creation kept the surface of verbalized ideas among the several Ohio librarians who were gathered in the meetings bubbling furiously at all times. The temperature of the creative mix was governed by the common-sense observations of A. Robert Rogers, the practical views of Bob L. Mowery, the all-angles approach of Arthur T. Hamlin, the wise synthesis of Lewis C. Branscomb, and the urge toward action of Robert F. Cayton.

The members of the Ohio College Association Committee of Implementation sensed that they were onto something big, but never in their wildest dreams and far-ranging discussions did they conjure up any image that would have had the form of the presently enormously successful genie called OCLC, no matter what the initials then and now denoted.

From the very beginning, it was the hope of the Committee of Implementation to improve library service in Ohio. From the beginning too, these men looked beyond Ohio, first to academic libraries, then to public libraries, and eventually to all libraries in the nation. It was their fundamental belief that OCLC must improve library service throughout the nation. The Committees' timetable for achieving this zenith of library development, if there ever was a timetable, certainly did not include the astounding rate of progress OCLC made during its first decade.

The mid-1960s proved to be a propitious time when all the stars in the library world were in the right heavens. There was at hand the technological tool in the form of the computer. There was the right director in the person of Frederick G. Kilgour, who came equipped with appropriate experience and inventiveness. There were the Ohio academic librarians ready after many years of searching for new ways to cooperate in library service to be led into a full-length drama.

Again we think of Henry James when he wrote that "any drama worth speaking of can develop but in the air of civilization." There was in the Ohio academic world in the 1960s that air of civilization that allowed for the founding and rapid developing of OCLC. The perspicacious Ohio academic librarians supported their leaders, Kilgour and his staff and the members of the early Boards of Trustees, by providing a favorable climate characterized by openness and, of prime importance, by a willingness to take a risk. This climate also included the great essential basic to any achievement on a large scale: firm, friendly financial support.

In its early years, the greatest asset of OCLC may have been its ability to respond to its clients' demands. The response was not always as swift as the clients wished, but nevertheless the saving grace of OCLC was its ability to listen to them and to plan accordingly. By necessity the process was often slowed because any movement was made by trial and error. It must be remembered that there was no map or chart that Kilgour and his Board of Trustees might follow. Indeed these people were drafting the map to follow step by step as they moved ahead. Although there were no precedents to guide them, they remained flexible and resolute enough to push ahead and to bring the drama of OCLC into an exciting third act.

Providing vital information on the history of OCLC during its first decade, this book will stand as a reminder to all that the development of OCLC is the American Revolution of the library world. As with all revolutions, it will be many years, perhaps a century, before all the far-reaching consequences of OCLC's dramatic conception and early development will be fully known by a grateful world.

PREFACE

This book traces the development of OCLC from 1967 to 1977, the first decade of its existence. The order is chronological; the underlying theme is cooperation. An attempt has been made to create a comprehensive, compact, and accurate history by bringing together between the covers of one volume all the historical facts about OCLC. This wealth of information fills an important gap in library literature by recording the birth and evolution of the nation's first large-scale computerized library system.

Although other networks had begun to take shape concurrently, OCLC was unique in the library world as the first extensive, cooperative, and fully successful venture. This book, in a very real sense, deals with the history of library networking activities in the country. By pointing to the exciting past, the author conveys her vision of a still brighter future.

The story is an exposition and not an analytical discourse. Although the book's aim is to present a factual and unbiased history, the subjective element is inevitable not only in judgment but in the choice of facts and events treated in this short synthesis.

As a practicing librarian, the author witnessed the introduction of OCLC into the cataloging department at Kent State University (Kent, Ohio). Along with the hundreds of other Ohio librarians who believed in the ideals of OCLC, she felt a sense of pride to be a part of it. Since the time of her contact with OCLC, the author did not want to lose sight of those early years. She did not want others who would follow her to forget that it all began in Ohio. This is especially significant because of the change in the meaning of the acronym, OCLC. Originally it stood for the Ohio College Library Center, founded in Columbus, Ohio, in 1967. Today it stands for the Online Computer Library Center. The Ohio identity is gone, but not forgotten. The book brings the reader back to OCLC's Ohio roots. Moreover, those early pioneers who shaped the Center's destiny and created for it a permanent place among library annuals are quickly disappearing from the scene. This book attempts to preserve their labors.

The purpose of this work is to provide librarians (especially those who are members of the OCLC family in over six thousand institutions in the United States and those who are participating through the Center's overseas branches in six foreign countries), library historians, and library school faculty and students with the complete story of OCLC's formative years as well as to provide specific information about the development of a particular service or procedure. To this end, the arrangement is chronological, and the text is furnished with detailed name and subject indices.

Each chapter is devoted to one fiscal year (i.e., July 1 through June 30), with the exception of chapter 1, which presents background information, and chapter 3, which covers a two-year time span. Chapter 10 extends beyond the fiscal year to include the new governance structure. Although for some readers it would, perhaps, have been more convenient to base each chapter on the calendar year as opposed to the fiscal year, the author chose the latter because the facts of OCLC were most often described in terms of the fiscal activities.

The book begins with a foreword by Dr. Robert F. Cayton (Marietta College librarian and professor, Marietta, Ohio). Before and after the inception of OCLC, he was actively involved with Ohio's cooperative activities, serving as secretary of the Ohio College Association Committee of Implementation (1965-1967) and as a member of the Director Subcommittee. For eight years he was a member of the Board of Trustees (1967-1974, 1977-1978) and secretary of the Corporation for six (1967-1973).

The foreword is followed by an introductory chapter by Dr. Lewis C. Branscomb (professor emeritus, The Ohio State University and former director of libraries, Columbus, Ohio) and Dr. A. Robert Rogers (dean, Kent State University School of Library Science, Kent, Ohio). In addition to his work as a member of various library committees laboring to bring OCLC to fruition, Branscomb was intimately involved as a member of the Committee of Implementation of the Ohio College Association. Following the founding of OCLC, he served as The Ohio State University representative to OCLC from 1967-1975. In the fall of 1967, he was elected the first vice-chairman of the Board of Trustees for fiscal year 1967-1968. With the death of Dr. A. Blair Knapp, first chairman of the Board, Branscomb was appointed acting chairman for the remainder of Knapp's term. During the next two years (1968-1969 and 1969-1970), he was chairman of the Board, and he was vice-chairman for yet another two years (1970-1971 and 1971-1972). Rogers, his co-author, was very active in OCLC from 1962 until 1967. During this period he served on a number of committees of the Ohio College Association, including the Committee of Implementation. He was also a member of the Board of Trustees during its early years (1967-1969). Branscomb and Rogers set the scene by providing background materials leading to the incorporation of OCLC in 1967.

The text closes with the epilogue written by Mr. Philip Schieber (public relations manager for OCLC and editor of the OCLC *Newsletter* since 1974). The book deals with the initial years (1967-1977) of the Center's development. The epilogue was added to enhance the practical usefulness of the volume, and to provide the reader with a more complete view of OCLC; it brings the story up-to-date, to 1982. A chronology highlighting major events of historical value, also by Schieber, follows the epilogue.

The historical growth and changes described in the text are further amplified and illustrated by the facts and documents contained in an extensive appendix. Although some of the materials may now be outdated, they are included for clarification of the text and for their historical value. Thus, a serious researcher cannot divorce the text from the appendix, and in a study of any given aspect of OCLC, the two should be viewed together.

Like OCLC itself, this work is a cooperative venture. The author wishes to express her deep gratitude to the following persons whose contributions made the book possible: Mr. Frederick G. Kilgour without whom there would be no OCLC today and to whom the writer is indebted for his invaluable support from the project's inception to its completion; Dr. Lewis C. Branscomb and Dr. A. Robert Rogers for their encouragement and most helpful counsel; Mr. Philip Schieber for editing the text; Mrs. Ann Ekstrom (archives and records manager, OCLC) for her expert advice and professional acumen in maintaining the integrity of the book and for supplying invaluable material; Mrs. Henriette D. Avram (director for processing systems, networks, and automation planning, Library of Congress, Washington, D.C.) for her professional assistance with the historical overview of national networking activities in chapter 2; Ms. Ann T. Dodson (manager, OCLC Library) for research assistance; Miss Patricia A. Becker (secretary to Frederick G. Kilgour) for her kind and generous help in securing the necessary materials; Mr. Chris J. Sullivan (director of Computer Center, Baldwin-Wallace College, Berea, Ohio) for his assistance in clarifying portions of the text; Susan L. Hambley (assistant music librarian, Baldwin-Wallace College, Berea, Ohio) for her skill and devotion in typing the manuscript; and the many OCLC members and staff, and the countless other individuals who in a variety of ways contributed to the book, and who due to the limited space have to remain regretfully unnamed.

A special word of gratitude is extended to Mr. Robert G. Cheshier (director, Cleveland Health Sciences Library, Case Western Reserve University, Cleveland, Ohio) for urging the author to undertake the project and for encouraging her throughout the process of writing the book.

The author would like to acknowledge the six translators of the résumés:

French   Dr. Richard K. Gardner (Directeur, École de Bibliothéconomie, Université de Montréal, Québec, Canada)

Mme Géraldine Mongeon (Secrétaire Administrative, École de Bibliothéconomie, Université de Montréal, Québec, Canada)

German   Dr. John R. Sinnema (Director, American-German Institute, Baldwin-Wallace College, Berea, Ohio)

Spanish   Mrs. Irmalicia B. Pianca (Department of Foreign Languages, Magnificat High School, Rocky River, Ohio)

Russian   Mrs. Katharina J. Blackstead (Assistant Head, Acquisitions Department, University of Notre Dame, Notre Dame, Indiana)

Mrs. Elsa Jarotski (Emerita Chief of Library Processing Services, Baker Library, Dartmouth College, Hanover, New Hampshire)

Chinese   Mrs. Tsung Tsung Hung (Reference Librarian, Baldwin-Wallace College, Berea, Ohio)

Japanese   Mrs. Ichiko Morita (Head, Automated Processing Division, University Libraries, The Ohio State University, Columbus, Ohio)

The author wishes to thank OCLC, Inc. for permission to quote extensively from both published and archival sources, and Baldwin-Wallace College (Berea, Ohio) for financial assistance in the final stages of the project.

1

THE CONCEPTION
AND BIRTH PANGS OF OCLC –
An Account of the Struggles
of the Formative Years
By Lewis C. Branscomb and A. Robert Rogers

The efforts at academic library cooperation that culminated in the creation of the Ohio College Library Center (OCLC, Inc.*) in 1967 really began no later than 1951. At that time a small group of head librarians from one municipal and several private colleges got together to cooperate among themselves so as to improve their resources and services. They were soon joined by others, including their counterparts in the largest state-assisted and private universities in Ohio. It required the strenuous, often agonizing efforts of academic librarians and college presidents, working through the Ohio Library Association and the Ohio College Association, to conceive and deliver OCLC sixteen years later.

From the perspective of the 1980s, it seems almost impossible to imagine contemporary American librarianship without the presence of this multi-million-dollar bibliographic utility which, octopuslike, has spread its tentacles to some 2,400 institutions in all fifty states and Canada. The period of phenomenal growth since 1967 has been well documented in numerous periodical articles and several monographs, but this information has not been brought together in one convenient source.[1] The earlier period of struggle to develop

*Present name is Online Computer Library Center, Inc. Lewis C. Branscomb is Professor of Thurber Studies, and former director of libraries, the Ohio State University. A Robert Rogers is dean, School of Library Science, Kent State University.

Reprinted, with one minor revision, by permission of the authors and the American Library Association from *College & Research Libraries* 42 (4): 303-7 (July 1981); copyright © 1981 by the American Library Association.

cooperative projects among the academic libraries of Ohio has not been so well chronicled. Thus, a few comments by two participants in those earlier years may be of interest.

In a sense, OCLC may be said to be the product of a century of cooperation among Ohio's colleges and universities. The Ohio College Association (OCA) was founded in 1867 with twelve charter members, including both state and private institutions.[2] The century that followed saw a fivefold growth in membership and a pattern of cooperation at the institutional level. It was within this general context that the librarians of Akron, Dennison, Kenyon, Oberlin, Ohio Wesleyan, and Wooster met in December 1951 and formed a group to explore cooperation among Ohio's academic libraries. At the time, all of these (except Akron, which was municipal) were private institutions — small, good, liberal arts colleges for the most part.

A Joint Committee on Inter-library Cooperation was formed in 1952, with representation from the Librarians' Section of the Ohio College Association and the College and University Round Table of the Ohio Library Association (OLA). The appointment of the joint committee brought several of the state university libraries into the effort, most notably Ohio State University, because Lewis C. Branscomb, director of libraries, was also chairman of OLA's College and University Round Table. Bowling Green State, Kent State, and Cincinnati (then still municipal) followed. Thus both public and private institutions became involved. Discussions centered around the need for a regional union list of serials, a book depository, and lending services — activities somewhat like those of the then relatively new (1949) Midwest Inter-Library Center (MILC), now the Center for Research Libraries. Other ideas included cooperative purchase and sharing of expensive sets and some linkage to MILC. Ralph Esterquest, then director of MILC, met with the group.

In 1953 the joint committee recommended to OCA that a survey be undertaken to determine to what extent Ohio college and university libraries could cooperate. OCA voted to sponsor the survey, but only if a foundation grant could be secured to underwrite it. The search for foundation funding was not successful, and this delayed the survey for a decade.

Another development of consequence was the formation of the Inter-University Library Council (IULC) in 1953. It consisted of the head librarians of the state-assisted university libraries in Ohio (at that time Ohio State, Ohio University, Kent, Miami, Bowling Green, and Central State). These were among the largest academic libraries in the state and their directors soon became heavily involved in the committee work that preceded the formation of OCLC.

The year 1957 saw a flurry of activity but no lasting accomplishments. A subcommittee of the joint committee (chaired by J. H. Lancaster, Ohio Wesleyan) wrote to Walter Brahm (then state librarian) in support of a new five-million-dollar building to be shared by the state library and the state historical society. Among the expanded services to be expected from the state library were: supplying to college and university libraries the same types of backup in collections and interlibrary loans furnished to public libraries; becoming a repository for infrequently used books and periodicals; promoting cooperative acquisitions among college libraries; maintaining a regional collection of federal and state documents that could relieve individual libraries of the need to retain seldom-used documents; a college library research specialist; photoduplication; coordination of the State Library Union Catalog with other bibliographic services that might become available; and studying the feasibility of a book-exchange program.[3] Nothing came of this grand design.

Another abortive effort in 1957 was the attempt to have a survey of Ohio's academic libraries included in plans for a Governor's Commission to Study Higher Education in Ohio.[4] Perhaps one clue to the failures in 1957 was opposition to a state repository from within the academic library community. John Nicholson, Jr., of Kent, in particular, was deeply concerned that the budget for such a cooperative endeavor would result in less money for the state-assisted university libraries.[5]

By 1960, matters had begun to take a more positive turn. Nicholson was appointed chairman of the joint committee and was to serve in that capacity for the next six years.

Foundation funding continued to be elusive, but the joint committee made progress in clarifying its ideas and expectations. The emphasis shifted to union catalogs as a basis for cooperation. Rivalry developed between Cleveland and Columbus as to whether the Cleveland Regional Union Catalog, primarily research-library-oriented, or the State Library Union Catalog, primarily public-library-oriented, should be the basis for further efforts. Ralph Esterquest conducted a study in which he recommended that the Cleveland Regional Union Catalog be discontinued on December 31, 1961.[6] Esterquest thought that a reduced scale of service to Cleveland and northeastern Ohio might be feasible and this was continued for several years.

Accelerated progress came in 1962 when OCA decided to use $10,000 of its own funds to finance a study to determine the feasibility of several programs of cooperation among Ohio's academic libraries. Wyman Parker, then librarian at Wesleyan University in Connecticut but familiar with Ohio through past service at Kenyon and Cincinnati, was appointed to conduct the survey. He spent two months in Ohio interviewing, traveling, analyzing returns from questionnaires, etc. He made four recommendations:

1. It is recommended that a Bibliographical Center be established by the Ohio College Association for the rapid location and procurement of books through interlibrary loan and purchase....
2. It is recommended that a separate building to house this Bibliographical Center be erected near a large university library....
3. It is recommended that a cooperative purchase program of generous proportions be inaugurated so as to secure as soon as possible a central archive of research materials on microprint....
4. It is recommended that a Director and staff for the center be secured as soon as is practical....[7]

The expenses for the bibliographical center were estimated as follows: land and building — $150,000; basic microprint stock — $150,000; possible annual budget — $60,000.[8]

In 1963 OCA approved the report in principle and then dissolved the joint committee, which was believed to have accomplished its purpose. It then formed a purely OCA committee charged with "implementation of the recommendations" made in the Parker report.[9] What could have been a problem turned out not to be. Most of the librarians were involved in *both* OLA and OCA. The new committee consisted of ten librarians, two presidents, and a provost. It was titled the Ohio College Library Project Committee.[10] It was not expected that the presidents and the provost would work actively on the committee, but their appointment was extremely important because of the weight they lent to the implementation of the recommendations. Through these top executives it was possible to have direct access to the powerful OCA Executive Committee. Without this access, it is doubtful the librarians would have succeeded in establishing the Ohio College Library Center. A. Blair Knapp, president of Denison University, was chairman and John Nicholson was executive secretary. Nicholson actually chaired most of the meetings of the committee. He resigned in 1966 and was succeeded by A. Robert Rogers.

The committee sought to publicize its work through OLA, OCA, and the institutional presidents. The latter were especially important in securing consent of college fiscal officers. The remainder of 1963 and the early months of 1964 were spent in study of various automation alternatives. No fewer than eight meetings were held in less than a year. The storm center of debate was whether there should be a microfilm-based union catalog or a computerized one. Proposals were received from IBM, Recordak, Remington-Rand, and Bibliomatics, Inc. After exhaustive review, the committee decided that the two most promising proposals were those of Recordak (microfilm) and IBM (computer). All members of the committee but one favored the Recordak proposal, partly because the estimated cost of initial installation ($383,683) was substantially lower than that proposed by IBM ($1,093,700). The advantages of each were listed by the committee as follows:

Recordak

1. Low cost of initial installation.
2. Speedy retrieval of information.
3. Ease of updating.
4. Possible location of three stations within the state.
5. Ease of operation from the operator's point of view.
6. Familiarity among librarians with Recordak film and equipment.
7. Ease of addition of new stations when desired.
8. Possibility of sale of film catalog to other libraries and other states.

IBM

1. Provision of a printed book catalog by author, subject, and title for each member library.
2. Elaborately complete updating process.
3. Complete computer system flexibility for the future.
4. Salability of printed catalogs to retrieve some of the initial cost.[11]

Because of the different views among committee members respecting the microfilm-based catalog versus the computerized one, the committee made no recommendation on this point in its proposal to the Ohio College Association in April 1964 or to the consultants, Ralph H. Parker and Frederick G. Kilgour, when they met with the committee in September and October of 1965.

When the committee's recommendations to establish a center were announced at the Librarians' Section of OCA, there were strong protests, but a majority voted to proceed. OCA itself cautiously endorsed the proposed center "in principle." Some librarians, opposed to the microfilm-based system, sent letters of protest to the presidents. A report by Verner Clapp, then president of the Council on Library Resources, to the Academy for Educational Development (for the Ohio Board of Regents) recommended that the issue be given more study. By the fall of 1964, it looked as though the whole project was dead.[12] A determined group of library directors in IULC was not about to let this happen. In 1965 they persuaded the OCA Committee of Librarians to accede to what several critics had requested — an appraisal by outside consultants respected in the library field for their expertise in library automation.

OCA agreed with this approach and provided $2,200, which enabled the committee to invite Ralph H. Parker, then director of libraries, University of Missouri, and Frederick G. Kilgour, then associate librarian for research and development, Yale University, to review the project and make recommendations. The consultants met twice with the committee in the fall of 1965 and read the considerable amount of documentation which by this time had accumulated. Parker and Kilgour proposed a new approach:

> The consultants are convinced that computerization of present library procedures on a piece-by-piece basis cannot be justified....
>
> The present proposal suggests the establishment of a cooperative, computerized regional network in which most, if not all, Ohio college libraries will participate....
>
> The first goal of the system will be to establish an effective, shared-cataloguing program based on a central computer store containing a catalogue for the current holdings of Ohio college libraries....
>
> The second function of the central store would be to provide a catalogue of holdings in Ohio college libraries which in effect would supply union catalogue information....[13]

The Committee of Librarians met in January 1966, endorsed the Parker-Kilgour report in principle, and raised some questions that were subsequently answered by the consultants. Among the more important of these were:

1. Will the machine record-kept catalog at the Center in time make the traditional catalog in each local library obsolescent?

   In all probability, the card catalog will become obsolescent in the next 15 years. But an individual library would be able to continue its card catalog with the cards prepared, ready for filing, by the regional center.

2. The Committee wished to re-check with the consultants on the possibility of any very recent developments in the automation field that would affect their thinking in this matter. In

particular, the Committee was concerned with the automation schedule of the Library of Congress.

The Library of Congress appears to be progressing rapidly in the design of its over-all automation program.

3. What format will the output in each individual library be? Will it be tape print-out, or card print-out, or will it take some other form?

The output to each individual library can take a wide variety of forms to meet the needs of a particular member. The cataloguing output might be in the form of traditional cards, might be complete catalogs in book form, or might be simply a printed index to the magnetic catalog in the Center.

4. Even though the report states that regional centers are more practical, do the consultants ever envision a time when larger libraries in Ohio would have direct lines to the Library of Congress?

With the type of organization suggested, there would be no reason why a library need have direct connections with the Library of Congress. The regional center would automatically transfer the message to the Library of Congress whenever needed.

5. Why are serials being left out initially?

The consultants have recommended the omission of serials at this time since there are problems peculiar to them both in cataloguing and in mechanization of holdings records.

6. Should contributions by local libraries to the existing state union catalog be discontinued now in view of the possibilities of this project?

Individual libraries should consider the question of discontinuing contributions to the state union catalog, but the consultants would prefer not to give a categorical *Yes* or *No* to this question.

7. The Committee is desirous of clarification of acquisitions procedures in connection with the Center. What *specifically* would be the utilization of the Center in acquisitions searching?

The individual library would have instantaneous access to the bibliographic records of all libraries in the Center from all access points now available in the traditional card catalog, from the Library of Congress card number, and from various other points such as date and place of publication.

8. The Committee would like for the consultants to be more specific concerning foundation grants. Which definite foundations might be amenable to the idea of the Center?

The consultants have been of the opinion that specific study grants ... might be obtained from either private or public sources, for example, the Council on Library Resources, the National Science Foundation, or the United States Office of Education. A grant for system design might be obtained from a combination of these same sources or possibly from Title II B of the Higher Education Act. In some cases granting agencies require that part of the cost of a project be borne by the grantee.[14]

In March 1966, the committee endorsed the plan for the Center, commended it to OCA for adoption, and authorized two of its members (Branscomb and Rogers) to meet with Chancellor John Millett of the Ohio Board of Regents to explore the regents' interest in the Center.[15] In April, incoming OCA President Novice G. Fawcett (Ohio State University) asked that information be disseminated to all presidents and librarians of OCA and this was done, with a view to seeking early endorsements from OCA institutions. By summer, a digest of the consultants' recommendations and a plan for prorating costs for the first two years had also been prepared and distributed.[16]

"On October 30, 1966, the Ohio College Association approved The Ohio College Library Center as recommended by the Committee of Librarians, the Committee of Presidents and the O.C.A. Executive Committee."[17] OCA also empowered President Fawcett to appoint a Committee of Implementation with power to: form a nonprofit corporation; employ a director; choose a location; make funding arrangements; and develop procedures for appointing a board of trustees.[18]

Victory was sweet. The Committee of Implementation and its various subcommittees worked diligently during the ensuing months and by the summer of 1967 the Ohio College Library Center was a reality, with Frederick G. Kilgour as its first director.[19]

NOTES

1. An excellent starting point is the annotated bibliography at the end of *OCLC: A National Library Network*, edited by Anne Marie Allison and Ann Allan (Enslow, 1979). OCLC's annual reports and newsletters will enable the reader to keep abreast of current developments.

2. Kathleen Lynn Post, "A History of the Ohio College Library Center, 1967-1972" (Master's research paper, Kent State University, School of Library Science, 1974), p. 9.

3. J. H. Lancaster to Walter Brahm, March 23, 1957.

4. J. H. Lancaster to the Ohio College Association, April 6, 1957.

5. John B. Nicholson, Jr., to J. H. Lancaster, April 4, 1957.

6. Ralph T. Esterquest, *The Cleveland Regional Union Catalog: A Survey*, 1961.

7. Wyman W. Parker, "The Possibility of Extensive Academic Library Cooperation in Ohio," *Transactions: Ohio College Association* (1963), pp. 26-27.

8. Ibid., p. 27.

9. Ibid., p. 3.

10. Charles S. Wesley to Lewis C. Branscomb, April 11, 1963. The Ohio College Library Project Committee was composed of: A. Blair Knapp (chairman), president, Denison University, Granville; Wanda J. Calhoun, librarian, Heidelberg College, Tiffin; John B. Nicholson, Jr., executive secretary, librarian, Kent State University,

Kent; Lewis C. Branscomb, director of libraries, the Ohio State University, Columbus; Richard K. Gardner, librarian, Marietta College, Marietta; Dorothy Hamlen, librarian, University of Akron, Akron; Arthur T. Hamlin, librarian, University of Cincinnati, Cincinnati; Mollie E. Dunlap, librarian, Central State College, Wilberforce; Lois E. Engleman, librarian, Denison University, Granville; Lyon N. Richardson, director, University Libraries, Western Reserve University, Cleveland; A. Robert Rogers, acting director of libraries, Bowling Green State University, Bowling Green; Thurston Manning, provost, Oberlin College, Oberlin; and Robert I. White, president, Kent State University, Kent.

11.   "Recommendation of Committee of Librarians of the Library Cooperation Committee to the Executive Council of the Ohio College Association." *Transactions: Ohio College Association* (1964), pp. 12-13. For more detailed information on the alternatives evaluated by the committee, see "Summary of Information Gathered and Studied by the Ohio College Association Committee of Librarians" (Ibid., pp. 6-17).

12.   For more detailed information of the controversy, see the following articles: Walter Wright, "Ohio College Association Seeks Accord on Union Catalog: Background Notes," *OLA Bulletin* 35:8-9 (July 1965); Walter D. Morrill, "A Semi-Sophisticated Machine-Assisted Union Catalog," *OLA Bulletin* 35: 10-11 (July 1965); and Frederick L. Taft, "Why Automate Without Appraisal?" *OLA Bulletin* 35:13 (July 1965).

13.   Ralph H. Parker and Frederick G. Kilgour, "Report to the Committee of Librarians of the Ohio College Association" (unpublished manuscript, OCLC Archives, 1965).

14.   Robert F. Cayton to Ralph Parker, January 17, 1966. Ralph H. Parker and Frederick G. Kilgour to Robert Cayton, February 3, 1966.

15.   "Minutes of the Meeting of the Committee of Librarians, Ohio College Association," March 11, 1966.

16.   "Ohio College Library Center," *Transactions: Ohio College Association* (Oct. 1966), p. 13.

17.   A. Robert Rogers to OCA Committee of Librarians, November 8, 1966.

18.   Ibid.

19.   Novice G. Fawcett to Presidents and Executive Committee Members, November 15, 1966.

2

ORGANIZING
THE RESOURCES
1967-1968

Before one can fully appreciate the drama of the development of the Ohio College Library Center (OCLC), one must examine the historical roots that governed its conception. A major spark that ignited the fire of activities and kept it burning was the Library of Congress (LC). (A list of acronyms is found in appendix 3 on pages 341-346.) Referred to as "the hub of the nation's bibliographic apparatus for monographs and serials,"[1] it housed a mammoth collection of materials representing a cross section of the world's knowledge. Moreover, it had gained national acclaim as the largest receiving and processing center for library materials in the nation. It offered a wide range of services to the country's libraries—the Card Distribution, the Machine-readable Cataloging (MARC) Distribution, and production of the *National Union Catalog* (*NUC*), to name but a few. Although it was never officially recognized as the national library for the United States, its involvement in nationwide networking activities was unmistakably that of a leader. Without LC there would be no OCLC.

Drawn into this whirlwind of activities were many other groups including the federal government, the Council on Library Resources, Inc. (CLR), the American Library Association (ALA), the Association of Research Libraries (ARL), together with many other professional library organizations and the whole alphabet of library networks that appeared. In varying degrees the events at LC and elsewhere overlapped, intertwined, or in some other way affected the development of OCLC from 1967-1977. The following brief historical overview of these events places the story of OCLC's first decade in its proper historical perspective.[2] The activities are grouped under four general headings: creation, acceptance, and application of machine-readable data; distribution of machine-readable data; retrospective conversion; and national networking efforts.

CREATION, ACCEPTANCE, AND
APPLICATION OF MACHINE-READABLE DATA

CLR was created and funded in 1956 by the Ford Foundation. The original intent of this independent, nonprofit organization was to support research and development in the field of libraries by providing grants either to individual libraries, library networks, or to organizations such as LC. One of its major contributions to library networking was its support of LC's Information Systems Office (ISO) MARC Pilot Project (January 1966 to June 1968), which tested the feasibility and effectiveness of LC distributing its cataloging information in machine-readable form. Under the direction of Henriette D. Avram, the project led to the creation of the MARC II format in 1968. At that time, LC was interested both in distributing its records in machine-readable form and in creating a standard format to accommodate exchange of records, a first step toward the creation of a national network. The designing of the comprehensive MARC II did, indeed, set the standard for future exchange of bibliographic information among the nation's libraries.

The year following the creation of the MARC II format was a landmark in the history of efforts toward the worldwide exchange of bibliographic data. In 1969 the International Federation of Library Associations (IFLA) called its International Meeting of Cataloguing Experts to discuss a standard bibliographic description. The result was the creation of a working party to prepare an international standard bibliographic description for monographs, establishing "a standard set of descriptive elements in a standard order using standard punctuation to separate the elements."[3] It would cut across language barriers and facilitate the identification of the elements of a record. Several years later in 1971 the first draft of the International Standard Bibliographic Description (ISBD) was published. The first standard edition was published in 1974. In the United States the drive toward standardization was given impetus by the 1974 revision of the *Anglo-American Cataloging Rules* (*AACR*) incorporating for monographs only the provisions of ISBD. Since LC used AACR as the basis for its cataloging, it was directly involved with the application of ISBD to machine-readable data.

ALA and LC had a long-standing relationship dating from 1899 when Herbert Putnam, then president of ALA, was nominated for the position of the Librarian of Congress. In 1967 this tradition continued as the fourteenth division of ALA, the Information Science and Automation Division (ISAD), was created.[4] In the early days of the MARC Distribution Service, the MARC Users Discussion Group (MUDG) was formed within ISAD. The Division was also responsible for two publications, the *Journal of Library Automation* (*JOLA*) and the *JOLA Technical Communications*. The *Journal* began with a three-year grant from CLR, and in March 1968 its first issue appeared. Frederick G. Kilgour served as the first editor. The second publication began in October 1969, and in 1973 was absorbed into *JOLA*. In cooperation with LC's ISO, ISAD published *MARC Manuals Used by the Library of Congress*, a tool to aid librarians and computer programmers in the use of the MARC II format. Over the years LC worked closely with ISAD to sponsor a number of gatherings including conferences and institutes related to library automation. Sixteen MARC institutes took place between 1968 and 1972.

Perhaps the Division's greatest contribution to the library community was its advocacy of acceptance of the MARC II format. In November 1967, a committee of ISAD unanimously recommended endorsement of the MARC II format as an ALA standard. It should be added that the MARC format structure was adopted by many other national and international agencies. Its acceptance by the library community at large was a main factor in the development of the earliest networks, including the New England Library Information Network (NELINET), the State University of New York (SUNY) Biomedical Network, Washington Library Network (WLN), and of course OCLC. The latter's first newsletter succinctly expressed the feeling of the nation's libraries with regard to the MARC II format: "The ISO staff of the Library of Congress has achieved an accomplishment that would be impossible to praise too highly. Library computerized developments, such as those envisaged by OCLC, can now move forward with much greater confidence."[5] With each year OCLC came to depend more and more on the MARC II records as the foundation for building its data base. In January 1973, Kilgour spoke to the MARC editorial staff on the value and importance of the MARC records not only to OCLC but to all the libraries in the United States.

In March of 1969 a significant event occurred that affected both LC and the library community. At this time, the United States of America Standards Institute, Sectional Committee Z39, Library Work and Documentation, approved the publication of the document entitled "USA Standard for a Format for Bibliographic Information Interchange on Magnetic Tape." On July 14, 1970, it was adopted as a United States National Standard by the American National Standards Institute (ANSI). Kilgour was a member of the Sectional Committee.

A month before the approval of the American National Standard by ANSI, LC underwent a noteworthy internal change. In June 1970 the MARC Development Office (MDO) was created with Henriette D. Avram as appointed chief.[6] It signaled a swing in emphasis at LC from the distribution of MARC data to the automation of its own technical processes. The program encompassed three areas: the expansion of the MARC Distribution Service, the creation and implementation of a core bibliographic system, and a consideration of products and services that LC provided for itself and the nation's libraries.[7]

With establishment of MDO the scene was set for the Co-operative CONversion of SERials Project (CONSER). The seeds for CONSER were sown in June 1973 at ALA's annual conference in Las Vegas. The Ad Hoc Discussion Group on Serials Data Bases (also known as the Toronto Group) held its first meeting under the financial auspices of CLR. The birth of project CONSER reflects the common interest among librarians in building a cooperative serials data base. OCLC was selected as the location for the construction of a *de facto* national serials data base. For two years it provided the computer facilities to establish and maintain the project. CLR was designated as the temporary manager of the cooperative data base until a permanent arrangement was made. The goal was to build a data base of one hundred thousand records the first year and another one hundred thousand the second. By the third year it was hoped that a permanent arrangement would be established.[8]

The CONSER project was clearly conceived:

As the project gets under way, it will work like this: a set of detailed written guidelines for establishing the record and creating the input will be promulgated, and agreement to abide by them will be a prerequisite to participation. Selected libraries with known excellence in serial records will be asked to participate; others may request participation. Those selected who already have or can arrange for terminals on the OCLC system will participate on line. This is the preferred method, but it may be possible to permit record creation off line, such records to be added to the data base in a batch mode. It is very difficult to merge serial files from different sources in this way, so an attempt will be made to find a large serials data base in machine-readable form for use as a starting point. This file would be read into the OCLC system. ...CLR will, from time to time, report progress to the community.[9]

The data base for the project was composed of machine-readable records from the LC MARC Serials data bases and the Minnesota Union List of Serials (MULS). The Pittsburgh Regional Library Center (PRLC) file was added later along with others. In 1976 the project was fully operational at LC. It was a joint American-Canadian venture. Each not only input its own records but also updated and authenticated records added by the other participants. Verified records were then distributed through LC's MARC Distribution Service.

As use of the MARC II format expanded, there was a need to create an advisory body to LC. ALA's Resources and Technical Services Division/Reference and Adult Services Division/Information Science and Automation Division (RTSD/RASD/ISAD) Committee on Representation in Machine-readable Form of Bibliographic Information (MARBI) partially met this need. It was responsible for recommending new formats and additions and changes to existing ones. Its recommendations affected not only networks but individual systems as well. In 1973, through the suggestion of LC, the MARBI committee also appointed itself the ALA MARC Advisory Committee.

There is no doubt that MARC changed the face of librarianship. Perhaps its most lasting influence was the stress it placed on standardization:

> The interest of libraries in the computer for library operations was increasing in the 1960's. The availability of cataloging data in machine-readable form supplied by LC, the need to input cataloging data locally (data not within the scope of MARC or titles not cataloged by LC), the possibility of sharing these locally generated records, the potential for using computer programs across organizations to reduce the high cost of designing and writing software, and the need for hardware capable of handling large character sets were all factors that put increased emphasis on the establishment of and conformity to standards.[10]

The creation of the OCLC Committee on Implementation of *Standards for Input Cataloging* in the early years of the Center's development proved that standardization was utmost in the minds of the country's network architects. A number of LC's standards were widely adopted by the evolving systems. Its expanded Roman-alphabet character set was one example. It was accepted by ALA, subsequently used by OCLC, and eventually applied to systems around the world. It led to the manufacture of a typewriter sphere, a print train, and a number of cathode-ray tube terminals (CRT). The country of publication and language codes created initially by LC for use in the MARC Pilot Project and modified for the MARC Distribution Service were a part of the MARC II format and were accepted as the codes for other systems.

DISTRIBUTION OF MACHINE-READABLE DATA

Following close behind the creation of the MARC II format was the founding of the LC MARC Distribution Service to handle distribution to libraries of magnetic tapes containing MARC records of currently cataloged English-language monographs. The first tape was issued in March 1969. Each tape contained approximately one thousand records.[11]

In July 1971, LC received a grant from the National Endowment for the Humanities (NEH) and CLR to launch its Cataloging in Publication (CIP) Program. Under the guidelines of CIP, books were published with prepublication bibliographic data on the verso of the title page. The records then became a part of the MARC Distribution Service. The purpose of CIP was to expedite the delivery of bibliographic data to libraries. In 1974 Congress approved the allocation of government funds to the project.

The MARC formats were gradually expanded. By 1973 LC was distributing records for films, serials, maps, and French-language monographs. LC had not yet begun to put records for either music or manuscripts into machine-readable form. The UNIMARC format was published in 1977 for international exchange.[12] In 1975, LC began to distribute records for German, Spanish, and Portuguese books. In June 1975, LC agreed to exchange machine-readable records with the National Library of Canada. The National Library of Canada distributed its own records in the Canadian format. Through the agreement with LC, it would send its records to LC, which would then distribute them to U.S. subscribers in the U.S. MARC format as one of its distribution services. In August 1975, LC signed a similar exchange agreement with the Bibliothèque Nationale in Paris. The National Library of Australia also signed a similar accord with LC the next year (April 1976), followed by the British Library (October 1977).

RETROSPECTIVE CONVERSION

Soon after the completion of the MARC Pilot Project, LC embarked on a new one. There was great interest at LC in expanding the scope of the MARC tapes to include its retrospective cataloging data. The success of the MARC Distribution Service led not only LC but many libraries in the nation to consider the conversion of their entire catalogs to a machine-readable form. In November 1968, CLR approved a grant to LC to support a three-month project to determine "the feasibility of a large-scale centralized conversion of retrospective cataloging records and their distribution to the library community."[13] The same month an advisory committee was appointed at LC to provide guidance. Kilgour served on this committee. With funds it received from CLR and the U.S. Office of Education (OE), LC launched the REtrospective CONversion Pilot Project (RECON) in August 1969. The two-year experiment allowed LC to convert to machine-readable form a total of fifty-eight thousand records not included in the ongoing MARC Distribution Service. Together with RECON, LC became the first to create and use automatic identification of data elements in a machine-readable record (format recognition).

Beginning in December 1972, CLR sponsored a series of meetings attended by representatives from eleven organizations, including OCLC. The group gathered "to discuss the implications of bibliographic data bases being built around the country and the possibilities of sharing these resources."[14] The outcome of these discussions was the formulation of recommended modifications and additions to the MARC format that created the basis for a national exchange of bibliographic information. The meetings prompted LC to submit a request to CLR for funds to coordinate the CO-operative MAchine-Readable Cataloging (COMARC) Project.

In 1975, LC began its pilot project COMARC. It was designed "to test the feasibility and utility of accepting from outside sources, records in the MARC format for books cataloged by LC but outside the scope of MARC."[15] It involved a process of comparing and updating:

> The access points will be compared and updated against the LC official Catalog, and the records distributed as a separate service. Participants will be selected on the basis of record completeness in bibliographic content and adherence to the MARC format. In addition, if the NUC symbol for the holding library is included in the record, it will be posted to LC's automated Register of Additional Locations (RAL).[16]

The project ended in May 1978 proving that retrospective conversion of LC cataloging records through a cooperative project was possible, but not cost-effective in the environment in which the project took place. When it began, a number of OCLC member institutions were involved in local conversion activities. The Center had been unable to sponsor its own concerted conversion program. However, in 1977 it became a significant participant in the project.

NATIONAL NETWORKING EFFORTS

Attempts to harness the nation's bibliographic resources and create a national information network gained momentum in the 1970s. A number of events contributed to the movement. The National Commission on Libraries and Information Science (NCLIS) was established in 1970 as the President's Commission to advise him on information services across the United States. It was composed of librarians, information scientists, and other notables in the field.

Also in 1970, the Conference on Interlibrary Communication and Information Networks was held to set goals for library cooperation. Jointly sponsored by OE and ALA, it laid the intellectual foundation for large-scale cooperation.

Another significant event was the Conference on National Bibliographic Control held on April 17-20, 1974. Sponsored by the National Science Foundation (NSF) and CLR, it was attended by individuals representing a diversity of interests related to national bibliographic control. It included librarians, publishers, and those active in formulating standards. Quite naturally, OCLC was among those represented. The objective of the conference was "to provide a solid, progressive framework of approved objectives to constitute a series of working programs for all concerned in the foreseeable future. These programs would be codified and widely circulated and would facilitate participation by producers, disseminators, and using agencies or individuals."[17] The purpose was to increase "understanding and acceptance of the logical role each has to play."[18]

Based upon the recommendations of the Conference attendees, the Conference grew into the Advisory Group on National Bibliographic Control, sponsored by CLR, NSF, and NCLIS.[19] The Advisory Group established a number of working parties. The first two were the Working Party on Formats for Journal Articles and Technical Reports and the Working Party on Bibliographic Name Authority Files. The Formats Working Party met for the first time on July 15-16, 1975. The next month the Working Party on Files met. The importance of the parties was succinctly stated in an article appearing in the December 1975 issue of *JOLA* that read in part: "The activities of these and future parties constitute efforts leading toward the development of some of the building blocks from which ultimately will evolve a national system."[20]

A national information web began to be formed around the mid-1970s. *Toward a National Program for Library and Information Services: Goals for Action* was released in 1975 by NCLIS. It advocated the creation of a national system to bind the wide variety of information systems at all levels. LC was seen as the vital link to its creation: "The participation of the Library of Congress is crucial to the development of a National Program and to the operation of the nationwide network because it has the capacity and the materials to perform many common services in both the areas of technical processing and reference and because it can set the national bibliographic standards for the program."[21] The report was designed to serve as a springboard for seeking federal legislation and financial support to accomplish its recommendations.

In the fall of 1975, LC and NCLIS received funds to conduct a study to define in what areas and to what extent LC would be involved in a national network. As the calendar year drew to a close, LC was completing work on *The Role of the Library of Congress in the Evolving National Network* (published in 1978). The report clearly suggested that LC become the prime coordinator in the network development activities. Moreover, it recommended that a series of meetings be held to develop the specifications for the telecommunications and computer architecture for the system as well as to determine its organizational structure.

The creation of an office for the Special Assistant for Network Development, which was later renamed the Network Development Office (NDO), and the appointment of Henriette D. Avram as its head in 1976 signaled a serious intent by LC to participate actively in the creation of a national network blueprint.

In 1976 a giant step forward was taken. Acting on the invitation of the Deputy Librarian of Congress, William J. Welsh, representatives from major operational networks, including OCLC, and leaders of the major forces in the nation's networking activities met at LC to discuss a variety of network issues. At the second meeting in August 1976, Welsh asked the group to serve as an advisory body to LC. From that date forward the group became known as the Network Advisory Group (NAG).

One of NAG's earliest recommendations was the creation of a task force of technical experts to design the network architecture. In addition it recommended that LC conduct a study to ascertain the hardware requirements for the system, along with a number of other details. Another recommendation called for the creation of a subcommittee to examine the organizational and managerial aspects of the system. After nearly a year of working together, NAG met for the last time on April 11-12, 1977. Shortly thereafter, the Librarian of Congress, Daniel J. Boorstin, created the Network Advisory Committee (NAC).

NAC first met on November 28-29, 1977. The membership remained unchanged from that of NAG except for the addition of some new members. Many subcommittees were created; Kilgour was a member of one working on the legal and organizational structure of a nationwide network. NAG was important because it represented a concerted effort on the part of the various groups to talk to one another about the complex issues involved with the national coordination of library and information services.

In March 1977, before the dissolution of NAG, its preliminary edition of a working paper was released under the title *The Library Bibliographic Component of the National Library and Information Service Network*. It was followed by a revised edition issued in June entitled *Toward a National Library and Information Service Network: The Library Bibliographic Component*, which was presented and discussed in an open session at the ALA annual meeting in Denver in July 1977. It was based on the document originally produced by NCLIS (*Toward a National Program*). However, it was more limited in scope, covering primarily the exchange of bibliographic resources among libraries.

While NAC was busy establishing its goals, objectives, and agendas for future meetings, several other activities were underway. CLR was preparing "a five-year development plan for a comprehensive, computerized bibliographic system for review by several foundations that had an interest in library service."[22] Members of CLR served on NAC, and its proposed program can be traced to the advisory committee's planning paper and work in progress at NDO. The plan received the necessary funding, and in November 1978 CLR's Bibliographic Service Development Program (BSDP) was established.

Upon the recommendations of NAC, the Network Technical Architecture Group (NTAG) was formed to formulate hardware and telecommunications needs for a national library network. Kilgour represented OCLC as a member of NTAG. It was composed of technical experts from the various network organizations using automated systems. In 1977 and 1978, NTAG met a number of times and in 1978 published its general requirements in the *Message Delivery System for the National Library and Information Service Network*. Submitted to NAC for review, it was approved in May 1978. The group was then charged with formulating the detailed requirements, and as a result, a proposal was sent to CLR for funding. In time the project became a part of CLR's activities related to BSDP. NTAG's general requirements were used by CLR as a basis in developing BSDP.

The Research Libraries Group (RLG) Pilot Project was of direct interest to NTAG:

> The Research Libraries Group, whose members include the libraries of Columbia University, Harvard University, and Yale University and the New York Public Library, has established a computer-to-computer link between the facilities at the New York Public Library and the Library of Congress. After searching their own data bases, users at RLG libraries can direct queries to the LC MARC data bases via on-line terminals; if the record is found, it is transmitted on-line to the computer facility at the New York Public Library, where it is subsequently processed and added to the RLG data base.[23]

NTAG saw in the project a valuable source of data relative to its own work and the formation of the national network design, particularly if such a project could be expanded to include other systems. From the technical standpoint the project was significant as "the first step toward bidirectional links between library computer systems."[24]

The outcome of events described in the previous paragraphs represents the writing of a new chapter in librarianship. By 1977, the manuscript remained unfinished. To bring together all of the nation's bibliographic resources contained in its libraries under the aegis of one national network seemed an insurmountable task. The two necessary ingredients were still lacking: a willing and capable coordinating agency and assiduous cooperation.

Consider now the activities in Ohio in 1967 and the vital and exciting role that OCLC took upon itself in library history. The ten-member Committee of Implementation[25] was composed of academic librarians and administrators. In the formative stage of OCLC its role was paramount. The selection of Frederick G. Kilgour as its first director was perhaps its most monumental and far-reaching decision. Lewis C. Branscomb, a member of the Director Subcommittee[26] of the Committee of Implementation, prepared a working paper entitled "Search for a Director of the New Ohio College Library Center." It outlined the basic qualifications of a director. He or she should be a librarian of national repute who understood the problems and potentials of library computerization, and who had both knowledge and interest in information science or computer programming. Thirty-eight persons were invited to consider the position. The group of candidates was narrowed to nine, then to five, and finally to two. The Subcommittee then made a recommendation to the Implementation Committee. On July 11, 1967, Kilgour accepted the position as director of OCLC. His arrival marked the first major event in OCLC's history.

The second such event took place at Denison University on October 25, 1967, when the first annual meeting of the membership was called to order. As of that date, OCLC had forty-eight paid members.[27] The intent of the meeting was to fulfill the corporate organizational requirements of the Center according to the laws of the State of Ohio. It recognized the Articles of

Incorporation and adopted the Code of Regulations of the Center.[28] This meeting established OCLC as a corporate organization. As stated in the Articles of Incorporation, the Center's purpose was

> ...to establish, maintain and operate a computerized regional library center to serve the academic libraries in Ohio (both state and private) and designed so as to become a part of any national electronic network for bibliographical communication; to develop, maintain and operate a shared cataloging program based upon a central computer store; to create, maintain, and operate a computerized central catalog (inventory) of books and journals in the participating libraries; and to do such research and development related to the above as are necessary to accomplish and to extend the concept.[29]

The meeting elected the required nine members to the Board of Trustees.[30] The Code of Regulations of the Center provided that the members of the Board hold staggered three-year terms. The Board held its first meeting following the first annual meeting of the membership. The trustees elected A. Blair Knapp (Denison University) as chairman; Lewis C. Branscomb (The Ohio State University) as vice-chairman; Robert F. Cayton (Marietta College) as secretary; and Bob L. Mowery (Wittenberg University) as treasurer. Kilgour reported at the meeting that he had visited one third of the member libraries since assuming the post of director. He presented a detailed development program for the Center in five major areas: shared cataloging, bibliographic information retrieval, circulation control, serials control, and technical processing.

The shared cataloging system would be implemented first because it was the foundation on which the total library system was to be constructed. It would result in the creation of a large data base of bibliographic information recording the holdings of each member library, and was viewed as a way to once and for all eliminate duplicate descriptive cataloging in Ohio academic libraries. Kilgour believed that a fully implemented program of shared cataloging could be operational by 1970, and he strongly urged that members begin immediately to explore the possibilities for data processing in their respective member libraries. He urged librarians to keep themselves well-informed on new library techniques by continuously reviewing the literature in the field, and to be prepared for impending changes.[31]

The remaining four development areas would be logical outgrowths of the shared cataloging system. A bibliographic information retrieval system would enable library users to secure, with speed and accuracy, references on subjects. However, before subject retrieval could be achieved, all of OCLC's member libraries' holdings would need to be a part of the huge data base used in the shared cataloging system. Automated circulation control, serials control, and technical processing systems[32] would complete the picture of a library system built upon a central data base and computer technology. In an automated circulation control system, the computer would serve as the bookkeeper. The vast amount of record keeping involved in maintaining and updating a library's serial records file could be alleviated by computer applications. Serials records could be stored in the shared cataloging memory bank. A member library would access the memory bank by using a computer terminal console; it would be able to input its holdings and receipts. The combined record of all members would create a second large data base. An automated technical processing system could offer relief to the clerical aspects of acquisitions by again making use of the shared cataloging memory bank.[33]

A research program was also an integral part of the system. Kilgour shared with the membership at the first meeting his belief that there was a great need for research in such areas as "duplicate processing, identification of a statewide core collection, and a local library's extrainstitutional information activities."[34]

The Board of Trustees gave its stamp of approval to the detailed program for development that Kilgour had presented *in extenso* to the membership. It also approved the research program and a budget for 1967-1968 for the expenditure of $66,428 from an anticipated income of $66,462. Most importantly, in June 1968, the trustees approved a statement of two principal goals of OCLC: to increase resources for education and research to faculty and students, and to decelerate the per-student cost in member colleges and universities. To achieve these goals the Board foresaw the need to use library and new library-like information servicing techniques, which included dial-up installations, audiovisual centers, television stations, closed-circuit television, computation centers, and computer-assisted instruction. Since the traditional library was prevalent among OCLC members, the Board agreed that the emphasis in planning and development had to be on services associated with traditional library operations.

In April 1968, the director presented a paper at the Sixth Annual Clinic on Library Applications of Data Processing at the University of Illinois.[35] The main purpose of the Clinic was to provide a forum for discussion and reports on major advancements and experience in the field of data processing. Kilgour's vision of the early stages of system design at OCLC was almost prophetic.

According to him, OCLC was using a newer system design approach. As the classic library system differed from the modern system so did the newer system's design differ from older varieties of management planning. The choice of appropriate objectives was especially important. Three objectives for OCLC were cited: academic library participation in educational and research programs; development of OCLC as a prototype node in a national network; and system design capable of evolvement into a more complex system containing bibliographic information and textual material.[36]

To accomplish its first objective, the Center would have to work on a system that would enable academic libraries to become directly involved in their institutional programs. In the words of Kilgour, "Resources necessary to attract research-oriented faculty and to support independent work by undergraduates were identified in the early stages of design of the OCLC system."[37] Availability of bibliographic resources would have to be augmented both within an institution and without it. Data would have to be furnished to a researcher or a student whenever and wherever he or she needed it. Two anticipated projects would achieve this: the bibliographic information retrieval system and the circulation control program operating remotely from the library.[38]

The second objective, that of a nationwide network, had always been a librarian's dream. The concept involved nodes containing unique information, along with interwoven subnets with smaller nodes. To undertake the design of OCLC as a regional system that could be a node in a national network was one of the Center's early decisions. Care was taken to ensure that in future years hardware, programs, and data could be duplicated in another region with minimal costs. Thus, OCLC would be a system for Ohio academic libraries that could equally operate for public or special libraries, inside or outside Ohio.[39]

In sum, OCLC was envisioned as a regional computerized library network that would fulfill three needs. First, it would make resources available to users in a manner that separately computerized libraries could never achieve; second, it would greatly expand computer capabilities as libraries joined in their computer activities; and third, it would minimize duplicate processing and thereby reduce costs of duplication and costs for the computerization of major processes in a library.[40]

The shared cataloging activity, as described by Kilgour, was the first step toward the full participation of academic libraries with their faculty and students. It was described in detail at the Conference, and in all probability was met with some raised eyebrows in the light of library tradition. As Kilgour put it, "A century ago the objectives of Ohio academic libraries were to collect, catalog, and conserve printed material; ... the real objective of an academic library is to participate in the educational and research missions of the institution of which it is a part."[41]

As described by Kilgour, the shared cataloging system would first and foremost require a competent computer. A stand-alone system using a computer was chosen. Catalog card production would be the main product. Magnetic tape records containing cataloging data for all member libraries would be used to reproduce catalog cards. After a day's business, the tapes would be remounted on a tape drive of a large computer, and the appropriate cards would be produced. Each librarian would specify how the cards were to be produced for his or her library. Cards would be promptly sent to member libraries in alphabetically arranged packs, ready for filing, with a single pack designed for a specific catalog. The system was being engineered to meet individual cataloging needs as well as to maintain a format that would be useful to other members.[42]

The Ohio State University Libraries proposed to OCLC the development of a remote catalog access and circulation system, a possible prototype for OCLC. The system was to be based on conversion of many of the data elements in each catalog record. The Ohio State University Libraries' system was to use the same machine-readable library record as the OCLC shared cataloging system. Therefore, it would not only greatly increase the value of the OCLC shared system, but would also expedite the activation of it.

According to Kilgour, the OCLC system had two inadequacies that were being resolved. The principal one was the lack of a method for organizing a tremendously large file of bibliographic records; the other was the absence of a terminal to perform the prescribed work. A CRT terminal was favored as most serviceable to a cataloger. In 1968 such a terminal was nonexistent.[43]

Kilgour's closing statement at the Clinic made it clear that OCLC's designers predicted a decade of continuous evolution. "The actual design as presented is not the final design, but only the current organization of an evolving system. The only guarantee that can be made about the design is that it will be different within a month after this article appears."[44]

The financing of the OCLC system was of paramount concern to all members. Library administrators had to present a convincing case to their college or university administration to participate in OCLC. In addition, they had to believe firmly themselves that joining OCLC was in the best interest of their institutions. Kilgour's scheme was truly radical. He was proposing to introduce technology into an American institution that had witnessed no major changes since LC began to print and distribute catalog cards to libraries around the turn of the century. In agreeing to commit fully to Kilgour's plan, the Ohio librarians were embarking on nothing less than a totally new phase of librarianship.

OCLC's financial policy stated that each member was to pay for operational costs prorated by the use of the system. It was hoped that funds for development would be secured through granting agencies. Thus, members were to support operation of the system, while outside funds would be used to develop and activate major system segments. A special meeting of the members of OCLC on April 17, 1968, led to the approval of a formula for calculating members' assessments based on the number of titles cataloged in each library during 1966-1967. Of a possible sixty-six members, fifty-four paid assessments for fiscal year 1967-1968.[45]

Believing that development of OCLC required outside funds, the Center prepared a draft of a research proposal, "Development of a Computerized Regional Shared-Cataloging System," and sent it to OE for preliminary review. Although interest was shown in the formal submission of the proposal, no assistance was offered. In the spring of 1968, CLR expressed a desire to see the proposal. The first prepared text was revised, and plans were made to send a copy to CLR.

Another aspect of the financial picture was the OCLC staff. At the time of the first meeting of the membership, the staff consisted of a director and an administrative assistant. The budget provided for a position of a chief of development. As the Center's first year ended, only a few qualified persons were available, four of whom were invited to consider the position. None accepted.

Kilgour had an extremely active first year. From the fall of 1967 to the spring 1968, he crisscrossed Ohio visiting campuses of forty colleges and universities to meet library staffs and present the dream of OCLC. Groups of librarians gathered to meet him and to hear his presentations. He addressed faculties on several occasions. He attended a dozen meetings in Ohio, two OCLC-sponsored meetings and ten regional ones.

During this first year, the director was involved in the activities of several organizations that had a direct bearing on the development of OCLC. As a member of the United States of America Standards Institute, Sectional Committee Z39, he contributed to the passage of the American National Standard for Bibliographic Information Interchange on Magnetic Tape. OCLC adopted this standard from the very beginning.

In 1968, OCLC became a member of the Interuniversity Communications Council (EDUCOM), a nonprofit consortium of colleges and universities founded in 1964 to promote the use of computer and communications technology in higher learning. EDUCOM was proposing a prototype information-handling project called EDUNET. It was to link, through a computer network, a group of more than sixty universities and colleges in the United States and Canada to exchange information in education, science, and technology.

A sad note in the history of OCLC's first year was the death on May 28, 1968, of A. Blair Knapp, the first chairman of the Board of Trustees. For a long time, he had zealously advocated statewide cooperation among academic libraries. Indeed, he had been appointed chairman of the Implementation Committee of OCA that brought OCLC into being.

The year closed with the good news that OCLC would be moving to more spacious quarters. The Center had been housed throughout the year in the space made available by The Ohio State University Libraries. In the spring, The Ohio State University offered twenty-four hundred square feet of space in the University's Research Center.

In summary, OCLC's freshman year was one of planning and preparation for future development and activation. There was an air of excitement as Ohio librarians began to formulate plans, dreams, and hopes for their regional system. Although, not all of them reached fruition, those that did left an indelible mark on librarianship.

NOTES

1. National Commission on Libraries and Information Science, *Toward a National Program for Library and Information Services: Goals for Action* (Washington, D.C.: Government Printing Office, 1975), pp. 66-67.

2. The author gratefully acknowledges the generous assistance of Henriette D. Avram (Director, Processing Systems, Networks and Automation Planning, Library of Congress) in compiling and organizing the information in the historical overview.

3. Henriette D. Avram, *MARC: Its History and Implications* (Washington, D.C.: Library of Congress, 1975), p. 22.

4. ISAD is currently the Library and Information Technology Association (LITA). Kilgour was a founding member and past president of ISAD.

5. Ohio College Library Center, *OCLC*, 18 December 1967, p. 2.

6. In 1970 MDO was a part of the Processing Department. In 1976 it was transferred to the Bibliographic Systems Office, Administrative Department, and was subsequently disbanded.

7. Op. cit., Avram, p. 25.

8. OCLC assumed the role of manager of the project in 1975 through a December 1974 agreement between itself and CLR.

9. "A Composite Effort to Build an On-line National Serials Data Base (A Paper for Presentation at the ARL Midwinter Meeting, Chicago, 19 January 1974)," *Journal of Library Automation* 7 (March 1974): 63-64.

10. Op. cit., Avram, p. 20.

11. Ibid., p. 9.

12. UNIMARC (also called SUPERMARC) was an international system for the exchange of bibliographic data. Each country was responsible both for translating its machine-readable data into the UNIMARC format and for translating the UNIMARC records into its country's format.

13. Op. cit., Avram, p. 13.

14. "Sharing Machine-Readable Bibliographic Data: A Progress Report on a Series of Meetings Sponsored by the Council on Library Resources," *Journal of Library Automation* 7 (March 1974): 57.

15. Op. cit., Avram, p. 20.

16. Ibid.

17. "National Bibliographic Control; A Challenge," *Library of Congress Information Bulletin* 33 (June 21, 1974): Appendix III, A-108.

18. Ibid.

19. Subsequently changed to the Committee for the Coordination of National Bibliographic Control that held its first meeting on February 1975.

20. "Advisory Group on National Bibliographic Control Establishes First Two Working Parties," *Journal of Library Automation* 8 (December 1975): 339.

21. Op. cit., National Commission on Libraries and Information Science, p. 67.

22. Lenore S. Maruyama, "Nationwide Networking and the Network Advisory Committee," in *The Management of Serials Automation in Current Technology & Strategies for Future Planning* (New York: Haworth Press, 1982), p. 248.

23. *Annual Report of the Librarian of Congress for the Fiscal Year Ending September 30, 1977* (Washington, D.C.: Library of Congress, 1978), p. 5.

24. Ibid.

25. The Committee of Implementation included: Lewis C. Branscomb (director of libraries, The Ohio State University), Gordon B. Carson (vice-president for business and finance, The Ohio State University), Robert F. Cayton (librarian, Marietta College), John J. Kamerick (vice-president for academic affairs, Kent State University), A. Blair Knapp (president, Denison University), Bob L. Mowery (director of libraries, Wittenberg University), Paul L. O'Connor, S.J. (president, Xavier University), A. Robert Rogers (director of University Library, Bowling Green State University), Phillip R. Shriver (president, Miami University), and Emerson Shuck (vice-president for academic affairs, Ohio Wesleyan University).

26. The Director Subcommittee consisted of Robert F. Cayton, Bob L. Mowery, Phillip R. Shriver, and Emerson Shuck. Lewis C. Branscomb and A. Robert Rogers were included later.

27. The forty-eight paid members were: Antioch College; Ashland College; Athenaeum of Ohio (The); Bluffton College; Borromeo Seminary of Ohio; Bowling Green State University; Capital University; Case-Western Reserve University; Cleveland State University; Central State University; College of Mt. St. Joseph on the Ohio; College of Wooster (The); College of St. Mary of the Springs; Defiance College (The); Denison University; Findlay College; Heidelberg College; Hiram College; John Carroll University; Kent State University; Kenyon College; Malone College; Marietta College; Miami University; Mount Union College; Muskingum College; Oberlin College; Ohio College of Applied Sciences; Ohio Northern University; Ohio State University (The); Ohio University; Ohio Wesleyan University; Otterbein College; Our

Lady of Cincinnati College; Pontifical College Josephenum (The); Rio Grande College; Sinclair College; University of Akron (The); University of Cincinnati; University of Dayton; University of Toledo; Ursuline College; Western College for Women; Wilberforce University; Wittenberg University; Wright State University; Xavier University; and Youngstown University (The).

28. See appendix 1, Exhibits B and C, for the complete documents.

29. Ohio College Library Center, "Articles of Incorporation of the Ohio College Library Center" (Columbus: Ohio College Library Center, 5 July 1967), p. [1].

30. See appendix 1, Exhibit D, for a list of the members of the Board of Trustees.

31. Ohio College Library Center, "Minutes of the Members Meeting" (Columbus: Ohio College Library Center, 25 October 1967), p. 5.

32. The technical processing and the acquisition systems are two different terms used for the same system. The two were cited interchangeably in the literature. The term *technical processing system* is used throughout this book.

33. Ibid., pp. 5-6.

34. Ibid., p. 6

35. Soon after the first meeting of the membership in October, Kilgour wrote a document entitled "Preliminary Description of the Activities of the Ohio College Library Center" (November 11, 1967). His presentation at the Clinic included many of the ideas found in the document. Its full text appears in appendix 1, Exhibit A.

36. Frederick G. Kilgour, "Initial System Design for the Ohio College Library Center: A Case History," in *Clinic on Library Applications of Data Processing, University of Illinois* 6th, 1968 (Champaign, Ill.: University of Illinois, 1968), p. 87.

37. Ibid., p. 82.

38. Ibid.

39. Ibid., pp. 83-84

40. Ibid., p. 84.

41. Ibid., p. 82.

42. Ibid., p. 85.

43. Ibid., p. 87.

44. Ibid.

45. See appendix 3, Exhibit E, for a complete list.

3

LAYING
THE FOUNDATIONS
1968-1970

The purpose of OCLC was clarified and amplified in a "Statement of Academic Objective, Economic Goal, and Missions to Achieve These Ends," approved by the Board of Trustees in spring 1969. The document was important because it brought together in one declaration what previously had been stated by a variety of people in a variety of ways. It included the Center's principal objective, its economic goal, and a description of its activities, including the five major subsystems.[1] The closing paragraph summarized what OCLC hoped to accomplish through the use of computers and the application of wide-scale cooperation:

> In effect, these systems furnish the advantages of computers to faculty members, students, and the library. They take advantage of existence of materials in other institutions and of effort accomplished in other institutions without increasing costs to such institutions. Of equal importance, the system is based on labor-saving machines which will make it possible to bring exponentially rising library per-student costs into a linear relationship with costs in the general economy before it will be possible to bring rising per-student costs in other areas of college and universities into a linear relationship.[2]

From this statement emerged three major projects for the fledgling organization in 1968-1970. They included the following: a simulation study, conducted as a means of pretesting the effectiveness of the planned computer-based system; activation of off-line catalog card production; and creation of an efficient file system to handle the large volume of catalog records in the OCLC data base.

Each project involved both OCLC staff in Columbus and personnel in member libraries and brought into focus the unprecedented large-scale cooperation underlying the OCLC system. The united efforts of Ohio librarians dramatized their faith in cooperation as the most economical and mutually beneficial way to realize the envisioned library system.

SIMULATION

OCLC's use of simulation was a limited case of the general procedure.[3] The initial design for OCLC equipment and communication systems included installation of terminals in each of the Ohio academic institutions, together with a single terminal at the Library of Congress. All terminals were to be connected by telephone lines to a central computer in Columbus. Attached to the computer would be various types of external memories, including magnetic tape drives, a small, fast, random access file, and a large, medium-speed, random access memory file containing the central catalog for member institutions. The complexities of the system obviated any attempts at manual design, as the OCLC *Newsletter* stated in January 1969:

> There is no doubt that the simulation route is the most rapid and least expensive for OCLC to follow. The complexity of data processing equipment and programmed operating systems is so great that only computer simulation can give assurance that manufacturers' proposals will perform the job required. The only alternative is manual over-design of the system which would take longer and require greater expenditure. Obviously an over-designed system is unnecessarily expensive. An under-designed system which would function satisfactorily for an on-line, shared-cataloging operation alone would require use of different equipment several years later because it could not handle some modules as the technical processing system. A change in equipment would undoubtedly mean reprogramming of earlier systems, such as the shared-cataloging activity, and this expense might be so great as to necessitate the decision not to activate completely the OCLC system as planned. The choice seems to be between simulation and over-design to obtain insurance for growth in the future.[4]

The OCLC simulation was made possible thanks to a matching grant from the Board of the State Library of Ohio (Library Services and Construction Act, Title III, Special Project Grant Funds). The sum of $18,588 was to be coupled with the same amount from the Center.

Before selecting a simulation firm, the Center completed two preliminary tasks. It formulated a design for the equipment system and submitted requests for equipment proposals to ten manufacturers. The replies were reviewed, and those proposals that appeared technically and economically feasible were used in the simulation study. Before the study, monthly rentals for equipment were expected to range from twenty thousand dollars to thirty-five thousand dollars.

Philip L. Long joined the OCLC staff as senior programmer and systems analyst on January 2, 1969. Although Long's primary responsibility was to develop the hardware/software complement for the on-line system, he did a great deal of work with the simulation project. He created the design for a reliable equipment system to handle the anticipated traffic.

Once the equipment proposals were received and studied, OCLC chose Comress to conduct the simulation. Comress used a program called the Comress Systems and Computers Evaluation and Review Technique (SCERT). It was a data processing-directed simulation system to evaluate computer applications and hardware/software capabilities. Upon completion of the simulation, the SCERT system models would become the property of OCLC, which would make them available to other centers and libraries to simulate and evaluate equipment for similar systems.

The envisioned OCLC system was a vanguard, with a large percentage of operations involving the exploration of uncharted areas. The simulation activities, as outlined in the Comress SCERT program, did not fully meet the needs of the Center. Adjustments had to be made. The original SCERT program included simulation of proposals by three manufacturers. Since the Center had already elicited proposals from ten companies, Comress agreed to simulate all ten proposals for nearly the same cost as that for three.

Following its first meeting with Comress analysts, OCLC realized that simulating only the shared cataloging and the remote catalog access and circulation control projects would be insufficient. All five OCLC projects had to be subjected to the test conditions. The result would be higher overall efficiency for both manual and computer segments of the entire system. The shared cataloging project was to be simulated first, including catalog card production.[5] The Comress SCERT program was leased for three months. Beginning on June 9, 1969, Michael Crawford, Comress analyst, gave his full time to the Center.

Long received proposal data from the computer manufacturers and furnished Crawford with file designs and other relevant information. Simulation demanded a complete and detailed system design. Each file had to be fully described including record size in every file and identification of each field to determine whether it would be submitted to character manipulation or arithmetic calculation. Configurations for the communication system contained data, giving type and number of communication lines, kind of terminals to be placed in member libraries, and anticipated volume of traffic for the system.[6]

By August the Comress analyst had simulated the five major projects and the computer system model. Moreover, definitions of the system were being refined to prepare for testing of proposals. The following breakdown of the relative burden of each project on a central processor was based upon the assumption that the five projects represented 100 percent of the work load:

Remote catalog access and circulation control	79%
Bibliographic information retrieval	17%
Shared cataloging	2%
Serials control	1%
Technical processing system	1%

It was assumed that user-oriented projects (remote catalog access and circulation control, and bibliographic information retrieval) would consume a far greater amount of the central processor's time than would the cataloging-processing tasks.[7]

The equipment that OCLC was searching for would have to supply the computing power to meet a peak loading average of five requests per second over an hour's time.[8] When the manufacturers' proposals were challenged by the simulation network, all ten proposals fell short of expectations because of the inefficiencies of the operating systems of the computer simulation. The manufacturers proposed to OCLC and Comress that they modify the operating systems. The changes were then made and accepted. The next series of trials showed that over half of the computers or external memory files would be used more than 100 percent of the time to handle the planned traffic. Consequently, one computer manufacturer rescinded its proposal, and five others modified theirs by upgrading the systems. The percentage of computer use for the proposals ranged from 19.70 percent to 114.31 percent.[9]

A study that followed demonstrated that if the equipment were to handle peak traffic loads, computer use would have to be below 30 percent during periods of heaviest employment. A trade-off study was made of the three manufacturers who were able to meet this requirement. Additional factors that were considered included cost, expansibility, memory requirements, size of application program needed, support available from the manufacturer, and availability of lease-with-purchase option.

On February 12, 1970, the Board of Trustees agreed to purchase a Xerox Data Systems Sigma 5 computer. Among those on the market, it was both the least expensive and the best suited to OCLC's needs. Soon after, a lease agreement was signed that included the option to purchase the computer at a later date. It was scheduled to arrive by the latter part of August and to be operational by September 1, 1970. Monthly rental for the computer and its peripheral equipment was estimated at $15,146.

Before the decision was made to acquire a Sigma 5, the Center began to study and evaluate CRT terminals. They would serve as the link between the various institutions and the main computer in Columbus. By June 1970, twelve different terminals were under consideration. The following year, trade-off studies were conducted on three.[10]

Summing up, simulation was a success. Through its application, the economic and technical feasibility of a centralized, computerized, on-line library network for Ohio's academic institutions was ascertained. This, in turn, enabled OCLC to establish a firm plan to develop its systems. In addition, results of the study could be applied to other regional planning efforts. As of March 1969, computer simulation of computer systems for individual libraries or for library networks had never been done. OCLC was a pioneer.

OFF-LINE CATALOG CARD PRODUCTION

The principal objective of the OCLC off-line[11] catalog card production project was implementation of an on-line computerized shared cataloging system. The on-line system would be the necessary step to the planned bibliographic information retrieval. As cards were manufactured off-line from machine-readable data, records were accumulated for use in both the shared cataloging and information retrieval systems. The beginning of off-line catalog card production signaled commencement of events culminating in fulfillment of OCLC goals.

Off-line activity similar to that at OCLC was occurring elsewhere. The Georgia Institute of Technology, the New England Library Information Network (NELINET), and the University of Chicago had released reports describing off-line catalog card production. Improved cataloging was the objective for all three. OCLC was hoping to accomplish not only this goal but also to establish a system encompassing the major facets of library activity.

The decision-making process was put to full use in planning for off-line production. Since it was a cooperative venture, both OCLC and its membership had to make some crucial decisions. Before off-line procedures could commence, the membership had to decide upon specifications for catalog cards. Meetings were held on February 21 and March 7, 1969, at Ohio Wesleyan University. Approximately one hundred members attended each session. These twelve specifications were added to the original description including the identification of over twenty-three hundred options:[12]

- Cards for each member would come in alphabetical, ready-for-filing packs.
- For each type of heading, a member could decide to print it at the far left of the card, at the first identation, or at the second identation.
- Each type of heading could be printed in full caps or in uppercase and lowercase, depending on each member's wishes.
- Specific types of cards in specific packs could be produced with or without the tracing being visible, as requested by a member.
- Three lines at the top of the card could be allowed for headings.
- Any one card could contain multiple call numbers.
- For all call numbers in the master file, a record could be made of library and location holding information.
- The following elements could be updated (changed later): call number, location, holdings information, notes, main entry, body of title, imprint, collation, and tracings.
- Upon request, extra main entry cards could be produced.
- A note concerning any specific copy a member might hold could be recorded on both the machine-readable record and the catalog cards.
- Permalife or other comparable paper stock could be used for printed cards.
- If a library used the dropped heading technique, cards could be produced showing headings at the bottom.[13]

This list was significant because it illustrated the kind of flexible and personalized system OCLC's designers had in mind. Catalog cards would be produced to suit the needs of over fifty different catalogs. That libraries could maintain their separate identities and yet share in the common goals of OCLC was a revolutionary idea to Ohio's academic librarians.

The Center had to choose supplies and equipment that would best meet the requirements of card production. Because catalog cards were being designed for individual catalogs in a variety of library settings, such production, without a doubt, would be both complex and costly. However, it was reasoned that one-time costs were program-related. New options would continue to be added, and members were free at any time to make suggestions.

To reduce programming expenses existing computer programs were used. Of the three programs that could meet the Center's specifications, the Yale Bibliographic System (YBS) was chosen nationwide.[14] The OCLC off-line system was designed to operate on four Ohio State University computers: IBM's 360/75, 360/50, 7094, and 1620. In order for YBS to become operational on the computers, a second set of programs, the Maryland Michigan Operation System (MAMOS), had to be installed to schedule and allocate computer resources. The MAMOS program would determine which terminal was to receive what resources and would resolve conflicts when multiple terminals needed the same resource simultaneously. In the spring of 1970, the job of embedding MAMOS under the main operating system of Ohio State's IBM 7094 was completed.

While the YBS project was in progress, numerous smaller searches were made to refine the plans. The Center conducted a search for a computer print chain and forms, eventually supplied by the University of Chicago and modified by OCLC. The printer used a mylar ribbon. Chosen for its longevity of more than three hundred years, Permalife card stock was to be used to produce the standard 75-by-125-mm catalog cards.

The precoded punch cards used by members for ordering the card sets were designed in cooperation with LC, which assisted OCLC in the precoding process. LC used a similar system of coding in its *NUC* to identify libraries owning particular titles and participating in its cooperative cataloging program. The LC codes were of variable lengths, interchanging uppercase and lowercase letters. The OCLC codes were always three letters and always uppercase. For example, the LC code for Bowling Green State University was OBgU. OCLC's code for the same institution was BGU. These codes were invaluable in the off-line stage. They facilitated the return of the requested catalog cards to the correct library. They were also important as location symbols for the titles stored in the computer's central file.

As a prerequisite to participation in off-line production, a member had to agree to convert its cataloging records to a machine-readable form. It also had to be willing to become involved in the initial activation of the shared cataloging project. Once preliminary agreements were reached, a member was required to complete a Profile Information Questionnaire stating its options for the production of catalog cards. OCLC then assigned the library a unique three-letter uppercase code for each holding library within a library system. A holding library referred to a catalog file. Each institution generally had at least two and often three or more such files including the main, reference, and departmental collections. The holding library codes were assigned in addition to the general three-letter codes used in the union catalog feature.

One striking characteristic of the OCLC computer-based card production system was its ability to adhere to existing relevant library standards, and yet to allow for individual personalities of the member's catalogs. The catalog cards contained fixed and variable elements. Fixed elements were predetermined and unalterable. Variable elements were controlled by the member library. For example, the order of the information on a catalog card was fixed. The main entry would always have to precede the title, which would always be followed by the author statement. However, indentations on the cards, arrangement of call numbers, and upper- or lowercase printing of subject headings were variable elements. At the outset, catalog cards for one title could be produced in thirty-four hundred different combinations of elements.

Early in its development, OCLC launched an educational and communication program for the membership. Massive education was necessary because the use of computer technology was a new experience for academic librarians. Moreover, the pull of tradition was strong within the profession and retarded change. On December 18, 1967, the first OCLC newsletter, issued under the title "OCLC," reached the librarians and began what was to become a steady stream of communication between the Center and its membership. The second communication, dated June 19, 1968, was issued under the official name of *Newsletter*. The OCLC staff's first major document sent to the membership was entitled *Preliminary Description of Catalog Cards Produced from MARC II Data* (September 1969). Its purpose was to describe in detail the OCLC-produced catalog cards. Copies were sent to a few institutions for a test reading. An amended draft then went to all members. As a further aid to members, the Center offered a series of seminars on library computerization. The first meeting was held in the spring of 1969 at the University of Toledo Library. Representatives from nine institutions attended.

Although off-line production for the membership did not begin for nearly two years after the release of *Preliminary Description*, the Center made it a point to keep librarians informed well in advance of forthcoming events. They were first of all to limit the books they cataloged to those written in the English language and those bearing an LC card number that began with the digits "69" or higher. All other titles were to be cataloged manually. Local notes (for example, an author-autographed copy note) would be recorded on a precoded punch card. Lastly, librarians would order catalog cards from OCLC by writing the LC card number on another precoded punch card.

Off-line production began in the autumn of 1969, and by April 1970, cards first appeared in the catalogs of Oberlin College, Ohio University, and Wittenberg University. Request cards were mailed to Columbus in weekly batches, where the new requests were combined with those previously unfilled and run against the MARC II file. Images were produced on magnetic tapes for all requested cards. Individual cards were formatted to meet an institution's options, produced from magnetic tapes, and then sent out.

In the beginning some LC card numbers were incorrect. Consequently, before cards were filed, librarians instructed staffs to compare a computer-generated card from each pack with information on the title page of the matching book to ensure correctness. Staff members were also asked to transcribe call numbers from computer-produced catalog cards to corresponding books before shelving them. Wittenburg University was the first institution to receive off-line-produced catalog cards. A subject card from the first set is shown on page 32.[15]

APOLOGETICS – 20TH CENTURY.

BT 1102
.R3313   Rahner, Karl, 1904-
          [Glaubst du an Gott? English]
          Do you believe in God? Translated
    by Richard Strachan. New York, Newman
    Press [1969]
          vii, 114 p.   22 cm.
          Translation of Glaubst du an Gott?

          1. Apologetics - 20th century.   I.
    Title

OSH   WITpa   70-77644

Before off-line production, libraries were receiving catalog cards that were similar in appearance to the off-line-produced cards through the Card Distribution Service at LC. LC-generated cards closely resembled those produced by OCLC:

Ikime, Obaro.
          Niger Delta rivalry; Itsekiri-Urhobo relations and the European presence 1884-1936.   [New York] Humanities Press [1969]

      xxi, 301 p.   illus., maps (part fold.), ports.   23 cm.   (Ibadan history series) 10.00

      Bibliography: p. 285-290.

      1. Jekri (African people)   2. Sobo (African people)   I. Title.   II. Series.

DT515.42.I47   1969   966.93   68-54522
                                          MARC

    Library of Congress

Each OCLC-generated catalog card would allow for a maximum of seventeen lines of print with forty-nine characters to a line (or ten characters to an inch). Characters would be of upper- and lowercase Roman alphabetical symbols together with Arabic numerals, diacritical and punctuation marks, and other special markings.

The first run of cards for the first library demonstrated that some errors were inevitable, and that the blame for such errors would fall both on librarian and computer, with the computer faring better.

The *Newsletter* of 16 October, 1969 warned that errors would occur in the early operational period of catalog production, adding that the errors would be human errors, not machine errors. The first batch of cards prepared for Wittenberg confirmed the prediction, but the machine seemed to take on a benevolent anthropomorphism. A repeated error manifested itself in the form of subject headings concocted from various sections of the data. It almost appeared that the machine had made an effort to help the user, and since some of the gratuitously added headings were class numbers, it seemed that the machine was setting about to establish a classed catalog as well for Wittenberg users.[16]

Off-line production was well under way by spring 1970, with some fifty-four hundred cards having been produced. Initial cost per card was estimated at 9.5¢. By June 1970, it was evident that the cost would be lower than anticipated. As a result, the Board of Trustees decided that the charge for cards for any given billing period would be determined on the basis of actual cost along with 0.5¢ per card. The total cost per card would not exceed 9.5¢. Billing was to start in July 1970.[17]

During its second year (1968-1969), OCLC formed a new committee, the "Committee to Determine Data Elements in Converted Library Records," with Alan B. Hogan (systems automation librarian, Wright State University Library) as chairman.[18] The Committee compiled a document entitled "Draft Statement of Data Elements in Converted Library Bibliographic Records."

In the spring of 1969, The Ohio State University Libraries began to convert current cataloging to machine-readable form. The project was part of a larger one, to design a remote catalog access and circulation system. On June 19, 1969, the conversion project became operational; by September some five thousand records had been converted. The system was being developed in such a way that OCLC could adopt it. On September 1, 1969, a fifteen-month contract was signed with IBM to design and activate it.

For OCLC, LC's two-year RECON project was a catalyst. The pilot project began in August 1969 and ended exactly two years later. During the first year of its on-line operations, the Center would be able to take advantage of the fifty-eight thousand newly converted catalog records available on the MARC tapes.[19]

The Advisory Cataloging Committee was created in the winter of 1970. Its purpose was to assist with design of the on-line system and to help complete work on the off-line project. On June 17, 1970, the first meeting took place at Case Western Reserve University.[20, 21]

FILE DESIGN

In the early stages of simulation it became evident that a competent file organization was needed. There were two avenues available. Neither mimicry of library manual files nor application of standard computer techniques could efficiently process envisioned peak traffic loads of the OCLC system. Many hours were channeled into research in the hope of finding a solution to the management of the theoretically enormous data bank.

The dilemma of rapid access to records using derived search keys was of interest not only to OCLC but also to the entire library community as it labored to find more efficient and economical ways to handle knowledge. A derived search key is "a search key derived from bibliographic information in the entry and from which the physical address in the file is computed."[22] In October 1968, Kilgour presented the findings of a research project that he and Long conducted on derived search keys at the Columbus meeting of the American Society for Information Science (ASIS).[23] Their findings showed that the work on the OCLC file organization had only begun. If a user was to employ the system to its fullest, additional files would be needed. In addition to the main file, subject, title, and added entry indices had to be created. The subject index would prove to be the most difficult of the three.

In the spring of 1969, the Center entered into a contract with the National Agricultural Library, which provided $4,182 for continuation of research on retrieval of single entries from very large bibliographic files. The investigation would determine the efficiency of using truncated name-and-title search keys in the retrieval process.

A three, three name-title search key seemed a likely solution to the file organization problem. It consisted of the first three letters of the first nonarticle word of the main entry, followed by a comma, and the first three letters of the first nonarticle word of the title. For example, if a user was trying to locate bibliographic information on Charles Dickens's novel *A Tale of Two Cities*, he would search on the CRT terminal under "Dic,Tal."[24] In a data base of 132,808 name-and-title entries, 99.08 percent of the time, five or fewer entries would appear on a library computer terminal. Over four-fifths of the academic libraries in the system owned fewer than 132,000 monographic titles. The solution, indeed, was close at hand. Research indicated that if twenty entries were the optimal maximum number of replies to a query, this maximum would be exceeded on the average only three times in ten thousand requests.[25]

A description of the investigation and its results was prepared by Kilgour, Long, and Eugene B. Leiderman, an additional investigator, not a permanent member of the staff.[26] The paper, read at the October 1970 meeting of ASIS, presented the research findings.[27] If a reply produced more entries than the optimal maximum of twenty, what would be done? The problem was difficult, and the authors admitted it would require ingenuity. It would later be solved by a method called the extended search. How would truncated search keys perform on files ten and one hundred times the size of those used in the experiment? Undoubtedly, an augmented file would increase the probability of retrieving more entries than the optimal maximum of twenty. Previous studies showed that most academic library patrons sought documents by searching card catalogs under name-title entries. Therefore, a three, three name-title search key warranted further investigation and application.

In June 1970 the Center received news that the National Agricultural Library was extending its contractual grant in the amount of $1,750. Although the amount of the grant was small, it would help OCLC continue research on title-only entries in a large bibliographic file. OCLC was on the threshold. File design for the system was the key to widespread accessibility to the cataloging data.

The OCLC system was a revolution that evolved; many changes would shape its final destiny. Both internal and external forces would play a part in the process. Externally, the Center received grants. The National Agricultural Library's extension of its grant for OCLC to continue the file design was followed by receipt of the largest grant to date. OE granted OCLC $90,135 for "Development of a Computerized Regional Shared Cataloging System." Funds were available from January 1, 1970, through June 30, 1971. A $14,133 grant from CLR further aided development of on-line shared cataloging, enabling the Center to acquire supplies and materials needed for the on-line project. The same funds made it possible to lease computer terminals to be placed in member libraries and telephone lines to transmit messages between Columbus and the membership. The funding period began June 1, 1970, and ended June 30, 1971.

The OE grant enabled the Center to establish the OCLC Advisory Committee. Its purpose was to examine OCLC's plans in general, and its program for shared cataloging in particular. Five eminent authorities in library automation and regional networks comprised the membership: Henriette D. Avram (MARC Development Office, LC, Washington, D.C.), Richard E. Coward (head, Research and Development, The British National Bibliography, London, England), Richard M. Dougherty (acting director of libraries, University of Colorado, Boulder, Colorado), Peter Paulsen, (technical processes librarian, The New York State Library, Albany, New York), and Josephine Pulsifer (chief, Technical Services and Development, Washington State Library, Olympia, Washington).

On April 30, 1970, the Advisory Committee met. It was generally agreed that the five major projects should proceed. The Committee believed, however, that the serials project would require more time and energy than anticipated. It also expressed a concern for the problems the Center might encounter in the shared cataloging project. The immensely varied requests from the large number of libraries participating could present difficulties as could the lack of capital to begin the project.[28]

A strong commitment to cooperation and firm financial backing were necessary for launching the shared cataloging system. Although there was more than an adequate supply of cooperative spirit, it could not compensate for the lack of funds. Libraries would have to undergo a period of financial adjustment. It was calculated that in the cooperative effort affecting library operations in their entirety, the gross savings would exceed a million dollars. To realize the savings, members would have to reduce amounts being spent on salaries for cataloging and to channel the funds into OCLC. Not all institutions could take advantage of a normal staff attrition, and many would, therefore, lack start-up funds.[29]

The OCLC member institutions held three meetings beginning in fall 1969. In the spring of 1970 the Ad Hoc Committee on Financing was appointed. After its first meeting the Committee knew that the on-line system could not begin solely with the financial support of the membership. Outside assistance had to be found.

The same grant that created the OCLC Advisory Committee made possible an increase in the size of the Center's staff. The organization had moved in October 1968 from the Main Library on The Ohio State University campus to the University's Research Center at 1314 Kinnear Road. The twelve hundred square feet of space made possible an expansion of the staff and an increase in the Center's activities. Almost from its beginning, OCLC had searched for a Chief of Development. Unable to fill the position, it decided to look instead for personnel competent in computer system analysis and development, and in application system analysis and development. Philip L. Long and Curtis E. Higgins were both senior programmers and systems analysts. Long was responsible for the computer system, and Higgins headed activity applications. Long would be in charge of simulation, and Higgins would be responsible for catalog card production. (Higgins resigned in May, 1969.) In January 1970, four programmers were hired. The larger staff was a boost toward activation of on-line shared cataloging.

Once the on-line shared cataloging system was in operation, it was theorized that the amount of material available through interlibrary loans would grow rapidly. In the course of OCLC's second year (1968-1969), thirty-two institutions formally entered into an agreement whereby each would make direct library loans to faculty members of all OCLC institutions. The rules established by the Dayton and Miami Valley Consortium, and the Inter-University Library Council (IULC) were adopted.[30] The accord was a major step in accelerating sharing of resources.

Still, on paper, OCLC was unique. Nationwide, it was the only large-scale computerized library system in existence. The idea of expanding the Ohio network into a regional one was a part of the OCLC blueprint. The first step was to extend it across state boundaries. The glimmerings of an interstate network appeared in the spring of 1970, when the Pittsburgh Regional Library Center (PRLC) inquired about receiving services from the Center. In addition, it asked about the possibility of participating with OCLC in a network. The Board of Trustees approved entering into talks with the PRLC. As the fiscal year terminated, an agreement was being drafted to establish a formal relationship.

From 1968 to 1970, OCLC witnessed changes in its membership and in the Board of Trustees. In 1968-1969, fifty-four members paid assessments. The next year the number dropped to fifty-two. Due to an administrative error, Mount Union College did not renew its membership in 1968-1969, but it did so the following year. Dyke College in Cleveland became a new member in fiscal year 1969-1970. The same year Borromeo Seminary of Ohio, Cuyahoga Community College, Mary Manse College, and Ursuline College for Women did not renew memberships. In November 1968 the Board of Trustees elected its officers: chairman, Lewis C. Branscomb; vice-chairman, Phillip R. Shriver; secretary, Robert F. Cayton; and treasurer, Bob L. Mowery. The following year the officers remained the same with the exception of the vice-chairman's seat that was filled by Charles C. McDonald.[31]

The two years of history told in this chapter are summarized in a 1969 report by Lewis C. Branscomb, director of libraries, The Ohio State University, and newly appointed chairman of the Board of Trustees.

> In my considered judgment, as Chairman of the Board of Trustees and as the Director of Libraries of one of the member institutions, the Center is making good progress in a new, daring, largely uncharted cooperative venture. In such an enterprise reasonable men will not expect too soon too much. The tremendous potential is there and we are moving prudently and steadily towards the goals which have been established.[32]

The Ohio adventure called OCLC was quickly becoming a reality. Many librarians discovered that by using the computer technology and by working cooperatively toward a common goal they could accomplish together what would be impossible to do alone.

NOTES

1. See appendix 1, Exhibit F, for the complete document.

2. Ohio College Library Center, "Statement of Academic Objective, Economic Goal, and Missions to Achieve These Ends" (Columbus: Ohio College Library Center, 9 April 1969), pp. 1-2. (Mimeographed.)

3. See appendix 2, Glossary of Terms, for a definition.

4. Ohio College Library Center, *Newsletter*, 9 January 1969, p. [2].

5. Ohio College Library Center, *Newsletter*, 25 June 1969, p. [1].

6. Ohio College Library Center, *Annual Report 1968/1969* (Columbus: Ohio College Library Center, 1970), p. 3.

7. Ohio College Library Center, *Newsletter*, 29 August 1969, p. 2.

8. The OCLC system in 1982 handled over forty-four messages a second.

9. Ohio College Library Center, *Annual Report 1969/1970* (Columbus: Ohio College Library Center, 1970), p. 3.

10. See chapter 4 for details on the terminals.

11. See appendix 2, Glossary of Terms, for a definition.

12. Op. cit., Ohio College Library Center, *Annual Report 1968/1969*, p. 4.

13. Ohio College Library Center, *Newsletter*, 25 April 1969, pp. 2-3.

14. Frederick G. Kilgour came to OCLC from the Yale University School of Medicine with extensive experience in computer applications to libraries. At Yale he and colleagues from Columbia and Harvard organized the Columbia-Harvard-Yale Medical Libraries Computerization Project in 1961. As Yale's first associate librarian for research and development from 1965-1967, he continued work on the application of computers to libraries at Yale.

15. Ohio College Library Center, *Newsletter*, 3 March 1970, p. 2.

16. Ibid.

17. Op. cit., Ohio College Library Center, *Annual Report 1969/1970*, p. 6.

18. The other members of the Committee were: James A. Damico (University of Dayton), Sul Lee (University of Toledo), John Linford (The Ohio State University), Leo R. Rift (Bowling Green State University), Jack Scott (Kent State University), and Morgan I. Temple (Case Western Reserve University).

19. See chapter 2 for a full description.

20. Those present included: John Demos (The Ohio State University), Mildred Dugas (Ohio University), Barbara Gates (Oberlin College), Esther Greenberg (Case Western Reserve University), Will Rogers (Ohio University), Ruth Rose (Hiram College), Eva Schroeder (Heidelberg College), Bonnie Seiss (Wittenberg University), and Duncan Wall (Kent State University).

21. Since no minutes were kept at this meeting, no details were available.

22. Frederick G. Kilgour, Philip L. Long, and Eugene B. Leiderman, "Retrieval of Bibliographic Entries from a Name-Title Catalog by Use of Truncated Search Keys," in *Proceedings of the American Society for Information Science* 7, 1970 (Washington, D.C.: American Society for Information Science, 1971), p. 79.

23. Frederick G. Kilgour, "Retrieval of Single Entries from a Computerized Library Catalog File," in *Proceedings of the American Society for Information Science* 5, 1968 (New York: Greenwood Publishing, 1968), pp. 133-36.

24. Op. cit., Ohio College Library Center, *Annual Report 1969/1970*, p. 7.

25. Op. cit., Ohio College Library Center, *Annual Report 1969/1970*, p. 7.

26. Eugene B. Leiderman was a full-time graduate student in The Ohio State University Department of Computer Science & Information. His research with OCLC was incorporated into his thesis written in partial fulfillment of the requirements for an advanced degree.

27. Op. cit., Frederick G. Kilgour, et al., "Retrieval of Bibliographic Entries," pp. 79-81.

28. Op. cit., Ohio College Library Center, *Annual Report 1969/1970*, p. 4.

29. Ibid., pp. 4-5.

30. See appendix 1, Exhibits H and I, for the list of participants and the rules adopted by the Dayton and Miami Valley Consortium and the IULC.

31. See appendix 1, Exhibit D, for a complete list of the Board of Trustees members.

32. Lewis C. Branscomb, "Progress Report to the Ohio College Association, Executive Committee" (Columbus: Ohio College Library Center, 11 April 1979), p. 4.

4

ON THE BRINK
OF THE NEW ERA
1970-1971

The experience with off-line catalog card production proved beneficial. It allowed the build-up of the union catalog and gave the Center a chance to see if card production would run smoothly. Moreover, it manifested the need to implement off-line production before undertaking the on-line system. To attempt both off-line and on-line activities simultaneously might have resulted in a fiasco. The off-line system was a stage in the on-line shared cataloging project, and not a separate program. The beginnings of the on-line shared cataloging project and of the OCLC network of library systems were guideposts directing the Center in its "new, daring, largely uncharted cooperative venture."[1]

OFF-LINE

Off-line catalog card production began in July 1970, and 440,711[2] catalog cards were produced the first twelve months. During this first year, cards could be requested off-line *only* by LC card number. The ability to make requests by LC card number, *or* author and title, *or* title was an on-line activity planned for the summer of 1971. Once the on-line system was operating, a member library was free to furnish OCLC with its own original cataloging from which the Center would produce cards.

Off-line production proved to be economical and efficient. The more efficacious were the operations, the greater were the dollar savings. A number of hardware improvements, including a switch in computers and in the print train, increased the efficiency of operations.

As mentioned in the preceding chapter, the original off-line system operated on four Ohio State University computers located in two different computer centers on campus. During the spring of 1971 the programs running on the four computers were redesigned and recomposed for OCLC's Sigma 5. Converting from four computers to one increased efficiency. For example, the speed of the program that formatted catalog cards for printing was increased fivefold from the original system. This meant cost savings for libraries. The initial cost to format catalog cards, without printing them, was 2.27¢. The new programs written for the Sigma 5 would format cards at a cost of 2.21¢ per card.

Plans were underway during the year to use smaller printed characters to print up to twenty-three lines per card. This, in turn, would reduce costs to member libraries that were being charged on a per-card basis.

A comparative cost analysis of computerized versus manual procedures in cataloging was presented in an article by the director entitled "Evolving, Computerizing, Personalizing." The analysis was followed by an explanation. The off-line experience proved that it was, indeed, more economical to use computerized rather than manual procedures. The saving was more than half the cost of manual production. As table T-1 shows, the first catalog cards produced yielded an average cost of 6.9¢.

TABLE T-1
Comparative Costs of Manually and Computer-produced Catalog Cards[3]

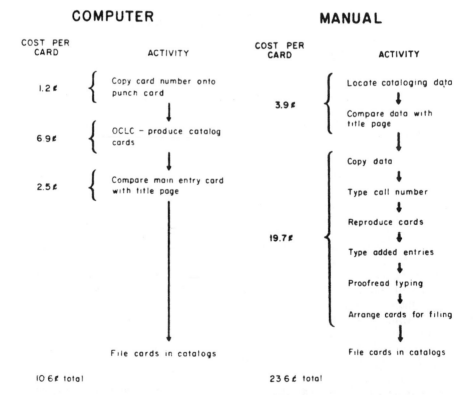

COMPUTER

COST PER CARD	ACTIVITY
1.2¢	Copy card number onto punch card
6.9¢	OCLC – produce catalog cards
2.5¢	Compare main entry card with title page
	File cards in catalogs
10.6¢ total	

MANUAL

COST PER CARD	ACTIVITY
3.9¢	Locate cataloging data → Compare data with title page
19.7¢	Copy data → Type call number → Reproduce cards → Type added entries → Proofread typing → Arrange cards for filing
	File cards in catalogs
23.6¢ total	

In the same article, Kilgour described in detail the economics of off-line card production.

> The costs for computerized production come from experience with the OCLC system. Ohio University found that subprofessionals receiving $6,000 a year were transcribing LC card numbers from books to punch cards and shelving the books in an ordered arrangement at an hourly rate of forty-three. The 1.2¢ was calculated from these observations. The cost of 6.9¢ was the actual cost of producing 358,007 cards from July 1970 through April 1971. The auditing firm of Haskins & Sells has reviewed the OCLC costing procedures (over twenty separate cost items are included) and have reported that these costs include all costs except for costs of space occupied by staff. The calculation of the cost of 2.5¢ was based on the assumption that the hourly rate of comparing finished catalog cards with books and transcribing call numbers from cards to books by subprofessionals could not be less than half the rate of transcribing LC card number to punch cards and shelving books. Hence, twenty per hour was assumed, and the cost is 2.5¢....
>
> Clearly, computerized catalog production is reaching such low cost levels that not much would be saved if no charge were made for computer usage. The majority of the cost of computer-produced cards is incurred by associated manual procedures not yet mechanized.[4]

The cost to OCLC members of producing individual catalog cards fluctuated from week to week. Twenty-four elements were considered in computing the cost. The fixed and variable costs together accounted for the varying cost per card per week.[5] The more cards produced, the lower was the cost.

Activity in member libraries focused on participation in off-line production. At the Center the new requests for catalog cards submitted on punch cards would be run weekly against LC's MARC II data base of cataloging records. If a record could not be located the first time, it would be recycled and sent through the MARC II file one or more times. Each library chose a recycling period of from one to thirty-six weeks. After the Center had recycled a request with no success, it was returned to the requesting library where a decision was made to catalog the book without LC copy or to return the request to OCLC for recycling. As a result of LC daily adding new records to the MARC II data base, and the weekly additions to OCLC's data base, more and more requests were being filled.

To assist libraries in the use of off-line procedures, OCLC staff prepared and distributed to member institutions a *Manual for OCLC Catalog Card Production* (February 1971) that provided an informal course of instruction.

The Advisory Cataloging Committee, established during the previous year, was instrumental in redesigning catalog production for greatest efficiency. It met frequently during the year. As users of the off-line system, the Committee members supplied OCLC with advice and information from the real world.[6]

ON-LINE[7]

As the librarian at Brown University from 1841-1847, Charles Coffin Jewett, established one of the first library card catalogs. His rearranging and cataloging of the collection brought him recognition at home and abroad. Jewett had a dream for his catalog that he described in an article in *Proceedings of the American Association for the Advancement of Science* (August 1850).

> By means of it every student in America would have the means of knowing the full extent of his resources for investigation. The places where every book could be found, would be indicated in the Catalogue.... A system of exchange and of general loans might, with certain strigent conditions, be established so that all the literary treasures of the country would be measurably accessible to every scholar. When the loan of the book would be impossible, extracts might be copied, quotations verified, and researches made through the intervention of the Smithsonian Institution, which would, in many cases, be nearly as valuable to the student as the personal examination of the book.... Again, this general catalogue would enable purchasers of books for public libraries to consult it judiciously for the wants of the country.... Another important benefit of this system is that it allows us to vary the form of the catalogue, at will, from the alphabetical to the classed, and to modify the classification as we please. The titles, separately stereotyped, may change their order at command ...
> Another great benefit of this system would be that it would secure *uniformity* in catalogues. A good degree of uniformity would be absolutely indispensible to the success of the plan....[8]

A hundred years later modern technology was creating a means to fulfill Jewett's dream. Although there are palpable vestiges of Jewett's original plan in the OCLC on-line shared cataloging project, its success depended not on uniformity but on standardization. Each member's catalogs were to be unique, but at the same time, they were to be based on a standard format.

In 1970 the era of the on-line interactive computing machine was only commencing. Many machines were operating, but none had been designed specifically for library use. The library literature of 1970 describes only one on-line cataloging system at the Shawnee Mission Public Schools in Shawnee Mission, Kansas. The system produced uniform cards from a fixed-length, non-MARC record. In contrast, OCLC was using a variable-length MARC II record to produce individualized cards.

Five components constituted the OCLC on-line system. The first was the data base, representing a catalog of information about documents held in members' collections. The second was a secondary storage device that housed the data catalog; OCLC used disk storage. The third component was a collection of computer programs needed to retrieve the data. The fourth was a set of control programs designed to manage the flow of information throughout the system. Finally, to use the computer, CRT terminals, very similar in appearance to an ordinary typewriter, were purchased. They permitted a dialogue between the user and the main computer. An important feature of the on-line interactive machine was that it enabled the user to make decisions and to plan his retrieval strategy, allowing him to interrupt and to alter his program at will. Since the OCLC on-line system used the time-sharing method, a multitude of users could simultaneously query the data bank in Columbus.

The OCLC on-line system was designed to speed cataloging and reduce cataloging costs in member libraries. This was accomplished by making use of cataloging performed elsewhere (eliminating duplication) and by using labor-saving machines. Production rather than reproduction characterized the system. Reproduction was providing duplicate copies of a card by copying or printing. Production meant creating catalog cards, based on a generalized record, in finished form ready for filing in a catalog.

The economic realities of the late 1960s made the on-line system attractive. As the wholesale price index had climbed at a rate of less than 1 percent per annum since 1951, the operating cost for each student in college and university libraries had risen at the rate of 5.1 percent per year.[9] A by-product of faster, less costly cataloging was an improvement in the speed with which newly cataloged items would be made available for library users. One book ready for circulation was far more valuable than two sitting in the uncataloged backlog.

Creation of a master file of catalog records was essential. It would represent both a growing bank of cataloging information to be shared and an ever expanding union catalog of data about materials in member libraries. The file would be fundamental to production of catalog cards, the shared cataloging system, and creation of such products as accession lists, selective dissemination of information (SDI) notices, bibliographies, reference lists, spine labels, and book cards.

The principle behind the card production system was to convert a member's current cataloging into machine-readable form. This would be accomplished by adding call number and member library holdings data to an extant machine-readable record. When the on-line system became operational, the contents of the file would then be a combination of the LC MARC II data and the original cataloging. During 1970-1971, several libraries began to convert their retrospective holdings. The converted records would be fed into the data file, thus helping to build a fuller, more useful master file.

Implementation of on-line activities involved acquiring equipment, designing and leasing the telephone network, activating computer programs, and coordinating equipment, communication, and programs into an efficient system. Most importantly, to accomplish the on-line goals, member libraries' staffs would need continuous instruction in the intricacies of the system.

The cost of operating a system on the scope of OCLC was high. The minutes of the meeting of the Board of Trustees on November 13, 1970, included the estimated cost of operations for July 1, 1971, through June 30, 1972:[10]

Center Costs (personnel, equipment, supplies, etc.)	$132,167
Computer Costs	186,000
Terminal Costs	136,320
Communication Costs	102,300
Loop Charges	18,000
Modem Installation Costs	6,800
	$581,587

The largest investment of operating funds would be for the computer, which arrived at the end of August 1970. The major components of the Sigma 5 were the central processing unit (CPU), three banks of core memory, a high-speed disk secondary memory, ten disk-pack spindles with a total capacity of 250,000,000 bytes plus two spare spindles, two magnetic tape transports, two multiplexor channels, five communications controllers, a card reader, a card punch, and a printer.

Two immediate changes were made in the computer: the operating system was redesigned and the monitor program that controlled the execution of programs was reworked. The alterations in the operating system enabled the computer to run two programs simultaneously. It could run batch jobs while, at the same time, operating the on-line system with no degradation of on-line performance.

Third generation computers, like the Sigma 5, were characteristically inefficient. They were designed to adapt to a variety of programs. Consequently, the operating system had to go through a complex series of operations that lengthened running time to execute any one program. After tailoring, the Sigma 5 was transformed from a general purpose machine into a more efficient, specifically OCLC computer.

The second largest cost, after that of the computer, was the estimated terminal cost of $136,320. Beginning in the fall of 1969, the Center studied over twelve terminals in its search for the best one available at the time. The terminal would have to meet certain requirements including:

- displaying both upper- and lowercase characters and diacritics
- producing highly legible and visible images on its screen
- handling a large repertoire of editing capabilities
- interacting smoothly and swiftly with the central computer and files
- accepting and generating ASCII (American Standard Code for Information Interchange, Department of Commerce) code
- making minimal demands for message transmissions to and from the central site
- operating with at least a score of other terminals on the same dedicated line

The Center was hoping that the cost, including service at remote sites, would be around $150 per month per terminal.

In the final analysis, thirty-one characteristics were used for evaluating prospective terminals. Near the end of the search a trade-off study was made of three terminals. In the fall of 1970, OCLC decided on the Spiras Systems, Inc. Irascope Model LTE, which surpassed or equaled other contenders in twenty-eight characteristics. The Irascope was a CRT terminal that used an electron tube to emit a beam of electrons onto the various parts of a phosphor-coated screen, forming a visual display. The Center was given the opportunity to advise the company on a review and revision of specifications. The OCLC staff, working with the Advisory Committee, formulated an Irascope designed solely to manipulate bibliographic data of the Center. Two Irascopes were ordered in September of 1970, and the remaining sixty-eight were requested in January 1971. Initially, the number of terminals per member varied from one to five.

Member library staffs had to orientate themselves in various aspects of computer language. Procedures such as installation and use of a CRT terminal were new to librarians. The OCLC *Newsletter,* for June 11, 1971, explained the terminal equipment that would be installed in member libraries. It is interesting because it describes in detail the physical size of equipment that librarians would have to make room for.

> The CRT terminal equipment will consist of three items: (1) the telephone system interface unit (MODEM); (2) the visual display unit; and (3) the keyboard.
>
> The MODEM measures 8 inches high by 18 inches wide by 12 inches deep, and it is to be located within 10 feet of the visual display unit.
>
> The visual display unit measures 17 inches high by 20 inches wide by 22 inches deep. It is most important that this unit be situated in freely moving open air; it should not be placed under a low shelf or smothered under a pile of publications.
>
> The keyboard unit will be connected to the visual display unit by a cable that is 5 feet in length. The keyboard is portable and is designed so that it can be located to provide maximum comfort for the user.[11]

The OCLC telecommunication network was in the forefront of national library telecommunications, and near the forefront of the American Telephone and Telegraph Company's (AT & T) networking activities. Initial efforts toward designing the OCLC telephone network began in November of 1970 when the Center placed its order with AT & T's Long Lines Division. The Center hoped to have the network ready for use by July 1, 1971, giving the telephone company over seven months to complete the work. Through the network the majority of Ohio's academic libraries would be linked to the central computer in Columbus. With the CRT terminals located in the libraries, and connected via telephone lines, institutions would be able to carry on a "conversation" with the main computer. Despite efforts to have the lines ready by the target date, the telephone system was not ready for use until the middle of August 1971. The network was a multiple party line operating in synchronous mode. The method was effective and economical although not yet in wide use. The telephone company was working on a system with which it had had little prior experience. Moreover, the communications web crossed the territorial lines of several non-Bell System telephone companies that also were relatively inexperienced in computer-data networking.

The resolution of the problem of designing a mammoth file of bibliographic entries from which a single entry could be rapidly retrieved was facilitated by Long in collaboration with Kunj B. L. Rastogi, a programmer for OCLC; James E. Rush, associate professor, Department of Computer and Information Science, The Ohio State University; and John A. Wyckoff, senior programmer and systems analyst for OCLC. The findings were reported by Long in late August of 1971 at a meeting of the International Federation for Information Processing Societies in Ljubljana, Yugoslavia. The paper bore the title "Large On-Line Files of Bibliographic Data: An Efficient Design and a Mathematical Predictor of Retrieval Behavior," and its research and findings served as a basis for construction of the Center's on-line files.

Research continued on access to large files employing truncated, derived search keys. OCLC staff wrote two papers on the subject that were ready to go to the press in the spring of 1971: "Title-Only Retrieval from a MARC File" and "A Truncated Search Key Title Index." The findings were directly applicable to the OCLC system, containing over 150,000 catalog records by the end of the year.

As the year drew to a close, three indices were operational on-line: a name-title index containing a truncated name-title-date record, a truncated title index, and a nontruncated LC card-number index. The name-title index employed the three,three search key.[12] The title index also consisted of six characters, the first three characters of the first, nonarticle word of the title, plus the first character of the next three words. This was called the three,one,one,one search key. For example, if a user was searching for bibliographic information on Ernest Hemingway's novel *For Whom the Bell Tolls*, he would type in "For,w,t,b" using the CRT terminal keyboard. Work was under way on author, added author, and call number indices.

Truncated search keys were not new. The Ohio State University Libraries were the first to use truncated key indices in the design of their remote catalog access and circulation control system, which was operational in December 1970 with a four,five key. This experience represents one example of how OCLC was willing to use and share successful research conducted elsewhere.

The linking of the academic libraries in Ohio to a central computer site, with each library being able to use and input information, was a major undertaking involving people and machines. Librarians were novices. Therefore, the training of member library personnel was an ongoing responsibility of OCLC. *Creation of Machine-Readable Catalog Entries; an Adaptation of the "Data Preparation Manual, MARC Editors"* (May 1971) and *Cataloging on a Cathode Ray Tube Terminal* (June 1971) were written as training tools by the OCLC staff. A brochure, entitled *Ohio College Library Center*, presented a brief description of OCLC. Two day-long instructional meetings were held in June 1971, with approximately 340 staff members from Ohio universities and colleges attending. One meeting covered the preparation of bibliographic data to be input on terminals, and the other dealt with use of terminals. In July 1971, five half-day clinics were arranged to instruct terminal users. A maximum of ten participants were accepted for each. Practice time on the terminal plus further instructions constituted the clinic training. One person from each institution was sent as a representative to instruct his or her co-workers. Additional plans were being made to hold a dozen regional clinics in member libraries during the summer of 1971. The OCLC *Newsletter,* begun in December of 1967, continued as the main vehicle of communication between the Center and member libraries. Information was interesting, often mentally taxing, but always useful. Publication of the *Newsletter* facilitated a smooth conversion to on-line cataloging.

Carlos Cuadra, Manager of the Library and Documentation Systems Department at System Development Corporation (SDC), composed a paper based on observations of other on-line systems. His remarks were shared, in part, in the *Newsletter* for January 14, 1971. For OCLC members the comments were directly related to their future activities.

> Terminals of some on-line systems have been set up in public or semi-public locations. Operations of a terminal in such a location has proved distracting to others and public observation has deterred users of the terminal. For most people, operation of an on-line terminal is not a completely comfortable experience during the first hours or days. Feeling that one is in a fish bowl enhances discomfort. It is hoped that members can set up terminals in locations where the terminal user does not feel that he is distracting library patrons and other staff members.[13]

Membership status for the year was as follows: fifty institutions paid 1970-1971 assessments; Dyke College, St. John College of Cleveland, and Wilberforce University failed to renew memberships; the College of Steubenville became a new member; and the United Theological Seminary informed OCLC of its plans to join. In November 1970 the Board of Trustees elected Hyman W. Kritzer as chairman, Lewis C. Branscomb as vice-chairman, Robert F. Cayton as secretary, and Bob L. Mowery as treasurer.[14] The Executive Committee was established at the September 3, 1970 meeting. First members included the chairman, the secretary, and the treasurer of the board. A later amendment resulted in the addition of vice-chairman. The committee had the power to act on significant issues whenever action was required between the bimonthly meetings.

RESEARCH AND DEVELOPMENT

With the development and growth of the field of information science over the past twenty years, the role of research and development (R & D) in librarianship increased. From the onset, R & D was an integral part of OCLC's activities. Through its application many new avenues were explored. The Center's assessments supported a cooperative research and development program. Consequently, OCLC was able to undertake R & D efforts that no single library could afford, but many were able to underwrite. Lacking this kind of backing, some American libraries were spending as much as one hundred thousand dollars a year on research.

Major plans in 1970-1971 called for R & D on three new systems: remote catalog access and circulation control, serials control, and technical processing. The Board of Trustees on July 21, 1971, adopted a resolution establishing R & D priorities for the three systems. Serials had top priority, then technical processing, and finally, circulation control. Files and indices for these systems were to be blended with the existing shared cataloging system.

OCLC submitted research proposals to OE and CLR. Favorable results followed. OE granted $125,000, and CLR provided $75,000. Both grants were to be used for prolonging research to develop a computerized regional library system.

OUT-OF-STATE COOPERATIVE
ACTIVITIES AND NETWORKING

Plans also encompassed another library system outside of the state, the Cooperative College Library Center (CCLC) in Atlanta, Georgia. CCLC was incorporated in 1969 as a nonprofit corporation. Sponsored by the United Board for College Development and funded initially by the Carnegie Corporation, the Center was established to meet the library needs of eighteen black colleges.[15] The Center, operating with a staff of nine full-time employees and five student assistants, offered centralized purchasing, cataloging, and processing of materials.

OCLC served both colleges and universities, within Ohio whereas CCLC served only four-year, liberal arts colleges in ten states. However they were alike in a number of ways. They had experienced rapid growth in their successful efforts to reduce duplication in cataloging and to lower costs through cooperation. The two had discovered the need for a feasibility study before becoming operational, and the necessity of seeking outside funds for continued development. Both were interested in cooperation, although on different levels: OCLC on the shared level and CCLC on the centralized level.

From the OE grant, $50,000 was allocated to demonstrate that an OCLC interface with CCLC was possible. The demonstration was intended to prove that the OCLC system could lower processing costs in a centralized processing center.

The experiment's progress in 1971 was recorded in a document entitled "A Proposal for Library Support for United Negro College Fund Colleges,"[16] written by Hillis D. Davis, director of CCLC. Before its relationship with OCLC, CCLC cataloged materials conventionally. Under terms of the experiment, CCLC became a full participant in the OCLC on-line shared cataloging project. If the experiment proved successful, a permanent relationship with OCLC would be established.

OCLC was expanding its interests not only south, but also east to Pennsylvania. On November 27, 1970, an agreement was signed with PRLC.[17] Under its terms OCLC would provide off-line catalog card production services to members of PRLC. In an on-line phase of the project, a CRT terminal would be located in Pittsburgh. It was anticipated that future agreements would lead to the involvement of PRLC in the Center's on-line shared cataloging system.

The invitation extended to PRLC was a geographical and historical milestone. The OCLC system was communicating interstate — a national information web was being spun. The prototype linkage changed the Ohio information network into a superhighway of information networks, based on the methods and services developed by OCLC, and encompassing other regional library systems. It was only four years earlier that OCLC's founders had hoped to create a regional library system. Now, for the first time, a dramatic new possibility for a national system emerged.

OCLC proposed that cooperation with PRLC be on one of three levels. PRLC could be a unit serviced by the Center, or an OCLC satellite, or an independent node linked to the Center. At the close of the year they agreed to cooperate as a satellite. In an unpublished paper, Frank Ziaukas, executive director of PRLC, wrote that the interstate status for which OCLC would qualify meant a significant saving in the cost of communication lines. Instead of having to operate under the fee schedules of a dozen local Ohio telephone companies, OCLC could take advantage of a single telephone rate structure. Moreover, the new arrangement was a passport for OCLC in applying for funds to develop a national library network. It enabled PRLC to acquire catalog cards more economically, and to have full access to the union catalog through its own CRT terminal. Under the terms of agreement, the PRLC was free to use its CRT for both library operations and experimentation. Additionally, it would secure tapes, programs, and expertise from the Center to evolve a Pittsburgh-based regional library system.[18]

For OCLC, the year ended with a sense of achievement. The on-line shared cataloging system was on the verge of implementation. Librarians were training on the system. The actual shared cataloging project was scheduled to begin operation on July 1, 1971. A network of library systems was germinating.

NOTES

1. Lewis C. Branscomb, "Progress Report to the Ohio College Association, Executive Committee" (Columbus: Ohio College Library Center, 11 April 1979), p. 4.

2. Ohio College Library Center, *Annual Report 1970/1971* (Columbus: Ohio College Library Center, 1971), p. [1].

3. Frederick G. Kilgour, "Evolving, Computerizing, Personalizing," *American Libraries* 3 (February 1972): 145.

4. Ibid.

5. See appendix 1, Exhibit G, for a list of the fixed and variable costs of catalog card production.

6. Op. cit., Ohio College Library Center, *Annual Report 1970/1971*, p. 8.

7. See appendix 2, Glossary of Terms, for a definition.

8. Charles Coffin Jewett, "A Plan for Stereotyping Catalogues by Separate Titles," in *Proceedings of the American Association for the Advancement of Science* (s. l.: s. n., August 1850), pp. 12-13.

9. "The Costs of Library and Informational Services," in *Libraries at Large*, eds.: Douglas M. Knight and E. Shepley Nourse (New York: R. R. Bowker, 1969), p. 196.

10. Ohio College Library Center, "Minutes of the Board of Trustees Meeting" (Columbus: Ohio College Library Center, 13 November 1970), p. 3.

11. Ohio College Library Center, *Newsletter*, 11 June 1971, p. [2].

12.　See chapter 3 for an example of the three, three search key.

13.　Ohio College Library Center, *Newsletter*, 14 January 1971, p. 1.

14.　See appendix 1, Exhibit D, for a complete list of the Board of Trustees members.

15.　See appendix 1, Exhibit J, for a list of the CCLC membership.

16.　Hillis D. Davis, "A Proposal for Library Support for United Negro College Fund Colleges," 15 November 1971, p. 8. (Typewritten.)

17.　See appendix 1, Exhibit J, for a list of the PRLC membership.

18.　Frank Ziaukas, "Potential Cooperation with the Ohio College Library Center: Report," p. 3. (Typewritten, undated.)

5

OCLC GOES ON-LINE:
Laying the Cornerstone
to Grand-Scale Cooperation
1971-1972

As early as 1963 librarians were ambivalently anticipating the coming of computers into libraries. One librarian, Burton W. Adkinson, likened the situation to the ancient parable about the camel who entered the tent uninvited. According to it, the more of the animal that got in, the worse things were to become. Adkinson added a fresh twist to the story. "With the computer 'camel,' however, as I have shown, his 'nose' of the mechanization of various clerical-type routines already is proving immensely valuable in library operations."[1] He concludes, "It is up to people and groups like us to see to it that his further invasion of the librarian's professional 'tent' is accomplished in an intelligent, effective manner that will bring greater and greater benefits rather than disaster."[2] Nearly a decade after the publication of Adkinson's words, the camel had, indeed, gained full entrance into the tent of Ohio libraries. Ohio and OCLC's response was not only to welcome it in but also to enlarge the tent to accommodate it in every possible way.

OCLC activities in fiscal year 1971-1972 were focused on two main areas: the implementation and operation of the on-line union catalog and shared cataloging system and exploration of out-of-state cooperative possibilities. These activities, of course, had direct bearing on what Ohio academic libraries were doing.

ON-LINE IMPLEMENTATION
AND OPERATION

The on-line shared cataloging system got under way without much fanfare during July and August 1971. The installation of the terminals in each member library signaled the start of on-line dialogues between Columbus and curious librarians throughout the state. The terminals were the medium for retrieving cataloging records from the OCLC data base and editing them in accordance with library preferences. In the off-line system of card production, all libraries had to accept the MARC II records in their full form, which could not be edited. Therefore, the ability to edit records greatly expanded the usefulness of the system. Moreover, the terminal proved to be a key that unlocked a wealth of bibliographic information that could be used not only for cataloging purposes but also for book selection, preorder searching, interlibrary loan requests, and pure bibliographic information.

On October 13, 1971, the on-line union catalog feature became available. For the first time on a CRT screen, institutional holdings were shown as part of the catalog record. The addition of the holding symbol to a record was initially an automatic by-product whenever a record was used for requesting cards. Prior to October, only the LC MARC II records could be used for either off-line or on-line production. On October 18, however, the system began to accept cataloging input by participating libraries. By the end of the year the major capabilities of the system were in operation. Member libraries had cataloged 336,307 titles using the system. An annual catalog card production at a rate of over 3.4 million was calculated from January to June.

July 1971 to June 1972 was a momentous year for Ohio's academic libraries, with totally new experiences occurring regularly. This summary of the year's accomplishments serves as a backdrop for the following detailed monthly unfolding of events.

JULY, 1971

According to the Center's plans, a prototype of the on-line shared cataloging system was projected for activation on July 7, with implementation of the operational system scheduled for 7:00 A.M. on July 12. Capabilities were to include all those of a fully operational on-line system, with the exception of the production of catalog cards. The prototype system would be interfaced with the catalog production system on the morning of the twelfth. OCLC's computer was ready to go. All that was needed to begin operations was the installation of the terminals in the member libraries and the completion of the telephone network.

Fulfillment of the planned schedule would depend heavily upon installation of forty terminals by July 9. However, the terminals were late due to problems at the factory, and on-line operation had to be postponed until July 19. The already late arrival of the terminals was further delayed. As of July 17 only twenty had been delivered, seventeen of which were ready for use. By July 22, the company was to have shipped six more, with the remaining fourteen due on July 30.

A second problem developed with the telephone network. A telephone workers' strike further deferred the inception of the on-line activities. An additional complication was the incorrect installation of many of the data sets, which were crucial to the total communications system for each library. A single incorrect installation could obstruct receipt of messages from Columbus to all libraries on one circuit. Moreover, the multiple party line network allowed one obstruction to multiply quickly. More communications problems surfaced. One of the more unusual of these occurred when a bullet was fired into a cable carrying an OCLC circuit.

By the end of July only eleven terminals were installed and working. Youngstown State University, using the system in training mode, experienced nearly an hour's wait from the time it made its original request to Columbus until a response was received. The delay was not attributable to the malfunction of the system but rather to the misbehavior of the telephone data set at the College of Wooster.[3] This incident was not an isolated case. Many more bizarre, fantastic, and often trying events took place in those early weeks of on-line operations.

Proper preparation and instruction in the details of the on-line procedures was the best insurance for a successful on-line beginning. The massive training efforts begun several years earlier intensified. Supplemental to the clinics at which a single representative from each institution was present, the Center also provided for statewide regional meetings to be held after the middle of July. They would be especially beneficial since full staff participation was possible either from an individual institution or from several neighboring ones. Three meetings were scheduled. The first was held at Bowling Green State University on July 20. On July 28 Oberlin College hosted the second gathering. Ohio Wesleyan University held the final one on September 13. Cleveland State University and Ohio University also called meetings. Their importance was underscored by the fact that either Judith Hopkins, Bibliographic Editor for OCLC, or Kilgour himself conducted all of the sessions.

AUGUST, 1971

The month began with deliberations between OCLC and AT & T's Long Lines Division over problems with the leased line network. It ended victoriously with the implementation of on-line cataloging on August 26.

The data sets and communications circuit were the two main trouble areas. Due to malfunctioning data sets, information transmitted from a member library would arrive in Columbus in an amended and often unintelligible form. The condition affected libraries that were sharing the party line. Data set problems were less common than those associated with communications circuit. They were often related to incorrect options for the production of catalog cards in a particular library or to the malfunction of communications units. If an undesired option was mistakenly installed in one data set, a communication blockade could shut out the local terminal as well as others on the same party line.

In the early part of August, libraries that had received terminals could practice on them. The training system was available from 7:00 A.M. to 7:00 P.M., Eastern Standard Time, Monday through Friday. The Center urged librarians to use the training system as much as possible. It gave them the opportunity to adjust to the new operational procedures of the on-line system, including hands-on experience with the terminal keyboard. The Center reasoned that the practice sessions were the necessary prerequisite to the smooth transfer to the on-line mode. The prototype system proved to be beneficial not only to terminal users but also to OCLC, which tested operations before full on-line production began. Many malfunctions were detected and corrected in this pre-on-line stage.

LC had begun its CIP program in July 1971 and by August the Center had to make adjustments to it.[4] OCLC received the CIP catalog records included on the weekly LC-distributed MARC II computer tapes. They would appear on the terminal screen as nearly complete catalog records except for the absence of the collation, which described the books as a physical object (the number of volumes, the pages, and the type and character of illustrations). Once the collation was completed, the records were totally acceptable for production.

While the training mode was still operational, the on-line cataloging resulting in card production at OCLC was initiated on August 26. Ohio University was its first participant. On the first day it cataloged 147 titles while simultaneously 36 other institutions made use of the terminals in the training mode. As the system's first user, Ohio University automatically became the first contributor to the union catalog.

By affixing its three-letter holding symbol in a designated place on the catalog record, Ohio University communicated to the Center's archival file that it owned a copy of a particular title. In the beginning the file was solely a storage bank, inaccessible to the terminal user. This was no longer the case in October when the holdings information began to appear on the bibliographic record. The early system allowed for only one holding library and one copy to be registered on a record. It was adjusted in October to include the recording of additional libraries and copies.

A particularly useful facet of the system was its SAVE function. The save area was a part of the computer memory that was shared by all libraries. Each terminal had approximately twenty save slots that permitted retrieved records to be preserved by the system for later viewing the same day. At first records could be saved daily from 7:00 A.M. to 7:00 P.M., Eastern Standard Time.[5] The function was particularly useful to a trainee cataloger, especially when it was necessary to leave the terminal for further checking of bibliographic information.

For OCLC and libraries the first day's operation of on-line cataloging was an unruffled success. But on the second day, lightning struck, literally, as the September 1 OCLC *Newsletter* (page 2) reported:

> *Disaster:* Throughout the first day of live operation, the system functioned smoothly, but soon after the computer system was made active at 7:00 A.M. the next day, smoke began to billow out of the Sigma 5. The computer was immediately taken out of operation. Investigation revealed that the power pack in the core bank had failed, and there was some possibility that the failure might have been associated with a severe electrical storm during the previous night that caused a power outage for an hour and a half. This catastrophe was the first major emergency that had occurred in a year of computer operation.

Despite the interruption, Ohio University cataloged 156 titles on its second day on-line, averaging 10 titles per terminal-hour for the two days. The following Saturday, 1,803 catalog cards were printed from the first two days of on-line activity.

SEPTEMBER, 1971

September was characterized by an increase in card production and an expansion of the system's capabilities. By the first week of the month twenty libraries were on-line, with over two thousand catalog cards being generated each evening. The Center anticipated activation of two libraries each day until all of the membership had at least one terminal installed.

The importance of the OCLC *Newsletter* cannot be overstated. It was an indispensable tool for the librarian. In the start-up stage, it enabled the Center to keep members aware of problems, procedures, and results of early on-line implementation. The communications system established between OCLC and the membership, which included the *Newsletter*, made it possible for the Center's on-line work steadily to proceed.

Many of the bugs were removed from the system as September came to a close. The system's finer components were introduced to the users through written instructions sent from the Center. They were taught to interpret and use supplementary screen space, and contents notes features. In August, a terminal operator could extensively edit a MARC II record for catalog card production but could not see the entire set of changes. In September the Center added a reformat function, whereby an operator could instruct the computer to rearrange the cataloging information on the screen in its edited form. Thus, editorial changes to any record were visible on the terminal screen. As librarians became more comfortable using the terminals, card production rose. For the week of September 23, 1971, it surpassed the four thousand mark. When on-line production exceeded twenty thousand cards per week in the months ahead, the Center had surpassed the peak production rate of the off-line system.

OCTOBER, 1971

October marked the commencement of a new and highly desirable on-line function — the capability to add original cataloging data to the extant data base. It also was the month in which the membership held its first general meeting where members could share with one another what they had been experiencing.

For input cataloging, the system provided the display of a work form outline of the MARC II format on the terminal screen.[6] On Friday, October 18, 1971, at 7:00 A.M., the Center began to accept input cataloging. Subsequently, members were asked to do all monographic cataloging on-line except for materials published in non-Roman alphabets. After the original record was input at the terminal, the operator sent the message via communications lines to Columbus to instruct OCLC to produce a set of catalog cards for its library's card catalog. The system was programmed to record daily the received data onto the tape used for nightly card production. A second program put the record into the master file (to which the terminals had direct access) and added it to the holdings information in the archive file. Most importantly, within seconds the record was available to any library.

With the influx of the new cataloging information, the Center found it necessary to discontinue temporarily addition of the MARC II records to the data base. The activity would be resumed when the complex programming was developed to detect whether a MARC II record duplicated one already input by a member. The decision to halt the addition of MARC II records was based on the Center's belief that the system would be more beneficial to its users if they felt free to catalog *any* book regardless of its publication date and language.

Five days before the start of the input cataloging function, the terminals began to display holdings information, by institution. As of October 13, 1971, a library could call up any record and see at the bottom of the screen who owned a copy of the particular title.[7, 8] The new procedure was a step toward fulfilling one of the Center's primary goals: the widespread availability of library resources.

The month was characterized by more "firsts." The first meeting of the Advisory Committee on Serials Control was convened on October 1, 1971, when approximately thirty people from OCLC member libraries and participating regions met to define the products and processes to be developed for the on-line serials control subsystem, one of the five originally conceived OCLC subsystems. Discussion centered around a document entitled *A Brief Description of the Serials Control System: A Preliminary Report* (September 1971), prepared by Ann Ekstrom.[9] It outlined a comprehensive serials control system that would include all of the products and functions necessary to satisfy the requirements of member libraries.

The first general meeting of the OCLC membership was held on October 29, 1971. All of the member library staffs were invited. Its main purpose was to fulfill the legal obligation to meet annually as a body. Part of the meeting was set aside to allow librarians to share their on-line cataloging experiences. The speakers, all member librarians, were Barbara Gates of Oberlin College; Philip Wei of the College of Wooster; Helen Cheadle of Kenyon College; and Milton E. Hodnette of Ohio University. Each described the procedural alterations that resulted since his or her library's participation in the on-line cataloging system. The gathering reinforced the communications channel between OCLC and its users.

NOVEMBER, 1971

On-line cataloging continued to grow, and a daily record was set on November 11, 1971, when forty-two members cataloged a total of 1,868 titles. On the same day 483 original catalog records were converted into a machine-readable form, and 12,254 catalog cards were produced. For the first time, cards were being shipped with the date of shipment stamped on the card packs. The new procedure let a library know if more than two days, the expected lapse time, passed since the day when the cards had been requested.

Members spent the month learning more of the finer points of system procedures, such as cancelling holding codes, formatting call numbers, spacing, reformatting records, and avoiding input of duplicate records.

The preceding chapter mentioned the award of $200,000 from OE and CLR to OCLC to support R & D from July 1971 through December 1972. An unforeseen reduction of the total amount to $150,000 in fiscal year 1971-1972 altered the original development schedule. Work had to be halted on one of the three systems covered by the original grant. Based upon a membership poll, a decision was made to proceed on the technical processing and serials control systems and to postpone the development of the remote catalog access and circulation control system. Thus, work was transferred from development of remote catalog access and circulation control to technical processing and serials control.

During November, the Center set up an Advisory Committee on Technical Processing. Invitations were sent to seventeen institutions who were to nominate staff members to serve on the Committee. In all, there were twenty-five representatives. Through its efforts, a system design was constructed from which the Center's programming staff could begin to formulate the new system.

The Ohio State University Libraries agreed to provide four programmers in the early part of September 1972 to work on the technical processing system. The Ohio State University Libraries had already decided to develop an on-line circulation system to include technical services. Rather than continue its work independently, Ohio State chose to cooperate with OCLC.

The OCLC technical processing system was to begin on April 1, 1973.[10] The cooperative effort to write the computer programs would be advantageous not only to OCLC and The Ohio State University Libraries but also to the academic libraries in Ohio that were members.

The on-line shared cataloging system created novel methods of handling library materials. Many library activities were being done in new and unpredictable ways. The Ohio State University Libraries were using the system to fulfill a variety of needs:

> The instantaneous availability of authoritative cataloging copy and greatly speeded card production are only the two most obvious benefits of this new shared-cataloging system. The ability of pre-catalog searchers to search by LC card numbers and titles has made the determination of main entry much easier. The utility of the remote access terminal to determine statewide holdings for inter-library loan purposes has already been established here. Cataloging activity has reached a new level at The Ohio State University Libraries with the successful implementation of on-line computer techniques.[11]

The Advisory Committee on Serials Control worked assiduously during November to define the serials control system. The first stage of the system was the serials check-in module, scheduled for operation in December 1972.

The annual meeting on November 12, 1971, witnessed the election of Hyman W. Kritzer as chairman of the Board of Trustees, Lewis C. Branscomb as vice-chairman, Robert F. Cayton as secretary, and John H. Becker as treasurer.[12]

The membership roster reflected some changes. The United Theological School of Dayton joined at the start of the year. An expression of the intent to join in the next year came from the Medical College of Ohio. John Carroll University and Mount Union College terminated their memberships. Capital University, a charter member, rejoined the Center at the start of the year, but did not renew its membership for 1972-1973. Forty-nine members were active during the year, one less than in the previous year.

At the 1971 annual meeting the membership approved a change in the calculation of membership fees. Earlier in April 1968, the membership had approved a method for determining membership fees. During 1971, fees were essentially based on this 1968 formula: assessments were drawn from the number of titles each library cataloged during 1969-1970. The fees assessed in the spring of 1971 were based upon the 1969-1970 figures since they were the most recent available. After the end of the year, the 1971-1972 fees were to be adjusted according to the actual use of the records in the system for cataloging purposes. Thus, the extent to which a member used the system would be the criterion for the following year's fees.

DECEMBER, 1971

During December OCLC was deeply involved in maintenance of the system. Besides routine debugging and correcting work, OCLC was working on several projects scheduled for completion by mid-January. The Center decided to invoke a moratorium on visits from staff members of non-OCLC libraries. The temporary halt ran from December 17, 1971, through January 10, 1972. The visits were resumed in January with one change. Beginning January 17, non-OCLC visitors were to be received on Mondays only. Visitors from all parts of the world were coming daily to satisfy inquisitiveness, to find solutions to a particular problem, or to learn more about the replication of the system. Many were also interested in The Ohio State University Libraries' remote catalog access and circulation control system. The OCLC library automation tour was later revised to include a stop at The Ohio State University Libraries in the morning and a visit to the Center in the afternoon.

Before activation of input cataloging, members began to be concerned about the disparate quality of cataloging coming into the system from member libraries. Differences in both quality standards and internal library policies accounted for the variety. An additional factor was the availability of a wide spectrum of catalog card options. The outcome of this concern was reactivation of the Advisory Committee on Cataloging, which held meetings from mid-December into April 1972. Discussions centered around the methods available for improving the quality of input cataloging while at the same time maintaining input costs at the lowest possible level.

A standard form and procedure for reporting mistakes was established in December. Previously, errors on bibliographic records in the data base were reported directly to the Center as they were identified by members.

Problems related to the communications equipment plagued the system in December. Members reported occasional instances of screen images from another library appearing unexpectedly on their terminal screens. The Center's staff investigated this strange phenomenon. On December 2 the problem was isolated, and an emergency programming effort was made to correct it. Unfortunately, the problem had spread until the system was overrun with scrambled and misplaced records. On the afternoon of December 3, the SAVE file had to be totally purged. During the next three days OCLC staff worked around the clock to remedy the situation. By the fourth day the repaired system was back in use. Hardware difficulties further delayed actual start-up by several hours.

A modified version of ALA's print train was purchased in December. The new train was a vast improvement over the former one. It printed eight rather than six lines to the inch. Thus, more data could be printed on fewer cards, and the need for extension cards diminished. The modified model contained nearly all of the diacritics and special characters contained in LC's MARC print train plus a script "el." It also printed Greek letters as well as subscript and superscript numerals, parentheses, and plus and minus signs.

Libraries generally greeted their terminals warmly. One library went so far as to personify its CRT.

> 'Bruce' sounds pretty, doesn't it? Our CRT 'Bruce' was named before I came to the Ohio Wesleyan University Library. Judy and Sephronia, our assistant catalogers, said that the 'CRT' sounds so cold, cruel and improper. Also it would not stand for what they really liked and loved, so they thought if they loved to operate the CRT so much, they would name and treat him as a person.[13]

Other terminals across the state were christened "Charlie," "Curt," and "George and Georgina" (a pair).

The Advisory Committee on Serials Control continued to meet monthly. By December a *Manual for Checking-in, Binding, and Claiming of Serials on a CRT Terminal—Draft of Preliminary Procedures* (December 1971) was completed. It laid the foundation for further refinement of system design.

For several years the Center had been working to finance the early on-line system. In fiscal year 1969-1970 the Ad Hoc Committee on Financing was appointed to explore the problem. One theme permeated the Committee's deliberations: OCLC could not operate without outside financial assistance. Efforts toward securing outside funds culminated in November 1970 when the Center presented the Ohio Board of Regents with a development proposal entitled "Implementation of a Computerized Regional Library System." The Center requested $581,587 over a two-year period. The amount was equal to the OCLC budget for one year of operation. Two-thirds of the funds would be available during the first year, and the remaining third would be expended in the second year. The membership would have to pay one-third of the first-year's expenses, two-thirds in the second year, and the full costs for the third year. With the subsidy, OCLC would begin operations with a sound financial footing. The members would realize the net savings in start-up costs. At the same time, they would take advantage of the two-year period to allow for normal attrition of staff members and transfer of resulting savings as payments to OCLC.

The Board of Regents approved the request in fiscal year 1970-1971. However, it was not until December 1971 that the State Legislature released the funds. The first payment arrived in February 1972. Late receipt of the funds could have created problems for OCLC had not some of its creditors been willing to accept deferred payments. A bank loan of $77,000 filled the financial gap until the first of February. The OCLC membership was deeply indebted to the Board of Regents for helping to cushion the financial burden of supporting its own staffs in addition to making payments to a new system.

JANUARY, 1972

In January, OCLC added a fourth retrieval index, the OCLC control number, to its existing indices. Each record in the bibliographic data base automatically received an OCLC control number when it entered the file. The Center activated that number index and made it available to all members. As opposed to the OCLC control number index, the LC card number index was a supplementary one whose use was limited to the records that contained an LC card number.

The same month the system experienced card production problems. One of the more interesting cases involved the printing of the word "rocksoulblues-jazzsickjewblackhumorsexpoppsych," which appeared on the title page of a book entitled *Freakshow* by Albert Harry Goldman. If any word in a record were too long to be printed on a single line of the card, the system refused to print the card for the title. The problem was resolved by inserting a hyphen in the middle of the word.

FEBRUARY-MARCH, 1972

On February 23 the Advisory Committee on Technical Processing held its first meeting with Ann Ekstrom and reviewed a paper prepared by her entitled *OCLC Technical Processing System—A Preliminary Outline* (February 1972). The Committee's first task was to design a system compatible with the needs of the membership. The system, according to the document, was to offer five basic services: issuance of purchase orders, maintenance of an outstanding order file, maintenance of a committment register, automatic issuance of claims for material not received, and clearance of invoices for payment. Each participating library maintained its financial records differently. The heterogeneity of financial bookkeeping among members increased the difficulties of designing the system.

Catalog card production steadily increased, and by February the entire system was functioning well. The February *Newsletter* described a promising situation:

> Member libraries cataloged 44,158 titles using OCLC during the month period that extended from 18 January through 17 February. This monthly rate yields a total of 529,896 titles cataloged for a year; this total is fifty thousand more than the total titles processed by OCLC Members in 1969/70, the total on which present membership fees are based. At no time during the month was the system more than minimally used.
>
> The daily average of titles cataloged during the month period was 1,920.
>
> The first day in which catalog card production exceeded 15,000 cards was February 1st, when 15,136 were produced.
>
> The month period analyzed followed addition to the data base of MARC records that had accumulated since mid-October.

Hence, the sample is probably abnormally high when viewed as representative of a year's production. However, the sample does show that the system can comfortably function at the same or higher level than Members' total volume in cataloging.[14]

Much time and effort were exerted to perfect the on-line cataloging system. As spring arrived the Center was adding two new features. An error checking feature would automatically verify the correctness of new data added to the base, would upgrade the quality of cataloging in the base, and would indirectly improve service to users.

The other feature was the extended search for bibliographic data. Whenever a search key yielded more than 50 truncated entries, the system would automatically go into the extended search mode enabling the user to view all of the entries (up to 256) in the data base under a specific search key. Through a dialogue of questions and answers between the computer and the operator, the search for a specific record would proceed by quickly narrowing the options until the desired record (assuming it was in the data base) was located in the data base and subsequently retrieved and displayed.[15] Activated in February 1973, the feature was in great demand. Like error checking, its addition would further enhance the system's worth.

The error checking and extended search features were the last two added before OCLC placed a temporary moratorium on system changes and enhancements. The fabric of the on-line system had been stretched to its limit by heavy use and programming additions and modifications. The result was degradation of performance. The system was being forced to digest new tasks that it was unprepared to handle. The moratorium gave the Center's staff the time to consolidate, solidify, and properly document the terminal support program.

APRIL-MAY, 1972

The activities during April and May focused on the development and implementation of input standards and on the expansion of the membership to nonacademic libraries in Ohio. In the spring of 1972, the Advisory Committee on Cataloging generated a series of recommendations for input cataloging standards that were reviewed and approved by the membership at a meeting on May 17 in Columbus. The draft document was entitled *Recommendations for Standards for Input Cataloging*. The final one, *Standards for Input Cataloging* (June 1972), was prepared by staff members from a number of libraries.[16] These standards were to be applied and followed by all members as well as new or affiliate members who had to agree to abide by them.

At the same meeting, the Committee on Implementation of Standards for Input Cataloging was appointed by the chairman of the Board of Trustees to devise procedures for implementation of the standards. The members, under the chairmanship of Thompson M. Little of Ohio University, were: L. Ronald Frommeyer (Wright State University); Herbert F. Johnson (Oberlin College); Richard J. Owen (Heidelberg College); and Frederick G. Kilgour, OCLC, ex-offico. The Committee was to report its recommendations at the fall membership meeting.

The Advisory Committee on Serials Control was also concerned with cataloging standards. In anticipation of the serials control system, it had prepared *Recommended Standards for the Cataloging of Serials* (May 1972).

The Advisory Committee on Technical Processing worked through the winter and into the spring to design the technical processing system. *The Technical Processing System — The Ohio College Library Center* (May 1972) was issued in the spring, setting the stage for further discussions on design and definition of the system.

On May 17, 1972, a landmark decision was made by the membership when it instructed the Board of Trustees to amend the Articles of Incorporation to permit nonacademic libraries in Ohio to be eligible for membership in OCLC.[17] From the beginning, the founders of OCLC had wanted to include nonacademic libraries. The widening of the membership circle would be yet another move toward fulfilling the goal of large-scale accessibility of bibliographic information.

The Center had been established as a nonprofit organization, and it wished to retain this status. As a result, libraries in profit-making institutions in Ohio were not eligible for membership, thereby closing the door to another potential group of users. The nonacademic libraries that joined as a result of the policy change were the Dayton and Montgomery County Public Library, Geauga County Public Library, Lakewood Public Library together with the Lakewood Board of Education, the Public Library of Youngstown and Mahoning County, and the Toledo-Lucas County Public Library.

Also in May, Philip L. Long, senior programmer and systems analyst, was promoted to the position of assistant director. His responsibilities included the general operations of the entire system in addition to research and development.

During the first year of the Center's incorporation, the Board of Trustees convened only three times. In 1971-1972 it met ten times. The role of the Board had changed from a constitutional body to an advisory one. At the time of the May membership meeting the Trustees initiated a move to broaden the professional composition of the Board to include people possessing special skills in such fields as law, economics, and computer science.

JUNE, 1972

The Center spent the summer perfecting the system and preparing for future activities. The economic realities of the first year of the on-line system were evident. Ideally, the system would offer economic incentives to its members while providing for wide dissemination of bibliographic information. In fiscal year 1971-1972, the membership did not experience a net saving. The 1969-1970 *Annual Report* included a savings estimate that was to be realized when the system was in full operation, i.e., at the end of the second operational year, when member libraries could on-line catalog an average of six titles per hour. A daily average of 1,460 titles was projected to be cataloged during 1972-1973. From January through June 1972, the membership had fulfilled 82.6 percent of the original estimate. The Center believed that after another year had passed the union catalog would have reached a size adequate to meet its original use predictions.[18]

Further encouragement came when the members reported in 1971-1972 that they could on-line catalog from 5.9 to 20 titles per hour per terminal. Thus, the original figure of six titles per hour was an underestimation. All indicators led the Center and its membership to believe that although the system was not yet cost beneficial, it soon would be.[19]

The strongest link in the OCLC communications chain was the telephone network. The weakest was the terminals. "Operation of the terminals revealed weaknesses in two modules, and the manufacturer was currently in process of replacing these modules with new circuits that would give improved performance."[20] The fourth *Annual Report* summarized the work of OCLC at the close of the year as follows: "The outstanding accomplishment of the year was the implementation, operation, and enhancement of the on-line union catalog and shared cataloging system."[21]

OUT-OF-STATE COOPERATIVE ACTIVITIES AND NETWORKING

During the year Kilgour worked in cooperation with five regional library centers outside Ohio: Pittsburgh Regional Library Center (PRLC), Union Library Catalog of Pennsylvania (ULC), Five Associated University Libraries (FAUL), New England Library Information Network (NELINET), and Cooperative College Library Center (CCLC). The agreements that were reached were designed, with the exception of one, to implement an OCLC-like system in another regional center.

The costs continued to mount as the Center expanded its operations. Replication of the system in other regions absorbed a portion of the costs. Efforts to coordinate the Center's programs with those in other geographic locations were producing a skeletal library network. Perhaps in the future the centers would be linked telephonically. At this point, however, the pool of bibliographic records and the storehouse of information in the union catalog would be increased many times over by participation of libraries outside Ohio.

The year witnessed the signing of a new agreement with PRLC. At the end of 1970-1971, OCLC and PRLC had agreed that since PRLC was too small to support its own system, it would operate as a satellite of OCLC. The agreement provided for direct access by PRLC libraries to the OCLC network services. Off-line catalog card production began in 1971-1972 and was to be followed by the on-line services. Pursuant to the agreement, in October 1972 (the next fiscal year), eight PRLC members expressed their intent to purchase terminals.

A second agreement to establish a cooperative relationship with ULC was in the process of completion. ULC was a nonprofit corporation serving over one hundred libraries as a bibliographic and a locator service for library resources, primarily in eastern Pennsylvania. Established in the 1930s, it was originally a manual catalog card system based in the University of Pennsylvania Library, containing over four million records dating from 1936. Fifty thousand titles were added yearly to the catalog. Although no formal agreement was reached during the year, the two centers agreed to continue to work toward a mutually satisfying arrangement.

A test and a demonstration of the compatibility of the OCLC and ULC systems was begun in fiscal year 1971-1972. In August 1971 interest in the

OCLC system was expressed by libraries in the Philadelphia area. Upon the invitation of Richard DeGennaro, director of the University of Pennsylvania Libraries, and with his personal participation, library administrators from Bryn Mawr, Drexel, and Temple Universities spent a day at the Center visiting the site and talking with Kilgour. As a result of the visit, all of the institutions showed interest in using the system for experimental and demonstration purposes. Under the auspices of ULC, an experiment using the OCLC system in three libraries was begun in January 1972. The trio included the University of Pennsylvania, Drexel University, and Temple University. (Bryn Mawr decided not to join at this time.) Funds were partially provided by the libraries, supplemented by a grant from the Pennsylvania State Library under the Library Services and Construction Act, Title III. The libraries paid full communication and terminal costs, but only one quarter of the fee was spent for use of the Center's facility; the remainder was covered by the grant. Each library planned to test the system according to its own design. During the test period an outline for a new regional consortium was sketched that resulted in the founding of the Pennsylvania Area Library Network (PALINET) in December 1972.

Two more agreements were nearly ready for signing at the close of the year. One was with FAUL and the other with NELINET. Both agreements stipulated that the regional center outside Ohio was to participate only in the on-line shared cataloging system for a maximum of three years. At or before this time, each center would then acquire its own computer. A national network was the goal. OCLC would serve as one node, FAUL as another, and NELINET as still another one. It was also agreed that each center would reimburse OCLC for expenses and for its share of the use of the central installation. Moreover, the Center would be paid for any necessary additional communications expenses. Each center would provide its own terminals.

The FAUL, NELINET, and other out-of-state linkages would mean a double bonus for Ohio academic libraries. The membership fees would be reduced as the group of participating institutions expanded. Furthermore, the increase in the number of cataloging records in the data base would translate into more information for more libraries to share.

Founded in 1964, FAUL represented the libraries of five of the largest universities in upstate New York: SUNY-Binghamton, SUNY-Buffalo, Cornell University, Syracuse University, and the University of Rochester. Most regional centers, including OCLC and FAUL, were born out of shared needs and aspirations. The objectives of FAUL typified those of many consortia. First, the five libraries believed that they could accomplish certain tasks in common at less cost than they could perform them separately. Second, through unity the quintet believed it would gain strength and meaning.

At the time, the arrangement between OCLC and FAUL represented one rung on a ladder leading toward a national bibliographic network. As with the OCLC/PRLC agreement, the two centers declared their intent to work harmoniously to build a model for a national information web based on the methods and services developed by OCLC. The accord contained nine points, two of which were extremely important as OCLC spread from Ohio. First, when the time was ripe for FAUL to replicate the OCLC system, the Center would supply it with the programs, the documentation, and the data files. All of the results of the system development would be shared and made available to each party because an OCLC contract was seen as interim until a local centralized system such as OCLC was set up. Second, FAUL would reimburse OCLC for the cost of using the OCLC central installation on a full-service basis. In addition, it would pay for the full communications cost and furnish its own terminals.

NELINET operated in the New England region, providing services to academic libraries in a way similar to the OCLC batch card production system. The project was administered within the New England Board of Higher Education (NEBHE). Its clientele was not restricted to academic libraries, nor were its geographical boundaries confined to the six New England states. In addition to the academic members, there were three affiliates: the New York State Library, FAUL, and the Consortium of Universities of Washington, D.C.[22]

In 1971-1972 NELINET was engaged in a six-month test of transferability of the OCLC system to other groups of libraries. Conducted under auspices of a $53,589 grant from CLR, the test was begun on January 1, 1972, and terminated on July 1, 1972. Phase I was a fifteen-week computerized simulation. Phase II was a twenty-six-week evaluation and demonstration of the system at the Baker Library of Dartmouth College. Since January 1971 NELINET and OCLC had held discussions among themselves and with representatives of the MARC Development Office of LC. The meetings were arranged to identify areas in which their separate programs could be integrated. The two systems were conceptually very close, with many of the same reasons motivating each one in its development.

COMRESS, Inc., which carried out the simulation for OCLC in 1969, performed the NELINET simulation. It was first done for 35, then 75, and finally 249 libraries. An IBM 370/155 computer was the major simulation tool. Thanks to the operation of the OCLC on-line shared cataloging system, COMRESS could validate the model by comparing computed results with observed ones. The simulation was done for three sets of systems and performed on the shared cataloging system alone. Next, shared cataloging was combined with serials control and technical processing systems. Finally, cataloging, serials control, technical processing, and remote catalog access and circulation control systems plus subject retrieval were tested together. The simulation results were all positive. Simulation proved that the OCLC system could perform the functions required by the NELINET consortium. The simulation included additional units that the present system could not handle without extra equipment.

During the second phase of the test, which involved Dartmouth College, cost records were kept before and after the on-line system was applied. In February the results were recorded in the 1971-1972 OCLC *Annual Report*:

> Dartmouth found full cataloging including card production cost to be $.38 per title if cataloging information was in the OCLC data base; this cost excludes the cost of the OCLC system and includes only costs incurred at the Baker Library. Cataloging costs for titles not in the OCLC data was $3.02. Moreover, Dartmouth was able to reduce its cataloging staff through attrition subsequent to implementation of the OCLC system by seven full-time positions and three full-time equivalent part-time positions. In reference to

paying full OCLC fees, Dartmouth concludes that 'with a savings of over $16,000 in rental charges or MT/ST and MCRS, with little loss in efficiency, plus the tremendous staff savings we can readily meet the projected costs and still show a budgetary decrease.'[23]

The previous year's activities (1970-1971) included an interface agreement between the Center and CCLC. Fifty thousand dollars of grant funds from OE were allocated to demonstrate that the two systems could be meshed economically. Hillis D. Davis, director of CCLC, in a paper entitled "A Cost Analysis of the Cooperative College Library Center: Using the Manual Method of Card Production as Compared to the Computer Method Used by the Ohio College Library Center," reported:

Table III is a floor chart of work flow using the OCLC CRT terminal. Five of the 19 required steps in the manual system have been eliminated. To date we have been able to call records up for an average of 80 percent of the titles purchased by our members. Then too, we have been able to find catalog copy for 19 percent of the remaining 10 percent in National Union Catalog. This means that we do less than one percent original cataloging. The feature of shared cataloging on the system should increase the 80 percent figure appreciably over a period of time.

On May 22, 1972, records for 352 volumes were called up and cataloged on the terminal. Since the amount of typing has been reduced, one typist can comfortably type charging materials for 300 volumes a day. It is quite apparent that we received a malfunctioning CRT terminal. Our down time is usually high. With this in mind the Director would estimate that we can comfortably catalog 200 titles during an eight hour work day from the existing bibliographic information. This computes out to 2.4 minutes per title using cataloging data already in the data base. This means that 52,000 titles could be processed comfortably through the system in a year. This would decrease the turn around time to five days (by one half).[24]

The early 1970s witnessed glimmerings of library networks — networks that possessed potential for growth into a national system. OCLC had pioneered the first successful on-line library network.

In the past, leadership in cooperative library development had originated with the public library sector. In the 1960s and 1970s academic libraries took the lead. The accent was on cooperation among *all* types of libraries. OCLC was in the forefront of those cooperative efforts. Quite naturally, its bold and imaginative system was the target for criticism as well as for praise. There were, however, common threads of trust and loyalty connecting its members. They agreed to join OCLC in 1967 not knowing where their decision would lead them. They were willing to wait five years for tangible results. This type of fidelity gave impetus to the Center's development.

NOTES

1. Burton W. Adkinson, "Trends in Library Applications of Data Processing," in *Clinic on Library Applications of Data Processing, University of Illinois, 1963* (Champaign, Ill.: University of Illinois, 1964), p. 7.

2. Ibid.

3. Ohio College Library Center, *Newsletter*, 4 August 1971, p. 1.

4. See chapter 2 for details.

5. The SAVE function was later extended. By 1982 a record could remain in SAVE for seven working days (excluding Sundays).

6. See appendix 1, Exhibit M, for a sample work form.

7. See appendix 1, Exhibit K, for an example of a catalog record displayed on a terminal screen. The holding symbols appear at the bottom of the record. Although the sample record was created by LC in 1978, the display format was basically the same in August 1971.

8. See appendix 1, Exhibit L, for a list of the union catalog location symbols as of March 17, 1972.

9. Ann Ekstrom joined the OCLC staff on August 2, 1971, to prepare functional specifications for the serials control and the technical processing systems. From 1972 to 1974, when she became director of the Library Systems Division, Ekstrom was the primary liaison between OCLC and system users. Through 1979 she was involved in the functional design of all subsystems.

10. The technical processing system finally began on April 1, 1981, despite efforts to implement it sooner.

11. Dan L. Kniesner and Betty J. Meyer, "On-Line Computer Techniques in Shared Cataloging," *Library Resources and Technical Services* 17 (Spring 1973): 230.

12. See appendix 1, Exhibit D, for a complete list of the Board of Trustees members.

13. Ohio College Library Center, *Newsletter*, 10 December 1971, p. 5.

14. Ohio College Library Center, *Newsletter*, 28 February 1972, p. [1].

15. See appendix 1, Exhibit N, for a screen display of the extended search.

16. Antioch College, Bowling Green State University, Case Western Reserve University, Cleveland State University, College of Wooster, Heidelberg College, Hiram College, Kent State University, Miami University, Oberlin College, The Ohio State University, Ohio University, Ohio Wesleyan University, University of Cincinnati, University of Toledo, Walsh College, and Wright State University.

17. See appendix 1, Exhibit B, for the amended Articles of Incorporation.

18. Ohio College Library Center, *Annual Report 1971/1972* (Columbus: Ohio College Library Center, 1972), p. 5.

19. Ibid.

20. Ibid., p. 1.

21. Ibid.

22.   See appendix 1, Exhibit J, for a list of the NELINET membership.

23.   Op. cit., Ohio College Library Center, *Annual Report 1971/1972*, pp. 4-5.

24.   Hillis D. Davis, "A Cost Analysis of the Cooperative College Library Center: Using the Manual Method of Card Production as Compared to the Computer Method Used by the Ohio College Library Center" (Unpublished report, Atlanta, Georgia, 30 May 1972), pp. 3-4.

6

GAINING MOMENTUM:
Toward a Comprehensive
Library System
1972-1973

By fall 1972 OCLC was providing services to forty-nine Ohio institutions and several out-of-state cooperatives. Over four thousand miles of telephone lines linked a network of eighty terminals. July 1, 1973, marked the passing of two-thirds of its first decade of life. During that time, its principal objective was attained. OCLC was, indeed, increasing availability of library resources in academic libraries while at the same time decelerating the rate of rise of per-student costs. The on-line union catalog and the shared cataloging system had been in operation since August 1971. Four million catalog cards were produced during the twelve-month period, and over 500,000 titles were cataloged on the system. Moreover, the size of the data base exceeded 652,000 records.

During the year, the system was enhanced by a number of new features and by the formulation of quality control standards. By spring 1973, programming was begun on the serials control system, while the technical processing system was being researched and developed. In December 1972, CLR awarded the Center a grant of $194,000 to define and improve the on-line union catalog and the shared cataloging module, and to develop and activate the serials control system. OCLC also expended $193,333, the third and final portion of the Ohio Board of Regents' grant.

Out-of-state involvement continued to grow during the year. As a result, the perimeters of the union catalog were expanded, the data base was enlarged, and access to library materials was improved. Moreover, a contract was signed with the Federal Library Committee for experimentation of on-line cataloging with the federal library community.

THE ON-LINE UNION CATALOG
AND SHARED CATALOGING SYSTEM

The OCLC data base, the wealth of information available to the membership, grew inordinately. In October the Center added 45,717 RECON 68 MARC II[1] records from LC, only 13 percent of which replaced existing OCLC records. The system was programmed to automatically transfer the holdings information from the OCLC record to the MARC II record that replaced it. On November 21, 1972, the Library of Pontifical College Josephinum input the 500,000th catalog record into the system.

In December 1972 an analysis of the 505,326 records in the file revealed that 42.9 percent were OCLC MARC records, and 57.1 percent were LC MARC II records. As additional MARC II records entered the file weekly, only 5 percent replaced OCLC records already in the file. LC was responsible for a little over half the records in the data base. Studies conducted by OCLC showed that even though only one third of the LC records were being employed, their use far exceeded all expectations. This was clearly demonstrated by the fact that OCLC recorded an average of 1.36 holding institutions per record while LC records averaged 4.07 holding institutions.[2]

The blending of member libraries' cataloging with LC's to create a shared information bank was a minor miracle since before joining OCLC, each library maintained its catalogs primarily for use by its own constituency. Now it had to create entries for a broad spectrum of users.

By June 30, 1973, the on-line system contained over 652,000 catalog records and over 1,090,843 location listings. Table T-2 records the number of titles cataloged on the system from July 1, 1972, through June 30, 1973, by the membership and the libraries in other regional centers. Note that the second column indicates only the first time that an existing record is used for catalog card production.

TABLE T-2
Titles Cataloged from 1 July 1972 through 30 June 1973[3]

Center	Total Copies of Titles Cataloged	Titles Cataloged Using Existing Records	Input Cataloging
Ohio College Library Center	436,413	278,043	128,664
Cooperative College Library Network	41,294	20,256	1,570
New England Library Information Network	32,649	23,643	5,809
Pittsburgh Regional Library Center	30,295	20,977	708
Union Library Catalogue of Pennsylvania	31,823	25,712	4,758
Total	572,474	368,631	141,509

Data Base

The on-line system was enhanced to enable libraries to conform to LC rules while at the same time benefit from automation. During the year several new functions were added to the system. The ability to create pseudonumeric class numbers for the LC "K" classification schedule (Law) was one of them. With the exception of "KF" (law of the United States), LC had not yet completed the classification system for legal materials, thereby posing problems for any library wishing to catalog them. The entire LC classification scheme is built upon an alpha-numeric call number. The numeric portion of the "K" schedule was lacking. The Center devised a technique whereby the system would accept pseudonumerics. The formatting programs accepted the numbers but the print programs suppressed them on printing. The pseudo "K" call numbers were not a part of the bibliographic record file and therefore would not be displayed when the record was retrieved from the data base. The suppression program would allow libraries eventually to receive full call numbers on their catalog cards as LC developed the various "K" classes. At the start of the fiscal year, LC had announced that it had prepared a draft for the "KD" schedule (law of the United Kingdom). The generalized procedure for the suppression of the "K" numerics went into effect on November 13, 1972.

Another new feature was the inclusion of a free-text call number field on a record. Before its availability libraries had only two choices for inputting call numbers: LC-type or Dewey-type. With the third option, the OCLC system could accommodate *all* types of call numbers. This feature would be particularly valuable to institutions with special collections and to the nonacademic sector.

Access to information in the on-line file depended heavily upon the system's searching capabilities. Four search keys were available: name-title, title, LC card number, and OCLC control number. As the storehouse of bibliographic records grew, the number of entries retrievable through these search keys was expanded. At first, a search key would display only two screens of entries. The two-screen boundary was imposed at the request of the Advisory Committee on Cataloging. By the fall of 1972, the Center was working on the implementation of the extended search technique that would eliminate the two-screen display limit by providing for the display of more entries for any search key. (The system contained over a million search keys.) The number of screens of entries was enlarged from two to nine in November 1972. On February 12, 1973, the full extended search procedure was activated displaying up to 256 entries per key. Eventually, the Center planned to increase the display up to 1,024 entries that would, it was estimated, retrieve all entries for all keys. The development of retrieval by derived truncated search keys was completed with the implementation of the extended search function.

By spring 1973, it became evident to the OCLC staff that nearly 10 percent of the index searches were extended searches, which added an unanticipated load on the computer's central processor. A large programming project would eventually have to be undertaken. Terminal users had already noted a degradation in response time.

The importance of maintaining a high-quality data base grew in proportion to the increase in digital traffic that daily flowed through OCLC. The addition of an automatic procedure for checking illegal field tags, and error report forms helped to upgrade the system. In May 1972 the automatic checking of illegal field tags started. Whenever a terminal operator keyed in a field and incorrectly labeled or tagged it, the system displayed the following message at the top of the screen: E1/ILLEGAL TAG. Before the new procedure was available, the system would produce catalog cards with illegal field tags, and the illegalities would remain undetected. The automatic error checking function continued to be expanded. By the end of October 1972, checks were being made for illegal indicators, illegal subfield codes, and illegal text characters. The system was programmed to reject any fields with errors and not to produce card sets until the correct data had been input. Even though the new checks were a great help, they were not a panacea; human errors not programmed for verification by the system persisted.

In January 1972, the Center sent LC approximately eight hundred error reports for its MARC II records, representing about 0.33 percent of the total MARC II data base. The member libraries had been instructed to send error report sheets directly to OCLC. When a record was corrected, a copy of the report sheet was returned with an explanation to the reporting library.

As of September 1972, OCLC had received approximately six thousand error reports for cataloging done by members along with errors from LC via MARC II. The error rate for the membership was slightly more than 3 percent. OCLC made a study of the 244 error report sheets it received on one morning. LC was the cataloging source on 19 of them. Excluding the LC errors, the following analysis was made of the remaining 225 records:

> One hundred sixty-nine errors (or 75% of 225) consisted of keying errors in the text. Of these 169, 29 involved changes in call numbers, three involved diacritics or special characters, and some 20 involved more serious changes in text in which whole words were added, changed, or deleted.
> Some 40 more records (17% of 225) required changes in designators: tags (18 records), subfield codes (11), indicators (9), and insertion of delimiters (2).
> The remaining 16 records consisted of 13 for which fields were added, and three for which duplicate fields were deleted.[4]

Through further analysis, the Center learned that 88.2 percent of the errors brought to the attention of the Center were reported by the library committing the error.[5]

The SAVE file, a temporary file where catalog records could be stored for later review and then used for the production of catalog cards, provided each terminal with a SAVE capacity of twenty records. Unfair use of the function was noted in early November. Some institutions seldom used it while others (with one or two terminals) stored up to one hundred records at a time. It was further noted that nearly 50 percent of the records had been in SAVE for more than seven days, and some had been there for over a month. The Center chose to alleviate the situation by revising the policy on the use of the file. The staff completely eradicated the past accumulation in the SAVE bank on the eve of November 10, 1972. One week later a scanning device was employed whereby the system was searched nightly for records that had been in SAVE for more than seven calendar days. Those exceeding the seven-day limit were erased. The new procedure provided incentives to get records out of the SAVE file.

System-produced accessions lists were undertaken in response to a request from members for a list of their recent accessions. The lists would be derived from each library's on-line cataloging and would be circulated to faculty and students of member institutions. By March 1973 the programming was in the testing stage. Individual lists would be produced from offset press masters. Entries would be arranged in LC subject heading order. In the spring, the regular printing of such lists was instituted for selected libraries. The lists were to be widely available by the fall of 1973.

Libraries have traditionally maintained authority files. They can be a record of the correct form of a personal name, a series, or a subject used in a library's card catalog. The function of the file is to assure uniformity in the catalog entries. The Advisory Committee on Cataloging, with the assistance of John Rather from LC, designed a computer record for a personal name authority file.

At the December 15, 1972 meeting of the Committee, Rather shared the results of the study. Approximately seven thousand records were examined. The frequency of name cross-references and the average length of the headings were among the topics analyzed. Following Rather's presentation, the Committee discussed the kind of authority record format that OCLC would be interested in implementing.

During the Committee's next meeting on January 19, 1973, John A. Wyckoff, an OCLC staff member, presented the Center's preliminary plans for an on-line, personal name authority file. Before it could be activated, the Center would first have to implement a personal author index to existing bibliographic records. By the time a personal name authority file was available, the Center planned to have the personal author index in operation. The file and the index were to be formulated and indexed independently.

The record deferral program dates to October 1971, when input from terminals began. Although the system was programmed to accept only one record for each title in the data base, it was incapable of detecting a duplication of bibliographic information. If two nearly identical records were input, they would be treated as two separate ones. The LC MARC II tapes that the Center received regularly from LC's distribution service[6] were slow in arriving. The contents of a tape was unknown until its arrival. A library would often decide to input original cataloging if it were unable to locate data on the system. Frequently, several weeks later, two nearly identical records for the same title would appear in the data base. One represented the original cataloging of the member, and the second, the cataloging done by LC as it appeared on the newly input MARC II tape.

A further complication resulted when LC decided to repair a record in error. Instead of preparing a replacement record for the one in error, it would delete the record one week and replace it with a new one several weeks later. The deletion of one record and the delayed addition of another meant that meanwhile a member library could conceivably input an original one, unaware that a very similar entry might soon be added by LC. Another problem was the loss of holdings information at the end of the record whenever LC deleted and replaced a record in the data base. Any library that used it in the past was listed as a holder.

The Center halted input of new weekly MARC II tapes to avoid rapid proliferation of duplicates. The tapes would again be added when the detection device for duplicate records was available. However, pressure from libraries forced the Center to resume adding MARC II records. The Center activated programming to place potential duplicate records onto a secondary magnetic tape for later examination. A MARC II record was substituted for an existing OCLC record when the LC card number, the author-title, and the title matched. If only two of the three criteria were met, the record was deferred for optical inspection. Unfortunately, the on-line programs had to be rewritten for optical examination. By spring of 1973, the Center had accumulated approximately three thousand deferred MARC II records. The programming for comparison and replacement of the duplicates was to be implemented by mid-July 1973. (It was implemented eventually in the winter of 1975.)

The compatibility of the records input by various libraries was a prime concern of OCLC. A record added to the data base by one library should be usable by another with minimal verification and alteration. The OCLC staff could correct errors, but there was no quality review for the incoming records. Quality control was a human problem, not that of a computer. Each user had to accept responsibility for quality of bibliographic information. *Standards for Input Cataloging* (June 1972) written by the OCLC Advisory Committee on Cataloging provided criteria for judging the quality of records.

Responsibility for implementing *Standards* rested with the special Committee on Implementation of *Standards for Input Cataloging*, appointed by the chairman of the Board of Trustees at the May 1972 membership meeting. The Committee was to report its recommendations at the November 10, 1972 meeting. Unfortunately, it did not meet until September 11, 1972. Nevertheless, the Committee's chairman, Thompson M. Little of Ohio University, did give a progress report at the November meeting. During the next twelve months it met seventeen times.

The Implementation Committee divided its work into two major areas: establishment of a hierarchy of record levels for information in the data base, and implementation and endorsement of the *Standards*. The various levels were formulated to categorize the contents of the data base and to facilitate enforcement of the *Standards*.

The Advisory Committee on Cataloging defined three levels. The Implementation Committee accepted two and modified the third. Level one represented the records that were in the MARC II format. Level two referred to those records input by the members according to the MARC II format as defined in the *Standards*. The definition of the third level of records was partially altered to include all bibliographic records that lacked certain data required in the other two levels. The incomplete records could be incorporated into the current file design. The technical processing and serials control systems would be likely to be used for this since neither required complete cataloging information. The incomplete records would be less costly and therefore all the more appealing.

The Implementation Committee formulated how tri-level records would interact with the total OCLC system. Another activity was preparation of a detailed definition of the third level. Levels one and two were covered by the *Standards*. The Committee felt that a similar document should be formulated for level three. Based upon *Standards*, a list of minimal requirements was compiled to blend third-level records with present and projected indices of the system.

Having devised a multiple-level record data base, the Implementation Committee turned its attention to implementation of *Standards* and appointed a Peer Council to investigate quality control:

> Basic to the Committee's deliberations was the concept that the implementation procedure *as finally adopted* should be positive and constructive rather than negative and punitive.
>
> Another basic principle was that, although of necessity involving the Center, the problems of implementation should be the responsibility of the membership rather than the Center or the Executive Director.
>
> From these considerations evolved the concept of a committee of members to review problems and to meet with member libraries as needed to investigate difficulties and hear the individual library's point of view. This group was referred to as the Peer Council.[7]

Support for the Peer Council concept was unanimous. It officially represented OCLC members and implemented standards and maintained quality control. The Council, which would report to the membership, would have six members serving staggered terms, plus at least one OCLC staff member ex-officio. Representation encompassed a cross section of library types, sizes, and locations. It included libraries using the LC classification as well as those employing the Dewey Decimal System.

The Peer Council assumed the following responsibilities:

- Receive quarterly an error report analysis and member reports or complaints.
- Review and evaluate reports and complaints.
- Advise the member library in question about the alleged problem.
- Investigate the problem. Consult with the member library.
- Guide corrective action to be initiated by the member library.
- Review the institutional action.
- Recommend some form of sanction for continued or continual noncompliance.

These decisions reached by the Committee on Implementation during 1972-1973 were incorporated in a document entitled "Ohio College Library Center: Implementation Committee Report" (October 1, 1973). Action was taken on the Report's recommendations in the fall of 1973.

Out of the new developments, there arose a need for user input into the planning and implementing of the programs. An ad hoc committee, the OCLC Patron Input Committee, was appointed to study ways of involving users in the Center's developments. At the November 10, 1972 meeting of the membership, the representatives voted to charge the chairman of the Board of Trustees with the responsibility of appointing the new committee. The next meeting of the membership, on March 26, 1973, reported that Herbert F. Johnson (Oberlin College) would chair the committee. The OCLC Patron Input Committee had five other members. Hyman W. Kritzer (Kent State University), Lewis C. Naylor (Toledo-Lucas County Public Library), Richard J. Owen (Heidelberg College), Patricia L. Lyons (Walsh College), and Robert Walker (Oberlin College student) completed the list. The executive director served as an ex-officio member. The Committee began to meet in the spring of 1973.

The OCLC system was in evolution. Keeping members aware of its capabilities and limitations ranked high among the Center's duties.[8] OCLC-sponsored tutorials on terminals, and several new publications produced by the Center effectively communicated information to the users. The bimonthly tutorials on terminals initiated by the Center in July 1971 continued. The meetings were especially helpful to library personnel totally unversed in the intricacies of the daily applications of the system. For library staff members already using the system, the tutorials served as review sessions.

In the spring of 1971, the Center staff produced two instructional manuals (generally referred to as the yellow and green manuals), *Creation of Machine Readable Catalog Entries* (May 1971) and *Cataloging on a Cathode Ray Tube Terminal* (June 1971). Twenty-two issues of the *Newsletter* from July 1971 through June 1972, and nine issues over the next twelve months, kept the manuals up-to-date by clarifying various procedures and explaining additional functions and changes in the system. Unfortunately, neither the manual nor the newsletter was indexed.

A new manual, *On-Line Cataloging* (1973), was warmly greeted. It revised the original two manuals and incorporated pertinent information from the *Newsletter* through April 13, 1973. *On-Line Cataloging* was supplemented by *Design of Formats and Packs of Catalog Cards* and *Off-Line Catalog Production* in 1973. All three manuals were published by The Ohio State University Libraries Publications Committee.

OCLC was gaining a national and international reputation. To satisfy a growing interest on the part of American librarians in developments at OCLC, demonstrations of the Center's on-line union catalog and shared cataloging system were presented both at the OCLC headquarters and to groups at various locations in and out of Ohio. The librarians who attended ALA's annual meeting in Las Vegas, Nevada, in June 1973, witnessed such a demonstration. The OCLC exhibit booth was manned by staff members of the OCLC membership. Over one thousand librarians were estimated to have visited it. The Xerox Corporation donated twenty-five hundred dollars to absorb some of the telecommunication cost between Las Vegas and Columbus.

Throughout the year, Kilgour and other staff members received an increasing number of invitations from librarians, educators, and others to present papers. In May of 1973 Kilgour gave a paper on the recent developments at OCLC, in Geneva, Switzerland, at a United Nations meeting.

Articles about individual experiences with the system also became part of the library literature. Librarians at Walsh College, Temple University, the University of Pennsylvania, and The Ohio State University published accounts relating the pioneering use of the system.

Equipment

During the year, OCLC purchased a printer, six disk drives, and a different terminal model. In addition, a new lease agreement for the Spiras Irascope terminals was negotiated, along with a purchase agreement for the Xerox Sigma 5.

In the latter part of 1972, Center staff successfully coupled an IBM 1403 N1 Printer to the Xerox Sigma 5 via a Spur 1403 Controller, thereby enabling OCLC to print cards independent of on-line activity. Producing four thousand cards an hour, the printer was operating four to five hours a day. It could be run simultaneously with the on-line activity without degrading on-line response time. Also, in the closing months of 1972 six Telefile disk drives were interfaced with the Xerox Sigma 5 to expand the on-line files.

The poor performance record of the irascope coupled with improved design characteristics of new models invited OCLC to find a new terminal. In the spring of 1973, OCLC and Beehive Medical Electronics, Inc. of Salt Lake City, Utah, signed a contract to produce specially designed CRTs. The OCLC Model 100 Display terminal (see plate II, page 78) was to be available in the summer of 1973. The staff and some representatives of the membership cooperated with Beehive to design the thirty-four hundred dollar terminal. Beehive would only produce the terminals; OCLC would retain the sole right to market them.

The terminal unit consisted of a detachable keyboard, a fifteen-inch CRT monitor, a character generator, a MOS memory, a MOS/LSI processor unit, and a power supply. It had a display repertoire of up to 2,000 characters in twenty-five lines with 80 characters per line. Not more than 192 characters were displayable. The terminal was connected to the telephone lines (the message carriers) via data sets. OCLC used the Ohio Bell 201C dataset, installed and maintained by the Ohio Bell Telephone Company.[9] The private-voice grade telephone lines would, in turn, carry the messages to the processor in Columbus.

Each terminal came with a twenty-five-foot cable enabling a library to connect up to seven terminals to the same dataset. The Center's communication system would accommodate as many as twenty-seven terminals connected to a single line. It had been demonstrated that response time would improve as the number of lines grew, even if the number of terminals per line did not change.

In March 1973, the Board of Trustees authorized purchase of the Xerox Sigma 5 computer from the Xerox Corporation. The Center by this time had built up an equity of $206,199 on the computer. The monthly bill from Xerox was $19,844.90, including maintenance. A saving of approximately $100,000 in cash flow per year would result from that purchase.

Plate II. Beehive OCLC Model 100 Display Terminal (Courtesy of OCLC)

Finances

Financially OCLC was enjoying good health. First, the members had persuaded their administrators that OCLC was a valuable investment of time, energy, and money. Second, support came from four directions: the membership, CLR, OE, and the Ohio Board of Regents. In 1971-1972, the Ohio members paid $234,167, and the Board of Regents contributed $386,676. In 1972-1973, the membership paid $444,871, and the Board contributed $193,333. Beginning with fiscal year 1973-1974, the Center would totally finance its own overhead expenditure.

In an effort to maintain its monetary well-being, the Center made several changes during the year. Two such changes involved the billing procedure for the membership fees and the use charges to the members. The Board of Trustees decided to have two billings for the 1972-1973 membership fees. It reasoned that if other regions took part in the system, and if other Ohio libraries joined, the fees for the OCLC members would drop during the year. The first billing would be in the fall for 75 percent of the total fee including debits or credits from fees and use in 1971-1972. The next billing would come during the second half of the year when a more realistic cost prediction could be made. The intent of the double billing was to avoid overcharges to the members.

The absence of the state subsidy in 1973-1974 would require a 50 percent increase in membership fees, which covered the cost of operating the system including use of terminals, telephone line charges, and expenses of the central facility in Columbus. The amount of records input by each of the participating libraries and the use of the data base for noncataloging purposes were factors that were not considered in the assessments. Members were asked to add the increase to the 75 percent of their membership fee for 1972-1973.[10]

In May 1973, the membership fee had to be increased 52 percent, raising the 1972-1973 cost per use of a record from $1.52 to a projected cost for the next year of $2.02. The approved budget for fiscal year 1973-1974 amounted to $1,577,500. The largest income would come from the membership fees ($604,500) and nonmember fees ($459,000). The new budget figure reflected a huge increase, nearly double the 1972-1973 figure of $842,322.

On July 13, 1972, the Board approved establishment of a basic minimum charge for new members. In addition, it endorsed an initial implementation fee, again for new members only. The basic minimum charge would be included in the membership fee. The implementation fee would be based upon the actual cost of implementing the system plus overhead.

At the October 1972 meeting of the Board, Kilgour presented his views on the future charges to all members for services rendered by OCLC. In the light of the forthcoming serials and technical processing systems, he believed that a restructuring of charges was likely. At the same meeting, the Board approved the preparation of a study for charging fees. Haskins & Sells, Certified Public Accountants, would undertake the project. The director would subsequently present it to the Board.

The Haskins & Sells report was discussed at the January and February board meetings. The cost for a library to maintain one terminal was five thousand dollars per year. Twelve libraries paid membership fees of less than this amount.[11] The Board debated the possibility of establishing an annual minimum fee. The twelve libraries whose fees might exceed what they could afford would be most affected. The Board then contemplated a special formula for small libraries. One Board member suggested the possibility of giving credit to libraries for their catalog input. The director sent a memorandum to the twelve small libraries asking for comments on the establishment of a minimum five thousand dollars per year membership fee. By the end of March, eight had replied that if the policy was enacted, they would be unable to participate.[12]

In addition to the question of a minimum membership fee, another issue surfaced, that of charging for total use of the system. Under the current system, members paid only for the catalog cards that they produced, even though the system was being used for purposes beyond cataloging. At the January meeting, the Board charged Kilgour with the responsibility of gathering data relative to the total use of the system by the membership. The data would be used as a basis to study the possibility of institution a usage charge. The collected data revealed that the use of the indices for noncataloging purposes exceeded those for cataloging by 150 percent.

Kilgour offered evidence that savings were forthcoming in an article entitled "The Shared Cataloging System of the Ohio College Library Center" (September 1972).

> The original cost benefit studies were done on the basis of a calculated rate of six titles per hour for those books for which there were already cataloging data in the system. The net savings will be realized when the file has reached sufficient size to enable the largest libraries to locate records for 65 percent of their cataloging and for the smallest to find 95 percent. To reach this level, members collectively would have to use existing bibliographic information to catalog 350,000 titles in the course of a year, or an average of approximately 1,460 titles for the total system per working day. It was thought that this rate would be attained by the end of the second year of operation. However, at the end of the first month of on-line operation, over a thousand titles per day were being cataloged.[13]

On January 24, 1973, members cataloged over three thousand titles on the system. The OCLC on-line system was proving to be cost-effective.

In the course of the year the Center assumed two new rental payments: its residence at The Ohio State University and its new off-campus facility on Henderson Road in Columbus. The Ohio State University was in the forefront of the activities related to the operations of OCLC. During the first five and a half years of the Center's existence, the University gratuitously allocated space on its campus, but in March 1973 OCLC started paying rent.

At about the same time, some of the Center's operations were moved to offices on West Henderson Road. The research and development staff required additional space. The new quarters offered twenty-four hundred square feet of office space to house the executive, administrative, and research and development offices. The machine operations would continue to be located at the Kinnear Road site. In mid-March the move was completed. On May 1, 1973, the thirty-fifth meeting of the Board of Trustees convened for the first time in the Conference Room of the Ohio College Library Center at 1550 West Henderson Road.

Organization

The year was highlighted by a change in the privileges for borrowing library materials among member institutions. The membership also dealt with governance issues such as the reorganization of the composition of the Board of Trustees and a definition of its duties.

The ad hoc committee on extending direct borrowing privileges to graduate and undergraduate students of OCLC institutions, appointed by the Board of Trustees, decisively attempted to increase access to library materials in November 1972 at the annual meeting by introducing the following proposal:[14]

> ... the Members instruct the Director of the Center to take appropriate action within the next month to invite each academic Member of the Center to enter into a general agreement extending direct reciprocal borrowing privileges to all students, both graduate and undergraduate subject to the standard rules of borrowing in effect at the lending institution; and further, that this general agreement be similar to the agreement now in effect which extends reciprocal direct borrowing privileges to faculty of signatory academic Members of the Center; and further, that each academic Member of the Center be given the option to participate, or not to participate, in this general student agreement, and further, that this general student reciprocal borrowing agreement take effect January 1, 1973; and further, that other academic Members of the Center be eligible to join at a later date upon their acceptance of the conditions specified in this general agreement.[15]

The new proposal was an extension of the one adopted by the membership at its November 8, 1968 meeting. Privileges were now to be extended not only to faculty members but also to all students of the OCLC member institutions. The call to vote resulted in a unanimous acceptance of the motion. Kilgour was then instructed to send a memorandum to the individual members outlining the rules and asking them to indicate participation or non-participation. Twenty-six libraries agreed to include undergraduate and graduate students of other OCLC institutions as borrowers.[16]

The OCLC membership and the Board of Trustees wanted to alter the structure of the present Board to a more specialized body. The appointment of the Subcommittee on Reorganization of the Board of Trustees, on June 8, 1972, was a direct result of this common concern.[17]

The "Progress Report of the Subcommittee on Reorganization of the OCLC Board of Trustees" was presented to the Board on July 13, 1972. The chairman of the Subcommittee referred to the membership meetings of November 12, 1971, and May 17, 1972, that had expressed a desire to change the current board structure. In September 1972, a document describing proposed duties of the Board was circulated.

At the meeting of the membership on November 10, 1972, Joseph M. Denham, a member of the Subcommittee, proposed enlarging the Board from nine to thirteen members. Three of the thirteen were to be specialists whose residences and institutional affiliations would in no way affect their seats on the Board. The fourth member was to be the director of the Center who would hold a nonvoting position

After months of debate among the membership, the Board in December 1972 decided to postpone further discussion of reorganization until the role of OCLC in a national library network was more clearly defined. Such a network would, no doubt, prompt an adjustment in the present organization of the Board.

The new board members were elected at the annual meeting on November 10, 1972, along with the new officers. James V. Jones was elected chairman and president; H. Paul Schrank, Jr. was elected vice-chairman; Robert F. Cayton was to serve as secretary; and John H. Becker as treasurer.[18]

At its November meeting the Board paid tribute to several of its members for their distinct contributions to the development of OCLC. One of those honored was Lewis C. Branscomb. His term as a member of the Board and as its vice-chairman expired on November 10, 1972. Branscomb was library director of The Ohio State University Libraries in 1967 when OCLC was incorporated, and will be remembered as one of the most influential figures in the Center's early development. It was only fitting that the Board adopted a resolution on his behalf recognizing his important achievements.[19] Others were also honored in this manner. Joseph M. Denham, professor of chemistry at Hiram College, was the subject of a similar resolution. He, too, was a member of the Board from its inception on October 25, 1967, through November 10, 1972. Hyman W. Kritzer, assistant provost and director of libraries at Kent State University, served the Board as a member from November 14, 1969, and as chairman from November 13, 1970, through November 10, 1972. He held his office during a crucial period of development, a time when the Center had achieved national recognition. The Board expressed its gratitude to him through a third resolution.

The membership list continued to grow as three new institutions added their names. The Cincinnati Bible Seminary, the Cleveland Health Sciences Library, and the Medical College of Ohio at Toledo joined as academic institutions. The membership of Lake Erie College, a charter member, was not renewed.

ON-LINE SYSTEMS

Work proceeded on development of the on-line serials control and the technical processing systems. Research and development in the on-line serials control system was possible through a $194,000 grant from CLR in December 1972. Although only a portion of the grant was earmarked for the on-line serials control system, the amount enabled the Center to make significant progress on its development. The rest of the funds were to be used to improve the on-line union catalog and the shared cataloging systems. The on-line technical processing system was being developed independent of outside funding, using only OCLC resources.

The first computerized serials control system was activated by the Library of the University of California at San Diego. It provided information on the Library's complete serial holdings, the issues it daily received, the binding status of any serial, and those serials that never arrived or whose subscription had expired. A prepunched card was manually removed from a file and sent to the computer center for processing. In 1963, the Washington University School of Medicine Library activated its own serials control system. Similar to the one at the University of California, it served as a model for others. The University of Minnesota Biomedical Library used the unprecedented technique of recording the receipts of individual journals on preprinted check-in lists. Check-in information was then keypunched directly from the lists.

A milestone was reached in 1965 with the production of the *Kansas Union List of Serials,* the first computerized union list registering holdings information for several different institutions. Approximately 22,000 titles were recorded for eight colleges and universities. The difficulties posed by all of these systems were overcome with the advent of the on-line system. Laval University, Quebec, was the father of the on-line techniques for serials. In 1969, its on-line system contained a file of 16,335 titles.

The OCLC on-line serials control system had two major goals. First, it was to create a union catalog of serials records that would increase availability of serials data to libraries. Second, it was to reduce processing costs for serials by eliminating the need to maintain several records. The system was designed to provide on-line maintenance of serials records, to predict the date of a forthcoming issue and its expected arrival date, and to enable a library to update automatically its holdings information.

The OCLC Advisory Committee on Serials Control met frequently during the year to complete the configuration of the system. Composed of thirty members from Ohio libraries and participating regions, the Committee had first met on October 1, 1971, to discuss the draft *A Brief Description of the Serials Control System: A Preliminary Report* (September 1971), prepared by Ann Ekstrom. The Committee's input into the design stage was crucial. The final blueprint would supply the products required by the system's users.

From October 1971 until December 1971, the Committee met monthly. In December, a *Manual for Checking-in, Binding, and Claiming of Serials on a CRT Terminal—Draft of Preliminary Procedures* was completed by Ekstrom. Additional monthly meetings throughout the 1972 calendar year led to the formulation of a more detailed system definition. *Recommended Standards for the Cataloging of Serials* was completed in May 1972.

It is important to note that serials cataloging was not a part of the serials control system but rather belonged to the cataloging system. However, the two separate systems were interrelated. Serials cataloging was an extension of the shared cataloging system already available. To set up a serial record for local check-in, a library had to establish a catalog record already in the OCLC file or create a new one. Once a library's holding symbol appeared on a serial record, the record would be stored in the master file, available to all members through the terminals. Most importantly, it could be used as the serial check-in record. The cataloging record therefore became a vital link in use of the serials check-in module. When a library subscribed to more than one copy of a title, the system was programmed to display a summary screen presenting brief data about all of the copies and a more detailed screen giving information about each subscription.

The Center's serials file would hold bibliographic records of its members along with the serials records in the MARC II format. LC had provided the start-up data base of monographic records for the on-line union catalog. The Committee looked for an outside source to provide machine-readable serials records. By December 1972 it had found only one option. The serials data base at the University of Minnesota, the Minnesota Union List of Serials (MULS), was compatible with the MARC serials format.

By December 1972, measurable progress had been made in design of the on-line serials control system. Design work was completed on the on-line union catalog as well as on input of serials cataloging, production of serials catalog cards, and procedure for on-line checking-in, automatic claiming, and report binding. Serials cataloging routines would be implemented first, followed by check-in and claim procedures. Check-in was to be done on a special serials work form displayed on the terminal screen. If the serial in hand was the anticipated next issue, the check-in process involved depression of the UPDATE and SEND keys. If it was a new title for a member, the information would have to be typed in to update the holdings information for the institution. The check-in procedure being developed by OCLC was a marked improvement over earlier serials systems using prepunched arrival cards.

Washington State University Library was the first to introduce a sophisticated on-line system for acquisitions. This major technological advance occurred as early as April 1968. Stanford University activated its on-line system in 1969. The University of Chicago was also in the forefront of the on-line developments. Other institutions making inroads into this largely unexplored area of librarianship included the University of Michigan, Texas A & I University, Brown University, and Oregon State University.

In the fall of 1969, the director presented a paper entitled "Effect of Computerization on Acquisitions." He emphasized that a new technology had to be found before the full-service on-line acquisitions system reached fruition. "The application of computers to acquisitions activities will be a technological advance that will require much new knowledge."[20] He continued, "the principal obstacle is the incompleteness of knowledge required to employ a new technology to produce new products, new organization, or new management methods."[21]

The OCLC on-line technical processing system was designed to automate the acquisitions procedures and to make available management and control reports on the overall technical processing operation. The Advisory Committee on Technical Processing spent the year providing input into the design of system products and on-line operation.

The technical processing system included financial records and a monitor to issue notices to staff whenever an item was delayed in purchasing, serials, cataloging, or physical processing. Its goals were rapid and accurate processing of library materials, reducing of staff hours in technical processing, accumulating of data in one central record, and reducing of unnecessary duplication.

As originally conceived, on-line technical processing was to provide libraries with four basic operations: creating a technical processing record and producing purchase orders, on-line updating of records once materials had been received and again after they were cataloged, automatic claiming of overdue orders, and producing accounting records.

The Advisory Committee on Technical Processing met for the first time on February 23, 1972; twenty-five representatives from seventeen institutions attended. Representatives from participating regions also attended subsequent meetings. The Committee reviewed *OCLC Technical Processing System—A Preliminary Outline* (February 1972). In the spring, *The Technical Processing System—The Ohio College Library Center* (May 1972), a detailed description of the system, was issued.

Also in the spring, an agreement had been reached between the Center and The Ohio State University whereby the latter would donate the services of four programmers to write OCLC computer programs and associated documentation for the Center's on-line technical processing system. The programmers would be among those working on The Ohio State University Libraries on-line circulation system. Unfortunately, this cooperative effort did not materialize. For budgetary reasons, The Ohio State University had to withdraw its offer. This change in the course of events resulted in a delay in the programming.

A proposal for mandatory participation of members in the on-line serials and technical processing systems was discussed at the October 5, 1972 meeting of the Board of Trustees. A number of problems surfaced. Some members were already using automated serials systems that might not be compatible with OCLC. Also, the larger libraries were departmentalized and, therefore, had no central serials check-in procedures. It was subsequently decided that when the serials and technical processing systems were available, participation was to be optional.

OUT-OF-STATE COOPERATIVE ACTIVITIES AND NETWORKING

A major decision was made on March 26, 1973, when the membership voted to invite regional library groups outside of Ohio to use the Center's services. The original concept of cooperation, upon which OCLC had been founded, had reached a new plateau.

A chain of events set the stage for this historic decision. The rumored possibility of a national library network was discussed at the October 5, 1972 meeting of the Board of Trustees. There were questions. Should the Center assume a leadership role in such a network? What form should it take? How should one proceed to establish it? Following the discussions, the Board asked the director to prepare a paper outlining a plan for the Center's role in designing and developing a national network.

The plan was presented at the Board's next meeting on November 10, 1972. It included two options. The first option placed OCLC at the center of a national network. To operate at this level, it would need additional computers in Columbus. The second option suggested that OCLC be a central node, or network authority, for a system of nodes placed throughout the country. The Board agreed that the subject should be presented to the members at their annual meeting that same afternoon. They recommended that the membership be asked to endorse, in principle, further study regarding the Center's leadership in design and development of a national library network. If the members approved, the Board would detail a plan to present to them at a special meeting held for this purpose.

That afternoon, Lewis C. Branscomb, vice-chairman of the Board, presented to the membership the idea of the Center's assuming a leadership position in national networking activities. The Board hoped to secure an expression of interest on the part of the members to explore the possibilities of expanding services beyond Ohio. After considerable discussion, the membership granted full approval to the Board, which would report its recommendations at the next special session.

The director and assistant director, Philip L. Long, in consultation with the Board and with the assistance of legal and financial advice, proceeded to devise the plan. Further details were presented to the Board in December. They included information on general design of the network with OCLC as the central control unit, an organization chart for governing and staffing, an estimate of staff requirements, a tentative budget for operations and for research and development, an enumeration of functions of the Center outside of Ohio, and costs to regions with non-Ohio-based computers, as well as those not currently on-line.

At the January 1973 Board meeting, Kilgour outlined methods by which OCLC might assume a leadership position in a national library network. With the advice of Haskins & Sells, he reported that a six-year projected budget forecast for OCLC as headquarters of a network was in preparation. The establishment of differential rates for service and the inclusion of the cost of research and development (derived from nonmember income) were also to be a part of the budget projection. In addition, the director stated that he was considering three types of agreements. They would cover the relationship of the Center with a region having a computer, with a region without one, and with a region not possessing a computer currently but with plans to acquire one in the future.

The proposed plan was approved by the Board on February 14, 1973. A special membership meeting convened on March 26 to decide its final fate. Kilgour's report included answers to questions asked in the past by the Board and membership as they considered the possibilities of networking and expanding on a large scale. The seven basic questions that permeated the discussions, together with their answers, follow.[22]

What, if any, investments would be needed on the part of the Ohio members? Extension of services outside Ohio would require no further investment for the members.

How would such an outreach affect the cost of services to the Ohio members? The extended services would lower the cost to Ohio users. The biggest economic risk would be the possibility of a competition from firms that would attempt to operate a network commercially. Haskins & Sells believed that if OCLC were the focus of a national library network, it might recover three hundred thousand dollars that members paid in research and development costs in the pre-on-line stage. It also felt that the Center's services lent themselves to differential charging, with the Ohio members receiving services at a lower rate.

How would the move affect the current research and development activities of OCLC? It would not only speed up research and development on the programs in progress, it would also provide sound financial footing for the future. As an added benefit, OCLC would become independent of grants for research and development.

How would it be possible to provide adequate staffing to implement and operate the extension? Financial projections indicated that OCLC would be able to meet the staffing requirements.

Was such a move legally feasible? It was illegal for OCLC to extend its services outside of Ohio to individual libraries. Specialized research collections such as those found at the Eastman School of Music Sibley Library, the Union Theological Seminary, and the John Crerar Library would, unfortunately, be excluded. The Center did, however, have a legal right to extend services to library consortia. Although regional agreements were economically and administratively the most advantageous, OCLC was interested in eventually being able to extend services to individual libraries, too.

Would the OCLC governance structure have to be altered? The governance of OCLC would still remain in the hands of the Board of Trustees of the Center, regardless of the composition of its corps of users. Some arrangements would have to be made for the representation of regional network affiliates in the governing of the Center. At past Board meetings, three possibilities were discussed. The first gave them representation on the Board. The second offered representation through an advisory committee to the Board. The third was representation on an advisory committee to the director, who would present their concerns to the Board.

Would not such an extension adversely affect operations of the Center? It already gives informal advice and help to newly created library cooperatives. The operations of the Center would not be degraded by the extension. On the contrary, if OCLC were the center of a national network, it could provide more efficient and effective library service to *all* of its users. Of course, the risk of failure on a national level was inescapable.

Following a lengthly discussion, the membership unanimously approved the plan to extend OCLC services outside of Ohio. This historic decision allowed the Center to offer services to consortia on three unprecedented levels. It could assist in the replication of the system, it could provide services directly from Columbus, or it could initially provide services from Columbus and then assist in a replication. One of the obvious advantages of such grand-scale cooperation was the widening of the spectrum of library holdings available to all individual libraries, irrespective of the type of regional agreement they had with OCLC.

Apropos of regional affiliates, CLR allowed OCLC to expend $11,000 that had not been spent from a previous grant scheduled to end on December 31, 1972. The funds helped to cover the expenses of setting up agreements with the other regions.

The agreements with FAUL, NELINET, and PRLC remained intact during fiscal year 1972-1973. FAUL and NELINET were participating in the on-line union catalog and the shared cataloging system for up to three years; at the end of that time, each would establish its own on-line system. During fiscal year 1972-1973, PRLC continued to operate as a satellite of OCLC. The agreements with CCLC and ULC renewed relationships. The operational expenses of CCLC were paid by an OE grant. Under its terms, the grant funds would terminate on December 31, 1972. CCLC wanted to continue its affiliation with the Center on the understanding that it would assume its own financial responsibilities. An agreement was drafted patterned after the OCLC/ PRLC one. CCLC accepted it, and in January 1973 the Board approved the continuation of the relationship.

Beginning in January 1972, ULC experimentally used the system for one year. Before the fall of 1972, it did not have a written agreement with the Center. Such an agreement was formulated during fiscal year 1972-1973 to continue the relationship. The Center anticipated that more ULC members would eventually be on-line to Columbus. Drexel University, Temple University, and the University of Pennsylvania, the original affiliates, would continue to participate, with Temple University and the University of Pennsylvania using one more terminal. Drexel University was the first of the three to make full use of the OCLC system. Its entire operations were channeled through the Center.

While the ULC experiment was in progress, a new regional network was created in Pennsylvania that became known as PALINET. Its formation was initiated by the original trio that had participated in the ULC experiment; two of the three directors were board members of ULC. ULC was the umbrella under which PALINET was founded.[23] The evolution of PALINET was unrelated to PRLC. An organizational meeting was held in December 1972. The first board of directors included the directors of the Pennsylvania Union Library Catalogue, the University of Pennsylvania, Drexel University, Temple University, the University of Delaware, and Bryn Mawr. PALINET evolved over the next several years as a consortium of academic and research libraries in eastern Pennsylvania, Delaware, Maryland, and New Jersey.[24]

Also, the Educational Testing Service (ETS) and the Interuniversity Communications Council (EDUCOM) had shown interest in replicating the Center as a mid-Atlantic regional library center. Inquiries came also from the states of Illinois, Indiana, Maryland, Michigan, Texas, and Wisconsin. In addition, the Province of Quebec inquired.

Early in the spring of 1973, the Assistant Director attended a meeting in Washington, D.C. with the Federal Library Committee (FLC) whose agent was LC. Long helped to draft an agreement with FLC that provided for "the experimental use of an on-line cataloging system that will have potential in improving shared cataloging among federal libraries."[25] The experiment, commonly referred to as FLECC (Federal Libraries' Experiment in Cooperative Cataloging), would run for twelve months, beginning January 1974. Start-up costs were estimated at sixty-six thousand dollars to be paid by the agent to OCLC. The libraries of seven United States agencies appropriated funds to LC.[26] The experiment involved a telecommunications arrangement with Tymshare, Inc. of Cupertino, California, for low-speed, dial-up connection of terminals.[27] The entire agreement, signed in the late spring of 1973, was subject to renewal for experimental purposes for one year after December 31, 1973. It enabled the federal library community to perform on-line cataloging and to receive OCLC-printed catalog cards.

The idea of cooperative federal library activity dates to 1964 when FLC was formed for the purpose of pulling together the intellectual resources not only of the federal library but also of the library-related community. In order to achieve better utilization of library resources and facilities, the committee hoped to provide more effective planning, development, and operation of federal libraries. This goal could be reached by maximizing the exchange of experience, skill, and resources.

FLECC resulted from a survey conducted by FLC that clearly showed the advantages of networking. The federal libraries were geographically scattered and inadequately financed. Most of them were small and most operated under high labor costs.

The year closed with the Center completing its first full year of on-line operations. Its body of users continued to grow as its services spilled across state lines. The system offered new capabilities, and the data base increased in value as more and more bibliographic data were available. Financial support was strong, and the development of the serials and technical processing systems was well underway. Plans for a national library network were being discussed. There was an excitement and suspense at this rapid growth. Members, participants, and curious observers carefully watched as OCLC gained momentum.

NOTES

1. See chapter 2 for details.

2. A holding institution is a member library that owns one or more copies of a particular title. When a record was used by an institution to produce catalog cards, its three-letter holding symbol was added to the list of holding institutions at the bottom of the record.

3. Ohio College Library Center, *Annual Report 1972/1973* (Columbus: Ohio College Library Center, 1973), p. 2.

4. Ohio College Library Center, *Newsletter*, 29 September 1972, pp. 2-3.

5. Op. cit., Ohio College Library Center, *Annual Report 1972/1973*, p. 2.

6. See chapter 2 for details.

7. Ohio College Library Center, "Ohio College Library Center: Implementation Committee Report" (Columbus: Ohio College Library Center, 1 October 1973), p. 9.

8. Judith Hopkins, the Center's bibliographic editor, resigned in November 1972, and Phyllis Bova was hired as library systems analyst in February 1973.

9. Ohio Bell was a subsidiary of AT & T.

10. In addition, members were to add 20 percent to the total resulting from the additional 50 percent. The 20 percent represented the cost for the activation of the technical processing and serials control systems. As an example, Wittenberg University's membership fee for 1973-1974 would be $13,599.13, calculated as illustrated:

75% of membership fee for 1972-1973	$7,555.07	(1)
50% of line 1	3,777.54	(2)
Total of lines 1 and 2	$11,332.61	(3)
20% of line 3	2,266.52	(4)
Estimated membership fee for 1973-1974;		
Total of lines 3 and 4	$13,599.13	

(Source: Ohio College Library Center, *Newsletter*, 22 November 1972, p. 4.)

11. Ohio College Library Center, "Minutes of the Board of Trustees Meeting" (Columbus: Ohio College Library Center, 10 January 1973), p. 5.

12. Ohio College Library Center, "Minutes of the Board of Trustees Meeting" (Columbus: Ohio College Library Center, 26 March 1973), p. 2.

13. Frederick G. Kilgour, Philip L. Long, Alan L. Landgraf, and John A. Wyckoff, "The Shared Cataloging System of the Ohio College Library Center," *Journal of Library Automation* 5 (September 1972): 181-82.

14. The ad hoc committee on extending direct borrowing privileges to graduate and undergraduate students of OCLC institutions included: James V. Jones, chairman (Case Western Reserve University); Patricia L. Lyons (Walsh College); Herbert F. Johnson (Oberlin College); and Martha Cox (Malone College).

15. Ohio College Library Center, "Minutes of the Members Meeting" (Columbus: Ohio College Library Center, 10 November 1972), pp. 6-7.

16. They included: Ashland College, Athenaeum of Ohio, Bowling Green State University, Bluffton College, Central State University, Cleveland State University, College of Mt. St. Joseph, College of Steubenville, College of Wooster, Defiance College, Heidelberg College, Hiram College, Kent State University, Malone College, Miami University, Oberlin College, Ohio University, Otterbein College, Pontifical College Josephinum, Rio Grande College, University of Akron, University of Toledo, Urbana College, Walsh College, Wittenberg University, and Xavier University.

17. The Subcommittee was chaired by Lewis C. Branscomb (The Ohio State University). Other members included Betty Wasson (Western College), Joseph M. Denham (Hiram College), and the director, ex-officio.

18. See appendix 1, Exhibit D, for a complete list of the Board of Trustees members.

19. See appendix 1, Exhibit O, for the resolution.

20. Frederick G. Kilgour, "Effect of Computerization on Acquisitions," *Program* 3 (November 1969): 95.

21. Ibid., pp. 95-96.

22. Ohio College Library Center, "Minutes of the Members Meeting" (Columbus: Ohio College Library Center, 26 March 1973), pp. 4-6.

23. PALINET was originally the acronym for the Pennsylvania Area Library Network of the Union Catalogue of Pennsylvania. Although PALINET began as a subunit of ULC, by 1975 the situation was reversed. As its membership and reputation grew, PALINET had become the dominant organization reducing ULC to the category of a subunit.

24. See appendix 1, Exhibit J, for a list of the PALINET membership.

25. "FLC and OCLC Enter into Cooperative Cataloging Experiment," *Law Library Journal*, 68 (February 1975), p. 106.

26. The agencies included: the departments of Agriculture, Army, Commerce, Housing and Urban Development, Interior, Labor, and Transportation. Additional funds were contributed by The Bureau of Standards, the Corps of Engineers, and the Smithsonian Institute.

27. See appendix 2, Glossary of Terms, for a definition.

7

EVOLUTION THROUGH CONTINUOUS EXPANSION 1973-1974

In the fall of 1973, OCLC executive director,[1] Frederick G. Kilgour, received the Ohio Library Association's "Librarian of the Year Award." The laurel was presented "in recognition of his outstanding contribution in providing courage, vision and leadership in the conception and vigorous development of the Ohio College Library Center ..."

The vigorous development of OCLC resulted in internal and external expansion. No longer confined to its Ohio boundaries, OCLC's sphere of service encompassed several new consortia. A new growth pattern emerged from that expansion, making greater demands on the Center's personnel and hardware. In fiscal year 1973-1974, OCLC made plans to add fifteen new positions to the staff, and in the spring the Board of Trustees approved a $2,218,000 budget for fiscal year 1974-1975, an increase of $614,000 over the previous year's budget.

THE ON-LINE UNION CATALOG
AND SHARED CATALOGING SYSTEM

The OCLC *Annual Report 1973/1974* included four tables that depicted the growth and nature of the data base. Table T-3 shows the number of titles cataloged by the Ohio libraries and the consortia from July 1, 1973, through June 30, 1974. Three of the participants were active for only part of the year: FAUL, FLC, and IUC. As shown in table T-3, 1,194,287 books were cataloged on the system. This figure contrasts with the 572,474 books cataloged during 1972-1973. Seven networks across the country accounted for more than half of the books cataloged. Among the out-of-state consortia, NELINET cataloged the greatest number of titles and IUC the least. NELINET also made the heaviest use of the data base, next to OCLC, for catalog card production and contributed nearly one-fifth of the total input cataloging to the system. Its input added to that of the other six consortia accounted for almost one-half of the total. Near the end of the fiscal year, the OCLC system daily handled nearly one hundred thousand communication messages.

TABLE T-3
Titles Cataloged from 1 July 1973 through 30 June 1974[2]

Center	Total Copies of Books Cataloged	Chargeable First-Time Uses of Records	Input Cataloging
Ohio College Library Center	587,481	348,457	107,734
Cooperative College Library Center	48,700	20,237	1,217
Five Associated University Libraries	117,068	81,943	24,199
Federal Library Committee	9,300	5,519	2,307
Interuniversity Council of the North Texas Area	4,780	4,337	208
New England Library Information Network	302,159	236,580	36,768
Pennsylvania Area Library Network	71,645	56,899	9,185
Pittsburgh Regional Library Center	53,154	25,003	3,942
Total	1,194,287	778,975	185,560

Table T-4, page 94, recorded the monthly cataloging activitity for the year. In July 1973, 58,853 copies of books were cataloged. By June 1974, the figure had more than doubled. The Center had hoped for an even greater growth, but because of a fire in February at Beehive Medical Electronics, the number of Model 100 terminals that could be put into the field was sharply restricted. Cataloging activity was heaviest in the spring, with the largest volume recorded for May.

TABLE T-4
Month-by-Month Cataloging Activity from July 1973 through June 1974[3]

Month	Year	Copies of Books Cataloged	Chargeable First-Time Uses of Records
July	1973	58,853	38,145
August		67,235	45,674
September		65,438	44,217
October		90,708	62,512
November		91,863	62,078
December		81,528	54,332
January	1974	109,445	72,172
February		112,573	73,969
March		121,718	78,841
April		130,501	83,019
May		139,642	88,690
June		124,843	75,388

Table T-5, page 95, clearly illustrates that OCLC was making it possible for libraries to lower the rate of rise of per-unit cataloging costs while enjoying the benefits of an expanding union catalog. A rise in the use made of the data base for cataloging purposes resulted in an increase in the economy of scale for users. For example, libraries increasingly used the records input by their colleagues for catalog production. Utilization climbed from 79,141 records in July 1973 to 166,426 records in July 1974, a 91 percent rise. LC continued to be a major contributor to the data base, accounting for 44.2 percent of catalog production by July 4, 1974.

The on-line union catalog grew by nearly 70 percent over the twelve-month period. The total number of materials with a publication date of 1967 and older increased from 290,916 records in July 1973 to 423,468 records a year later. The increase was due, in large measure, to the input of participants' original cataloging—358,748 records input as of July 4, 1974.

The number of titles published before 1800 jumped from 11,481 in 1973 to 16,726 in 1974 also as a result of the participants' input. The input of LC was notable, although less remarkable. The 1973-1974 *Annual Report* stated that:

> Libraries are using the union catalog increasingly. Small libraries are receiving interlibrary loan requests from large libraries, an event that rarely occurred before implementation of the on-line union catalog. Also, more libraries are searching interlibrary loan requests on the system. Since the union catalog is currently growing at a rate that approaches seven thousand new location listings a day, its usefulness is rapidly expanding.[4]

TABLE T-5
Analysis of On-line Catalog Record File (6 July 1973 and 4 July 1974)[5]

	6 July 1973	4 July 1974
Catalog records in system	652,114	935,314
Source of records:		
Participating libraries	321,242 (49.3%)	521,797 (55.8%)
Used for catalog production by non-source libraries	79,141 (24.7%)	166,426 (32.0%)
Library of Congress	330,872 (50.7%)	413,517 (44.2%)
Used for catalog production	137,818 (41.7%)	207,387 (50.2%)
Average usage per record by other than source library:		
Records input by participating libraries	2.91	3.63
Library of Congress	4.55	5.80
Date of publication:		
Before 1800		
Participating libraries	11,481	16,726
Library of Congress	238	365
Total	11,719	17,091
1800–1899		
Participating libraries	18,026	34,174
Library of Congress	695	1,022
Total	18,721	35,196
1900–1967		
Participating libraries	213,225	307,848
Library of Congress	47,251	63,333
Total	260,476	371,181
1968–1973 and 1974		
Participating libraries	78,075	162,590
Library of Congress	282,485	348,572
Total	360,560	511,162

By using a few figures, one can demonstrate the level of activity on the system. From October 19, 1973, through November 2, 1973, according to "Minutes of the Members' Meeting,"

... 20,437 records were used for catalog production; 3,792 records were input; 142,257 cards were produced; 137 terminals were in operation; and the system functioned 99.83% of the available uptime.[6]

Table T-6, page 96, illuminates the nature of the data base. Although eleven languages represented 99.46 percent of the on-line file, the prevalent one was English (87.67 percent), followed by German (3.73 percent) and French (3.61 percent). Low on the list were Polish (0.13 percent) and Indonesian (0.12 percent). One may safely assume that in subsequent years, the ratio of records in the English language in the data base to those in other languages will change, especially with the participation of large research libraries whose collections include a wide spectrum of languages. The list of languages would surely have to be expanded before total access to catalogs was realized.

TABLE T-6
Frequency of Records, by Language[7]

Language	Code	Count	Percentage of Total Records
1. English	ENG	815,634	87.67
2. German	GER	34,832	3.73
3. French	FRE	33,490	3.61
4. Spanish	SPA	22,993	2.47
5. Italian	ITA	7,544	0.81
6. Portuguese	POR	2,949	0.32
7. Latin	LAT	2,440	0.26
8. Russian	RUS	1,705	0.18
9. Dutch	DUT	1,521	0.16
10. Polish	POL	1,245	0.13
11. Indonesian	IND	1,146	0.12
Total		925,499	99.46

Data Base

The concerted efforts of the Committee on Implementation of *Standards for Input Cataloging* and the Patron Input Committee encouraged the growth of the OCLC system.

The Ohio membership, on November 9, 1973, approved "The Ohio College Library Center: Implementation Report," which contained nine recommendations from the Committee on Implementation. Quality control was the major concern. Three acceptable levels of bibliographic records were enumerated, and a Peer Council was recommended. The final recommendation dissolved the Implementation Committee. All nine recommendations were approved. The Peer Council played an influential role; the integrity of the data base rested upon its shoulders.

In the fall of 1973, the six-member OCLC Patron Input Committee,[8] chaired by Herbert F. Johnson (Oberlin College), began to meet. By November 1973, the group had met at each of the five members' libraries to discuss with patrons their library activities. These dialogues helped the Committee to accomplish its major task of finding ways of synchronizing most efficiently OCLC developments with the actual needs of library patrons.

At the Toledo-Lucas County Public Library, seven points emerged from this first encounter with patrons. First, there was a significant gap in patron awareness of OCLC's capabilities. Second, patrons were primarily concerned with getting information when they needed it. Third, ready access combined with ease of using OCLC influenced its acceptance. Fourth, patrons wanted a hard copy of the bibliographic data for many reasons, including sharing it with other faculty members at department meetings where curriculum decisions were made. They also thought that a hard copy could be presented to students to increase their awareness of what was available. Fifth, users requested that fugitive literatures (materials dealing with matters of temporary interest) and media materials be incorporated into the data base. Sixth, an access, by subject, to library materials would be an added incentive to using the system. Seventh, patrons asked that the subject contents of periodical articles be analyzed and made available.

At the March 19, 1974 meeting of the Board of Trustees, the Committee summarized the results of the series of meetings. It disclosed two salient findings. In general, patrons were unaware of OCLC. Moreover, priorities for service differed between patrons and library administrators. Patron priorities included interlibrary loans through OCLC, local call number displays on the terminals, subject and author searches, extended analytics for periodical articles, and access to additional machine-readable files, such as the Mechanized Information Center (MIC) data base at The Ohio State University. An unexpected outcome of the visits was the realization that communication between OCLC and the member institutions needed improvement. Therefore, the main challenges confronting OCLC with regard to patrons were the smooth mix of OCLC priorities with those of users, and improvement of communication between the two groups. These preliminary findings were embodied in the Committee's draft, "Interim Report of OCLC Patron Input Committee" (March 7, 1974).

The new and improved functions added to the on-line system heralded a more intellectual approach to librarianship. The pioneering technological advances of OCLC were freeing librarians to pursue a higher level of professionalism. After more than one hundred years of relative stability, librarianship finally moved on to an age of creative instability.

Response time directly affected the efficient operation of the functions of the system. It was approximately two seconds at its best, and thirty seconds at its slowest. With twenty-seven terminals on a line sending messages at a rate of ten per second, heavy traffic on the lines degraded the rate of communication between terminals and computer. Through statistics gathered at OCLC, it was demonstrated that working at one terminal, a cataloger generated approximately one hundred requests to the computer per hour. Of those requests as few as three or as many as twenty titles per hour were cataloged.

The Center's staff was reorganizing the data base to add a variety of new functions, including a personal author index, to the system as well as to increase overall operating efficiency. The name-title and title indices were also scheduled for expansion. By June average response time between terminal and computer dropped by 40 percent to 5.35 seconds.

During the twelve-month period under discussion, another important function was initiated, the on-line correction of input cataloging. It enabled libraries to correct on-line the records they themselves had input into the system, provided that no other library had used the record for cataloging. The correction procedure involved four steps.[9] Records already used by another library for cataloging, or which were originally input by another library, had to be corrected through the mail, using the error report forms.

The problem of duplicating catalog records in the data base persisted. Duplicate records increased search time, dissipated holdings information, needlessly expended valuable on-line cataloging time, and deceptively increased the size of the data base. The Center took several steps to alleviate the situation. A new form to report duplicate records to the Center was devised. Records chosen for deletion would appear on the terminal with a note "DO NOT USE THIS RECORD FOR CATALOG PRODUCTION." Users were advised to take full advantage of the author-title, title, and LC card number search keys. By trying all three access points, one could reduce the chances of recurring duplications. Terminal operators were asked to query the data base if a record had been in the SAVE file for one day or more. The February 28, 1974 *Newsletter* reported an unusual example of duplication:

> The most depressing example of duplication was the existence at one time of three records in the file for *On-Line Cataloging*. Of the more than three quarters of a million titles in the file, *On-Line Cataloging* should be the last one to suffer the fate of duplication much less triplication. The Center suspects that some terminal operators have not read carefully the second paragraph on page 32 of *On-Line Cataloging* stating that search keys 'do not contain ... punctuation.' Inclusion of the "-" in either the name-title or title search key for *On-Line Cataloging* causes an unsuccessful search and subsequent unnecessary duplication.[10]

In January 1974 a new function became available for the medical libraries. They could now add directly to a master record a National Library of Medicine (NLM) call number, a call number based upon a NLM number, and the Medical Subject Headings (MeSH). Previously, medical libraries were required to send OCLC the information on the call number and the subject headings, which the Center's staff would then add to the data base records. The new function not only expedited cataloging, it also made fuller information instantaneously available to other libraries in the system.

The production of accession lists began in September 1973. They cited in call number order or subject heading order books by a member library that had been cataloged on the system within a three-month period. The text of the lists was available on offset masters or on plain white paper for printing by a member. Charge for the lists was $.075 per entry, based upon the production costs. A minimum of $10.00 was charged for lists containing less than 140 entries.

In the spring of 1974, the capabilities of the on-line system were expanded to include cataloging of maps and films. *Maps: A MARC Format* and *Films: A Marc Format*, published by MDO, served as guidelines.

Many OCLC participants were also cataloging music scores. To date, MDO had not issued a machine-readable format for scores. To satisfy a request by the membership, the Advisory Committee on Cataloging approved the input of bibliographic records for scores. On-line score cataloging departed on a number of points from the book format. The form of a composition (sonata, symphony, étude, etc.), the format of the score (miniature score, score with parts, etc.), and the number of instruments for which the piece was written (brass quintet, flute solo, etc.) were elements unique to music cataloging. Nonetheless, scores were input according to the MARC format for books, pending release of a music format from LC.

Operation of the system both at OCLC and in libraries was starting to require more and more communication. The psychological aspect of communication was a determining factor in the system's success or failure. At the February 20, 1974 Board of Trustees meeting, a number of complaints were registered. Member libraries wanted a list of staff members to call about problems. They complained of a lack of knowledge as to when the system was down or when a new MARC tape was input and the paucity of information concerning the Board meetings. To improve communication with libraries, OCLC hired a full-time editor for the *Newsletter* and other communications.[11] Kilgour had written the first sixty-seven issues from December 1967 to April 1974. In 1973, the *Index to OCLC Newsletter* was published, covering all of the issues through number 61 (September 18, 1974).[12]

In June 1974, OCLC staff began systematic visits to Ohio libraries to become familiar with library procedures, to discuss specific problems and operations with library personnel, and to answer questions about OCLC. Information about OCLC was provided at exhibits and demonstrations at state and regional library association meetings. Thanks to a gift from Xerox Corporation, OCLC installed a telephone line between New York and Columbus, making it possible to exhibit the system at ALA's July 1974 meeting. Beehive Medical Electronics absorbed the rental expense of the booth. Two operators demonstrated their on-line terminals.

The Center used video tapes for instruction. A series of such tapes was prepared in conjunction with Kent State University's Television Center. They described the impact of OCLC automation on an academic library, the OCLC cataloging system, the procedure for the on-line bibliographic search, and the operation of a terminal.

A reference manual entitled *Specifications for Magnetic Tapes Containing Catalog Records for Monographs and Serials* was compiled. To be used in conjunction with *On-Line Cataloging, Books: A MARC Format* and *Serials: A MARC Format*, it described the communication format for machine-readable cataloging records.

The availability of the data base was crucial to its usefulness. Beginning on May 21, 1974, the on-line system was available from 7:00 A.M. until 8:00 P.M., Eastern Standard Time. The extension of hours was prompted by the participation of the Interuniversity Council of the North Texas Area (IUC).

In February 1974, the Board of Trustees encouraged the data bank to grow by resolving that new member libraries and regional affiliates had to input all of their current cataloging of Roman alphabet titles into the data bank.

The data base was being used for a variety of library activities other than the cataloging of materials. As the *Annual Report 1973/1974* stated:

Monitoring of the system in early May, during a 12-hour period when some six thousand seven hundred titles were cataloged, revealed that the LC card number, name-title, and title indexes were used twenty-three thousand times. It is most unlikely that these indexes were used more than thirteen thousand five hundred times for catalog production for cataloging sixty-seven hundred books. Hence, it is clear that libraries are making extensive use of the data base for preorder searching, searching for bibliographic information, searching for book selection purposes, and searching to locate interlibrary loans.[13]

The newfound uses for the data base would increase in value as the union catalog grew. Expanding daily, the on-line union catalog stored 2,162,021 location listings for the member libraries and 413,517 on the LC MARC II records at the close of the year.

Growing along with the data base was its corps of users. The year witnessed the addition of eleven new members. Seven public libraries added their names to the membership list, bringing the total number of public library members to twelve. The seven were: Akron Public Library, Cuyahoga County Public Library, East Cleveland Public Library, Findlay Public Library, Greene County District Library, Shaker Heights Public Library, and Upper Arlington Public Library. From the academic community, Cleveland Marshall College of Law (the Law School of Cleveland State University) and Lutheran Theological Seminary joined. In addition, the Shaker Heights City School District became the first school system in the country to go on-line with OCLC. Finally, the State Library of Ohio would bring into the OCLC fold over eighty Ohio public libraries. Urbana College, a charter member, did not renew its membership.

Although the data base was growing and becoming important to libraries, the users of libraries were still the raison d'être of OCLC and were very much on Kilgour's mind in 1974 when he wrote:

> An excellent example of making a catalog available to users when and where they need it is the remote catalog access and circulation system at the Ohio State University Libraries. This system eliminates the need to go to the OSU library. As a member of the OSU faculty, I can pick up a telephone, dial a person at a CRT terminal, and, by giving the author's name and the first word of the title, I find out whether or not OSU has a particular book. If it does and if it is not charged out, the book is on my desk within a day or two. This remarkable service is available to students, staff, and faculty alike.[14]

Kilgour goes on to say:

> Professional librarians become just as frustrated with library service as anybody else does. Whereas I will not spend half a day going to a library to discover that I cannot obtain what I want, I am entirely prepared to spend half a minute not to get what I want!

Half of the time, I do get what I want, and my personal use of the books has doubled or tripled since OSU implemented its remote catalog access system.[15]

One final subject belongs in this discussion of the data base. The Inter-University Library Council (IULC), the official coordinating agency representing the state university libraries in Ohio, approached OCLC in the fall of 1973. IULC asked the Center to cooperate with it on a shelf list conversion project for its member libraries as well as for other interested libraries in the state. OCLC was to convert the shelf list records to a machine-readable format and add them to the Center's data base. Thus, the data base would grow very quickly while, at the same time, libraries would make their holdings accessible to other libraries using the system. The project was conceived to accomplish total on-line cataloging in the future and eventually to replace the card catalog with an on-line catalog.

Kilgour envisioned the project as technically feasible, although it would require a generous investment of time. Each library was to choose a different area to input to ensure the balanced growth of the data base. Unfortunately, due to a number circumstances, the project lost momentum as the individual institutions independently negotiated with OCLC for shelf list conversions.

The only other similar undertaking had been the RECON pilot project at LC (see chapter 2), which began in 1969 and ended in 1971. By 1974, there was no concerted drive to continue this type of large-scale operation. Although the IULC project was not carried to its conclusion, it rekindled interest in converting catalog records to machine-readable format, and led to an enlarged data base for OCLC members.

Equipment

The OCLC system, from the start, was designed to accommodate change:

The system is not designed for present library practices. It is designed for future development. Our feeling is that we are right at the very beginning and although we are off the ground, we have not been off for a very long period of time.... Also, we are dedicated to an idea and that is to deliver the information; then cataloging information; and ultimately textual information to users when and where they need it. This is surely what we are going to have to do in librarianship.[16]

This attitude coupled with the growth of the system prompted the staff to plan carefully the acquisition of new equipment and the update of existing hardware. During the year, the equipment configuration was expanded and altered. The Center selected and ordered a second computer, a Xerox Sigma 9, to assist the Sigma 5. In addition, minicomputers were used to increase the system's efficiency. The telephone network was altered by addition of a Wide-Area Telephone Service (WATS) line and the statewide application of the Telpak telephone system. Beehive Medical Electronics, Inc. began production of the OCLC 100 Display. A major breakthrough in the processing of library materials was the ability of the new terminal to drive a printer.

The Sigma 5 had served the Center well for the past three years, but as system activity continued to rise, it became evident that a second computer would be required to handle the increased system load. A committee of key staff members selected the Xerox Corporation's Sigma 9. This machine could compute 40-90 percent faster than the Sigma 5, and it had a core memory that could be expanded to include up to four times the work limit of the Sigma 5. Moreover, it had built-in detection devices for better performance.

The Sigma 9 was scheduled to be installed shortly before the Sigma 5 would reach saturation, which was predicted to occur in the fall of 1974. In February 1974, the Sigma 9 was ordered along with additional core memory for the Sigma 5. The extra memory would be used as a secondary bank for the future storage of serial records input by the membership. By March, Xerox Corporation had set the delivery date for December 1974. OCLC procured an earlier date of October 1, 1974.

To prepare for the arrival of the new computer a staff committee had to design the simultaneous operation of the two computers. The committee was also considering acquiring a third computer and selecting a place that offered high security to all of this hardware. The Computer Security Committee was formed. In the spring of 1974, Kilgour, a security consultant, and the Committee worked to find a location that would accommodate up to four Sigma 9s. In June, the Committee recommended to Kilgour that OCLC eventually obtain three Sigma 9s and sell the Sigma 5. When the second Sigma 9 was on order, the Center would place the Sigma 5 for sale. If it were sold, the Center would use the funds to purchase a third Sigma 9. The third would be used to operate the production activity. If the Sigma 5 could not be sold, it would be used for production.

Ten additional Telefile disk drives were interfaced with the Sigma 5. The new drives brought the total capacity of the secondary memories to one billion characters. With member libraries wanting to convert all of their retrospective holdings to machine-readable form, the extra storage space would help to accommodate the increased input of bibliographic records.

The Center acquired two minicomputers during the year. According to a contract with FLC, OCLC would use the minicomputers to reduce the load on the Sigma 5. They would also enable government libraries as well as other libraries to have access to OCLC via teletype-like terminals. The goal was to make it possible for small libraries with an equally small amount of daily cataloging to use the system for cataloging and searching through a dial-up, in this case, Tymnet, network. A telephone call linked the terminal in the library with the OCLC computers.

On August 1, 1974, the State of Ohio began using the Telpak telephone system. Qualified to participate, OCLC expected to use it toward the end of the calendar year to reduce telephone rates and eventually OCLC fees for the Ohio members. The September 18, 1973 *Newsletter* informed its readers that the Center had added a WATS line for use throughout the continental United States, except in Ohio. Non-Ohio members would be able to call OCLC on a toll-free line.

The weakest link in the OCLC system was the terminals. During 1973-1974, both the Spiras Systems Irascope and the new OCLC Model 100 Display terminals were used. It was difficult to obtain spare parts for the Spiras terminals since the manufacturer did not sufficiently stock extra parts. The

Spiras terminals played a historic role in the development of OCLC. At the time of their original purchase, they were the only model with the terminal features OCLC sought. The fact that they were later superseded by another model in no way detracts from their role as the first bridge linking OCLC members to the computer in Columbus.

The story of the acquisition of the OCLC Model 100 Display terminals can best be described as an act of patience. In May 1973, Beehive Medical Electronics shipped two hand-constructed prototypes of the new terminals to Columbus. In August the production units were expected to be available. The original order called for 100 terminals. Beehive Medical Electronics was to deliver 90 terminals by September 30. By September, the prototypes were in operation at Syracuse University where some minor design problems were detected. In October, 100 more terminals were ordered, arriving somewhat behind schedule. By the end of the month, 137 were operating less than satisfactorily. On the average, three terminals a day were down, with downtime averaging three days per terminal. However, requests for the terminals continued to arrive at the Center. In response, the Board of Trustees approved a purchase order for 100 more terminals, and in February 1974, 100 more terminals were ordered, bringing the total order to 300. In March, Beehive had a fire that caused extensive damage at one of the company's two manufacturing sites. Unfortunately, the fire occurred where the OCLC Model 100 Display terminal was produced. Manufacturing had to be consolidated at one site. In April, the company committed itself to producing five terminals per week, beginning with the last week in April. It would produce five a week for two weeks, then ten a week until all orders were filled. It also announced that the price of the terminal would soon be raised from $2,675 to $3,076. The same month the Board of Trustees once again approved an order for 100 terminals. By May, Beehive had not met its commitment to ship to OCLC ten terminals per week. The lack of terminals in the field would immediately affect the first-time uses made of the records in the data base. (First-time uses refers to the first time a record already in the system was used for catalog production by a member that did not input it.) The Center had anticipated approximately 825,000 first-time uses. At this time, use provided a basis for the revised estimated total of 805,000 by close of the fiscal year.

From the viewpoint of users waiting for new terminals to arrive, May was disappointing. For the rest of the membership, however, May was record setting. On May 28, 1974, seven thousand records were cataloged on the system, the largest amount of cataloging ever done on any single day. In all, over forty-eight thousand catalog cards were produced. This high point was offset by a disaster on June 4 when all of the machine-readable cataloging records for that day were destroyed. All holdings information input on that day was also irretrievable. It was later discovered that two hardware failures and two human failures were to blame for the accident. In addition to the records that were destroyed, the Center lost fifty-four hundred dollars since it could not charge for the first-time uses on June 4.

There were 233 terminals in operation in 193 libraries as of June 28, 1974. The backlog of terminals on order numbered around 300. Beehive Medical Electronics was 30 terminals behind its production schedule. In June, Jack R. Vincent, the Center's comptroller, and Huntington Carlile, legal counsel, visited the company and received a new commitment schedule. Despite the negative aspects related to acquiring new terminals, the OCLC Model 100 Display proved itself reliable. It would eventually be found in libraries across the country. The *OCLC 100 Users Manual* was being prepared at the end of the fiscal year.

Originally, terminals were allocated to each member based upon the number of titles it cataloged per year. A new allocation formula was approved by the Board of Trustees in December 1973, whereby for each eleven thousand first-time uses made of the records, a library would be entitled to one terminal. (The serials control subsystem was not governed by this allocation procedure.) The formula would benefit the larger libraries by letting them use the system not only for cataloging purposes but also for book selection, acquisitions, and interlibrary loans.

In June the State Library of Ohio announced that it would grant OCLC $18,867 to acquire five test "public use" terminals to be placed in public areas of the State Library and selected Ohio academic and public libraries. The grant monies would cover the cost of the terminals, the telephone lines, and the necessary staff time. One portable terminal was to become the property of OCLC, and the remaining four were to remain permanently in the libraries where they had been originally placed. The funds were to be available as of July 1, 1974. The test period was one year. The experiment would yield useful information about the value of public access to the OCLC data base.

The production and distribution of forty-five thousand catalog cards per day was a major activity of the OCLC system. Approximately one mile of two catalog cards printed side-by-side was being produced daily. Each day six hours were needed to prepare the print tapes, and another eleven or twelve hours to print the cards. The Center used an IBM 1403 printer that could transfer data to cards at a rate of 1,100 lines per minute. To ensure precision, OCLC used a special library print chain, which reduced the speed to 450-550 lines per minute. With the expansion of services outside Ohio, the Center needed more printers. In February 1974, it placed an order for two IBM 1403s. One of the new printers was to reinforce the present one in the production of catalog cards. The other one was to be put in the machine room at the West Henderson Road location to serve as a backup printer for the catalog cards as well as to assist in other operations.

The Center was investigating a totally different type of printer that could be attached to a terminal to print labels for book spines, book circulation cards, and book pockets. A terminal operator, by typing certain commands at the completion of the cataloging process, could reformat the data on the screen into copy for a book spine label, a book circulation card label, and a book pocket label. Depression of a key would activate the printer and transfer data to it.

At the November meeting of the membership, Philip L. Long, newly appointed associate director,[17] distributed examples of the labels produced by two types of printers connected to the OCLC Model 100 Display terminals. Before the meeting he had sent a sample of type size to Ohio members, who were to indicate their willingness to use it on the labels.

In June 1974, the Center amassed a packet of information about the printers and distributed it to the members to help them choose a printer best suited for their libraries. There were two choices: The Centronics Model 306 Printer or the Holmes Tycom Model 38-KSR. The Centronics Model was a printer only; the Holmes Tycom Model had a keyboard, and any IBM Selectric typewriter could be used with it. When the printer was not needed, the typewriter could be used for normal typing. A pricing schedule for quantity was available with both. If a library chose the Centronics Model, the printer would cost $2,005. On the other hand, the Holmes Tycom Model would run $2,250.

The information packages also included samples of the labels. Their format was devised by the Advisory Committee on Cataloging. The sample here shows first what appears on the terminal and then what appears on the labels. The label on the far left would be affixed to the spine, and the other two would be used on the circulation card and the book pocket:

EXAMPLE OF LABEL FORMATS FOR HARD COPY PRINTER

U.S. National Business Council for Consumer Affairs.
Subcouncil on Performance and Service.
Product performance and servicing; an examination of consumer problems and business responses.

JK 1036 1959 .U56 P75 1974 v.2 no.5	JK1036 1959.U56P75 1974 v.2 U.S. National Business Council for Consumer Affairs Product performance and servicing;	JK1036 1959.U56P75 1974 v.2 U.S. National Business Council for Consumer Affairs Product performance and servicing;

At the June Board meeting, the Trustees decided to discontinue the option of off-line card production to new libraries. However, service to the four libraries using it would continue to be provided until they could go on-line.

Finances

One of the major objectives of OCLC was to lower the rate of increase in per-student costs for the library community. Since libraries across the nation were experiencing this rapid rise in costs, pursuit of this goal was valuable not only to OCLC but to the library profession as a whole. In *Economics of Academic Libraries*, William J. Baumol and Matityahu Marcus explain the reasons for this sharp increase. The analysis, the first of its kind, dispelled false notions and revealed new conclusions about the technology of library operations.

Their third chapter, "Cost Trends and Long-range Plans," was particularly significant in light of developments taking place at OCLC. It discussed postwar trends in library and computer costs, which, stated the authors, were diametrically opposed with regard to their cost behaviors. The cost per unit of library service had risen quickly and steadily, relative to the average cost of commodities in the country; the cost of electronic computers had dropped. Traditionally, it was believed that the cost of library services was directly related to inflation and increased enrollments in academic institutions. In reality, according to Baumol and Marcus, library costs per unit rose at a compound rate that far exceeded the general price level:

> Obviously, in a period in which the wholesale price index was increasing at an annual rate of less than 1 percent while library costs *per student* increased at more than 5 percent a year compounded, the growth in student body and the rise in price level still leave unexplained an annual rise of more than 4 percent.[18]

The disparity is clearly evident in table T-7:

TABLE T-7
Unit Costs in Fifty-eight University
Research Libraries in Comparison with Wholesale Price Index, 1951-69[19]

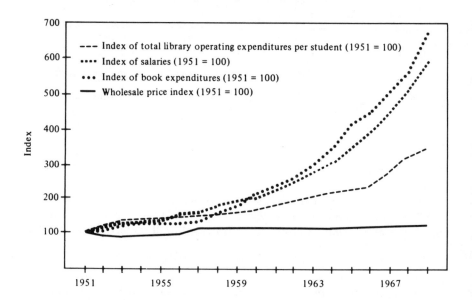

Reprinted by permission of the American Council on Education.

Table T-8 shows a cost decrease of about 55 percent a year (except between 1955 and 1960 when it was about 20 percent) for computer systems:

TABLE T-8
Comparison of Cost of Computation with Wholesale Price Index[20]

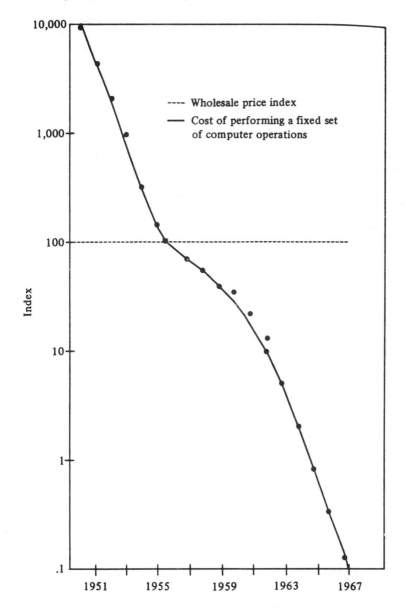

Reprinted by permission of the American Council on Education.

The authors cautioned that these trends did not necessarily beckon an era when any particular library operation would become less costly by virtue of its being automated. By 1969 libraries faced a dilemma of grand proportions as a result of several factors occurring simultaneously. To begin with, the per-unit cost in academic libraries rose at a rate of 6.3 percent from 1951 to 1969. During the same period the wholesale price index rose only 0.9 percent per year. On the other hand, the cost of computerization dropped 55 percent a year from 1951 to 1969 (with the exception of the years 1955 to 1960 when the drop was approximately 20 percent). Some profound modifications were inevitable.

The authors pointed out that libraries were inflexible, labor-intensive service organizations; salary increases in libraries did not mean an equal increase in productivity. The result was an increased strain on already stretched library budgets. Library mismanagement or inefficiences were not totally responsible for the increases in library budgets. Other reasons were the postwar expansion of book production and the rising prices of books and journals. The authors concluded "that the rising costs of library operations emanate from what may be described as the technological structure of library operations."[21] Electronic systems were less applicable to the complex library operations than its proponents had hoped. The profession's conservative nature was another factor.

Amazingly, OCLC had hurdled these obstacles to library automation, including perhaps the major one, the cost.

> Yet, a major impediment to a change in library operations turned out to be the cost of the electronic equipment itself and of its operation. The investment in purchase or rental of the equipment is enormous, and rapid obsolescence does not make matters easier. Moreover, sophisticated equipment requires the use of highly skilled personnel for maintenance, operation, programming, and so on, and such personnel are never cheap. As a result, the use of electronic equipment for the performance of library functions has been, for the most part, financially prohibitive.[22]

The authors did not claim that computers could or would replace all manual library operations. Rather, they believed that a noteworthy portion of library operations would be computerized because computerization would become affordable. The implications of their analysis of the current cost trends led them to conclude that "some fairly radical changes may become inevitable within a matter of decades."[23] Although *Economics of Academic Libraries* was limited to colleges and universities, Baumol and Marcus's conclusions were, in a large measure, applicable to any type of library.

The economic climate described in the preceding paragraphs influenced the financial operation of OCLC in a number of ways. One area where change was needed was the method for collecting fees for members and nonmembers. Some libraries were paying quarterly while others were delaying their annual payment until the next fiscal year. The Board of Trustees agreed to consider a monthly billing procedure to reward institutions that paid quarterly or annually with a discount. The details of the plan were prepared by the executive director with the advice of Haskins & Sells, Certified Public

Accountants. In November 1973 the Board received that firm's report recommending that OCLC continue the annual billing procedure at least for the immediate future.

Historically, OCLC had charged both the Ohio members and the nonmembers in advance at the start of each fiscal year. Billing was done on the basis of the cataloging activity in a library during the previous year. This procedure provided the Center with adequate working capital, but engendered budgetary problems for nearly one-half of the members and nonmembers who found it difficult to pay in advance. OCLC had to borrow operating capital from $500,000 to $750,000 halfway through the year. Apart from the fact that advance payments were illegal in some states, continued growth necessitated a modification in the current policy. A second plan was presented to the Board of Trustees by the comptroller, Jack R. Vincent.[24] Based upon an annual billing system, it offered flexibility and options. An added surcharge would cover any loan expenses. Discounts encouraged early payments:

TABLE T-9
OCLC Membership Fee Payment Options (1974-1975)[25]

OPTION	DISCOUNT ALLOWED	PAYMENT DUE DATES
Annual-in-advance	6%	August 15
Semiannual in-advance	4.5%	August 15 January 1
Quarterly in-advance	3%	August 15 October 1 January 1 April 1
Monthly after-the-fact payment	None	30 days

The following example illustrates how the policy would operate for a library that cataloged ten thousand titles during 1974-1975:[26]

			OHIO MEMBER	NON-OHIO MEMBER
First-time-use charge, per 74/75 budget			$ 1.69	$ .850
Add: Administrative Service Charge (6.383%)			.11	.054
Revised First-time-use Charge			$ 1.80	$ .904
Estimated Membership Fee -- 10,000 title example			$18,000	$9,040

Payment Option	Discount Allowed	Payment Due Dates		
Annual-in-advance	6%	August 15	$16,920	$8,497.60
Semiannual-in-advance	4.5%	August 15	8,595	4,316.60
		January 1	8,595	4,316.60
			$17,190	$8,633.20
Quarterly-in-advance	3%	August 15	4,365	2,192.20
		October 1	4,365	2,192.20
		January 1	4,365	2,192.20
		April 1	4,365	2,192.20
			$17,460	$8,768.80
Monthly-after-the-fact	None	30 Days	$18,000	$9,040.00

The Board approved the new billing procedure, as presented, effective July 1, 1974.

At the meeting of the members in May, the executive director announced that the first-time-use charge was dropping from $2.02 to $1.69. The decrease was due to the fact that there were more records in the system and that there was a reduction in the Model 100 Display terminal lease and service costs. An additional factor was an 80 percent equity that had accrued from Spiras terminals, which had been refinanced for purchase. The first-time-use charges in 1975-1976 would not, in all probability, drop any further since OCLC needed to replace some terminals.

In calculating their 1974-1975 membership fees, institutions were asked to plan on adding 15 percent to the first-time-use charges for the serials subsystem and another 5 percent if the technical processing system was activated.

At the September 18, 1973 meeting of the Board of Trustees, a revision in the charge policy for catalog cards was approved. The policy had stated that the charges for catalog cards were based on the actual cost of the cards plus 0.75¢ for overhead. The new policy set a flat rate of 3.4¢ for each catalog card produced. It allowed libraries as well as the Center to forecast more accurately their financial obligations.

Other charges were amended. In March 1974, the Board of Trustees approved a reduced charge for the on-line reclassification of titles. A number of institutions were converting from the Dewey Decimal to the Library of Congress classification system or making other in-house classification changes. Before the change, charges for reclassification were identical to those for initial cataloging. Under the new policy, the Center would charge half of the current first-time-use charge for any reclassification involving the use of the records currently in the system and not input by the library during reclassification.

By early spring, a new pattern in on-line activity had become evident. Some institutions wanted to participate in on-line cataloging without receiving catalog cards. Ultimately, a charging formula for this type of use would have to be established.

OCLC also offered a special service to users, the production of tapes of machine-readable cataloging records input or used by libraries. In the spring, the price structure was reviewed by the Board of Trustees. By the close of the year, no decision had been made to change the current rate.

In 1974, Inforonics, Inc. and Butler Associates published the *Survey of Library Automation Systems. Phase II. Final Report: Volume 5. Ohio College Library Center.* The book includes a table (see table T-10, page 112) that depicts the seven-year financial history of OCLC. The analysis contains a detailed expense breakdown of the past five years and a general overview of the operating budgets. Total incomes and expenditures, including grant funding, are also broken down. All figures are approximate. The expense and budget items were extracted from OCLC reports.

The analysis by Inforonics and Butler Associates painted a background picture for the 1974-1975 budget. As was true with all facets of the OCLC operations, the budget was steadily expanding to meet the growing needs of the developing library network. The budget for the coming year totaled $2,218,000 (excluding grants to support research and development) and included fifteen new positions: development specialist, editor, secretary, bookkeeper, administrative systems analyst, (two) senior programmers, computer operator, package wrapper, library systems analyst, and (five) engineers. In addition, ten full-time and three part-time positions were to be transferred from the CLR grant funds to the regular income. The increase in personnel was due to a number of factors including the unexpected number of public libraries joining the system, the advent of the serials check-in module, the increased effort needed to maintain the Ohio terminals, and the expansion of services outside of the state.

The remarkable thing about the new budget was that despite the increase in the final budget figure over the previous year's, the Center achieved a lower first-time-use charge than it had anticipated.

In December 1972, CLR awarded OCLC a grant of $194,000 to develop the on-line union catalog and shared cataloging system and to activate the serials control system. By November 1973, the grant period was extended to March 31, 1974. Furthermore, a grant of up to $43,000, effective April 1, 1974, through June 30, 1974, was authorized by the Council. Yet another grant of $57,250 for a six-month period commencing on July 1, 1974, was approved in principle. This last grant would depend upon the Center's successful expenditure of previous funds and the capability of CLR to provide the funds.

The fast pace at which the Center was growing necessitated the need to plan for the future. Working with Haskins & Sells, Jack R. Vincent prepared a five-year projection of OCLC income and expenditures. It was an indispensable tool for formulating the Center's activities in the next five years.

TABLE T-10
Combined Income and Expenses, Operating and Grant[27]

CLASSIFICATION	1.	1967-8	1968-9	1969-70	1970-1	1971-2[b]	1972-3[a]	1973-4	TOTAL
GRANT INCOME									
U.S. Office of Educ.	1			90,000	60,000	125,000	194,000		275,000
Council Lib. Resources	2				14,000	75,000	200,000		283,000
State of Ohio	3					400,000			600,000
OPERATING INCOME									
Member Fees	4	67,100	64,500	81,100	86,400	234,200	420,000	604,500	1,558,600
Catalog Card Fees	5				30,700	84,600	145,000	271,600	531,900
Terminal Charges	6					28,300	69,000	227,400	324,700
Nonmember Fees	7						30,200	459,000	479,200
Miscellaneous	8				600	700	29,000	15,000	45,300
TOTAL INCOME	9	67,100	64,500	171,100	191,700	947,800	1,087,200	1,577,500	4,107,700
Salaries, Taxes									
Operations	10	30,000	46,500	88,400	70,700	117,600	131,600	380,600	1,308,300
Grants	11			68,200	50,300	94,800	151,700	72,900	
Computer Rental									
Operations	12		1,100	8,200	20,400	349,900	446,600	455,000	1,338,600
Grants	13			9,300	4,300	13,000	20,800	10,000	
Telephone, Network									
Operations	14					138,200	159,600	347,000	644,800
Grants	15								
EDP, Card Supplies									
Operations	16					40,800	68,000	164,000	282,500
Grants	17				9,700				
Administration									
Operations	18	3,900	8,400	8,500	19,600	14,500	15,000	244,000	376,900
Grants	19			10,600	2,800	14,700	23,500	11,300	
Travel, Consultants									
Operations	20	1,800	10,200	2,600	3,800	3,300	3,500	8,000	51,200
Grants	21			2,600	3,600	3,500	5,600	2,700	
TOTAL EXPENSES	22	35,600	66,500	198,400	190,200	790,300	1,025,900	1,695,600	4,002,300

a) 1972-73 income estimated from nine-month statement
b) 1972-73 and 1969-70 grant income distributed to expenses at 1971-72 reported allocations

Reprinted by permission of the author.

The economics of libraries was to be the main topic of discussion during a half-day workshop to be held during the next annual meeting in November 1974. It was to be open to all libraries. In May the Board of Trustees granted the executive director permission to proceed with the plans.

Organization

The expansionism that characterized the year also affected the organization of the Center. Aside from the anticipated changes in the composition of the Board and the new members, OCLC underwent an internal metamorphosis that would have an enduring affect on its operations. The changes included a new purpose clause coupled with a new set of objectives, the activation of the Peer Council, the rebirth of the ad hoc committee on extending direct borrowing privileges to graduate and undergraduate students, and organization of the Center into five divisions under the office of the executive director.

In November 1973 the new Board of Trustees members were elected.[28] The Board then elected the following officers: James V. Jones (Case Western Reserve University), chairman and president; H. Paul Schrank, Jr. (University of Akron), vice-chairman; Richard J. Owen (Heidelberg College), treasurer; and Thompson M. Little (Ohio University), secretary.

On May 21, 1974, the membership unanimously voted to replace OCLC's purpose clause in the Articles of Incorporation with a more general one reflecting the organization's growth and the possibility for future involvement in national and perhaps even international networking. The 1967 Articles of Incorporation, clause number three, reads:

THIRD. The purpose or purposes for which this corporation is formed are to establish, maintain and operate a computerized, regional library center to serve the academic libraries of Ohio (both state and private) and designed so as to become a part of any national electronic network for bibliographical communication; to develop, maintain and operate a shared cataloging program based upon a central computer store; to create, maintain and operate a computerized central catalog (inventory) of books and journals in the participating libraries; and to do such research and development related to the above as are necessary to accomplish and to extend the concept.[29]

The 1974 Articles of Incorporation, new purpose clause, states:

The purposes for which this corporation is formed are to establish, maintain and operate a computerized information processing and research center for development of programs, systems, and improved operational procedures in the field of library service and to gather, collect, maintain, index, and codify a central store of information, and furnish information from such central store, and provide services and products for the benefit of libraries and library users.

The term 'library' or 'libraries' shall mean those libraries and groups of libraries wherever the same may be situated, which shall be operated exclusively for educational and scientific purposes and which shall qualify as exempt organizations within the meaning of Section 501 (c) (3) of the Internal Revenue Code of the United States or other like legislation to which libraries outside the United States may be subject.[30]

This new statement of purpose represented a culmination of many months of deliberation dating to the fall of 1973. From October 1973 to January 1974, the Board of Trustees worked to create long-range plans for OCLC. As a result, a revised set of objectives was formulated, the list of total systems to be activated was enlarged, and plans were laid for fulfilling the objectives. The Board hoped to have a statement of goals on paper early in 1974.

The Board had asked Kilgour to delay final negotiations of any agreements with regional networks outside of Ohio until the Board had formulated definite goals for the expansion of OCLC. The executive director reported that interest in the Center had come from many directions. Representatives from Quebec Province, California, Indiana, Illinois, Kansas, Michigan, Oregon, South Dakota, Utah, and West Virginia had made inquiries.

Three documents, written by Kilgour, provided source material for discussions by the Board of Trustees in December and January: "Planning OCLC Goals for a National Information Network" (November 5, 1973), "Notes for Planning OCLC Goals" (December 15, 1973), and "Statement of Objectives, Projects and Plans for Attaining Objectives" (January 16, 1974).

On December 11, 1973, the Board of Trustees met and decided to hold a three-day conference to formulate new purposes, goals, and objectives of OCLC. The special conference took place on January 14-16, 1974. Besides the Board members, those present included the chancellor of the Ohio Board of Regents, a representative from the governor's office, Hugh C. Atkinson (The Ohio State University), Herbert F. Johnson (Oberlin College), L. Ronald Frommeyer (Wright State University), and representatives from the Council on Computerized Library Networks (CCLN).[31] Before the meeting, each member had received a copy of the "Statement of Purpose, Objectives, Systems, and Plans for Attaining Objectives."

For the purpose of conducting business, the Board of Trustees constituted itself as a committee of the whole. Testimonies were presented by a number of those present. The conference reached its acme with the creation and unanimous approval of the "Statement of Purpose, Objectives, Systems, and Plans for Attaining Objectives." These long-range plans became a beacon for the Center's future development.[32]

During fiscal year 1968-1969, the Board of Trustees had approved a similar statement entitled "Statement of Academic Objective, Economic Goal, and Missions to Achieve These Ends."[33] A comparison of the two statements leads one to conclude that OCLC in five years had become a much broader system that could envision its place in the world of libraries and computers.

At the same meeting, by another motion, the Board unanimously voted to discourage replication of the OCLC system. Over the recent months, the

Center had come to understand itself better. It saw itself as a centralized library system offering economic and technical advantages to its members. Only a year earlier, OCLC had offered its regional members a choice of either replicating or receiving OCLC services. Up to the time of the change, no consortium had opted for replication.

Another change in the OCLC organizational structure occurred late in 1973 when the report of the Committee on Implementation, "Ohio College Library Center: Implementation Committee Report," was approved by the membership. At the November 9, 1973 meeting of the membership, each recommendation was brought to the floor and voted upon separately. All nine recommendations and the Peer Council slate were approved.[34] The Peer Council was composed of representatives from the Ohio membership. One of its main duties was to enforce the input cataloging standards as stated in *Standards for Input Cataloging*. No doubt, the non-Ohio networks using OCLC would eventually have to address the same issue of standards.

During the year the reactivated ad hoc committee on extending direct borrowing privileges to graduate and undergraduate students of OCLC institutions held a number of meetings. The original committee was appointed by the Board of Trustees during 1971-1972. At the November 1972 meeting of the membership, the committee presented a proposal to include graduate and undergraduate students as borrowers. It passed, but not unanimously. In March 1973 a new committee was appointed. Chaired by Hugh C. Atkinson, it met with the twenty-two members who did not approve the original plan, which was to be reconsidered in light of objections. During 1972 the Committee heard concerns about overuse of collections in institutions located geographically close to each other, and occasional problems of retrieving lent items.

The final organizational change was the restructuring of OCLC in the spring of 1974 into five divisions under the executive director. The new structure, as depicted in chart C-1, page 116, was formulated in full awareness that it would change as the personality of the Center evolved. Comptroller Jack R. Vincent now also assumed the duties of chief of the Administrative Division; Larry L. Earn headed the Engineering Division; and Steve Beam was operations supervisor. Ann Ekstrom was in charge of the Library Systems Division, and James E. Rush was chief of the Research and Development Division.

CHART C-1
Restructuring of OCLC into Five Divisions under the Executive Director[35]

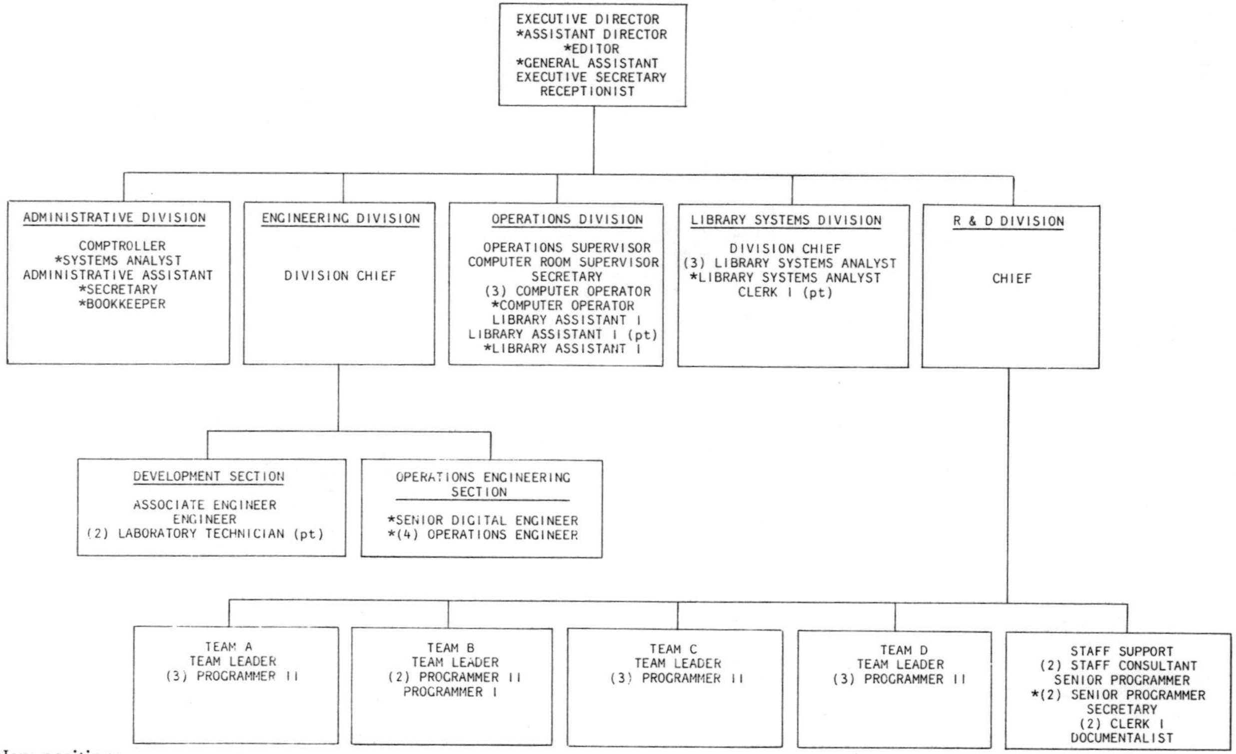

EXECUTIVE DIRECTOR
*ASSISTANT DIRECTOR
*EDITOR
*GENERAL ASSISTANT
EXECUTIVE SECRETARY
RECEPTIONIST

ADMINISTRATIVE DIVISION

COMPTROLLER
*SYSTEMS ANALYST
ADMINISTRATIVE ASSISTANT
*SECRETARY
*BOOKKEEPER

ENGINEERING DIVISION

DIVISION CHIEF

DEVELOPMENT SECTION

ASSOCIATE ENGINEER
ENGINEER
(2) LABORATORY TECHNICIAN (pt)

OPERATIONS ENGINEERING
SECTION

*SENIOR DIGITAL ENGINEER
*(4) OPERATIONS ENGINEER

OPERATIONS DIVISION

OPERATIONS SUPERVISOR
COMPUTER ROOM SUPERVISOR
SECRETARY
(3) COMPUTER OPERATOR
*COMPUTER OPERATOR
LIBRARY ASSISTANT I
LIBRARY ASSISTANT I (pt)
*LIBRARY ASSISTANT I

LIBRARY SYSTEMS DIVISION

DIVISION CHIEF
(3) LIBRARY SYSTEMS ANALYST
*LIBRARY SYSTEMS ANALYST
CLERK I (pt)

R & D DIVISION

CHIEF

TEAM A
TEAM LEADER
(3) PROGRAMMER II

TEAM B
TEAM LEADER
(2) PROGRAMMER II
PROGRAMMER I

TEAM C
TEAM LEADER
(3) PROGRAMMER II

TEAM D
TEAM LEADER
(3) PROGRAMMER II

STAFF SUPPORT
(2) STAFF CONSULTANT
SENIOR PROGRAMMER
*(2) SENIOR PROGRAMMER
SECRETARY
(2) CLERK I
DOCUMENTALIST

*New positions

ON-LINE SYSTEMS

By 1973-1974, the overall design of the on-line system included a total of six major systems: on-line union catalog and shared cataloging, serials control, interlibrary loan communications, technical processing (acquisitions), remote catalog access and circulation control, and bibliographic information retrieval (access by subject, title, author, or editor).

The advisory committees on the serials and technical processing systems met often throughout the year. Although the interlibrary loan system was planned for use after serials and technical processing systems were in operation, members were already beginning to take advantage of the holding symbols, which followed each catalog record in the data base, to facilitate interlibrary lending. This informal use of the system laid the foundations for the design and implementation of a fully on-line interlibrary loan communications web. Such a network would make the rapid sharing of library resources among the OCLC membership a part of a library's daily on-line routines.

The serials control system was to be fully operational in 1975. It included provisions for serials check-in, automatic claim, and binding control as well as for eventual evolution into an on-line union catalog of serials holdings. The OCLC Advisory Committee on Serials Control held a number of productive and well-attended meetings throughout the year. Work on the detailed design of the system continued, as did efforts to obtain suitable machine-readable files of serials cataloging records. The Ad Hoc Committee on Serials Data Bases was created to assist in the project.

The Advisory Committee on Serials Control together with sixty representatives present at a November 1973 meeting reviewed the specifications of the system and finalized the standards for input of serials data and terminal operation procedures for serials check-in. *The Recommended Standards for Input Cataloging for Serials* (revised draft, October 1973), comparable to the *Standards for Input Cataloging* (June 1972), was also accepted.

The Ad Hoc Committee on Serials Data Bases spent the fall of 1973 searching for serials data bases that would generate serials cataloging data for start-up of the serials system. The Committee examined MULS, based at the University of Minnesota, the Northwestern University Serials List, the Chemical Abstracts Service Source Index, the Serials Master File at the University of California, the Pittsburgh Regional Union List of Serials, (the Pittsburgh Regional Library Center's serials file), the LC Serials Data Base, and LC's MARC Serials Data Base. As a result, the Center began negotiations with the University of Minnesota and the Pittsburgh organization. LC's MARC Serials records were to be received regularly by the Center.

The groundwork for activation of the on-line serials system took more time than originally anticipated. In November 1973, the program to enable serials records to be fed into the system was in the final stage. The check-in module was nearing completion. A breakthrough was made in February 1974. Ohio University made history as the vanguard of the pilot project. On February 19, 1974, it began the on-line input of serial cataloging. Extension of the module to the membership at large was dependent upon two factors: its successful operation by Ohio University and the preparation of a draft manual for the inputting of the serials records. The draft, *Creation of Machine Readable Cataloging: Serials* (April 1974), was released two months later. On July 15, 1974, member libraries could start inputting serials records. Card production of serials cataloging was projected to begin in August.

At the June 1974 meeting of the Board, Kilgour reported that he had attended an Advisory Committee meeting for the CONSER project at the CLR headquarters in Washington, D.C. CONSER was a joint American-Canadian project to develop a machine-readable serials catalog that would house some three hundred thousand titles owned by American and Canadian libraries.[36] Kilgour foresaw further negotiations between OCLC and the Council.

The quest for mastery of the nation's serial resources began when LC launched its Serials Data Program in 1965. Several years later, the National Serials Data Program was established to create a machine-readable format for serials records. In 1969, the Association of Research Libraries (ARL) administered a two-year National Serials Pilot Project initially supported by LC, the National Agricultural Library, the Library of Medicine, and CLR. The first phase identified the data elements necessary for control of serials by machine-readable methods and created the MARC serials format, which later made possible the MARC Serials Distribution Service. The second phase of the project created a union list of serials for the three national libraries. In 1972, the project became the focus of a national center for the International Serials Data System (ISDS). The National Serials Pilot Project allocated International Standard Serial Numbers (ISSN) to each journal title. ISDS was only one part of a proposed United Nations Educational, Scientific, and Cultural Organization (UNESCO) system for the international exchange of scientific information. The project was delayed as a result, in part, of problems connected with establishing an acceptable title for each serial in the data system.

For library users, administrators, and those developing serials bases within the library community, serials had a sense of urgency. There was a pressing need for a national serials data file. The various interest groups had grown impatient with the slow pace of national developments, namely, the National Serials Data Program and the MARC Serials Distribution Service. The LC MARC serials format and the format used by the National Serials Data Program were incompatible. These differences would have to be reconciled before any progress could be made. At this time, CLR entered the scene.

The technical processing system was scheduled for implementation in the latter part of 1975. It would result in the computerization of most acquisitions and processing tasks. The data base would include information on materials ordered and on orders already in progress.

The Advisory Committee on Technical Processing met frequently during the year. In February 1974, *Recommended Workflow for Technical Processing and Cataloging through the OCLC System* (February 1974) was produced as a supplement to *The Technical Processing System—The Ohio College Library Center* (May 1972). The two opening paragraphs explain its purpose:

> To provide a guide for efficient use of the OCLC technical processing and shared cataloging systems, the Advisory Committee on Technical Processing has developed a workflow integrating the procedures for receiving new acquisitions and cataloging those

items for which catalog records already exist in the data base. By combining these activities, libraries will eliminate much duplicate searching of the data base and repeated handling of materials.

The Center is distributing this recommended workflow well in advance of implementing the technical processing system to allow administrators adequate time to consider the implications of TPS within their own libraries and to plan for reorganization and reassignment of staff responsibilities.[37]

Paralleling developments in Columbus was the on-line acquisitions activity at Stanford University known as Bibliographic Automation of Large Library Operations Using Time-Shared Systems (BALLOTS). It was the most intricate and sophisticated on-line technical processing system in operation on a daily basis anywhere. Unlike OCLC, it began as a technical processing system and evolved into a combined technical processing and cataloging system, with plans calling for inclusion of circulation control. Founded in 1967, the same year as OCLC, it began to operate its system in 1972, beginning with the first stage of the acquisitions system. By 1974, eleven terminals were used jointly by the acquisitions and cataloging departments. One of its strongest features was its searching capability, which was made possible by a powerful set of indices known as Stanford Public Information Retrieval System (SPIRES).

The capability to communicate interlibrary loan requests through the OCLC system remained an unfulfilled dream. During the year, activity related to interlibrary loan transactions was overshadowed by utilization of the system for pre-order verification and cataloging. However, two noteworthy trends were evident. First, smaller libraries received more interlibrary loan requests. Many came from large libraries that traditionally did not turn to a small library for this kind of assistance. Second, libraries increasingly tended to go to the closest owning library. The result of this trend was faster service for library users.

In fiscal year 1973-1974, Kent State University placed an OCLC terminal in its interlibrary loan office. Upon the receipt of a request, a staff member queried the terminal to determine which member library owned a copy. This initial step reduced the staff's searching time and increased the speed at which patrons received materials.

OUT-OF-STATE COOPERATIVE ACTIVITIES AND NETWORKING

In March 1973 the OCLC membership voted to extend services outside Ohio. Nearly a year later, the Center had agreements for on-line services with seven organizations—CCLC, FAUL, NELINET, PRLC, PALINET, IUC, and FLC. The newest agreements were those made with the last three. PALINET and FLC had formed relationships with OCLC during the previous year, although they were not listed as full participants until fiscal year 1973-1974. The only newcomer welcomed under the canopy of users was IUC. The remaining cooperatives agreed to full participation before 1973-1974. With the addition of the consortia, the Center's family of users totaled one hundred colleges and universities and nineteen public and special libraries. Only seven years earlier, OCLC had a family of only forty-nine-users.

During the interval from October to January, the Center's long-range plans were developed. On January 14, the decision was made to continue negotiations to extend services outside of the state.

In the spring of 1974, IUC announced its newly formed relationship with the Center. The three-year contract added to the system nearly twenty libraries in Texas and New Mexico.[38] The governance and operation of the network would emanate from the IUC Board of Directors and the regional Bibliographic Network Committee. The IUC Board represented presidents of member institutions; chief librarians constituted the membership of the Bibliographic Network Committee.

Preparations for the start of the Federal Libraries' Experiment in Cooperative Cataloging (FLECC) were completed during the year. On October 1, 1973, James P. Riley became the executive director of FLC. With Lillian Washington as the technical consultant, the project gained momentum. Hardware and software design work concentrated on the smooth interfacing of the OCLC system with the multitude of tasks that the project dictated. The contract signed between OCLC and Tymshare, Inc. gave users dial-up access to the data base. In addition, a direct leased line was established between Columbus and Washington, D.C. in January 1974 for greater flexibility in experimentation. By February, six federal libraries had terminals operating on the direct telephone line. Meanwhile, the Center continued to develop minicomputers to handle terminal communications and to interface with Tymnet, the Tymshare network. The linkage took place in July 1974.

Negotiations were in various stages with a number of other consortia. In the advanced or signing stage were negotiations with SUNY and SOLINET. At the September 18, 1973 meeting of the OCLC Board of Trustees, the agreement between SUNY and OCLC was presented for approval. The most significant outcome of the discussions was the adoption of a policy stating that there would be no differential charges for use of the central installation among the Ohio members and the regional members. An adjustment would become effective at the expiration of the present agreements. The intent of the policy was to keep the development of a national library network on a steady course. Moreover, it would protect the financial investment of the members in the research and development of the Center's programs. At the September meeting, Kilgour and the chairman of the Board were authorized to sign both the SUNY and IUC agreements. In October the agreement with SUNY was signed, although actual on-line participation did not commence until the next fiscal year. At the May Board meeting, the executive director was empowered to negotiate and to execute the final accords with SOLINET and the Illinois Research and Reference Center Libraries (IRRC).

Consortia and individual institutions continued to inquire about participation in OCLC at an unprecedented rate. The minutes of the April Board of Trustees meeting included a report by the executive director that served as testimony on that point. He related that agreements had been sent to the Wisconsin Board of Regents, the Michigan Library Consortium, the Illinois group, and the Higher Education Coordinating Council of Metropolitan St. Louis. Interest was also expressed by a group of libraries in St. Paul, as well as by the State Library of California and the University of California. The

Consortium of Universities in the District of Columbia was also interested. A library group from Quebec had also shown interest. Discussions with Quebec had to be deferred until the Articles of Incorporation were amended to allow participation of libraries beyond the geographic boundaries of the United States. A group of Scottish libraries also inquired. The high cost of tele-communications to Scotland and elsewhere on the globe created a temporary obstacle in the international growth of OCLC.

The early years of its development bore witness to the fact that evolution was integral to OCLC. The 1963 Parker report entitled *The Possibility of Extensive Academic Library Cooperation* planted the seeds that led to the birth of the Center in 1967, when its Articles of Incorporation were formulated. In 1963 OCLC was an idea. Four years later, in 1967, it became a reality. After that date the changes were rapid. From an off-line system it grew quickly into an on-line union catalog and shared cataloging system serving forty-nine academic libraries. During the next few years it expanded to over one hundred libraries of all types. From a shared cataloging system designed for academic libraries of Ohio it blossomed into a large-scale comprehensive on-line library system reaching beyond Ohio to encompass other consortia. This unprecedented growth turned out to be a trailblazing adventure in the development of our nation's on-line bibliographic networking.

NOTES

1. At the beginning of 1973-1974, the director was granted the title of executive director of OCLC.

2. Ohio College Library Center, *Annual Report 1973/1974* (Columbus: Ohio College Library Center, 1974), p. 2. The number in the first column of each row does not equal the sum of the second and third columns. The second column indicates the first time an existing record (one not input by the cataloging library) was used for catalog production.

3. Ibid., p. 3.

4. Ibid., p. 6.

5. Ibid., p. 5.

6. Ohio College Library Center, "Minutes of the Members Meeting" (Columbus: Ohio College Library Center, 9 November 1973), p. 7.

7. Op. cit., Ohio College Library Center, *Annual Report 1973/1974*, p. 7.

8. The members of the Patron Input Committee were: Herbert F. Johnson (Oberlin College); Hyman W. Kritzer (Kent State University); Patricia L. Lyons (Walsh College); Lewis C. Naylor (Toledo-Lucas County Public Library); Richard J. Owen (Heidelberg College); and Robert Walker (Oberlin College student). Executive Director Kilgour served as an ex-officio member.

9. The four steps of the on-line correction of input cataloging were: (1) Call up the catalog record on the CRT screen; (2) Check the cataloging source and the holdings display at the end of the record. The cataloging source must be the same as the library making the correction, and the holdings display must contain only the symbol of the cataloging source library; (3) Correct the record as one would edit an existing record for catalog production. Be sure to SEND each field altered; and (4) When all corrections

have been made, place the cursor at home position, type *rep*, then depress the UPDATE and SEND keys. The computer will respond with the message *Record replaced.* (Source: Ohio College Library Center, *Newsletter*, 28 February 1974, p. 3.)

10. Ibid.

11. Philip Schieber assumed the post on May 1, 1974.

12. Esther Greenberg (Case Western Reserve University) prepared the *Index.*

13. Op. cit., Ohio College Library Center, *Annual Report 1973/1974*, p. 6.

14. Frederick G. Kilgour, "Library Networks: What to Expect," in *Institutional Interface: Making the Right Connection* (Washington, D.C.: American Association for Higher Education, 1974), p. 25.

15. Ibid., pp. 25-26.

16. Frederick G. Kilgour, "Networks: Demonstrations of Operational Systems— The Ohio College Library Center," in *Networks and the University Library; Proceedings of an Institute* (Chicago: Association of College and Research Libraries, American Library Association, 1974), pp. 16-17.

17. Effective July 1, 1973, Philip L. Long became associate director of OCLC. As an electrical engineer he joined OCLC in its early days and soon became the prime systems designer. His responsibilities included the development, installation, and operation of the OCLC network. On January 1, 1974, his association with OCLC ended when he accepted the position of associate for Library Systems Development at the State University of New York. Although Long's direct involvement in OCLC activities had come to a halt, his contributions were lasting. In 1982, he received the ALA Library and Information Technology Association's (LITA) award for his "Achievement in Library and Information Technology."

18. William J. Baumol and Matityahu Marcus, *Economics of Academic Libraries* (Washington, D.C.: American Council on Education, 1973), p. 45.

19. Ibid., p. 46.

20. Ibid., p. 48.

21. Ibid., p. 56.

22. Ibid., p. 55.

23. Ibid., p. 60.

24. A new position of comptroller was created in January 1974 and assumed by Vincent. His responsibilities included accounting, budgeting, financing, personnel, and space allocation.

25. Ohio College Library Center, *Newsletter*, 7 June 1974, p. 2.

26. Ibid.

27. Inforonics, Inc. and Butler Associates, *Survey of Library Automation Systems. Phase II. Final Report: Volume 5. Ohio College Library Center* (Maynard, Mass.: Inforonics, Inc., 1974), p. 86.

28. See appendix 1, Exhibit D, for a complete list of the Board of Trustees members.

29. Ohio College Library Center, "Articles of Incorporation of The Ohio College Library Center" (Columbus: Ohio College Library Center, 1967), p. [1].

30. Op. cit., Ohio College Library Center, *Annual Report 1973/1974*, pp. 11-12.

31. See chapter 10 for background information on CCLN.

32. See appendix 1, Exhibit P, for the entire document.

33. See appendix 1, Exhibit F, for the entire document.

34. Richard J. Owen (Heidelberg College) and William Chait (Dayton and Montgomery County Public Library) would serve for one year (1973 to 1974). Two-year terms (1973-1974 and 1974-1975) were to be served by Melville Spence (Bowling Green State University) and Joseph M. Denham (Hiram College). Patricia L. Lyons (Walsh College) and Harold Schell (University of Cincinnati) were elected to serve from 1973 through 1976.

35. Ohio College Library Center, "Budget Request 1974/75" (Columbus: Ohio College Library Center, 1974). See also appendix 1, Exhibit B.

36. See chapter 2 for further information.

37. Ohio College Library Center, *Recommended Workflow for Technical Processing and Cataloging through the OCLC System* (Columbus: Ohio College Library Center, 1974), p. 1.

38. See appendix 1, Exhibit J, for a list of the IUC membership.

8

THE FUTURE
THROUGH
COORDINATED GROWTH
1974-1975

OCLC grew at an unprecedented pace during 1974-1975. By the close of the year the system was producing more than a million catalog cards per month and providing services to 577 institutions in 35 states and the District of Columbia.[1] Northeastern University in Boston became the first institution to input a millionth record into the data base when, on September 6, 1974, it input a 1960 edition of *Collier's World Atlas and Book of Facts*. The membership was bolstered when four out-of-state consortia and seven independent institutions joined along with 14 Ohio institutions. The expansion in geographic coverage and number of libraries served prompted the Center to reorganize its internal structure into five new divisions. Reflecting the growth, an unprecedented budget figure of $10,456,000 was approved together with an increase in rates. A new phase of computational power began with the arrival of the Sigma 901 and 902 computers. To accommodate the Center's growth, a project to relocate its facilities was spearheaded.

Efforts were made to improve accessibility to the data base, including the addition of new search key structures and index files. Steps toward in-depth subject searching began with imbedding of Battelle Memorial Institute's BASIS 70 indexing system in the OCLC system. The Peer Council and OCLC staff successfully upgraded the quality of the data base. Thanks to a grant from the State Library of Ohio, plans were laid to test terminals in a public service setting.

With OCLC as a participant, LC's COMARC project commenced. Participation in the CONSER project, sponsored by CLR, served the Center well in its efforts to implement the serials system. The Center exhibited at a large number of gatherings and received many visitors, including an entourage of international guests representing ten countries. Kilgour traveled to places as distant as Australia to demonstrate OCLC operations.

That OCLC grew rapidly was, no doubt, important. However, more significant than the rate was that it expanded in a logical, planned fashion.

THE ON-LINE UNION CATALOG
AND SHARED CATALOGING SYSTEM

Data Base

The information-rich OCLC data base continued to reach new levels of bibliographic sophistication. Accessibility to its contents was a top priority on the OCLC agenda for 1974-1975. Steps were taken to bring its information closer to those who needed it.

Response time was critical to the effective use of the system. Accessibility to the data base and user productivity were enhanced by rapid response time at the terminals; thus, they were deterred by slow response time. The goal of the OCLC staff was to increase accessibility by reducing response time. By February 1975, it exceeded twenty seconds on the average, whereas eight seconds was considered an acceptable time.

The root of the problem lay in a number of activities that were occurring simultaneously. The Center had introduced major hardware modifications. In July 1974, approximately $350,000 worth of new equipment was installed including a line printer, three 16-K banks of additional core memory, a disk controller, four new disk drives, and a multiplex input-output processor. To accommodate these additions the computer room had to be rearranged. The Sigma 5 had to be moved to make room for the Sigma 9, which arrived in February 1975. The computer's intricate and delicate circuitry was upset in the shift. To complicate matters, the Center lacked sufficient engineering personnel.

By February 1975, 475 institutions were participating members or had signed accords to do so in the future. At the close of the year, over 700 terminals were on-line. The growth of catalog card production from July 1974 to April 1975 was rapid. Over 10,000 books a day were cataloged on the system by June; more than 70,000 catalog cards were printed daily.

TABLE T-11
Monthly Catalog Card Production (July 1974-April 1975)[2]

Month	Total Cards Produced
July 1974	975,423
August.	881,696
September	1,018,656
October	1,285,767
November.	1,112,061
December.	1,097,879
January 1975.	1,426,039
February.	1,449,383
March	1,949,561
April	2,123,683

On-line searches of the data base totaled nearly 50,000 a day. The Sigma 5 was processing up to 100,000 requests within a six-hour period, which equaled 4.63 requests per second. The type of requests also affected the system. Data base searching, which required a great deal of computer time, degraded response time far more than the cataloging of materials on the terminals.

The number of terminals on each telephone line also affected response time. The permissible number of terminals per line was thirty, assuming that each terminal was used not more than 70 percent and no less than 50 percent of the time. Response time varied from line to line, especially when lines extended across time zones.

Terminal service, although not affecting response time, was another concern of users. There was also a lack of spare parts, which was partially solved when the Center extensively analyzed terminal failures and ordered large quantities of those parts that the analysis predicted would be most likely to fail. A new service agreement was drawn up with Syntonic Technology, Inc. that included a contract for three thousand service calls.

The Center continued to attack the response time problem. On February 18, 1975, Kilgour submitted a report to the Board of Trustees outlining the course of action.

Up until the day before the meeting, the minicomputers were handling seven lines, and they were adding about 600 milliseconds of latency to the polling time that considerably degraded response time. During the previous evening, programming had been completed that would lower the latency to about 350 milliseconds. Later in the week, the staff will transfer four of the six lines on the Sigma 5 to the minis; two lines overburdened with terminals will remain on the Sigma 5 until the end of the week when they will be transferred to the Sigma 9 over the weekend. The engineering staff will reconfigure the computer hardware over the weekend so that the Sigma 9 will be operating on-line as of Monday, February 24th. Since the Sigma 9 is about 60 percent faster than the Sigma 5 and since the Sigma 5 processing unit is nearly saturated, it is expected that the operation of the Sigma 9 will considerably lower response time.

The next steps will require three to four weeks and will consist of transferring all of the polling activity from the Sigma 9 to the minis and reconfiguring the overburdened telephone lines so that they can go onto the minis. With all polling on the minis and the Sigma 9 operating on-line, response time should return to an acceptable level.

Next in the schedule will be the linking of the Sigma 9 with the Sigma 5 so that both will work on-line. It is intended that staff will accomplish this linkage by June. Once the linkage has been accomplished, the on-line system will have at least another 60 percent increase in power.[3]

Several months later, the Board recorded further action recommended by Kilgour:

> Mr. Kilgour stated that there appears to be an inverted rela-tionship between system use and response time. OCLC's Computer Facilities Division is studying this phenomenon in which response time degrades during low system utilization and quickens when message traffic increases. Mr. Kilgour described the measures the Center is undertaking to alleviate high response time: 1) on the weekend of June 12 the Center increased the number of CATologing programs from 12 to 17, resulting in a drop in average response time from 14.8 seconds to 11.8 seconds; 2) the Center intends to utilize a fourth controller during the week of June 16; and 3) the Center will analyze the effect of additional CATologing programs and 4 controllers as well as distribution of lines over the mini-computer.[4]

By June 1975, response time was eventually reduced to less than seven seconds. Work on further resolution of the problem would continue in the year ahead.

The Center also improved access to the system by increasing the number of hours it was available to patrons, thus encouraging libraries to avoid using the system during peak periods. Beginning March 3, 1975, the on-line hours were extended into the evening. The system was available from 7:00 A.M. to 10:00 P.M., Eastern Standard Time, Monday through Friday. Although use of evening hours at first proved to be less than anticipated, it still justified the need for the longer hours.

The reorganization and expansion of the data base was perhaps the most important improvement made during 1975 to increase access to it. The name-title and title entries index files were expanded from 1.25 million to 2.5 million entries. The doubling of the index file spaces improved searching and access speed to the files and, consequently, also reduced response time. The reorgani-zation continued from February to the end of March. Every single record in the file was re-indexed and assigned a file space.

On February 10, 1975, the on-line personal author index file was installed in the data base. Ohio University, in its traditionally pioneering spirit, was the first institution to test it. Its installation made it possible for users to retrieve works in the data base by a given author. Any one of six search key structures could be used: 4,3,1; 4,2,1; 4,1,1; 4,3, (blank); 4,2, (blank); and finally 4,1, (blank). To use the 4,3,1 search key, an operator keyed in the first four letters of the author's surname, a comma, the first three letters of the forename (if known), a comma, and the middle initial (if known). The other search keys were used in a similar manner. By February 18 the new index was operational. In the ensuing months, it was expanded to include both corporate and added entries.

Three more index files were added to the data base in the spring of 1975. The ability to obtain information from the file by the International Standard Book Number (ISBN), the International Standard Serial Number (ISSN), and the CODEN identifier improved the usefulness of the data base and lessened search time by making it easier for a user to retrieve a specific record. The ISBN is a unique nine- or ten-digit number; the ISSN uses eight digits; the CODEN employs five or six letters.[5] The three new search structures brought the total number of search strategies to eight: LC card number, author-title, author, title, OCLC control number, ISBN, ISSN, and CODEN.

Two of the eight search keys were expanded on February 1 and 2, 1975, Developed by the Center's Research and Development Division, the new structures for the name-title and title indices provided more flexibility in searching and expedited the process. Four new search key structures were created for both files. The name-title index was accessible through the following key structures: 4,4; 4,3; 3,4; 3,3. The search key structures created for the title searches were: 3,2,2,1; 3,2,1,1; 3,1,2,1; and 3,1,1,1.

The capability to execute a subject search of the OCLC bibliographic file was a dream shared by librarians, library users, and OCLC. By October 1974 the Center had located three possible subject search systems: Lockheed's DIALOG, System Development Corporation's ORBIT, and the Battelle Memorial Institute's BASIS 70. Factors such as operational costs, availability of the system, and the schedule for updating new records were all considered.

In December, Kilgour brought before the Board of Trustees the Battelle Memorial Institute's BASIS 70 proposal for inverted indices of the data base. (By this time, the two other firms' proposals had already been presented to the Board.) BASIS 70 was selected as the most useful because of its powerful indexing capabilities and its ability to interweave gracefully with the Center's Xerox equipment. It carried strong recommendations from OCLC management. It permitted the free-text searching of words in the data base using a variety of combinations of search terms. It was planned to increase the value of a continuously expanding treasure of bibliographic information. The Board of Trustees authorized Kilgour to formulate and sign an agreement with Battelle Memorial Institute. At the same meeting Kilgour suggested and received approval to form the Users Advisory Group to decide what data on the records should be indexed. Such a committee would include students plus reference and public service librarians.

In January, Kilgour reported to the Board of Trustees that a project contract was ready for signing. He also disclosed that the National Center for Educational Media and Materials for the Handicapped (NCEMMH) at The Ohio State University, had obtained funding from OE for a project with OCLC. The Center was the headquarters for the first national clearinghouse for special education information known as the National Instructional Materials Information System (NIMIS). NIMIS was an on-line information retrieval system available to teachers and schools for locating data on instructional materials in special education. NCEMMH was interested in having the NIMIS network accessible through the BASIS data base. OE was to furnish OCLC with forty-eight thousand dollars the first year and twenty thousand dollars the second. Of the forty-eight thousand dollars, twenty-eight thousand dollars was earmarked for BASIS 70 indexing of the data base.[6] The remaining twenty thousand dollars was to be used for services to NCEMMH including inputting of records, searching of the data file, furnishing the organization with magnetic tapes containing input records that would be transplanted into The Ohio State University Libraries' circulation system, and furnishing NCEMMH with up to two terminals.

By March, the contract with Battelle Memorial Institute was signed, and NCEMMH had received the funds it requested to support the project. A month later, staff from OCLC and Battelle's Columbus Laboratories began to work on the initial stages of installing the BASIS 70 program. Implementation of BASIS 70 was estimated to last nine months, and on-line testing of subject searches was predicted for the first part of 1976. Also in April, the Advisory Group met with the OCLC staff and personnel from the Battelle Memorial Institute. In the spring, Kilgour submitted a grant proposal to CLR for $24,000 to support the remainder of the project. Kilgour said, "This development of OCLC is by far the most exciting for me, for it will be the first application of major benefit to library users toward which I have been working for eight years."[7] At the May 20 Board of Trustees meeting Kilgour announced that OCLC had received the CLR grant. In addition to the $24,000 requested for the subject indexing project, the Center received an additional $100,250 to be used to design the on-line authority files and to develop the acquisitions system. This grant, totaling $124,250, was the fourth one provided by CLR.

An authority file was designed to record the authoritative form of names and to provide cross-references to other versions of names as found in bibliographic records of the file. The Council funds enabled the Center to make cost studies of various designs of the authority files as well as to conduct studies on the value of authority files in on-line systems to library patrons.

Two more tasks were completed that also led to the improvement of the data base. The Research and Development Division worked on the modularization of the system operation. The programs used to operate the system were redesigned into modules. The technique obviated modifying huge programs later. The division also redesigned the SAVE file function. The change enabled a member library to store up to one hundred records, a vast improvement over the previous thirty to forty.

Moreover, in October 1974 OCLC implemented a new screen message to be displayed when the system was down. By depressing the SEND key, users received instantaneous information on the status of the system without having to call the Center.

Relative to the subject of accessibility was the problem of duplication of records in the data base. Beginning in 1972, libraries found in increasing numbers exact or nearly exact duplicate bibliographic records in the data base. Steps were taken to correct the situation. The most recent was the establishment of the deferred record file by OCLC in 1972, which served as a temporary refuge for possible duplicates. In December 1974 the deferred record file stored 90,800 records.

Despite all efforts, the problem reached the breaking point in 1974-1975. Due to an error in computer logic, records that should not have been deferred were deferred. In reality, 52,300 records had become bogus deferrals. The remaining ones were legitimate duplicates. The deferred record technique was ineffective for many reasons apart from the fact that it was time-consuming. Time would vary depending on the number of records to be reviewed and the number of holding symbols attached to them. On the average, twenty to twenty-five minutes were required per duplicate record.

In December 1974, the divisional directors approved a proposal for a new on-line SAVE file into which the deferred records would be written from the magnetic tapes. The OCLC staff would then use two terminals to compare records and reach final decisions. One terminal displayed the deferred record, and another the record in the on-line data base that corresponded to it. This dual terminal technique was a success.

To further reduce the chances of libraries generating duplicate records in the file the Center devised the NEW command function. The Library Systems Division sent all members a memorandum dated May 21, 1975, entitled "Technique for Generating a New Data Base Record from an Existing Record." Whenever an existing record closely matched an item being cataloged, the terminal operator used the NEW command to display a work form containing a large portion of the data from the existing record. The new information was then input on the work form and the cards ordered from it. The NEW command function was installed on June 3, 1975.

A streamlined method of reporting duplicate records was created soon after the start of the NEW command. Libraries were instructed to report duplicates only when at least one record had an OCLC control number exceeding 1368739. Each record input by a member was automatically assigned an OCLC control number, and as of June 2, 1975, the highest number was 1368739.

During the year, the Center also explored a number of approaches to enlarge the on-line file. In the spring, it submitted a proposal to the Ohio Board of Regents for retrospective conversion of holdings of selected Ohio academic libraries at a cost of nine hundred thousand dollars; the project was not funded.

The Center also held preliminary discussions with The Ohio State University Libraries to use its machine-readable data base. In addition, the idea of subject concentrations was examined by the Board of Trustees. Portions of the shelf lists from institutions with strong subject emphases were to be fed into the OCLC data base. OCLC also began preliminary discussions with the State Library to convert heavily used nonfiction titles in many Ohio public libraries. A proposal to this effect was prepared and submitted to the State Library. In December, Kilgour reported to the Board of Trustees that the Florida Computer Output Microform Union Catalog (COMCAT) project would soon be underway. It was a large-scale cooperative effort by fifteen Florida libraries, all members of the Southeastern Library Network (SOLINET),[8] to use the contents of the OCLC data base for converting local holdings to machine-readable format. From the viewpoint of OCLC the project assured a growing data base. For the Florida participants it created a machine-readable union catalog that would facilitate cooperative resource sharing in the state. Funded by a grant from the State Library of Florida Library Services and Construction Act, the project ran one year, terminating in December 1975.

Any discussion of improvements made in the quality of records in the data base should include the OCLC Peer Council. The Council set out to reduce the number of error reports, duplicate records, and LC updates (the upgrading of records to the cataloging standards of LC when LC cataloging was available). In December, the Council reported it was receiving some one thousand error reports each quarter. The overall error rate for the first nine months of 1974 was 1.85 percent, based on number of errors reported and number of records input for the period. The OCLC Library Systems Division corrected between ten and twenty records per week. Besides dealing with the errors, the Division had to handle the duplicate record reports. The LC updates created even more work for the Division. With good response time on the terminal, ten updates per hour were possible.

The first document written by the Council was "Requirements for Improvement of Quality Control" (November 7, 1974). To assist libraries in reducing the number of duplicate records in the data base the Council in "Requirements" recommended three basic principles for all libraries to follow. First, they should do a thorough search of the data base. Second, if a record was put in SAVE, it should be re-searched before cards are produced to guarantee that another library had not input an identical or nearly identical record. Third, they should use caution when editing an existing record to avoid creating a new one. A strong statement on the matter was issued by the Council: "No matter what the reason, altruistic or self-serving, the continuing creation of duplicates may necessitate the levying of a fine on those institutions responsible for their creation."[9] With regard to the LC updates, libraries were told that "if standards for input cataloging are observed by all institutions, the arrearages in the LC updates can be eliminated as the quantity being reported should be drastically reduced."[10]

"Requirements" also included the Council's method for reducing the error rate in the data base.

> Beginning in 1975 the Peer Council will send a quarterly report to the librarian of each Ohio institution and each non-network affiliate outside of Ohio, stating the system error rate and the institution's error rate. Those over the allowable rate (double the system-wide error rate) will be expected to take steps to reduce the number of errors being made in input records. A member of the Peer Council will contact any institution over the allowable rate for two successive quarters to discuss the problem. If an institution exceeds the rate for three successive quarters, the Peer Council representatives will arrange to visit the library to help the library staff work out more satisfactory procedures. Network peer groups should serve the same function for their affiliates.[11]

Its closing paragraph summarized the attitude of the Council:

> It is of prime importance that the quality of the data base be improved as soon as possible. However, improving the quality of

the records now in the data base will be a useless exercise unless participating institutions cooperate in improving the quality of records currently being added to the base. OCLC's reputation, and therefore the reputation of all networks and all participating institutions, is at stake. It is essential that all participants contribute to the maintenance of the good reputation of OCLC.[12]

The Peer Council and the Library Systems Division, headed by Ann Ekstrom, worked hand in hand. Nearly one-half of the Division's time was devoted to maintaining the quality standards as prescribed by the Council. It was the main link between the Center and the member institutions. In addition to handling all of the errors, duplicate record, and LC update reports, it was responsible for demonstrating the operations of OCLC to visitors, training personnel in the new member libraries, creating the documentation for the users, and accepting special assignments, including visits to libraries to resolve problems.

The discussion thus far has centered on the accessibility of the information in the OCLC data base to librarians. Although librarians were the first to use OCLC, the system was clearly being developed as a means to increase the availability of resources to library users. The data base was extended directly to users with a $18,867 grant from the State Library of Ohio (under the Library Services and Construction Act, Title III) to test the terminals in a public service environment. The main question to be answered was: would terminals in such areas be helpful to those who use the library resources?

The OCLC staff developed a special computer program to monitor the activity on the terminals. Questionnaires were also sent from OCLC to each institution to be placed beside the terminals. The State Library of Ohio, two public libraries (Dayton and Montgomery County Public Library and Toledo-Lucas County Public Library), and four academic libraries (Case Western Reserve University, Oberlin College, The Ohio State University, and Ohio University) participated in the test. Each of the seven libraries received one nonediting terminal for locating information about books. At the end of the project the terminals became the property of the libraries, which then had to assume the use and communications costs.

Library users formulated their own search strategies based on a set of operating instructions posted near the terminals. Availability of the terminals depended on the operation hours of each library. The data collection process began in February 1975, a month late. Because the enhanced searching capabilities were available only after January, the delay turned out to be beneficial. Originally, the project was to terminate at the end of the fiscal year (June 30, 1975). As a result of the delay, the project was extended three months into the next fiscal year.

Before library users could conduct experimentally their own searches on the terminals, another facet of OCLC's efforts to increase the accessibility of library materials began in 1968 with reciprocal borrowing among the member libraries. Although originally limited to faculty members at academic institutions, it was a laudable first attempt to expedite the union of users and information. In 1972 borrowing privileges were extended to graduate and undergraduate students. Since the privileges were not supported by all OCLC member libraries, an ad hoc committee on extending direct borrowing privileges to graduate and undergraduate students was appointed. At the November 8, 1974 meeting of the membership, the "Report of the Ohio College Library Center: Committee on Direct Borrowing" (June 1974) was approved as presented by Hugh C. Atkinson, chairman of the Committee on Extended Borrowing.

The report suggested that all members participate in a two-year experimental direct borrowing program, i.e., borrowing by students of OCLC institutions from other OCLC institutions according to the rules and regulations of the home library. At the end of the two-year period, it was anticipated that Kilgour would present a proposal to the Ohio Board of Regents to fund a statewide direct borrowing system. Statistics would reveal the cost per circulation and total number of loans transacted. Most importantly, the results of the two-year experiment would be useful in preparing the proposal to the Board of Regents for funding the next phase of the project. The two-year period would also allow libraries to decide whether they wished to continue the program.

The project had five basic tenets:

1) ... that each member of OCLC be assessed 10¢ per student (based on fall enrollment) and that such assessment be collected by OCLC and held for the remainder of the year,

2) that all OCLC institutions provide the ability for direct borrowing by students from other OCLC members,

3) that each institution keep track of the number of circulations to nonhome students in total,

4) that losses of material not recoverable by ordinary means be reimbursed from the assessment, and

5) that at the end of the year the committee will request that direct borrowing statistics be sent to it. The pool formed from the 10¢ assessment plus whatever interest might have been generated, less cost of lost material, will be divided among the institutions on the following basis:

> The total number of nonhome circulations will serve as a base. The pool will be divided according to the percentage of the total nonhome circulations lent by each institution.[13]

OCLC users kept themselves informed through a number of channels. The annual meeting of the membership, held on November 8, 1974, was prefaced by a seminar entitled "The Economics of Libraries." Conducted by Richard Tybout, Professor of Economics at The Ohio State University, it was based on *Economics of Academic Libraries*. A one-day workshop on resource sharing was hosted by SUNY in Albany, New York, on May 15, 1975. In the spring, the *Index to OCLC Newsletter* was updated to include the issues of the *Newsletter* (s) 1-80. The technical manual for the OCLC Model 100 Display terminals was also published in the spring.

During the year the directors from each of the divisions at OCLC held weekly in-house meetings. Their minutes became a part of the Center's archives. Due to a previous decision, the minutes of the meetings of the Board of Trustees, the agendas for the Board meetings, and other documents were sent to the regional directors. In March, the divisional directors also agreed to send their minutes to the regional directors.

Knowledge of OCLC and what it had accomplished was disseminated through several media. As in years past, OCLC exhibited at ALA's annual meeting. In July 1974, thirty-six hundred librarians visited the OCLC booth in New York City. Funds for the rental of the booth were paid for by Beehive Medical Electronics, Inc. The Xerox Corporation covered the cost of the telecommunications between Columbus and the booth in New York. During the year, OCLC exhibited at meetings in Wisconsin, Michigan, Utah, Texas, Washington, D.C., and California. The Special Libraries Association, the Medical Library Association, the American Society of Information Science, the California Library Association, and the Southwestern Library Association were organizations at whose annual meetings the Center exhibited. A high point of these exhibits was the one held from November 18 through November 20, 1974, at the International Federation of Library Associations (IFLA) Conference in Washington, D.C. Several days before the conference forty-nine delegates from ten foreign countries visited the Center. The stop was a part of the IFLA preconference tour of Columbus. Academic, public, school, state, and municipal libraries were represented by visitors from Australia, Austria, Belgium, Canada, Czechoslovakia, France, the Federal Republic of Germany, Malaysia, the Netherlands, and Spain.

Kilgour in 1974-1975 visited Australia, Yugoslavia, and Austria. In Sydney, Australia, on August 20, 1974, the on-line system was demonstrated at the Library Automation Systems Information Exchange Conference (LASIE).

> The communication between the Australian CRT and OCLC's computer in Columbus traveled a somewhat circuitous route of 15,000 miles via submarine cables and microwave transmissions. Conference participants stayed up late in Sydney to view the demonstration. While the demonstration ran from 9 a.m. to 12 p.m. EST, the time in Sydney was 11 p.m. to 2 a.m. Although the communications route went almost half-way around the world, response time was comparable to that achieved by libraries in the United States.[14]

In the latter part of March 1975, Kilgour traveled to Yugoslavia as a UNESCO consultant to advise the country on library networks. The following month he participated in a seminar on computerized libraries in Vienna, Austria, where the on-line union catalog and shared cataloging system was once again demonstrated.

Videotape and television also communicated information about OCLC. Through the courtesy of Kent State University, a series of videotapes about the Center were produced. During National Library Week, OCLC received its first television news coverage when it was featured in a local newscast on April 11, 1975.

Only some areas of the Center's rapid growth were visible. System improvements, new and upgraded equipment, and organization modifications were less obvious changes. One reason for the unforeseeable rapid growth was that most of the new members were affiliated with consortia. In 1974-1975, 14 Ohio institutions joined.[15] These added to the previous 64 Ohio members brought the total to 78. Four new regional groups and 7 independent institutions not associated with a regional center also began to participate. The total number of participants by the close of the year was 577 institutions in over thirty states, in contrast to 49 Ohio institutions that began the on-line operations in 1971.

Another avenue for participation opened in the course of the year. A library school could become an educational affiliate of OCLC. Some library schools of member institutions employed terminals for instruction. Two schools expressed interest in obtaining their own terminals. Kilgour proposed a policy to handle a terminal used solely for instructional use. The Board adopted the policy that library schools be permitted to use OCLC terminals for instructional purposes with the proviso that they reimburse OCLC for terminals and communication costs. The Drexel University Graduate School of Library Science in Philadelphia was the first library school to become an educational affiliate of OCLC.

In June 1975 the Board of Trustees approved service to for-profit organizations at a higher rate than to not-for-profit institutions. The rate was set at 20 percent higher for all services, products, materials, and equipment. The regions that belonged to OCLC were free to do business as they saw fit, but the network representatives were urged to consult legal counsel before they began to offer such services. It was important that this type of service would remain a low percentage of the total OCLC services; in Ohio it was less than 2 percent.

In January 1975, the Board of Trustees approved a proposal presented by Kilgour to provide terminals to not-for-profit library bibliographic journals published by national library associations. *Booklist* and *Choice*, both published by ALA, expressed interest. According to the terms of the agreement, a terminal was provided at cost, and there was a three hundred dollar per year charge for overhead. If cards were requested, the current rate per catalog card applied.

LC and OCLC were involved in an experiment that called for the Center to supply LC with copies of input cataloging by its members that transcribed the LC cataloging from 1956 to date. Its purpose was to test the mechanical updating of the *National Union Catalog: Register of Additional Locations*. The *Register*, a supplement to the *National Union Catalog* (NUC), records additional locations for library materials listed in the NUC. NUC contains bibliographic data for works cataloged by LC and by libraries contributing to its cooperative cataloging program. LC hoped to expand the update procedure to include non-LC cataloging input by OCLC members. The name of the institution responsible for the cataloging was included in the *Register*.

In the course of the last half of 1974, LC began the pilot project called COMARC (CO-operative MAchine-Readable Cataloging Project).[16] When COMARC began, many OCLC member institutions were involved in local conversion activities; the Center had been unable to sponsor its own concerted conversion effort. However, it later became a significant participant in the LC project.

Equipment

The terminals located in the member libraries and the computers at OCLC shared the spotlight in the Center's activities. The surge in the size of the membership, in particular the addition of four new consortia, influenced the decision to order a large number of terminals. SOLINET alone had requested 156 for the coming year. On September 12, 1974, OCLC and Beehive signed a final agreement. Beehive would furnish OCLC with 1,125 OCLC Model 100 Display terminals over a two-year period. The fixed price for the terminals was $2,916 each. The total cost to OCLC ran over three million dollars. From December 1974 to April 1975, OCLC installed 8.3 terminals per week. In May, the rate jumped to 13 a week.

OCLC developed a two-point policy statement for the purchase of the terminals that was designed to improve the ordering process as well as to offer incentives to libraries to make advance payments.

(1) All orders for terminals must be firm, not less than 120 days prior to desired delivery date. This time period is compatible with the Beehive ninety-day release policies. Exemptions for shorter delivery periods will be dictated by the volume of terminals and inventory which will be maintained at lowest possible level consistent with the required Beehive production releases.

(2) To provide some cost savings for OCLC system users and improve OCLC's cash flow position, an incentive in the form of discounts for advance payments accompanying terminal purchase orders as follows: 4 percent discounts for delivery 120 days after date of order; 5 percent discount for delivery 150 days after date of order, and a 6 percent discount for delivery 180 days after date of order. Those discounts are based on an annualized percentage of 12 percent.[17]

During the previous fiscal year, the Board of Trustees approved a new formula for the allocation of terminals. In 1974-1975, it was further refined. A separate allocation system for distributing terminals to the public library sector was devised. Up to this time the number of terminals a library could receive was based on the formula of one for every eleven thousand first-time uses. Under the terms of the new formula, allocations to public libraries would amount to one terminal for each fifteen thousand "produces," i.e., the number of times a record was used to produce catalog cards. The allocations to academic libraries would remain the same. This more equitable distribution was based on the fact that public libraries made greater use of the produce function than academic libraries, cataloging from two-and-one half to five times as many added copies as did academic libraries.

Terminal maintenance and repair always presented problems. The quality of the OCLC Model 100 Display terminal was less than satisfactory: failure rate for new terminals during their first two weeks of use was 50 percent. Originally the Computer Operations Division was responsible for their upkeep. In November, when the Computer Facilities Division was created, the responsibility was transferred to its Engineering Department.

The Center had contracted with Syntonics Technology, Inc. to service the terminals. From July 1974 through June 1975 the Center reduced the number of on-site service calls, thereby realizing a monetary savings while improving service to the users. OCLC experienced a reduction of over 20 percent on service calls over the year, although the number of terminals added to the network was augmented by 22 percent.

Members could purchase either the terminals made by Spiras Systems, Inc. or those manufactured by Beehive Medical Electronics, Inc. In the fall, Spiras Systems notified OCLC that beginning January 31, 1975, it would cease operations. A meeting was held before the January deadline with Spiras Systems, USM Credit Corporation (OCLC had a contract with USM for the terminals), NELINET, and OCLC representatives to settle the terminal lease-with-option-to-purchase contract. The final accord stated that OCLC would pay the company eighty thousand dollars. Sixty-five thousand dollars was for the terminals, ten thousand dollars covered the OCLC spare parts, and another five thousand dollars would provide spare parts for NELINET. NELINET, which would reimburse OCLC for the spare parts, had purchased a large number of terminals and needed the extra parts to maintain and repair them. In return for the sum, OCLC received eighty terminals and spare parts. Eventually the Spiras Systems terminals would be phased out as they became nonrepairable or too expensive to repair. As long as the supply lasted, a library could purchase one for fifteen hundred dollars. The demise of the Spiras Systems marked the end of one phase in the history of OCLC's on-line equipment and the start of a new one beginning with the OCLC Model 100 Display terminal.

FLC's experiment in on-line services introduced another method of communicating with OCLC through teletype-like terminals connected on-line to OCLC through Tymnet. During 1974-1975, another avenue of communication was tested in the Columbus area. Direct dial-up access to the OCLC data base took advantage of existing telephone lines used for directly dialed telephone calls. Teletype-like terminals were employed, and a simple station-to-station dialed or push-button telephone call connected the terminal to the data base.

After the cost and the charging procedures were evaluated, the Center made plans to extend direct dial-up access to Ohio libraries beyond the Columbus metropolitan area. Charges for direct dial-up would depend on the distance of the library from the Columbus area. For branch and departmental libraries in Ohio it could make searching on the system financially feasible.

The computer power of OCLC grew in proportion to the number of members the Center served and the systems that were activated. In anticipation of expansion in both areas, the Board of Trustees approved the purchase of two more Sigma 9 computers, bringing the total to three. Sigmas 901, 902, and 903 represented an investment of $4.5 million.

Five minicomputer systems were activated. Four of them operated on-line, and the fifth was to be used in case of failure. Each minicomputer supported 275 terminals. Plans included the transfer of polling and other communication processes to minicomputers, thus relieving this burden from the Sigmas.

Sigma 901 arrived at its new home at The Ohio State University Research Center, 1314 Kinnear Road, on December 18, 1974, two-and-one-half months late. By the end of January, its hardware and software had been tested for their compatability with the system. In the beginning both the Sigma 5 and the Sigma 901 were linked, and either could be used to access the data base. The combined system could support an estimated maximum of one thousand terminals.

Sigma 902 arrived in May 1975, four months behind schedule. It was housed in temporary quarters on Chatham Lane in Columbus where its use was initially limited to research and development activities, engineering studies, accounting tasks, etc.

Sigma 903 was due for delivery in March 1975. Because of a lack of space for it, the date was reset to January 1976, when it would arrive at the Center's new facility on Kinnear Road.[18] Once Sigma 903 was installed, Sigmas 901 and 902 would be moved to the new quarters. At this point, the data base was to be transferred from the Sigma 5/901 to the Sigmas 901 and 902. The new union meant that the system could accommodate approximately 1,440 terminals. When all five minicomputers were operating on-line, the system was expected to support 1,500 to 1,600 terminals. The Sigma 5 would then be used in card production and other off-line activities, while the Sigma 9s would handle the on-line functions. Future plans for the Sigma 5 included using it to produce claims for periodicals and unreceived books, to process purchase orders, and to maintain financial records for libraries.

During the year, the computer center was reorganized into two separate areas: the on-line center for the Sigma 9s and the production center where the Sigma 5 would operate.

The delay in arrival of the Sigma 9 and its subsequently delayed operational date of February 1975 resulted in slower response time at the terminals. The Sigma 5 hardware/software configuration was operating at almost maximum capacity. In an attempt to alleviate the situation, early in 1975 OCLC established an in-house Task Force to detect and remedy some of the problems with the system that influenced response time. Additional cataloging programs and minicomputer were added. Once the Sigma 9 was in operation in February 1975, users began to experience faster response time: "On 18 February response time averaged 25.3 seconds. One week later, OCLC's Sigma 9 relieved the Sigma 5, and response time plunged to an average of 12.1 seconds. After other changes, response time averaged 7.8 seconds on 3 March."[19]

Finances

One of the more exciting events of the year was the search for a site on which to build a new facility or to improve an existing one. The project was initially undertaken by the Administration and Finance Division, and later included the Building Subcommittee of the Board of Trustees and consultants. Three pressing needs led the Board to approve the plan in June 1974. First, security was a major concern to the OCLC staff. The membership was becoming increasingly dependent on the data base for its daily operations. The Center felt compelled to protect the interests of its users. Second, with the advent of increased computer power came the need for more space for the expanding inventory of equipment. Third, as the year opened, the Center was operating from four different locations. The computer facilities were housed at The Ohio State University Research Center on Kinnear Road, but the majority of the staff was located five miles north of the Research Center in two separate office buildings. The leasing of more computer and office space in yet a fourth location further dissipated the staff. A new facility would unify staff and equipment and provide a more favorable climate for expansion.

The 1974-1975 *Annual Report* noted progress made on the project during its first few months and the amount of homework involved in selecting a new site:

> The Administration and Finance Division working with the Building Subcommittee of the Board of Trustees and with consultants drew up a list of criteria containing 15 major elements ranging from the most important—security, telecommunication, and electric power availability—to lesser points. Using these site criteria, the Division staff investigated and evaluated more than 25 locations, some having existing structures and others being unimproved parcels of land. After the staff had prepared preliminary specifications for the facility, the Center asked owners and contractors to submit proposals for building or remodeling. These proposals were thoroughly evaluated, and the list brought down to two sites: one with an existing structure; and one vacant parcel.[20]

By September, a six-acre lot on Kenny Road was selected as the first choice for the new building. A series of meetings with builders, architects, the homeowner's association, and the lending agencies followed. Robert Grant, architect, attended the September Board of Trustees meeting to present a preliminary plan for the building. The estimated cost was $2.5 million. The amount was divided between the cost of the land ($427,500), office space ($870,000), and a computer vault ($1,202,500). The computer vault was a new concept for OCLC, devised to provide the ultimate in security for the computer. It would be constructed with reinforced steel walls and a roof of steel netting. The Board unanimously approved the plot on Kenny Road and the architect's plan. The chairman of the Board was directed to appoint the Building Subcommittee, which would investigate the construction of the facility, the purchase of the property, and the finance of the project.

On October 1, 1974, the first meeting of the Building Subcommittee was attended by William Chait of Dayton and Montgomery County Public Library; Thompson M. Little, the president and chairman of the Board of Trustees; and Jack R. Vincent, director of Administration and Finance for OCLC. The Subcommittee directed Vincent to procure the assistance of a professional fund raising firm to help the Center collect the necessary capital for the building. The fact that historically OCLC was undercapitalized and had taken out loans to grow worked against it when it came to lenders. Three days later, a meeting took place with representatives from Nationwide Insurance Company. Its offer did not meet the approbation of the Subcommittee. Further negotiations were planned.

On October 16, 1974, the Subcommittee met with representatives of Brakeley, John Price Jones, Inc., a fund raising firm. Two weeks later, a letter was received outlining its proposal. At the November Board of Trustees meeting, it was approved. Brakeley, John Price Jones, Inc. estimated that the fund raising would take between eight and ten weeks to complete. The project was to commence on December 4. In the beginning, the firm concentrated on tapping resources to raise revenue and hoped to work later on a long-range plan of fund raising and public relations.

Vincent presented a five-year financial projection for the Center along with a new loan proposal from Nationwide Insurance Company. The company offered to finance a $3 million loan. In the event the Center received grant funds, it would then be committed to a minimum of $1,750,000. After considering both, the Board of Trustees passed a resolution to proceed. The document read as follows:

BE IT, AND IT IS HEREBY RESOLVED, that the Executive Director and the Director of Administration and Finance, or either of them be and they hereby are authorized, empowered and directed, in the name and on behalf of the Ohio College Library Center to:

1. Enter into the purchase of real property being 5.74 acres of land known by Street Number as 3331-3377 Kenny Road, Upper Arlington, Franklin County, Ohio, for and in consideration of the sum of $430,650.

2. Cause to be constructed upon such land an office building and computer center of 51,000 square feet, more or less, at an estimated and approximate cost of $2,870,000.

3. Employ, in connection therewith, architects, engineers, surveyors, consultants, contractors, brokers, agents, and other persons or entities as the circumstances may require.

4. Conclude with the Nationwide Life Insurance Company a long-term first mortgage loan in a minimum amount of $1,750,000 and up to the amount of $3,000,000 for a term of 25 years with interest at a rate not to exceed 11-½% per annum in accordance with the terms, provisions, and conditions set forth in that certain letter of November 5, 1974, from Nationwide Life Insurance Company to Nationwide Real Estate Services, Inc., referencing the Ohio College Library Center.

5. Obtain a construction loan or loans and acquire such other grants, borrowings or funds and make such other arrangements as may be required to purchase the land, construct the building and complete all other matters in connection therewith.

6. Execute and deliver applications, purchase contracts, loan commitments, agreements for services, promissory notes, mortgage deeds, security documents, and any and all other instruments as may be necessary or desirable, and do and act upon any and all other things which may be appropriate or reasonably related to any and all of the foregoing.[21]

In December, it was announced that the Nationwide Insurance Company would lend OCLC the total amount of only $430,000 to purchase the land. The property was bought in December, but a construction loan had not yet been obtained. Meanwhile, Brakeley, John Price Jones, Inc. began fund-raising efforts that continued into the spring and the early summer. The executive director had arranged appointments with several foundations. The firm planned to report its results by the start of the next fiscal year.

All work on the Kenny Road building project terminated in April 1975, when a fresh, new plan emerged. The cost of the structure was projected for $2.5 million, but as the Center worked with the architect and building contractor, the figure grew until it exceeded $4 million. By unanimous accord the OCLC staff, the Board of Trustees, and the lenders decided that the Center should pursue an alternative course of action. A new piece of property including the structures on it was to be purchased in Columbus at 1125 Kinnear Road. (The Kenny Road site was later sold.) The Board of Trustees adopted a resolution on April 15, 1975, that said:

> ... that the Executive Director and the Director of Administration and Finance, or either of them, be and they hereby are authorized, empowered and directed in the name and on behalf of the Center to continue discussions with long-term and construction lenders, enter a contract to purchase 1125 Kinnear Road and remodel the structures in suitable fashion, employing architects, engineers, contractors and other persons or entities and do all other things necessary in the premises including the execution of notes, mortgages, settlements and all other instruments as required.[22]

As the year closed, the Center was decisively following a new road to expansion. Progress on the building project, as recorded in the Board minutes of June 17, 1975, was as follows:

> Mr. Vincent stated it appears that OCLC has obtained financing for the real estate at the Kinnear Road site. The costs for the Kinnear Road site are as follows: $1,300,000 for real estate property and $1,075,000 for remodeling existing buildings on the site. OCLC has obtained a short-term loan from Ohio National Bank in the amount of $1.8 million for remodeling and construction. Nationwide Insurance will provide a permanent loan in January 1976 for $1.8 million. OCLC is still in need of a short-term loan for $575,000, which a bank has agreed to provide.[23]

Turning now to the OCLC budget for 1975-1976, one finds the Center at a crossroads in its financial history. The out-of-state membership expansion over the 1974-1975 fiscal year and the projected non-Ohio participation for the following year were larger than expected. This created a need for additional staff and computers. The Board of Trustees viewed the budget as a "planning document" to be used by the Center staff, the networks, and the Board to formulate long-range plans for growth. The inflationary costs of maintaining operations and the Center's lack of operating capital were major issues in the new budget.

On March 5, 1975, each Board member was sent a copy of the "Budget Proposal 1975/76." At the March 11 meeting of the Board the budget of $10,730,000 was approved as a planning document. The final approval of the budget was prefaced by a lengthy discussion of its contents. The OCLC staff members present were the target of a number of questions. The Board members as well as the network representatives expressed concern about the rapid expansion of the Center. Some believed that with the accelerated growth OCLC could not accomplish all it wanted to do within its budgetary constraints. Still other members believed that more sources of income were needed if OCLC was to continue to grow. A comparison of the budgets for 1974-1975 and 1975-1976 showed that OCLC was going through an adolescent growth spurt.

TABLE T-12
Budget Plan Comparison (1974/75 and 1975/76)[24]

	1974/75 $	Budget %	1975/76 $	Budget %	Proposal % (minus terminal and grants)
PROJECTED INCOME					
System Usage	$1,193,000	53.8%	$ 4,302,000	40.1%	48.9%
Terminals	144,000	6.5%	3,201,000	29.8%	15.8%
Telephone	412,000	18.6%	1,745,000	16.3%	19.8%
Catalog Card Income	462,000	20.8%	1,100,000	10.3%	12.5%
Grant Income	–	–	116,000	1.1%	–
Other Income	7,000	0.3%	266,000	2.4%	3.0%
Total	$2,218,000		$10,730,000		
EXPENSES TO GENERATE PROJECTED INCOME					
Staff	$ 682,000	30.7%	$ 2,459,000	22.9%	27.6%
Rentals	716,000	32.3%	2,522,000	23.5%	28.3%
Debt Service	286,000	12.9%	758,000	7.1%	8.5%
Operations	366,000	16.5%	1,651,000	15.4%	18.5%
Administration	128,000	5.8%	366,000	3.4%	4.1%
Nonrecurring Expenses	–	–	168,000	1.6%	1.9%
Capital Expenditures	–	–	445,000	4.1%	5.0%
Cost of Sales	–	–	1,811,000	16.9%	–
Contingency Fund	–	–	100,000	0.9%	1.1%
Working Capital Fund	40,000	1.8%	450,000	4.2%	5.0%
Total	$2,218,000		$10,730,000		

By the last half of the year it was evident that OCLC would soon be experiencing a one million dollar shortage of working capital. To complete the fiscal year in the black the center asked the networks for early advance payments, postponed payment on some of its current accounts, and borrowed three hundred thousand dollars on a short-term loan. This situation contributed to the Board's concern with regard to the proposed budget. As the year came to an end, the Center closed the books with over thirty thousand dollars excess revenue over expenses.

A natural outgrowth of the financial situation was the appointment of a standing Finance Committee of the Board of Trustees on May 20, 1975. Richard J. Owen, the Board's treasurer, served as chairman. The other members were William Chait and H. Paul Schrank, Jr. The new committee was assigned to study the financial affairs of OCLC and to report regularly to the Board. The proposed budget was its first task. After carefully examining it, the Committee reduced the total figure to $10,456,000 from the original $10,730,000. Expenses were expected to generate revenues of $10,058,000. The contribution to corporate equity would be $398,000.

Because the Center would need $550,000 for its new building, the budget was short of $152,000. In June the Committee recommended that the basic noninclusive first-time-use charge (this charge applied only to the networks outside Ohio and excluded the terminal cost charge, terminal maintenance charge, and telecommunications line charges) be increased $.04. The new basic charge of $1.024 would generate an income of $169,800, allowing the Center a sufficient operating capital. The inclusive first-time-use charge to Ohio institutions was set at $1.92. Kilgour succinctly expressed his feelings on the subject of working capital when he wrote in the *Annual Report 1974/1975*: "Working capital is the money needed to operate an organization, and insufficient working capital more often causes the demise of organizations than any other factor."[25]

Two days after the approval of these charges, the Center received the good news that the State Library of Ohio had granted it $56,000 to purchase terminals for Ohio members. As a result, the inclusive first-time-use charge in Ohio was reduced from $1.92 to $1.87. Ohio members who paid in advance received a 6 percent discount, thus paying only $1.76.

OCLC had one major financial priority at this point in its history: adding new participants to increase its income. This was reflected in the Budget Proposal for the next year:

> The major accomplishment in the budgetary year is the growth in chargeable first-time uses of data base records for cataloging. During the first seven months of the year the monthly compounded percentage increase was 5.9%, and if this rate of growth continues for the remainder of the year, there will be at least 100,000 first-time uses in excess of the number estimated in the Budget. This growth is directly related to the increasing number of participants in the system, but new functions such as the serials module and new accesses will further increase system utilization before the end of the year.[26]

The 1974-1975 budget included a projection of 1,328,000 first-time uses by June 1975. In contrast, the next year's budget figures estimated 3,841,000 first-time uses by the close of the fiscal year. Libraries already on-line were expected to increase their total first-time use by 20 percent. Tentative projections for some of the consortia were made. PALINET with twenty-five new terminals was expected to use the system for an estimated 46,000 additional first-time uses. IRRC libraries were expected to contribute 70,000 first-time uses. The Wisconsin Library Consortium planned to be on-line by the first half of the fiscal year and projected its first-time uses at 75,000. The largest number of first-time uses, 350,000, was expected to be made by SOLINET, followed by SUNY with 270,000, followed by the trio of the Bibliographical Center for Research, the Missouri Consortium, and the Michigan Consortium (all three were expected to join in the next year). The smallest number of first-time uses would, in all probability, be made by FLC, according to projections.

The impact of the out-of-state membership was great:

> Not surprisingly, fees from non-Ohio users accounted for more of OCLC's 1974-75 budget than in any previous year. Of $1,956,981 in total fees, over 62%, or $1,213,330, came from out-of-state users, compared to 30%, or $383,438, for 1973-74. By contrast, fees from Ohio libraries were up only $36,441. Since total revenues rose by $1,542,978 over 1973-74, fees from Ohio members dropped from 48% to 25% of the budget.[27]

Income from the steady increase in the catalog card production amounted to nearly $300,000 in 1973-74; a year later that figure had doubled.

In increasing numbers libraries were installing noncataloging terminals in their public service areas. On February 18, 1975, the Board of Trustees voted to establish charges for searching on such terminals at 4.3¢ per search on Ohio public terminals and 2.2¢ per search on cataloging terminals in the state. Regions outside of the state paid 2.2¢ a search. The new schedule was effective July 1, 1975. A 6 percent discount was offered for annual advance payments.

Due to unfavorable reactions from users about searching charges, implementation of the charges was delayed until the Finance Committee could study it. Until June the Committee discussed and refined the Board's proposal. On June 17, 1975, after hearing the report of the Committee, the Board of Trustees voted to charge for search-key searches only on public use terminals, i.e., querying the data base by using one of the available search keys. The rate of 2.2¢ per search key would be charged to all institutions with public use terminals. Total charges per terminal could not exceed $2,280 annually. The Board also approved the stipulation that public use terminals had to be purchased. The searching charges for cataloging terminals was dropped.

Searching activities taxed the system more than any other activity. Some librarians feared that such charges would discourage use of the system. Nevertheless, the Board felt it necessary to charge and believed that the charge would not deter potential users. During the year the Board also approved charges for serials check-in.

With regard to finances, one other decision was made. At the November 8, 1974 membership meeting, the executive director proposed to waive the requirement that those institutions, invited to join OCLC in 1967 but which did not join until after 1970/71, pay the assessment they would have paid had they been members during the year before the on-line system became operational. This action of goodwill helped build a more hospitable environment for those considering membership.

Organization

OCLC became a new organization every year. Through its organizational metamorphosis it was reborn to accommodate its expansion. Fiscal year 1974-1975 was no exception. The change in the composition of the Board of Trustees, the reorganization of the Center's five divisions and their departmentalization, the groundwork for a user services division, and several other related events attested to the transformation.

Changes in membership of the Board of Trustees was an annual fall event. On November 8, 1974, the membership elected its new members[28] and the Board elected its officers. James V. Jones (Case Western Reserve University) was re-elected chairman and president. H. Paul Schrank, Jr. (University of Akron) was to continue as vice-chairman, with Richard J. Owen (Youngstown State University) as treasurer and Thompson M. Little (Ohio University) as secretary.

One of the more pleasant duties of this Board was the passing of a resolution on June 17, 1975, on behalf of Lewis C. Branscomb as he completed his final year as a representative to OCLC. The resolution was especially meaningful as it marked the second occasion that the Board recognized his outstanding contributions to the development of OCLC. The first occurred on November 10, 1972, when he was honored for his many years of service to the Board and for his direct role in the Center's early development.[29]

OCLC was reorganized into five divisions under the office of the executive director in the spring of 1974. A new organizational configuration was created soon after that. The executive director's office, Library Systems, Computer Facilities, Research and Development, and Administration and Finance divisions comprised the new organization, as of November 1974.[30] The changes were intended to improve the coordination of the Center's burgeoning activities.

The reorganization of the internal structure of OCLC resulted in shifts in personnel. Larry L. Learn was appointed director of the newly formed Division of Computer Facilities. W. Stuart Debenham, Jr. became assistant executive director. James E. Rush became director of the Research and Development Division. Ann Ekstrom assumed the new title of director of the Library Systems Division. Her appointment was historical both in August 1971 when she joined the staff and in 1974. In 1971 she was hired as the first full-time professional librarian other than Kilgour. In her new position she again was the only professional librarian to head a major OCLC division. James Barrentine became assistant director of the Research and Development Division, and Jack R. Vincent was named director of the Administration and Finance Division. When Vincent accepted his new position, the seat of the comptroller was left vacant. It was filled by the appointment of Jordan R. Maple.

The foundations for a sixth division were laid on January 28, 1975, when the executive director proposed to the Board of Trustees that a user services division be established. The unit would deal directly with the users in resolving all types of problems related to system activity. Its creation would fill a gap in the divisional structure by creating a unit devoted solely to the direct daily needs of the users. In January, the Board approved the proposal, although the unit was not established until May 1976.

Although Kilgour presented the proposal for the new division, the idea was recommended by the accounting firm of Haskins & Sells, which OCLC had used from its inception. During 1973-1974, the firm prepared a five-year projection of income and expenditures for the Center. During fiscal year 1974-1975 the Board of Trustees formed a special committee to work with the Management Services Division of Haskins & Sells to complete a study of the present and future organization of OCLC. The results of the study were released in "Outline of Recommendations for Improvement to Support Continued Growth" (July 1975).

The Peer Council's sphere of influence was limited to quality control in the state of Ohio, leaving the out-of-state networks without a controlling unit. In the early months of 1975 Ann Ekstrom met with a group of representatives from the different networks to discuss the establishment of individual peer councils for them. The group continued to meet throughout the year, although no formal organization equal to the Peer Council was created.

The lack of network peer councils was only one issue facing OCLC as its services spread beyond Ohio. Another was the absence of networks in regions where participating libraries were located. These libraries joined as independents and therefore did not enjoy the support of a network. The first example of this problem occurred in the state of California. By the spring, a large number of California libraries, not affiliated with a regional organization, were joining or planning to join OCLC. As a stopgap measure until the Center could coordinate these activities on the West Coast, Patrick Barkey (director of libraries, Claremont Colleges) and the director of his computer center offered to serve as part-time coordinators. The temporary arrangement enabled OCLC to establish a close tie with the individual institutions through a central headquarters.

Originally, OCLC membership was limited to Ohio academic libraries. The expansion in the number and the nature of the users prompted the Center to alter the Code of Regulations. On December 17, 1974, the Board of Trustees unanimously resolved to amend the Code's Section 2 of Article II, to be acted upon at the next year's membership meeting. The revised version expanded membership in Ohio to include all types of libraries.[31]

ON-LINE SYSTEMS

Full activation of the on-line serials system was not realized during the fiscal year 1974-1975, although members had been told that the system would be available in 1975. The serials system required complex programming and testing. The tests began the previous year with Ohio University and continued into the next year. The new target date was for the latter part of 1976.

Implementation of the serials check-in module depended on OCLC's ability to locate existing serials data bases. By the close of the previous year, the Ad Hoc Committee on Serials Data Bases had concluded agreements to use MULS and the Pittsburgh Regional Union List of Serials. In April 1975, the software for the conversion of both lists was completed. The Pittsburgh file was to be added after the MULS file. The Center estimated a 68 percent overlap in the contents of the two files and had already begun to formulate a method of eradicating duplicate titles. Although the on-line input of serials cataloging, which began the year before with Ohio University, was important, the installation of the check-in module, in December 1976, signified that OCLC was on a course leading to the full activation of its second major subsystem.

Even though the check-in module was not yet ready for general use, the Board of Trustees proceeded to establish the charges. At the Board's February meeting they were set at 8¢ for each issue of a journal that was checked-in by an Ohio library. Libraries participating through regions with arrangements to purchase terminals and to pay for telephone lines for charged 3.4¢. A 6 percent discount was offered to institutions that paid annually in advance.

OCLC concluded negotiations with CLR in Washington, D.C. to distribute the CONSER data base. For two years OCLC would provide the computer facilities to establish and maintain the beginnings of a national serials data base.[32] There were ten invited participants, excluding OCLC.[33] As of December 17, 1974, OCLC officially became a part of a bold new adventure in bibliographic control of serials records.

In January, Kilgour established a CONSER task force at OCLC to begin the project. Fortunately, preparations for OCLC's system development were applicable to the establishment of the serials data base to be used by the nation's libraries. OCLC had already planned to use the MULS file and the Pittsburgh Regional Library Center's file to build its own data base. The MULS file contained seventy-five thousand machine records and thirty-five thousand cross-references and added entry titles. The actual loading of the serials records did not begin until the next fiscal year. Documents containing the bibliographic practices to be followed were completed, and a terminal-operating manual was circulated to participants for comments.

A special program to convert LC's serials MARC records to a format acceptable to OCLC was developed, and in May, a tape of 14,428 serials records was sent to Columbus to be loaded into the system. Thus, not only the MULS but also LC files constituted the basic files for the CONSER project.

In November 1974, before the final agreement was reached, the National Library of Canada and LC agreed to exchange and distribute each country's current imprints in machine-readable form. Already underway were talks for a similar arrangement with the Bibliothèque Nationale in Paris and the National Library of Australia. The data base was conceived as an authoritative source for local, national, and international use.

On April 11, 1975, the CONSER Project's Advisory Group met at LC to review the progress of the project and to discuss further cooperative arrangements. The University of Florida, with its Florida Union List of Serials, and the Boston Theological Institute were added as participants. In addition, CONSER and the National Federation of Abstracting and Indexing Services (NFAIS) reached an agreement. Under its terms NFAIS supplied up to twenty-five thousand science and technology surrogates (photocopies of the covers, title pages, and mastheads of the publications) to the CONSER file through the National Serials Data Program within LC. In return, NFAIS was granted full access to the CONSER data file.

Throughout 1974-1975, work continued not only on the on-line serials system but also on the technical processing module. The latter was to follow the serials system. Although it was scheduled for implementation in 1975, plans were delayed because OCLC concentrated on developing the serials program. The technical processing system came to be viewed as a long-range project. As the year ended, the preliminary design of the system was nearly 50 percent completed. Design work was accelerated in 1975-1976 by the $124,250 grant from CLR (1974-1975), which allotted funds to design of the on-line authority files, the technical processing system, and the subject search project.

The interlibrary loan system, like the technical processing system, received less attention than the total development of the serials system. OCLC began assiduously to design and develop an interlibrary loan communication system following receipt of a $108,575 grant from OE (spring 1975).

The Patron Input Committee, organized in 1972, completed its first draft document in 1974. Entitled "Interim Report of OCLC Patron Input Committee" (March 7, 1974), it contained preliminary findings of the Committee after a series of meetings with library users. At the November 8, 1974 meeting of the membership, the Committee's chair, Herbert F. Johnson, shared the second and final paper, "Report of the OCLC Patron Input Committee to the OCLC Membership" (October 31, 1974). This report was again based on visits made to each Committee member's library. It included a recommendation to establish two committees to help OCLC reach one of its fundamental goals, increasing the availability of library materials to users. An Advisory Committee on Interlibrary Loans similar to those organized for other OCLC subsystems was recommended, along with an Ad Hoc Committee. The latter was to investigate effective procedures, to be implemented still that year, for the delivery of materials primarily through interlibrary loans.

OUT-OF-STATE COOPERATIVE
ACTIVITIES AND NETWORKING

The number of OCLC regional affiliates continued to increase in 1974-1975. The Higher Education Coordinating Council of Metropolitan St. Louis (HECC), the Illinois Research and Reference Center Libraries (IRRC), SOLINET, and SUNY were added to the list of participants. Seven independent institutions not affiliated with a regional center also began to participate in OCLC.[34]

The HECC[35] and IRRC[36] agreements brought a total of eight new institutions on-line. By September 1974, 315 terminals were in use on the OCLC system. Approximately 158 terminals were needed to serve SOLINET's ninety-nine libraries in ten states.[37] SUNY added fifty-seven new users.[38] Although SUNY signed the official agreement with OCLC, not all of the SUNY libraries decided to participate. Non-SUNY institutions also joined the system through SUNY, including members of the City University of New York (CUNY) system. The U.S. Military Academy at West Point, a non-SUNY institution, was the first to receive a terminal. As of June 1975, 411 institutions were participating in OCLC. As the year ended, Kilgour was working on an agreement that would apply to individual libraries outside of Ohio.

During the year, the Center recorded the impact of the new regional participants. Table T-13 presents their system activities, reflecting the fact that because the Higher Education Coordinating Council of Metropolitan St. Louis, Illinois Research and Reference Center Libraries, Southeastern Library Network, and State University of New York joined OCLC in the course of 1974-1975, the amount of participation for each one during the year depended upon the starting date of its participation.

TABLE T-13
Titles Cataloged in 1973/74 and 1974/75[39]

	Total Copies of Books Cataloged		Chargeable First-time Uses		Input Cataloging		Percentage Cataloging Using Existing Records	
	1973/74	1974/75	1973/74	1974/75	1973/74	1974/75	1973/74	1974/75
Ohio College Library Center	587,481	806,594	348,457	409,925	107,734	98,012	76.4	80.7
AMIGOS Bibliographic Council	4,780	260,908	4,337	201,991	208	23,814	95.4	89.5
Cooperative College Library Center	48,700	38,429	20,237	14,618	1,217	216	94.3	98.5
Federal Library Committee	9,300	62,966	5,519	29,197	2,307	24,991	70.5	53.9
Five Associated University Libraries	117,068	160,343	81,943	109,946	24,199	34,354	77.2	76.2
Higher Education Coordinating Council of Metropolitan St. Louis		20,121		13,118		2,639		83.3
Illinois Research and Reference Center Libraries		85,143		46,779		4,716		90.8
Independent Organizations	302,159	24,289	236,580	17,567	36,768	444	86.6	97.5
New England Library Information Network		493,446		375,685		57,903		86.7
Pennsylvania Area Library Network	71,645	163,227	56,899	127,130	9,185	21,134	86.1	85.8
Pittsburgh Regional Library Network	53,154	91,316	25,003	56,410	3,942	6,096	86.4	90.3
Southeastern Library Network		107,289		89,309		10,820		89.2
State University of New York		240,984		195,196		19,388		91.0
Total	1,194,287	2,555,055	778,975	1,686,871	185,560	304,527		
Average							80.8	84.7

The AMIGOS Bibliographic Council, a new name on the list of participants, was an expansion of the Interuniversity Council of the North Texas Area (IUC). It was a consortium of fifty-eight university, college, medical, public, and school libraries in Texas, Arkansas, Oklahoma, New Mexico, and Arizona.[40]

The Center's out-of-state activities also included the Federal Libraries' Experiment in Cooperative Cataloging (FLECC). Initiated by the 1973 cooperative agreement between OCLC and FLC,[41] it continued throughout the year and concluded with a decision by the FLECC Steering Committee to renegotiate the original contract that ended on July 14, 1975.

In February 1974 communication with OCLC was established for libraries in Washington, D.C. through use of existing direct-leased telephone lines. The terminus for the lines was the Smithsonian Institution. Access was through the OCLC Model 100 Display terminals. By June 1974, there were seventeen terminals in sixteen libraries in the Washington area. Five months later, on July 15, 1974, the OCLC system was connected to the Tymnet communication system.

As the project gained momentum, guidelines were developed. *The FLECC Information Bulletin* was a means to disseminate information about the experiment. Representatives from the libraries involved formed the Steering Committee. An evaluation advisory group, composed of Committee members, was created to evaluate the year-long experiment and to publish the results. In January 1975, Systems Architects, Inc. was awarded a contract to determine the effectiveness of the OCLC system on the federal library community. Eight libraries were chosen to participate in the seventeen-week evaluation. Libraries using Tymnet and those using leased lines (or both) were selected. Results were published in *Federal Libraries Experiment in Cooperative Cataloging (FLECC): Final Report* (May 14, 1975). In the words of one participant "the undertaking has been a very successful experiment in real cooperation."[42] The system was used not only for monograph cataloging but also for preorder searching, data verifying, and interlibrary loaning. Some libraries began to input serials cataloging. During the fiscal year, federal libraries cataloged 62,966 titles using OCLC. Some used printer attachments to produce spine, book, and card labels. As a final note, an ad hoc committee on extended automation was established for the purpose of planning and developing cooperative automation programs. The programs would utilize future OCLC services or in-house computer facilities of federal libraries.

Events in 1974-1975 were leading OCLC down a difficult and uncertain path toward the future. The beauty of its historical development lay in the Center's ability to adjust successfully to changing conditions and to harmonize its varied functions.

NOTES

1. Federal Library Committee, *Newsletter*, 1 October 1974, p. 4.

2. Ohio College Library Center, *Newsletter*, 28 May 1975, p. [1].

3. Ohio College Library Center, "Minutes of the Board of Trustees Meeting" (Columbus: Ohio College Library Center, 18 February 1975), p. 3.

4. Ohio College Library Center, "Minutes of the Board of Trustees Meeting" (Columbus: Ohio College Library Center, 17 June 1975), p. 2.

5. CODEN (not an acronym) is a five- or six-character (alphabetic) code used to identify serial titles. Devised by Chemical Abstracts Service, it was created for use in on-line systems.

6. The total cost of the BASIS 70 indexing was estimated at forty-eight thousand dollars. Therefore, the twenty-eight thousand dollars represented only a portion of the funds needed.

7. Letter from Frederick G. Kilgour to Fred C. Cole (Council on Library Resources). (Undated.)

8. The following institutions belonged to COMCAT: Florida A & M, Florida Atlantic University, Florida International University, Florida State University, Florida Technological University, Jacksonville Public Library, Miami-Dade County Public Library, Orlando Public Library, State Library of Florida, Tampa-Hillsborough County Library, University of Florida, University of Miami, University of North Florida, University of South Florida, and University of West Florida.

9. Ohio College Library Center Peer Council, "Requirements for Improvement of Quality Control" (Columbus: Ohio College Library Center, 7 November 1974), p. 3.

10. Ibid., p. 5.

11. Ibid., p. [1].

12. Ibid.

13. Ohio College Library Center Committee on Direct Borrowing, "Report of the Ohio College Library Center: Committee on Direct Borrowing" (Columbus: Ohio College Library Center, 14 June 1974), p. 2.

14. Ohio College Library Center, *Newsletter*, 17 September 1974, p. [1].

15. Baldwin-Wallace College, Battelle Memorial Institute, Burton Public Library, Cleveland Heights-University Heights Public Library, Cleveland Public Library, Columbus Technical Institute, Lima Public Library, Lorain Public Library, Methodist Theological School, Mount Vernon Nazarene College, Riverside Methodist Hospital, Stark County District Library, University of Cincinnati Medical Library, and University of Toledo Law Library.

16. See chapter 2 for details.

17. Ohio College Library Center, "Minutes of the Board of Trustees Meeting" (Columbus: Ohio College Library Center, 15 October 1974), p. 3.

18. See page 141 for information on the new facility.

19. Ohio College Library Center, *Newsletter*, 12 March 1975, p. [1].

20. Ohio College Library Center, *Annual Report 1974/1975* (Columbus: Ohio College Library Center, 1975), p. 11.

21. Ohio College Library Center, "Minutes of the Board of Trustees Meeting" (Columbus: Ohio College Library Center, 22 November 1974), p. 3.

22. Ohio College Library Center, "Minutes of the Board of Trustees Meeting" (Columbus: Ohio College Library Center, 15 April 1975), p. 8.

23. Ohio College Library Center, "Minutes of the Board of Trustees Meeting" (Columbus: Ohio College Library Center, 17 June 1975), p. 3.

24. Ohio College Library Center, "OCLC Budget Proposal Fiscal Year 1975/76" (Columbus: Ohio College Library Center, 1975), p. [10].

25. Op. cit., Ohio College Library Center, *Annual Report 1974/1975*, p. 15.

26. Op. cit., Ohio College Library Center, "OCLC Budget Proposal Fiscal Year 1975/76," p. 2.

27. Susan K. Martin, *Library Networks, 1976-77* (White Plains, New York: Knowledge Industry Publications, 1976), p. 33.

28. See appendix 1, Exhibit D, for a complete list of the Board of Trustees members.

29. See appendix 1, Exhibit O, for the revised version.

30. Three of these units were departmentalized. The Library Systems Division had a Cataloging and Quality Control Department and a Library Systems Analysis Department. The Engineering, Data Processing, and Systems Departments were part of the Computer Facilities Division. The Research and Development Division contained a Systems Development Department. The Administration and Finance Division was not yet large enough to warrant departmentalization, although plans were being made to establish separate departments to handle accounting, personnel, administration, and purchasing.

31. See appendix 1, Exhibit C, for amended Code of Regulations.

32. See chapter 2 for details.

33. Library of Congress, National Library of Medicine, National Agricultural Library, State University of New York, New York State Library, Cornell University, Yale University, University of Minnesota, and University of California at Berkeley. The International Serials Data System would be involved through two national centers, the National Serials Data Program at the Library of Congress and the International Serials Data System/Canada at the National Library of Canada.

34. Claremont College (California), Kansas City Public Library, Kearney State College (Nebraska), Northeast Missouri State University, Pomona Public Library (California), Sunnyvale Public Library (California), and University of Wisconsin.

35., 36., 37., 38. See appendix 1, Exhibit J, for a list of the members of each consortium.

39. Op. cit., Ohio College Library Center, *Annual Report 1974/1975*, p. [2]. The numbers in the first pair of columns do not equal the sum of the second and third pairs. The second pair of columns indicates the first time an existing record, not input by the cataloging library, was used for catalog production.

40. See appendix 1, Exhibit J, for a list of the AMIGOS members.

41. See chapters 6 and 7 for details.

42. Federal Library Committee, *Newsletter*, September 1975, p. 4.

9

VARIATIONS ON A
THEME
1975-1976

During 1975-1976 the Center continued to change rapidly. Within the folds of the main theme of growth were a number of secondary ones, all closely interconnected. These variations on the main theme included: finding a remedy to poor response time, improving the quality of records in the data base, providing access to non-OCLC data bases, developing a network supervisor program, expanding membership, updating user education, employing technological advances, and planning future on-line systems.

Poor response time compelled the Center to undertake major steps during the year to improve it. Terminals were "feathered" (a procedure whereby a certain number of terminals were taken off the system temporarily for a part of each day), new Saturday hours were offered, and a moratorium on the installation of new terminals and software was enforced. Access to data bases outside of OCLC was a goal that would link users with information from the fields of medicine, law, chemistry, and biology. Membership continued to increase, reaching a new total of eighty-four Ohio libraries. Out-of-state participation expanded with the addition of five new networks. The need to keep informed gave birth to two distinctly independent organizations, the Health Science OCLC Users Group (HSOCLCUG) and the Music OCLC Users Group (MOUG). With activation of the new dual Sigma 9 computer, the stage was set to implement the quadruple processor system. The Western Service Center was established in Claremont, California, offering support to an area where no OCLC network affiliate existed.

Although OCLC was growing rapidly, the delicate balance between stability and growth was maintained.

THE ON-LINE UNION CATALOG
AND SHARED CATALOGING SYSTEM

Data Base

Response time has been defined as "the elapsed time between depression of the SEND key and the instant the last character of the reply is displayed on the terminal screen."[1] At the June 1976 Board of Trustees meeting, Kilgour went on record stating that "The current principal problem is increased response time." Two illustrations emphasize the point. First, virtually every issue of the *Newsletter* contained a contribution on the subject. The issue for February 9, 1976, included an article entitled "How the Center Calculates Response Time." The *Newsletter* frequently conveyed information to users on slow response time. Second, the subject was discussed not only among librarians but also among network directors and staff at OCLC headquarters. Minutes of many meetings included that topic. Although average response time was reduced to below the acceptable level of eight seconds at the close of the previous year, the blissful period was short-lived as response time rose again to nearly thirty seconds in 1975-1976. Indeed, poor response time left an indelible imprint on the year's events.

On September 4, 1975, Kilgour discussed response time with the Ohio membership. Exactly one week later the same subject was discussed at a meeting of the Council on Computerized Library Networks (CCLN) in St. Louis, Missouri. At the September 16 meeting of the Trustees, Kilgour shared with the Board members a plan to ameliorate the slow response time by a target date of December 1, 1975, when the Center's computer facilities would be consolidated at the new headquarters at 1125 Kinnear Road. According to Kilgour, the main reason for poor response time was the delay in joining Sigma 901 and 902 computers.

Another inhibiting factor was the need for the full MARC record display for the CONSER project. Most MARC records required two screens to display all of the information, a procedure that required three times the average number of message exchanges between terminal and computer. Productivity improved soon after September 18 when the Center altered the terminal screen displays. Changes included eliminating five blank lines from the display, which meant a reduction in two-screen records and modification of the "next screen" command to expedite the on-line editing process. If these improvements did not appreciably reduce response time by December 1, the Center would begin to feather terminals.

In October, the response time was still worsening. In an attempt to curb it, the Center introduced three changes. First, beginning October 4, 1975, the system was to be available on Saturdays from 9:00 A.M. to 5:00 P.M., Eastern Standard Time. This was a temporary situation to improve the accessibility to the on-line data base and to increase productivity. Should greater use of the system result, then Saturday hours might be continued. The hope was that the extra hours would no longer be necessary by December 1. Surprisingly, the response time was less than three seconds on Saturday, October 4. Moreover, approximately 2,800 titles were cataloged, and the Center produced 17,000 catalog cards for that day. One week later, terminal activity rose as libraries cataloged 3,700 books and OCLC produced 22,727 catalog cards.

The second change was initiated on October 8 with systemwide feathering of the terminals. Terminals were suspended from use for one hour a day the same time each day. The Center had studied response time the week before and the week after feathering. Results showed that the average response time had dropped from 19.2 seconds before feathering to 13.7 seconds after it. The third change occurred on October 21 when polling (querying) by minicomputers began. The new procedure shifted the polling from the Sigma computer to the communications processors.

During the week of November 3, response time climbed once more to a systemwide average of 15.1 seconds during peak use hours (9:00 A.M. to 3:00 P.M., Eastern Standard Time), but a strange phenomenon occurred. Despite low response time, system activity increased. Some 106,128 titles were cataloged, and over 720,000 catalog cards were produced from November 3 through 7. Moreover, 17,568 titles were input into the data base, and over 1,400 MARC records from LC were added. By that time over 900 terminals were on-line. Efforts to decline response time were thwarted by a disruption of electrical power on November 19. The *Newsletter* stated:

> Early that week there were hardware problems, and on Wednesday, 19 November, electrical power in the Kinnear Road area in Columbus was disrupted for 15 minutes. The Columbus and Southern Ohio Electric Company says that a lineman working on a pole south of Kinnear Road accidentally crossed some wires, causing lights to go off in an area of about 2 square miles in the Kinnear Road area. The disruption of electrical power led to power surges which caused substantial hardware damage at OCLC's computer center at the Ohio State University Research Center at 1314 Kinnear Road. The hardware could not be repaired on-line, and thus, the Center incurred substantial downtime in the process of recovering from an unfortunate chain of events.[2]

By the end of the month the situation worsened. Users were finding it increasingly difficult to transmit messages on the terminals. To affirm the Center's efforts to improve response time, the executive director wrote a letter to the participating libraries that filled the first page of the November 28 *Newsletter*. "An Open Letter from the Executive Director about Response Time" began as follows: "Response time is rising and my credibility is falling." Kilgour went on to explain that the two-computer system would not be available by December 1, due to unforeseen delays. The first computer was expected to be on-line by December 8, and the second by December 15. He assured users that OCLC was doing everything possible to reach an acceptable response time on the terminals. Before that goal would be reached, users should expect to experience variations in response time during the first few weeks of operation of the new system. The letter closed on a positive note: "Participating libraries have been most patient and understanding in putting up with clearly intolerable response time. Now I must ask you again to be patient and understanding for a few more weeks. OCLC's new dual computer system, when installed and fine-tuned, should have a meritorious effect on response time for libraries participating in the OCLC network system."[3]

During the month two announcements were made. First, because of delays in the installation of the two computers, feathering was to be continued until the new system stablized and response time reached an acceptable plateau. Feathering proved to be a temporary but effective way to assure acceptable response time. Second, effective November 28, the Center would stop adding new terminals to the on-line network until systemwide response time fell to eight seconds. The Center also requested the Board of Trustees to sign no agreements with new institutions until response time fell. Additionally, through the offices of the regional networks, OCLC asked the networks temporarily to do no searching during peak hours of activity.

The Center kept informing users of forthcoming plans and events through the *Newsletter*. An article published in the November 28, 1975 *Newsletter*, "What Libraries Can Expect during Installation of New Computer System," warned of downtime, sporadic service, and a delay in card production service. The transfer to the new dual system was referred to as a "shakedown cruise, the passengers being the on-line users." A week earlier an article appeared in the November 21 issue of the *Newsletter* entitled "Response Time Rises Again, but Relief Is in Sight." The computer switching was compared to "going from a Piper Cub to a 747."

On December 1 the Center announced that it would suspend installations of new computer programs and additions to or enhancements of the on-line system until response time improved. Prior to December, the Center's polling activities were executed by the Sigma computers. Beginning in December, the polling of the terminals was performed by minicomputers, thus relieving the load on the Sigmas. The result was frequent malfunctions or "crashes" of the communications processors handling the polling. This, in turn, caused fluctuations in response time. For example, on December 1, 1975, the average response time for the day was 16.4 seconds. At 7:00 A.M. it was 5 seconds, and at 11:20 A.M. it peaked to 70 seconds.

As was the case in November, productivity and good response time did not go hand in hand. A case in point was the activity recorded on December 8 and 9. On December 8, despite a poor response time of 11.99 seconds, participating libraries set a record for system activity. On December 9, although response time rose to 17.4 seconds, on-line activity was still high.

In December the Center transferred on-line operations to the most powerful system yet available. From the standpoint of response time, it was an important event because significant improvements in response time and on-line operation could now be rightfully expected. The new system did not become active on December 8, as planned. Exactly one week later, on December 15, it ran for one hour and then sustained two severe crashes. On December 16, it had to be shut down, and the following day an unsuccessful attempt was made to bring it on again. December 19 witnessed success as the system ran for over twelve hours. Then, hardware design flaws surfaced, and again it was deactivated. A victory was scored on the morning of December 29 when the system was again activated, this time using only one computer. Beginning December 30, 1975, the on-line system was available on a limited basis. Although only one computer was in use, it was still more powerful than the old system.

The dual computer system, using two Sigma 9s (901 and 902), was available in January. It was reported that "after two weeks of ups and downs, OCLC's new dual computer system is becoming more stable each day, and users can expect to see continuing improvements in dependability and response time."[4] As stability increased, system activity also increased. By the end of January, the on-line system was available 90 percent of its scheduled time. Statistics for November 1975 stand in contrast to those of January 1976. In November, 359,970 books were cataloged as compared with 514,901 in January. Catalog card production was at 2,440,796 in November and 3,408,428 in January. Because of substantial use of the system on Saturdays, the Saturday hours were retained. When response time fell to eight seconds or less, the Center planned to reanalyze the extra hours and decide whether to continue them.

On January 7 the moratorium on the installation of new software was lifted. On January 12 the moratorium on installation of terminals was lifted. Furthermore, the Center was free to consummate agreements with organizations wanting to participate.

On January 21, 1976, at the weekly meeting of the Center's directors of the divisions, Kilgour and the OCLC directors adopted a proposal for guidelines for the number of terminals on dedicated telephone lines. The guidelines stated that no more than twenty-five terminals should be in use on a dedicated line. If a dedicated line had over twenty-five terminals, it was to be split. Data should be transmitted at twenty-four hundred baud, and all equipment attached to the dedicated lines should be approved by OCLC. It was also proposed that the Center establish as one of its objectives a response time that would not exceed eight seconds during peak periods under normal operating conditions.

In February, lightning struck OCLC disintegrating a utility pole near the Center on the eve of February 18. Fortunately, the staff had prepared the computers for such an eventuality, and they remained intact, but restoration of on-line activity was a major task. The system was unavailable on February 19.

Nonetheless, February was characterized by an increasingly stable and reliable on-line network with only brief periods when it was unavailable. User activity rose. About 11.4 percent more books were cataloged in February than in January, and approximately 12.2 percent more catalog cards were produced. The data base was accessible 94.6 percent of the time.

Good news came for users when the Center announced that beginning February 14, 1976, the on-line system would be available Saturdays on a regular basis. The decision was based both on a use analysis and expressed desire of users. With the extended hours, the system was in service a total of eighty-seven hours a week. The new hours were Monday through Friday, 7:00 A.M. to 10:00 P.M., and Saturday from 8:00 A.M. to 8:00 P.M., Eastern Standard Time.

The road leading to the smooth operation of the on-line system was paved with the unpredictable. Judging by the activity in February, one would think that March would offer comfort and assurance. Such was not the case. Average response time jumped to twenty seconds on March 22 and 24 because a massive equipment failure forced the Center to use one computer to transmit messages to and from more than one thousand terminals. The new dual computer configuration proved itself, however, by demonstrating that even if one computer was down, the users could still fully utilize the system, a situation that would have been previously impossible. The problem as described by Larry Learn, director of the Computer Facilities Division, was "about the size of a shirt button and worth about a dollar." A transistor in one of the computer's modules was malfunctioning. It was replaced and the dual computer system restored.

A new polling procedure was installed on March 27 that carried with it the promise of improved overall response time. The "poll-all" procedure enabled the minicomputers to poll or query an entire chain (more than one terminal connected to a modem) of OCLC Model 100 Display terminals with one poll (inquiry) as opposed to "conversing" separately with each terminal in the chain. Users were warned to expect erratic or long response times, especially in the case of a lengthy chain of terminals. On April 13, the poll-all protocol was taken off the on-line system. Although it did improve response time for most users, it resulted in a slower response time for some. Following modifications, it was reinstalled in the on-line system in May. The revisions did reduce response time for all of the terminals.

The Center also installed a new message capability referred to as the "null message," which allowed it to pinpoint malfunctioning terminals. By the middle of April the average response time was 7.6 seconds. Work had begun on reducing the number of terminals per telephone line to no more than twenty-five. Twenty-seven new terminals were scheduled for installation in April, and forty in May.

On May 17 the Center installed several devices to enhance on-line activities. The corporate name index allowed users to search not only by personal name but also by corporate name, i.e., the name of a corporation, a conference, or a meeting. Moreover, one could now retrieve personal names from added entry fields. This new capability was most helpful when searching for a jointly authored book when only one author was known. Response time for author, name-title, title, and, particularly, extended searches increased as a direct result of the enhancements. Three hundred typical searches could be made in the same amount of time needed to execute one extended search. The condition was considered temporary. The search keys that used numbers exclusively continued to yield rapid response time during peak hours. The Center urged users to employ the LC card number, ISBN, ISSN, or the CODEN, whenever possible. The overall increase in average response time was still comparatively low in spite of the fact that it was high for certain types of searches. All in all, these alterations produced on the average nearly 200 percent more entries.

The enhancements were complemented by two changes, a revision in the truncated entry display and reorganization of the index files through compression of holdings symbols for records in the data base. Whenever a search key yielded a long string of truncated records, the records would be arranged in a logical pattern based upon the type of search that was conducted. For instance, a search by title would result in the listing of the truncated entries by title.

Implementation of the ALL PRODUCE function began on May 22, 1976, following its testing by the Dayton-Montgomery County Public Library. Thus, a library could request catalog cards for multiple holding libraries by using one PRODUCE command as opposed to an individual command for each holding library.

These new features combined to create a powerful system for users. Because of unacceptable response time, the Center once again placed a hold on the installation of new terminals in May. The moratorium would be lifted once the response time returned to an acceptable level, and the system could comfortably accept more terminals.

In conclusion, poor response time was a time-consuming and irritating aspect of the on-line activities throughout the year.

Expansion

Expansion of OCLC meant, among other things, an increase in the number of functions the system could perform. Four new ones were introduced during the year. In addition to the previously mentioned ALL PRODUCE command, corporate name index, and index of personal names from the added entry fields, a new MARC films format was implemented to catalog films and special instructional materials such as charts, games, and realia. Before February 1976, the system accepted only monographic cataloging. Catalog cards for films could not yet be ordered, but users could begin to learn the new format prior to producing cards. The Center had received all of the approximately thirty-two thousand MARC films records distributed by LC and would be adding them to the on-line catalog in the future. In February, the Center completed and distributed to the membership a draft of *Films Format: A Description of Fixed Fields, Variable Fields, Indicators and Subfield Codes* (February 1976). The creation of other types of formats would ride the wave of the films format. Early in June, the Center developed fields and codes for inputting maps, manuscripts, recordings, and music scores. The certainty that the data base would grow was guaranteed by the new formats.

Funds to implement subject access and an on-line authority file were supplied by a grant from CLR. The subject search project was also financed by NCEMMH. By February 1976, the Battelle Memorial Institute's BASIS Subject search programs were imbedded in the Sigma 901 and were undergoing tests. The subject search system began slowly with NCEMMH using it in testing mode. The creation of a small, experimental on-line data base composed of records from OCLC and those from the NIMIS file used by NCEMMH was viewed by the Center as a major technological breakthrough in the project. Quite naturally, the Center was not sure how much of a burden it would be on the system. The controlled test environment was important because it allowed small-scale observation. During the next three months a number of corrections and refinements were made. The implementation plans proceeded with the assistance and guidance of an advisory committee of librarians and patrons from participating libraries. A special consultant, Janet Egeland, SUNY Biomedical Communication Network director, was also brought in. The Center had begun to design the on-line authority file and to conduct an exploratory study on the value of on-line files to library patrons.

As OCLC looked toward tomorrow, it began to lay the foundations for other functions. In October 1975, the Advisory Committee on Non-Roman Alphabets developed a limited set of twenty-seven Hebrew characters. Still to be developed were character sets for Greek, Cyrillic, and Arabic. Programming for the on-line correction of errors by selected libraries had begun, and the Center was planning to install a broadcast capability that would inform the terminal users when the system was temporarily down. OCLC was also planning to alphabetize the holding symbols on the bibliographic records so that terminal users at a glance could determine who owned a particular title.

On February 11, 1976, a new vista opened when the directors of the divisions at the Center unanimously approved a policy to accept large files of cataloging data from external sources. The records had to meet certain criteria. They had to be in the MARC II format and to be of benefit to all of the system's participants.

As the system's functions expanded, problems of duplicate and deferred records became unwelcome companions to this growth. At the March 10 meeting of the directors of the divisions, Ann Ekstrom asked to be put on record "as advocating the assignment of first priority for R & D to resolve the problems of duplicate and deferred records."[5] The deferral of the possible duplicate records for later verification began several years earlier. Despite Research and Development's successful installation of the NEW command during the previous year, it failed to reduce duplicates effectively. Over eight hundred duplicate records were generated after its installation. In the fall, an ad hoc committee of the Cataloging Advisory Committee was organized to define a "unique record."

At the November 7, 1975 meeting of the membership, Patricia L. Lyons (Walsh College) presented the "Report of the Peer Council." Initially, the Council was formed to implement the bibliographic standards adopted by the membership and to assure quality control of the contents of the data base. However, as the fiscal year 1975-1976 began, Lyons reported that "In actual fact, the Peer Council monitors and enforces adherence to standards for input cataloging. Day-to-day quality control, that is, error corrections and editing, is handled by the Cataloging and Quality Control Department of the Center's Library Systems Division. This Department tabulates errors, compiles statistics and analyzes problems for presentation to the Peer Council."[6]

The report elucidated the major concerns of the Peer Council. First, the reporting mechanism for duplicate records was inadequate. The Center had designed a form that allowed a library to list up to twenty sets of duplicates on one report. The Peer Council transferred each set of duplicates to three-by-five-inch cards. Approximately twelve thousand cards were completed. As of November, the Center had not taken action on the processing of duplicates. Second, the high level of errors in the data base was disturbing. Ohio libraries consistently committed most of the errors. Third, deferred records were a major concern. Many records remained to be processed and returned to the data base. Fourth, several years earlier the Implementation Committee (eventually dissolved and replaced by the Peer Council) had recommended the creation of a level "K" record to add a lower level of cataloging to the data base. Although it was not yet in use, the system contained illegally added level "K" records. Fifth, improper use of the system continued unchecked. The Council advocated forming a method for one library to report a misuse of another. Sixth, there was a need to revise the standards for input cataloging and to implement standards for inputting serials. The report raised two questions: "To whom does it recommend that action be taken?" and "How will sanctions be imposed?"[7] Although the Council continued to meet quarterly throughout the year, these questions remained unanswered.[8]

Concern for the integrity of the data base by out-of-state users was expressed by their representatives present at Board meetings, meetings of the network directors, and elsewhere. The problem of duplicates was discussed at the December 1975 Board of Trustees meeting. One of the main obstacles to its resolution was the lack of a definition of a duplicate record. The Board members and the regional representatives agreed that something had to be done. Several methods were investigated. The first and second methods placed the burden on the Center, recommending that the system be programmed automatically to reject duplicates and to inform terminal users whenever the possibility for duplication was evident. The third method imposed suggested that a library should pay the costs of eradicating a duplicate record it had input. By January, it was reported that the Center was working on a matching procedure to reduce the number of deferrals. Other retailoring procedures of the programs were planned. The Center staff was convinced that the problems were solvable by using program manipulation. The Center also began a dialogue with LC to ascertain its definition of duplicate record.

On May 17, 1976, a crucial decision was made by the network directors. They unanimously requested that OCLC load all of the deferred MARC records into the on-line data base with full knowledge that such a decision would result in the creation of a large number of duplicates. The main reason given for such action was economical. They felt that the networks and OCLC were losing out as a result of the deferrals. Despite the opinion of the Center's staff that the action would both increase response time and tax the disk storage system, the processing was to begin soon. As the year ended, the Center had installed an additional tape drive to process deferred records. The computer programs were similarly prepared for the processing. The procedure would begin when adequate machine time was available.

Relative to the topic of expansion were four changes that mirrored the evolutionary nature of OCLC. First, the catalog card production system was redesigned to facilitate the high volume of production expected in the future and to prepare for production of cards for the cataloging of maps, serials, audiovisual materials, etc.

Second, a common SAVE area was created to provide users with access to their SAVE files in the event that one computer in the dual system was not functioning. An added boost to the usefulness of the SAVE file was the decision in November to increase the retention period for records in the file from seven to ten days.

Third, on July 1, 1975, OCLC expanded the institution codes from two to three characters. A fourth character (previously a third) represented the holding library code. Whenever cataloging was performed for a branch library, a fourth symbol had to be added. As an example, The Ohio State University used four different codes, one for the institution (OS), one for its main library (OSU), and two for its branches (OSP, OS$). Complying with the change, it continued to use four codes, although each was expanded. The new symbols were OSU, OSUU, OSUP, and OSU$.

Fourth, stemming from a growing number of requests from members, the Board of Trustees authorized OCLC in September to begin scheduling the development and implementation of access of OCLC to non-OCLC data bases. The network supervisor program could bring information in specialized fields such as medicine, law, chemistry, and biology to the Center's already data-rich on-line catalog. The implications of that decision for the growth of library services were obvious. The first question to be answered was: What was the feasibility of such linkages? OCLC began to explore the possibilities of an experimental hookup to Lockheed's DIALOG data base.

As an indication of the times and of the direction in which OCLC was headed, another decision was made by the Board at about the same time. As of fall 1975, only two libraries were using the Center's off-line catalog card production service, and both intended to go on-line. Beginning October 1, 1975, the Center discontinued the off-line catalog card production system. The decision signaled a clean break with those early days of cataloging activity that launched OCLC's pioneering voyage.

Throughout the Center's history, grants and special projects served as catalysts for growth. The year 1975 was no exception. In the spring, OCLC received a grant from the W. K. Kellogg Foundation (based in Battle Creek, Michigan) for $339,319 to develop a network supervisor program (later to be called Gateway) to function in a minicomputer. The Foundation was willing to supply funds for terminals for up to 200 institutions outside of Michigan and up to 150 terminals for institutions within the state.

In a letter dated March 17, 1976, James E. Rush, director of Research and Development, wrote to George Hanson, program director for the W. K. Kellogg Foundation:

> I may say that all of us here at the Center feel strongly the importance of the proposed project. OCLC's ultimate goal is the support of vastly improved library services, and the ability to interface with other systems will rapidly advance us toward this goal. Without a network supervisor to enable OCLC to link with other services, all but the largest libraries will be prevented from access to these services.[9]

The grant also provided eight thousand dollars to each participating library over an eighteen-month period (July 1, 1976, through December 31, 1977) to assist in the initial costs and a part of the on-line activities. A letter dated May 12, 1976, from Kilgour to Hanson reiterated the main goal of the project:

> The Ohio College Library Center is most grateful to the W. K. Kellogg Foundation for its generous grant of $339,319 about which you informed us in your letter of 30 April 1976. Yesterday I told the Executive Committee of the Board of Trustees about your generosity, and they were delighted with the good news. The development of a mechanism for interfacing the OCLC on-line system with other on-line systems will enormously enhance the availability of information to library users.[10]

The closing statement reemphasized the importance of the grant: "...we are tremendously grateful to receive this grant, and I can assure you that there will be thousands of library users who will be equally grateful..."[11]

A second project was launched with the assistance of a grant. In June, the State Library of Ohio granted OCLC $550,000 to convert to machine-readable form the retrospective cataloging of seven major Ohio public libraries and the State Library of Ohio. The septet included the Akron-Summit County Public Library, the Public Library of Cincinnati and Hamilton County, Cleveland Public Library, the Public Library of Columbus and Franklin County, Dayton and Montgomery County Public Library, Toledo-Lucas County Public Library, and the Public Library of Youngstown and Mahoning County. Catalog entries would be microfilmed first and then fed into the data base via operators at OCLC terminals. The two-year project was envisioned to reduce the duplication of public library materials in Ohio and augment access to information on the network. The Center predicted that upon its completion approximately 1.5 million entries and location listings would be added to the on-line data base.

Efforts to convert a library's holdings to a machine-readable format continued during the year. A case in point was the COMCAT project, begun the year before. The August 6, 1975 *Newsletter* reported on the progress of the project after nearly six months of activity. "In less than six months fifteen Florida libraries have input 43,495 bibliographic records and added their holdings symbols to 251,129 records in OCLC's data base. To accomplish this amount of on-line activity the libraries are using 52 cathode ray tube terminals 15 hours a day in a massive retrospective conversion project called Florida COMCAT."[12]

On a much smaller scale the University of Toledo Law Library converted its monographic holdings. From October 1975 through April 1976, 11,395 titles were converted to a machine-readable format.[13]

Another on-going project was extension of borrowing privileges among the membership. During fiscal year 1974-1975 the membership agreed, in principle, to make borrowing in Ohio as extensive as possible. The idea of a universal borrowing card was suggested. At the November 7, 1975 membership meeting, Hugh C. Atkinson (The Ohio State Univesity), chairman of the Committee on Extended Borrowing, reported that although the theory of extended borrowing was accepted by the membership, its implementation had not been achieved. Atkinson made two suggestions. He recommended that the borrowing among the academic libraries be enlarged to include all of Ohio, and that implementation become the Center's responsibility. From that date forward OCLC was responsible for the project.

Public use of OCLC terminals was the highest level of access, for it would directly unite patron and library materials. In the fall, the twenty-three-week experiment begun the previous year to test the OCLC terminals in a public setting was completed. Funded by the State Library of Ohio, it gave a total of 51,293[14] patrons the chance to do their own searching on the terminals. In June 1976 a report, written by three OCLC staff members (W. Stuart Debenham, Jr., Kunji B. L. Rastogi, and Philip Schieber), was released under the title *OCLC Public Use Terminals: Report of Survey of Users of OCLC Public Use Terminals 1974-1975* (June 1976). The unique feature of the experiment (and the report) was that it focused on patrons of the libraries rather than library staffs. Before the experiment, use of the terminals began and ended with the library staff. The OCLC goal to increase accessibility of library materials was one step closer to fulfillment as a result of the test. The data collection process employed two methods: a survey of the library patrons who used the terminals and the computer tabulation of the messages received from the terminals. In sum, the project proved that the terminals could be useful to patrons if readily available.

Ohio libraries continued to support OCLC with their membership. Six new institutions were added during the twelve-month period: Chemical Abstracts Service, Columbus Public Library, Euclid Public Library, McKinley Memorial Library, Warren Public Library, and Wright State University's School of Medicine Health Science Library. The new total membership was eighty-four Ohio institutions. The list of out-of-state participants grew as five new consortia became involved.

Education

Education was an integral part of the OCLC activities. From the early days of the on-line system the Center had a program to keep users and the public informed of its developments. In an effort to facilitate the exchange of data between OCLC and member institutions, the Center created a new publication, the *Technical Bulletin*, issued apart from the *Newsletter*. The first issue appeared on February 25, 1976, and dealt with the new MARC film format. Subsequent issues were addressed to other topics relative to the technical procedures such as changes on the on-line display, catalog card reruns, searching tactics, and addenda to *On-Line Cataloging*. Although a distinct series, the *Technical Bulletin* was to be indexed in the *Newsletter*. Besides the *Newsletter* and the *Technical Bulletin*, network directors received a variety of memoranda beginning in February 1976. The manual, *Dial-Up Access to OCLC* (May 1976), was released in the spring. The document gave basic instructions for establishing dial-up communications with OCLC.

To supplement information received through the printed word, librarians met together in a series of programs. The year opened with a one-day seminar, "Training the Trainers," sponsored by the State University of New York (SUNY) and held on the SUNY-Albany campus on August 18.

Several months later the annual membership meeting on November 7 was preceded by a seminar entitled "On-Line Retrieval Services from Non-Monographic Data Bases." Carlos Cuadra, general manager of SDC Search Service, System Development Corporation, and Kilgour gave presentations. Cuadra discussed "The Impact of On-Line Retrieval Services." Kilgour's topic was "Expanding Public Services of Network Libraries."

In February 1976, Kent State University held a five-day workshop on the effective use of OCLC. Attendees included representatives from fifteen states plus Canada, Nigeria, and Australia. In May, a similar workshop was held. The five-day session covered a spectrum of topics including the operation of the system, the use of the MARC format, and the effective utilization of terminals.

The Center contributed to these educational endeavors by beginning a quarterly series of forums in Ohio. Approximately seventy persons met in Columbus on January 27, 1976, for the First Educational Forum for Ohio Libraries. Its success was followed by another on May 2, 1976. The OCLC staff and the membership provided in-house speakers for both occasions.

Establishment of a user services unit within OCLC had been in the works for some time. Due to a lack of funds, its activation was postponed until the following year.

The education of the public was accomplished through a number of channels. Personal visits to the Center by individuals and groups increased during the year. The new facility was an added incentive to visit. Viewers came from around the globe. In October, the Center hosted guests from the Soviet Union. The Library Systems Division gave over fifty demonstrations throughout the year. In December, owing to the volume of visitor traffic, the Center established in-house procedures to handle visitors.

With regard to the printed information about OCLC, three noteworthy articles were published in library journals. In the January 1976 issue of *Library Technology Reports*, a significant research study of OCLC's cataloging system appeared. Entitled "The Ohio College Library Center System: A Study of Factors Affecting the Adaptation of Libraries to On-Line Networks," it contained data of special interest to libraries contemplating participation in OCLC. During March, Arthur Plotnik, editor of *American Libraries*, spent two days at the Center to prepare for an article on OCLC for the journal's May issue. The article appeared under the title "OCLC For You—and Me?!: A Humanized Anatomy for Beginners." A second article was published in the same journal. Written by Joe A. Hewitt, it was titled "The Impact of OCLC: The Good and the Bad, as Recorded by Researcher Joe A. Hewitt in an Epic Journey to Every Charter Library of the On-Line System." The articles presented a sound introduction to OCLC. The literature published about OCLC was growing rapidly. Publications appeared in other library journals, bulletins, reports, studies, and segments of books.

Kilgour played a personal role in the education of the public, both in the United States and abroad. On October 9, he traveled to New York to attend an institute sponsored by the Information Science and Automation Division of ALA where he spoke on "Innovative Concepts of Bibliography in an Automated Catalog." In the spring, he journeyed for three weeks in Great Britain and on the continent. In England he met with British librarians and addressed the Standing Conference of National and University Libraries (SCONUL) Committee. In Dortmund, West Germany, he attended a conference and gave a presentation entitled "On-Line Library and Network Systems." In March 1976, he was chosen to present the Miles Conrad Memorial Lecture at the annual conference of the National Federation of Abstracting and Indexing Services (NFAIS) held in Columbus. His speech was titled "Comparative Development of Abstracting and Indexing and Monograph Cataloging." Kilgour also took part in "Project: Knowledge 2000," a bicentennial program to explore the nation's needs for knowledge over the next quarter of a century. The three-day forum was held in Washington, D.C. on June 28-30, 1976, and sponsored by the National Science Foundation, the American Revolution Bicentennial Administration, and Xerox Corporation.

The efforts among member libraries to exchange information with each other culminated in the formation of two new groups, The Health Science OCLC Users Group (HSOCLCUG) and the Music OCLC Users Group (MOUG). The founding of these two organizations was a distinct achievement in the field of library cooperation.

The groundwork for HSOCLCUG was laid in January 1973 when two health science libraries, the Cleveland Health Sciences Library and the Medical College of Ohio at Toledo, began to use the OCLC system for cataloging. At the start of 1974, the number of health science users grew to ten. By the summer of 1975, it grew to twenty. This special group had its own set of problems in adapting to on-line procedures. Verbal exchanges among librarians on how the system was or was not working led to expanded sharing sessions, the first of which took place at the Medical Library Association's (MLA) 74th annual meeting in Cleveland in June 1975. Besides sharing experiences in the use of OCLC and the National Library of Medicine (NLM)/ Medical Subject Headings (MeSH), the librarians explored the possibility of creating a special interest group within the organizational structure of MLA or OCLC. Feelings ran strong for the creation of the formal communications channel among themselves. At this time, the Cleveland Health Sciences Library, with the active support of its director, Robert G. Cheshier, offered to collect and disseminate information by creating a newsletter, similar to the OCLC *Newsletter*.

Discussion continued in July at the Colloqium on OCLC for Medical Libraries held in St. Louis. Approximately forty persons were present whose institutions were either members of OCLC or were contemplating membership. Three objectives were formulated. First, that the creation of a special interest group within MLA should be explored. Second, that a clearinghouse for OCLC information related to the medical library community be established. Third, that the medical libraries should be recognized as a unique group of users.

To facilitate implementation of the first objective a Task Force was founded.[15] Twenty-six persons signed a petition to MLA. The second goal was fulfilled by the Cleveland Health Sciences Library.[16] *START OF MESSAGE* was compiled and produced by the Catalog Department of the Cleveland Health Sciences Library. The final goal would be executed by the publication of the group's three objectives in the OCLC *Newsletter* and in the Medical Library Association's *MLA News*. In August 1975, the first issue of *START OF MESSAGE* was published. Its first page stated:

(HOME POSITION) The Cleveland Health Sciences Library (CHSL) has offered to serve as a clearinghouse for news and developments about OCLC and its health science library members. This first issue summarizes pertinent events from the program of the 74th annual meeting of the Medical Library Association held in Cleveland May 31 - June 5, 1975. It includes news of later developments in OCLC activities as well as helpful suggestions and provocative questions. Also included is a list of the institutions and persons to whom this issue has been sent. Additional names and addresses of interested parties are welcome and should be sent to CHSL. Please return the tear sheet so we can keep accurate records for mailing and as a basis for statistics.

We propose to issue this newsletter as often as required until some regular pattern becomes clear. Suggestions for format, news items, proposals for OCLC improvement, member training, etc., are more than welcome. They are *needed* to make this a broad-based medium for the dissemination of information to all types of OCLC health science libraries, from the one (so far) hospital library to the largest university affiliated or independent health science library.

To start our messages, we shall call this *Start Of Message*, which provides a neat acronym both appropriate and familiar to users of OCLC terminals. (Henry Segal, Asst. Catalog Librarian, CHSL, made the suggestion.) In the same vein, we are using some OCLC terms to identify various parts of this issue.

We hope you find this publication informative and useful and that you will share your honest opinions about it and its aims. Your 'input' is 'mandatory' in all 'fields' and 'subfields' for which we have 'tags.'[17]

October 7, 1975, marked the birth date for HSOCLCUG. Fifteen librarians from health science libraries[18] in ten states met in Chicago to discuss the fashioning of an organization of health science OCLC users. This task force appointed a five-member steering committee to approach OCLC for recognition of HSOCLCUG.[19] Other appointed committees dealt with membership and publicity, continuing education, input standards, liaison with NLM, and with the Regional Medical Library (RML) program. A committee was also appointed to lay plans for a general membership meeting at the June 1976 conference of MLA. The committees met in Cleveland in January 1976 to share ideas and direct the future of the organization. Eighteen librarians from ten states attended and made plans for a program at the MLA 1976 conference. The October 1975 issue of *MLA News* included the organization's first news release. The second issue of *START OF MESSAGE* (December 1975) succinctly stated the group's objectives: "A sound structure will enable the HSOCLCUG to carry on toward its objectives of information exchange, progress toward better use of OCLC, and interrelationships with OCLC, NLM, RML and MLA, as well as to share information with potential health science users of OCLC."[20]

In the spring, *START OF MESSAGE* made a last call for members. The bylaws were prepared, mailed to the membership, and unanimously adopted in May. The first business meeting of HSOCLCUG was held on June 15, 1976, in Minneapolis at the MLA annual conference. The Task Force, chaired by Paul Olson, presented a roster of officers to the membership for approbation. The new unanimously elected officers were Patti Armes, chairperson; Susan Hill, vice-chairperson; and Janet Mixter, secretary-treasurer.

HSOCLCUG also presented a program that included the status of NLM's records in the OCLC data base and recent developments at the Center relating to the health science libraries. Moreover, future plans were also on the agenda. HSOCLCUG also offered a new continuing education course, "OCLC Utilization in Health Science Libraries," to instruct librarians with no past OCLC experience.

The founding of HSOCLCUG, an independent organization, was a result of the concerted efforts of a devoted group of librarians who believed in the need to create a special group of OCLC users. By June 1976, the membership included twenty-six active members (institutions who had contracted for

OCLC services), eleven associate members (institutions contemplating use of OCLC), and twenty-three individual members (individuals wanting to be kept informed, affiliated, or not affiliated with an active or associate institution).

MOUG pursued a different course from HSOCLCUG. The Music Library Association's (MLA) Automation Committee and the MARC Development Office at LC had worked earlier on the MARC music format, which would enable music libraries to convert hard copy cataloging records into machine-readable format for use in an on-line system such as OCLC. In October 1975, MLA proposed to OCLC the establishment of a joint working committee appointed by OCLC and the MLA Board. The committee would act as a permanent advisory body to OCLC. One member of the committee would transmit news of the committee via the *Music Cataloging Bulletin* and the OCLC *Newsletter*. OCLC rejected the idea in favor of a task force created by MLA to formulate the MARC music format. Plans included the dissolution of the task force once the format was devised.

The OCLC Task Force for the Cataloging of Music and Sound Recordings met for the first time in Columbus on February 10, 1976.[21] The representation gave Ohio librarians a strong voice. With Karl Van Ausdal as the group's appointed coordinator, the Task Force made recommendations to the OCLC Advisory Committee on Cataloging, which would then make all the final decisions. The Advisory Committee was composed of one representative from each Ohio institution and one representative from each network. A number of topics were discussed including the design of the terminal work form for inputting scores and recordings, the hardships encountered in searching for bibliographic data, and the need for quality control. The Task Force held its second meeting in Columbus on April 12 to continue discussions. Lenore Maruyama from MARC Development Office (MDO) was present to answer questions on the MARC music format.

In conclusion, although MOUG and HSOCLCUG were interested in different subject matters, and although they developed independently of each other, they both were dedicated to a common cause: to facilitate use of the OCLC system for special groups of users.

Equipment

A capstone to the year's events was implementation of a new multiple computer architecture for the OCLC system. During fiscal year 1975-1976, plans for increased computer power were realized with the operation of the new dual Sigma 9 computer system. It was a logical step toward the projected quadruple processor system fed by seven minicomputers.

OCLC's new architecture was unique. Unlike its predecessors, the system's computers operated parallel to each other rather than receiving orders from a master computer. Each of the four computers held equal status in the configuration and shared a common core memory. If one computer failed, service would continue. Moreover, the computers were programmed so that each knew what the others were doing. The Center projected that twenty-eight hundred terminals could run on-line when all four computers were in use, i.e., seven hundred terminals per computer. This figure was based on current activities.

The Sigmas 903 and 904 arrived during the year. Installation of the two large Sigma 9s operating in tandem was a bold and new experience. It was a concept that would enable OCLC to build its on-line system cost-effectively in stages as additional computing power was needed. Sigma 901 would be linked to the Sigma 902, then the 903 would be added, and finally the 904 would be connected as the final link that formed the quadruplet.

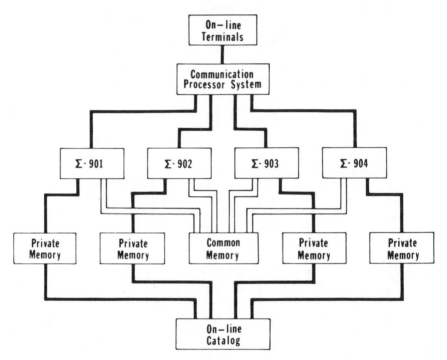

DIAGRAM D-1. OCLC Computer System Architecture[22]

By the end of December 1975, the dual processor was intact and operational. Terminal users were warned to expect the unexpected as the Center fine-tuned the system to create an amiable coexistence for the new twins.

In December 1975, the Sigma 903 arrived at the new facility on 1125 Kinnear Road. Subsequently, it was brought up for operation. As the year ended, the Sigma 904 had arrived, and preparations were being made to test it at the start of the next year. The Computer Facilities Division then began to develop an interim message switch between the minicomputers and the Sigma 9s to allow the system to use one instead of two machines when system activity ebbed, for example, on Saturdays.

The system's power was further bolstered by the purchase of a Sigma 7. On November 7, 1975, the Board of Trustees unanimously approved a proposal presented by the executive director to upgrade the Sigma 5 to a Sigma 7. The estimated cost of the new computer was seventy-five thousand dollars. The new piece of equipment would enhance the system by augmenting the Center's computer strength. By March, the Sigma 7 was being installed, and a month later it was operating. The new Sigma could handle a variety of on-line functions. It would be especially useful for the Center's internal data processing chores. It would also be used to produce catalog cards, accessions lists, and other related products. At night the Sigma 5 would also be used for production activities. During the day, it would assist with in-house data processing jobs.

OCLC in 1975-1976 began to test a new prototype model terminal, the OCLC Model 105, created by Beehive Medical Electronics, Inc. It was the Center's third model terminal, more powerful than its forebearers yet it cost no more than the Model 100 produced by the same company.

> The new terminal has a better packaging arrangement of internal parts; the skin is now cast plastic; it has a bonded, non-glare face plate; and the terminal should be more reliable, especially since it is more efficiently cooled. Beehive is also searching for another power supply source, and those recommended to date are being extensively analyzed by OCLC engineers.[23]

Maintenance of the Model 100 terminals was an ongoing concern. There was a shortage of spare parts, and consequently the average number of days to repair a terminal in the field was five. To remedy the situation fifty thousand dollars worth of spare parts were ordered from Beehive Medical Electronics and Syntonic Technologies, Inc. In an effort to curb rising costs for terminal service and maintenance, OCLC tried to get users to take better care of their terminals. A list of situations resulting from improper care of the terminal were commonly referred to by the staff as the "paper clips and potato chip crumbs" problems. Staples, rubber bands, and other foreign objects were found inside keyboards; control switches were improperly set; data cables were incorrectly attached to a power source, etc. Sometimes a terminal problem was reported and then subsequently resolved by the library without canceling the service call. These activities were driving up the cost of the terminal maintenance.

A new method for reporting malfunctions of terminals was begun during the year. Each terminal was assigned a unique identification number that was to be used to report terminal problems. It enabled the Center to know the telephone line to which the terminal was connected, as well as the location of the terminal by institution and in relation to the modem and other terminals, if it was part of a chain. The new procedure represented a diagnostic breakthrough for the Center. It would not only save staff time but would also accelerate repair.

The last pieces of equipment to be mentioned here are two IBM 2927 Print Stations, new printers for catalog card production. Before their arrival the Center printed catalog cards on an IBM Printer 1403 N1. Together, the stations provided enough power to run four printers, each printing at the rate of six hundred lines per minute. By year's end, three print stations had been bought. When card production exceeded the capacity of the three, a fourth would be purchased. As mentioned, the Sigma 7 participated in the production activities by executing programs to print catalog cards. The IBM 1403 N1 was used to print the tapes from the Sigma 7. The tapes were mounted on the Print Stations, which printed on the IBM 1403 N1. The new catalog card printing equipment improved efficiency, enabling the Center to keep down the cost of the cards.

With the increase in computational power and investment of funds in hardware the Center recognized the need for more security of the system. The new facility prompted the Center to invite a security consultant to Columbus. The consultant's report isolated three areas needing attention. First, the Center lacked a backup system in the event that the primary data base and the other vital areas of the system were destroyed. Second, there was a need for stricter control over the daily operations at the Center. The consultant recommended a system using badges and card-keys for employees. Third, he cited the need for an internal auditing team to monitor the security of all OCLC equipment. Other suggestions included the replacement of gas furnaces with electric ones for optimal heating and the construction of a concrete barrier wall to isolate the computer room. This concern was carried one step further with establishment of an in-house security committee.

Finances

As in the previous year, the Center's lack of operating capital and the inflationary costs of maintaining operations were issues in preparing the 1976-1977 budget. The Center's self-invoked moratorium on hiring needed personnel was the major factor that reduced expenses. At the same time, however, it increased pressures on the current staff. On December 10 the moratorium was lifted. The Center would begin interviewing to fill over thirty positions provided in the 1975-1976 budget. The need for personnel was further evidenced by the fact that during the preceding year, personnel expenses accounted for 34 percent of the total budget while in 1975-1976 it amounted to only 19 percent. The Board of Trustees was kept abreast of the financial picture through reports of the standing Financial Committee and those presented by Vincent. Financial statements were issued at the meetings that included monthly financial comparisons with the previous year. A portion of the report for the third quarter of the year, ending March 31, 1976, described the financial odyssey of the Center:

> The Comparative Balance Sheet comparing 31 March this year with the same date last year indicates the extent of the general improvements in the Center's financial condition. During the last twelve months, the Center added more than $4,800,000 in fixed assets to meet the demand for services. These additions increased the percent of fixed assets to total assets by only 8% from 66% at 31 March 1975 to 74% on the same date this year. A more dramatic change, however, has occurred in the liabilities and fund balance section. Current liabilities, as a percent of total liabilities and fund balance, has decreased from 59% to 33%, a drop of 26%. The 59% at 31 March last year is a reminder of the cash flow problem the Center had at that time. Normally, current liabilities classify those obligations that will be due in one year or less. Last year, because of the cash flow problems, we were delaying payables and asking networks for early advance payment to see us through until the regular advance payments were received. This wasn't enough, as

you will recall, because we had to borrow $300,000 short-term working capital from the bank. The Center has been able to repay this bank loan and get its accounts payable current and still maintain a reasonable cash flow balance. It probably will be necessary to borrow $200,000 to $300,000 from the bank in late May or June, or let accounts payable slip some, but we do not anticipate any major problems in cash flow comparable to last year.[24]

At the December 1975 Board meeting a resolution was passed authorizing the director of Administration and Finance or the Comptroller of the corporation to make short-term investments of funds not needed for current use. In the first part of the year, the executive director visited a number of foundations in search of financial support. These attempts were not fruitful. They reinforced the belief that OCLC needed to budget carefully and rely on revenues from operations to finance current operations rather than on the whims of external funding agencies. As it turned out, the Center closed its books on June 30, 1976, with a two hundred thousand loan to cover its cash shortage.

The 1976-1977 budget aimed at resolving the problems of undercapitalization and inflation. The total figure, as approved by the Board of Trustees, was $15,074,000, based on an equal amount of income and a projected first-time use of 6,023,000 (as opposed to 4,145,000 the previous year). Nearly one-half of the revenue would come from the first-time uses for cataloging. The personnel figure was increased by eighty new positions. A comparison of the 1975-1976 budget with the 1976-1977 budget in table T-14, page 174, illustrates the effects of rapid growth. The 42 percent increase in the total budget figure for 1976-1977 is staggering.

To counteract inflation several changes were made in the budget. In September 1975 the Board of Trustees voted to increase the first-time-use charge by ten cents for the coming year to create working capital. At the October 21, 1975 Board meeting, the chairman of the Finance Committee, Richard J. Owen, presented three proposals to fight inflation. OCLC had failed to keep astride with the economy by 2.2 percent. In 1974-1975 the nation's economic indicators reported a 15.5 percent increase in prices. OCLC had increased its charges only 13.3 percent for 1975-1976. The Board adopted the following resolution:

> Be it and it is hereby resolved that OCLC increase its basic first-time-use charge for 1976/77 by 8.7 per cent (2.2 + 6.5 = 8.7) in addition to the 10 cent increase to earn working capital and Be it further resolved, that in future years the increase, or decrease, in OCLC charges be determined in October for the subsequent fiscal year and that the determination take into account the difference between the originally estimated rate of inflation for the previous year and the actual rate plus the estimated rate for the current year.[26]

The increase in the basic first-time-use charge represented a concrete step toward capitalization of the corporation. Owen also presented a second

TABLE T-14
Budget Plan Comparison (1975/76 and 1976/77)[25]

	1975/76 Budget Plan		1976/77 Budget Plan	
Projected Revenue				
System Usage	$ 4,175,000	39.4%	$ 6,944,000	46.1%
Terminals	3,201,000	30.2	2,503,000	16.6
Telephone Income	1,745,000	16.4	2,405,000	16.0
Catalog Card Income	1,102,000	10.4	2,274,000	15.0
Grant Income	265,000	2.5	619,000	4.1
Other Income	120,000	1.1	329,000	2.2
TOTAL	$10,608,000	100.0%	$15,074,000	100.0%
Expenses to Generate Projected Revenue				
Personnel	$ 2,028,000	19.2%	$ 3,939,000	26.1%
General Operating Expenses	783,000	7.4	1,393,000	9.2
Computer and Support Equipment Maintenance	238,000	2.2	229,000	1.5
Data Processing Supplies and Expense	480,000	4.5	840,000	5.6
Data Communications and Tymnet	1,755,000	16.5	2,546,000	16.9
Terminal Costs	2,433,000	22.9	1,953,000	13.0
Physical Facilities Debt Service and Rental	235,000	2.2	272,000	1.8
Capital Equipment Debt Service and Rental	1,233,400	11.7	1,246,000	8.2
Capital Equipment - New	322,600	3.0	1,366,000	9.1
Capitalization	1,100,000	10.4	1,290,000	8.6
TOTAL	$10,608,000	100.0%	$15,074,000	100.0%

resolution to establish a 22.0 percent (15.5 + 6.5 = 22.0 percent) increase in all OCLC charges for 1976-1977, except for search-key searches on public use terminals, serials check-in, and telecommunication line charges set by the telephone company. The search-key searches and the serials check-in procedures were new for the Center and very experimental. The proposed prices would go into effect on July 1, 1976. Charges were divided into five categories: catalog cards, terminals, processing of catalog profile and pack definition table, off-line services, and access to the system through Tymnet. Terminal charges included the purchase price of the OCLC Model 100 and the terminal installation costs. Off-line services referred to accession lists and the purchase of magnetic tapes in the MARC II format. The Tymnet charges were based on logging-in costs and charges per connect hour.

The third resolution adopted by the Board advocated an increase of 22 percent for 1976-1977 in the terminal-cost-charge component of the inclusive first-time-use charge. It also suggested an increase of 6.5 percent for 1976-1977 in the terminal-maintenance-charge component of the inclusive first-time-use charge.

The price increases alone could not generate quick working capital. However, they would be a hedge against inflation. The Board working with the Center's management made these changes in the belief that the cataloging system alone should not be responsible for creating the needed capital.

The Finance Committee also recommended that OCLC sell its property on Kenny Road since it would not meet the future needs of OCLC. The six acres of land were being financed, and the property was no longer large enough to house the growing center. The Board voted to sell the property on the understanding that the Center would net not less than $425,000. (The Center paid $430,650 for the property.)

As previously stated, OCLC's Board approved a budget of $15,074,000 for the coming year. An unexpected trimming of the first-time-use charges was announced in March, reducing the estimated charges set by the Board on October 21. This was done at the request of Ohio members who wanted advance notice. The new lower rates were, of course, welcome. The first-time-use charges for Ohio member libraries dropped from an estimated $2.06 to $1.91. The *Newsletter* for April 2, 1976, contained a table summarizing the current charges, the estimated charges established on October 21, and the actual ones approved on March 16 and effective July 1, 1976. In most instances, the estimated charges were higher than those to be enforced on July 1. The categories were basically the same as those included in the October estimates.

The decrease in OCLC charges was counterbalanced by a decision of AT & T to increase its charges for interstate private line services by 3 percent. The new rates would go into effect on March 1, 1976. Unfortunately, the Center had no control over those charges.

In July 1975 OCLC announced that the property at 1125 Kinnear Road had been acquired and the necessary remodeling was about to begin. The land and buildings were bought for $1,300,000. Improvements and construction costs were estimated at $1,000,000. On January 28, 1976, the loan agreement was closed with Nationwide Insurance Company. The Center took out a $1,800,000 loan on the new facility to be repaid in twenty-five years. The remaining $500,000 was raised by the budget alterations during the year, namely, the increase in the first-time-use charges and cutbacks in expenses.

Organization

A large percentage of the reorganization of OCLC was funneled through the Board of Trustees. In November 1975, the Board elected new members along with a fresh slate of officers.[27] Its new officers were H. Paul Schrank, Jr. (University of Akron), chairman and president; Thompson M. Little (Ohio University), vice-chairman; Richard J. Owen (Youngstown State University), treasurer; and L. Ronald Frommeyer (Wright State University), secretary.

In the spring the Board announced the promotion of Thompson M. Little. Effective September 7, 1976, Little would assume the position of associate executive director of OCLC. He had served on the Board since 1973, acting as its secretary from November 1973 to November 1975. A second new position was approved. Donald Trotier would become the Center's first personnel manager in June 1976. The growth of the corporation and the subsequent increase in the staff necessitated the post.

At its July 1975 meeting, the Board announced that it would reorganize by appointing three new standing committees. The Personnel Committee was to be headed by James V. Jones (Case Western Reserve University). L. Ronald Frommeyer was appointed chairman of the Physical Facilities Committee. The new Network Relations Committee was to be chaired by Thompson M. Little. The chairman and each member of the committees were appointed by the chairman of the Board, and had to be on the Board before the appointment.

The Board was involved in another organizational move. During the past year, the Board unanimously voted to amend the Code of Regulations, Article II, Section 2. It received approval by the membership at its ninth annual meeting in November 1975.

The Board voted to reorganize OCLC not only internally but also externally. Services to the regional networks were improved in May 1975 with the establishment of support centers for regions where no OCLC network affiliations existed. During 1974-1975 a temporary arrangement was in operation in California. It was replaced in 1975-1976 by the first users' support center, the Western Service Center (WSC) in Claremont, California, which provided support services to independent participants in California, Washington, Oregon, and Nevada. The Service Center trained personnel, educated users, and prepared profiles for libraries. Patrick Barkey, director of libraries of the Claremont Colleges, who served the previous year as a temporary coordinator, became the first director of WSC. Myra White was chosen the coordinator librarian.

A major organizational change was in the wind: extension of the membership to other states. During the year, Kilgour explored the means for studying the advisability of extending membership to libraries outside of Ohio. The exploration was the result of a resolution passed by the Board on December 16, 1975. It was preceded by a resolution in November from the membership charging the Board to study the pros and cons of an extended membership and to report to the members at the next annual meeting of the representatives. By June, Kilgour stated he had met with a number of key persons including Robert Wedgeworth (executive director of ALA), Daniel J. Boorstin (librarian of Congress), Frederick H. Burkhardt (of NCLIS), and Fred Cole (president of CLR). The consensus was that OCLC should work with a management consultant to prepare a proposal for review by an advisory group. A national networking model would then be presented to the Board for approval, and finally to the membership. The real issue was the future governance of OCLC.

In June, the executive director presented a slate of seventeen prominent persons who would constitute an advisory council. It would recommend to the Board a plan to extend the membership and to reorganize the Center. The following thirteen persons who agreed to serve represent a diversity of fields from librarianship to management.

Thomas H. Anderson, partner, The Andersons

Frederick H. Burkhardt, chairman, NCLIS

William Chait, director, The Dayton and Montgomery County Public Library

Richard DeGennaro, director of libraries, University of Pennsylvania

Dan M. Lacy, senior vice-president, McGraw-Hill, Inc.

Barbara Evans Markuson, executive director, INCOLSA

Charles B. Maurer, director of libraries, Denison University

Roderick G. Swartz, state librarian, Washington State Library and director of the Washington Library Network (WLN)

R. L. Wagner, executive director, Data and Mobile Communications Division, Bell Laboratories

David C. Weber, director, Stanford University Libraries

Robert Wedgeworth, executive director, ALA

William J. Welsh, deputy librarian of Congress, LC

Ronald L. Wigington, director of research & development, Chemical Abstracts Service

The Advisory Council held its first meeting on July 9, 1976.

As OCLC evolved it collected a variety of relevant documents that could be termed an in-house library. The collection began in 1967 when Kilgour started shelving in his office articles and studies related to the development of OCLC. In the spring of 1973 when the Center's offices were moved to 1550 West Henderson Road, the library had a room of its own. Several futile attempts were made to organize and catalog the materials.

The minutes of the meeting of the directors of the divisions on July 16, 1975, contained one of the first recorded expressions of intent to create a full-fledged library:

> Mr. Kilgour said that the purpose of a 'corporate' library was to allow employees a place in which to read current publications and materials in their fields. He expressed concern that OCLC staff do not have the opportunity to go into a company library and sit down and read current literature related to their role in the

company. Mr. Kilgour agreed that the Division could maintain
their collections of documents and technical materials, but he
advocated placing OCLC's journal collection in one location
accessible by all employees.[28]

Although, no action was taken to establish the library, the seed for its germination was planted.

The remodeling of the four buildings on the six-acre tract of land at 1125 Kinnear Road began on July 7, 1975. By September, the Research and Development Division and the Administrative and Finance Division had relocated into the new quarters. As of October 1, 1975, the majority of the Center staff had made the shift.

ON-LINE SYSTEMS

Activation of the on-line serials control system continued to experience delays. The start-up date was revised for the latter part of 1976, when serials catalog card production would begin. The automatic check-in module would follow.

Case Western Reserve University was undertaking a project of interest to members contemplating involvement in the serials control system. For twenty-five dollars, it was offering libraries a copy of its serials printout. The list of current serials titles included the OCLC control number for about five thousand serial records to which were affixed the holding symbols for member institutions. It offered help to a library searching for or inputting an obscure title for the first time. The willingness of Case Western Reserve University to share its serials information with other libraries was an example of cooperation that had blessed OCLC.

In December, training sessions on the check-in component were held for members. The same month, the *Serials Control Subsystem: Users Manual* (December 1975) was circulated. In February 1976, there were educational sessions for representatives of the regional networks. These initial educational efforts on the part of OCLC were supplemented in the spring by the publishing of *Serials Cataloging for the Ohio College Library Center System: A Manual* (revised April 1976).[29] Once again libraries, with alacrity, brilliantly accomplished the Center's underlying theme of cooperation.

Closely tied to development of serials control was the CONSER project. By year's end, OCLC had added 80,000 records to the system from MULS, another 19,000 from LC's MARC serials records and Canadian MARC serials records, and still more from the PRLC records. The total contents of the serials file was approximately 140,000 records. CONSER would provide OCLC participants with an instant data base of value in the soon-to-be activated serials control system. This new influx of data kindled interest in the interlibrary lending of serials. However, more detailed information on specific holdings was needed before the system could actively serve the participants in this function. The next step for OCLC, after having loaded the serials records, was to complete the computer programming, thus enabling it to supply LC with machine-readable tapes of serial records.

This activity centering around serials control gained a deeper significance in the fall, when James E. Rush, director of research & development, met, in

Europe, with representatives from the International Serials Data System to discuss linking international centers via OCLC's on-line network. He believed that one day through modern technology OCLC and Great Britain would be joined for the international exchange of information. At the time the idea seemed farfetched.

Major support for the development of a technical processing subsystem came from a $124,250 two-year grant from CLR. Funds were to be divided between design of on-line authority files, subject search capability, and the technical processing system. Although preliminary design work was carried on prior to 1975-1976, the grant monies accelerated progress on the project. Grant funds were channeled into development of the preorder search and the order generation components. This first phase of the system provided each library with a separate on-line order file and simultaneously allowed cooperation among participants through sharing of bibliographic information. A portion of the grant provided funds for an acquisitions survey of OCLC participants to gather data on current policies, procedures, and practices in library acquisitions.

The Advisory Committee on Technical Processing continued to meet with OCLC staff to refine the system design for users. Its input would influence the final shape of the system. It was anticipated that by June 1976 some functions would be demonstrated in-house. Center management began pricing the technical processing system. The issue was still under study at the close of the year.

The last system under development was the Interlibrary Loan (ILL) Communications. Work on its development began with a grant of $108,575 from OE the previous year. Design work was done with the aid of the Advisory Committee on ILL, which mapped out the major blueprint and its finer details.

To prepare for the implementing and testing of ILL the Advisory Committee created a draft of a users' manual in February 1977. The Center had also readied an in-house test data base in which loan requests records could be created, searched, processed, and eradicated on a simulated network. The first phase of the system was to be tested in twenty-five libraries

OUT-OF-STATE COOPERATIVE ACTIVITIES AND NETWORKING

Although the Ohio members continued to govern OCLC, they were outnumbered one to ten by out-of-state participants. This majority was composed of libraries outside of the state that contracted for services usually through a network or individually in the absence of one. The independent institutions were a very small percentage of the total usership. The Center's out-of-state network grew rapidly as the following five cooperatives became actively involved in 1975-1976: Bibliographical Center for Research (BCR), Consortium of Universities of the Washington Metropolitan Area (CAPCON), Indiana Cooperative Library Services Authority (INCOLSA), Michigan Library Consortium (MLC), and the Wisconsin Library Consortium (WLC).[30] Incidentally, as of October 21, 1975, review of contracts and negotiations was placed in the hands of the Executive Committee of the Board of Trustees.

The out-of-state cooperative activities embraced yet another group. Following eighteen months of successful experimentation, FLC signed a new contract with OCLC on July 1, 1975, which ran through June 30, 1976. Its provisions were basically an extension of the current activities with one major difference. FLC became a formal participant in OCLC as it officially closed the experimental phase of the relationship. The final agreement was similar to those drawn up with other networks.

At the February 25, 1976 meeting of the Steering Committee, it was decided that FLECC needed to change its name since the experimental project had ended. The demise of FLECC led to the birth of the Federal Library and Information Network (FEDLINK). The FEDLINK Executive Advisory Committee was created to establish policies, advise the membership, and evaluate its involvement in cooperative cataloging. As did FLECC, FEDLINK would operate daily from the FLC office located at LC. In June 1976, the OCLC contract was renegotiated for another year.

Compared to computer-based networking activity in the United States, Europe was an unexplored wilderness. Throughout the year, Kilgour continued his dialogue with a number of European representatives.

In the history of OCLC, the year 1975-1976 was exciting. New performance records were set. On January 28, 1976, a record was established when over thirty thousand books were cataloged on the system. The second millionth record was added to the on-line union catalog on February 18, 1976, by the Boston University School of Theology library. The accelerated growth of OCLC was evidenced by the fact that it took three years to reach the first million records and only seventeen months to reach the second million. Card production in excess of one million cards per week[31] set a new record during the year. The August 26, 1975 issue of the *Newsletter* reported the phenomenal results of this growth.

> The growth of the OCLC network system has led, of course, to unparalleled system activity. Academic, public and special libraries now use OCLC's on-line system to catalog more than 15,000 books a day. The Center is producing catalog cards tailored for individual library catalogs at a rate of over 125,000 cards a day. The OCLC data base contains more than 1.5 million bibliographic records and grows at a rate of over 3,000 records a day. The on-line union catalog daily increases in size and utility and now provides more than 4.5 million location listings.[32]

The move to the new facility signaled the beginning of a new phase in the Center's history. Moreover, a number of innovative projects were in progress. James V. Jones, director of libraries at Case Western Reserve University, who had served as chairman and president of the Board of Trustees from November 10, 1972, to November 7, 1975, felicitously summarized the year. At the November 7 membership meeting he stated that OCLC's greatest period of growth and difficulties was not behind it and that "the future is exciting to behold."[33]

As in the life of any living organism, so it was in the life of OCLC, that the joy of growth was mixed with the pain of growth. Now the Center, the world's first large-scale cooperative library system, was coming to maturity.

NOTES

1. Ohio College Library Center, *Newsletter*, 21 November 1975, p. 2.

2. Ohio College Library Center, *Newsletter*, 28 November 1975, p. 4.

3. Ibid., p. [1].

4. Ohio College Library Center, *Newsletter*, 14 January 1976, p. 4.

5. Ohio College Library Center, "Minutes of the Directors of the Divisions Meeting" (Columbus: Ohio College Library Center, 10 March 1976), p. 5.

6. Ohio College Library Center Peer Council, "Report of the Peer Council" (Columbus: Ohio College Library Center, 7 November 1975), p. [1].

7. Ibid., p. [3].

8. At the November 1975 annual meeting of the membership, Melville Spence (Bowling Green State University) and Hyman W. Kritzer (Kent State University) were elected to the Peer Council.

9. Letter from James E. Rush to George Hanson, 17 March 1976.

10. Letter from Federick G. Kilgour to George Hanson, 12 May 1976.

11. Ibid.

12. Ohio College Library Center, *Newsletter*, 6 August 1975, p. 3.

13. Ohio College Library Center, *Newsletter*, 28 May 1976, p. 2.

14. W. Stuart Debenham, Jr., Kunj Rastogi, and Philip Schieber, *OCLC Public Use Terminals: Report of Survey of Users of OCLC Public Use Terminals 1974-1975* (Columbus: Ohio College Library Center, June 1976), p. 12.

15. Task Force members were Patti Armes (University of Texas Health Science Center Library at Dallas), Doris Bolef (East Tennessee State University College of Medicine), James Falasco (University of Illinois Medical Center), Paul Olson (Midwest Health Science Library Network), and Olyn Ruxin (Cleveland Health Sciences Library).

16. Olyn Ruxin, head catalog librarian, volunteered to be the first editor of the group's newsletter, *START OF MESSAGE.*

17. The Health Science OCLC Users Group, *START OF MESSAGE*, August 1975, p. [1].

18. These librarians were Patti Armes (University of Texas Health Science Center at Dallas), David Bishop (Midcontinental Regional Medical Library/University of Nebraska Medical Center), Doris Bolef (East Tennessee State University College of Medicine), Linda Baum (National Library of Medicine), Ted Caron (Mayo Clinic Library), James Falasco (University of Illinois at the Medical Center), Susan Hill (Cleveland Health Sciences Library), Lillian Kozuma (National Library of Medicine), Charles Lewis (Virginia Commonwealth University-Medical College of Virginia), Jean Miller (Medical Library Center of New York), Janet Mixter (Loyola University Medical Center Library), Paul Olson (Midwest Health Science Library Network), Olyn Ruxin (Cleveland Health Sciences Library), Sarah Salley (Medical College of Ohio at Toledo), and Deborah Yedlin (Washington University School of Medicine Library).

19. The steering committee members were Paul Olson (chairman), Patti Armes, Doris Bolef, Susan Hill, and Olyn Ruxin.

20. The Health Science OCLC Users Group, *START OF MESSAGE*, December 1975, p. [1].

21. The MLA-appointed members included Olga Buth (The Ohio State University), Barbara Denison (Cleveland Public Library), David Knapp (Oberlin Conservatory of Music), Mary Lou Little (Harvard University), Myrtle Nim (Carnegie-Mellon University), Donald Robbins (Cornell University), William Shurk (Bowling Green State University), Karl Van Ausdal (State University of New York at Purchase), and Margaret Wilson (University of Cincinnati). Also appointed, although not present at the meeting, were Fred Bindman and Lenore Maruyama (both from LC), Larry Dixson (University of North Carolina), Donald Siebert (Syracuse University), and David Urbanski (Lorain Public Library).

22. Ohio College Library Center, *Annual Report 1975/1976* (Columbus: Ohio College Library Center, 1976), p. 8.

23. Ohio College Library Center, "Minutes of the Board of Trustees Meeting" (Columbus: Ohio College Library Center, 15 June 1976), p. 2.

24. Ohio College Library Center, "Financial Report—Third Quarter Ended 31 March 1976" (Columbus: Ohio College Library Center, undated), p. [1].

25. Ohio College Library Center, "OCLC Budget Plan Fiscal Year 1976/77" (Columbus: Ohio College Library Center, 1976), p. 2.

26. Ohio College Library Center, "Minutes of the Board of Trustees Meeting" (Columbus: Ohio College Library Center, 21 October 1975), p. 3.

27. See appendix 1, Exhibit D, for a complete list of the Board of Trustees members.

28. Ohio College Library Center, "Minutes of the Directors of the Divisions Meeting" (Columbus: Ohio College Library Center, 16 July 1975), p. 2.

29. Written by Barbara Gates and published by the AMIGOS Bibliographic Council, the *Manual* was highly recommended by OCLC as an official document on serials cataloging until such time as a serials supplement to *On-Line Cataloging* would be available.

30. See appendix 1, Exhibit J, for a list of the members of each consortium.

31. Barbara E. Markuson, "The Ohio College Library Center: A Study of Factors Affecting the Adaptation of Libraries to On-Line Networks," *Library Technology Reports* 12 [1] (January 1976): 22.

32. Ohio College Library Center, *Newsletter*, 26 August 1975, p. [1].

33. Ohio College Library Center, "Minutes of the Members Meeting" (Columbus: Ohio College Library Center, 7 November 1975), p. 4.

10

REACHING FOR THE STARS 1976-1977

The year 1976-1977 culminates the history of OCLC's first decade. It leaves the Center's activities in various stages of development. Progress on the OCLC/Battelle Memorial Institute's BASIS system would continue as would the work on the network supervisor program. The Retrospective OCLC-MARC Project was gaining momentum, and the Ohio Public Library RECON Project still had one more year to go. An exciting new dimension of the OCLC hardware was unveiled as plans were laid for an OCLC II system to run on Sigmas 905 and 906. A new building was under consideration. The widespread use of direct dial-up access to OCLC using telephone lines was just over the horizon. The User Services Division added a new link to the OCLC/users communication channels, as did the founding of the OCLC/Special Interest Section (SIS) of the American Association of Law Libraries (AALL). The crowning event of the year was the creation of a new governance structure for OCLC, as recommended by Arthur D. Little, Inc., and approved by the Board of Trustees.

Although the 1976-1977 activities complete the first ten years of OCLC's existence, they by no means close the story. Instead, they bring the reader to a new point of departure. As the oldest and largest automated library network in the United States, OCLC created a firm base for the future application of the computer in a variety of library procedures.

THE ON-LINE UNION CATALOG
AND SHARED CATALOGING SYSTEM

Data Base

The data base numbered more than 3,000,000 records. Member libraries cataloged over 25,000 books per day, and OCLC produced more than 160,000 catalog cards daily. Over 12,000,000 location symbols provided users with up-to-date holdings information on the on-line file. The network of over 1,500 terminals beamed messages to OCLC during seventy-one hours a week of on-line operations.

One of the high points of on-line activities was the homage paid to the winner of the three millionth OCLC control number. The OCLC *Newsletter* reported the event as follows:

> SUNY-Potsdam captured OCLC Control Number 3000000 on 1977 May 27 at approximately 5:04 P.M., Eastern Time. Pushing the PRODUCE and SEND keys for the record that was to be assigned OCLC #3000000 was David Ossenkop, music reference librarian at SUNY-Potsdam.
>
> The "Three Millionth" bibliographic record in OCLC's on-line union catalog is *More Irish Street Ballads*, collected and annotated by Colm O'Lochlainn.
>
> According to Selma Foster, Head of Cataloging at SUNY-Potsdam, the cataloging staff saw how close the three million mark was on Friday afternoon and decided to try for it. 'We had hoped that our bibliographic record of Handel's *Messiah* would become the three millionth record,' says Ms. Foster. However, as luck would have it, *More Irish Street Ballads* achieved the distinction of having OCLC #3000000. Ms. Foster says that a bottle of champagne was on her desk the following Monday morning, and the cataloging department uncorked it at lunch in celebration of their inputting the third 'millionth' record in OCLC's on-line catalog.
>
> Runners-up in the race for OCLC gold were the University of Wisconsin—Parkside at Kenosha, Wisconsin (OCLC #2999999) and Loma Linda University Libraries at Loma Linda, California (OCLC #3000001).[1]

No subject was closer to the hearts of users than response time. The addition of a number of new enhancements the previous year and the growing list of users contributed to most of the poor response time during 1976-1977. At the October 13, 1976 meeting of the directors of the divisions, it was agreed that a group should be created to monitor average response time. The Corporate Committee on Response Time was composed of staff from the Computer Facilities, Library Systems, Research and Development, and User Services divisions.[2] Its purpose was "to assure an acceptable level of average response time on the OCLC system."

The two immediate assignments of the Committee were to review the moratorium on installation of new terminals and to develop recommendations to revise the author index. Prior to the formation of the Committee, there was a partial lifting by the Board of Trustees in July 1976 of the moratorium on new installations. Institutions could use the new terminals only during hours of favorable response time. Use was limited to the hours of 7:00 A.M. to 9:00 A.M. and hours after 5:00 P.M., Monday through Friday, and all day Saturday. The Center monitored activity to assure compliance. At the August 25, 1976 meeting of the directors of the divisions, it was agreed that the partial moratorium should continue until the Sigma 903 was installed and the triple processor system was functioning acceptably. At this time, a decision would be made concerning the moratorium.

The moratorium was finally lifted on December 1, 1976. The Corporate Committee on Response Time was directly responsible. The lifting necessitated imposing five guidelines for installing new terminals. The first limited the total number that could be activated in the on-line system by June 30, 1977, to eighteen hundred. The second projected twenty-four hundred terminals on-line by June 30, 1978. The third stated that OCLC would meet its schedule of adding new terminals in January through March 1977. The fourth limited the numbers of terminals to be installed in April, May, and June to sixty-six per month. The last guideline set the maximum to be installed throughout the fiscal year 1977-1978 at fifty terminals per month.

The lifting of the moratorium was short-lived. Increases in average response time led division directors to agree to follow a three-step plan to provide acceptable response time. Effective February 16, 1977, OCLC began delaying installation of terminals until the Center had the equipment available to add more terminals without endangering the acceptable level of average response time. As of February 17, 1977, OCLC would accept no new orders for terminals until the present commitments were fulfilled. Finally, the Center planned to accelerate the schedule for adding the fourth Sigma, the 904, to the on-line system.

Scarcely three weeks had passed when, on March 9, the Center approved once more the installation of terminals at a controlled rate. Response time had fallen almost immediately below the acceptable rate of eight seconds. The fourth computer was added without major problems two weeks ahead of the revised schedule.

The author search capability was temporarily suspended during August 16-21 so that its effect on response time could be observed. As suspected, there was a definite correlation between use of the index and response time. Average response time on August 16 fell to 5.19 seconds, and by the close of the week it was 4-5 seconds. Consequently, the index was suspended from operation for yet another week. The remarkable feature of the author search was that it represented only 3 percent of the total messages sent by the participants, and yet it claimed 35 percent of the total time used to process messages to the computer. In the months ahead, the author search was available only during nonpeak hours of system use until the third computer became operational in November 1976.

In early 1977 the Corporate Committee on Response Time was faced with the dilemma of how to reinstate the author search capability without degrading response time. Three avenues of action were recommended to the directors of the divisions. First, a two-level technique to reduce access time for derived search keys was suggested. Second, a study to find more specific algorithms for search keys that would cut down searching time was recommended. Third, a study of the concept of an authority file as an indexing tool was offered. The directors approved the first two recommendations.

The two-level indexing technique would not outwardly alter operations at a terminal. It was a procedure to reduce the number of internal computer transactions necessary to carry out a search-key search (author, author-title, and title) and to add records to the on-line catalog. Records were retrieved in groups as opposed to a separate retrieval. The results were reduced response time and improved efficiency.[3] This technique was not a truly new function; it was rather the redesigning of an existing one. As the year drew to a close, work on both recommendations was well on its way, with tangible results predicted for the next year.

Integrity of the data base remained a major concern. Like the problem of poor response time, it was well-known to OCLC users and staff. In the spring of 1976 the network directors, against the wishes of the OCLC staff, requested that the Center load all of the deferred MARC records into the on-line data base. The expected result was an increase in the number of duplicates in the on-line file, a total of approximately ninety thousand records.

Fortunately, in December 1976, the Center introduced a new procedure to detect and eliminate duplicate records in the on-line catalog. Through the application of sophisticated computer programs, the Center could process simultaneously the deferred records that were possible duplicates and the new weekly MARC II tapes from LC. The two separate files were automatically merged into one and put through a matching test. The records with the highest LC card numbers were run first.

A new and more detailed matching algorithm was the key. Records were compared by LC card number, name-title, and the first and the last sixteen characters of the title, place of publication, publisher, dates, and Arabic pagination. No records were deferred. An existing LC-MARC II record or records would be eliminated if an incoming, new LC-MARC II record matched all the criteria of comparison. In the case of an incomplete match, the incoming record would become a part of the on-line catalog. Whenever a record that was input by a member library was erased, the library's holding symbol and those of the other libraries that used it were automatically transferred to the incoming record. By June 1977, the Center was processing about six thousand LC-MARC II records per week; the number of deferred records awaiting processing had dropped to thirty-one thousand.

The monthly operational and catalog card production statistics for the year (see table T-15) reflect OCLC's progress toward resolving the problem of poor response time. Amazingly, response time fell from 12.1 seconds in July 1976 to 5.9 seconds in June 1977. The drop was even more dramatic because in July 1976 the number of terminals on-line stood at 1,219 while by June 1977 this number topped 1,670. Another remarkable feat was the steady increase in the number of records in the data base, in spite of fluctuations in the system's availability. Although not evident from table T-15, June was the first month in which over 200,000 books were cataloged each week.

TABLE T-15
Monthly Operational and Catalog Card Production Statistics
(July 1976-June 1977)[4]

Month	Terminals on Network	Average Response Time (Seconds)	Percentage of System Available	MARC II Records Added to On-Line Catalog	Records in On-Line Catalog	Catalog Cards Produced
July	1,219	12.1	94.4	10,997	2,349,003	4,300,481
Aug.	1,241	7.4	97.2	9,298	2,414,231	4,431,518
Sept.	1,287	6.6	99.0	7,633	2,477,876	4,840,931
Oct.	1,320	7.6	98.9	11,945	2,541,319	4,858,647
Nov.	1,338	6.4	89.8	10,412	2,599,501	3,631,949
Dec.	1,376	5.1	98.1	24,323	2,657,010	3,934,045
Jan.	1,470	6.1	98.7	14,515	2,722,671	5,171,137
Feb.	1,553	7.4	96.8	4,719	2,779,623	5,072,024
Mar.	1,560	5.8	94.0	17,407	2,855,930	6,118,314
Apr.	1,582	6.2	95.1	18,491	2,914,112	6,092,124
May	1,631	6.4	93.7	28,644	3,015,579	6,547,655
June	1,670	5.9	95.7	27,978	3,088,655	5,883,969
Summary	1,670	6.9	96.0	186,362	3,088,655	60,882,794

Since its birth in 1973, the Peer Council had played an important role in maintaining high-quality cataloging in the on-line file.[5] During 1976-1977 it directed its energies toward creation of a network peer council. The concept of an "umbrella peer council" among the networks was first introduced at the February 15, 1977 meeting of the Peer Council. In May the establishment of the Inter-Network Quality Control Council (IQCC) was the main topic of discussion.

IQCC would attack the immediate problems of duplicate records and quality of the data base as well as other relevant topics. Its three main areas of concern would be documenting, training in the use of the system, and monitoring quality control. It was to be composed of both network and Ohio representatives. The IQCC *esprit de corps* is reflected in the minutes of December 14, 1977:

> One last thought which could well be a keynote for IQCC. To paraphrase Barbara Markuson (Incolsa) — OCLC, as one on-line bibliographic system, is the greatest force for improvement of cataloging in the United States. We must take a positive approach to improve cataloging standards. Libraries can learn to trust and use each others cataloging.[6]

As the year closed, the idea for the creation of IQCC was approved by the network directors. The next step was to gain the approbation of the Board of Trustees.[7]

In the fall of 1976, all participants received copies of five documents explaining the additional MARC formats recently implemented by OCLC.[8] *On-line Cataloging of Audio-Visual Media and Special Instructional Materials — Preliminary Document* was a revision of the *Films Format* previously issued as part of the *Technical Bulletin* No. 1. All of the documents were called preliminary since the standards for input cataloging for each media had not been finalized. A final version of each would incorporate comments and suggestions of the task forces for the formats, the Advisory Committee on Cataloging, and users. Beginning in September 1976, OCLC users were able to input original cataloging for nonprint materials and manuscripts into the system using the MARC formats developed by the Center for audiovisual and special instructional materials, manuscripts, maps, music scores, and sound recordings. Two months later, in November, libraries were receiving catalog cards for all of the formats. As the year ended, more than 69,200[9] new records in nonbook format were input almost exclusively by participants. Compared to the total of over 3,000,000 records in the data base, this figure appears small. However, it was important because it represented the start of new cataloging activity.

At the December 21, 1976 Board of Trustees meeting, James E. Rush, director of the Research and Development Division, reported that forty-five projects of varying complexity were in progress to improve the on-line operations. Accomplishments included an increase of 35 percent storage area in the SAVE file. The institutional SAVE limit, the number of records each institution could place in SAVE, was increased to four hundred. (In 1971 the SAVE limit was twenty.) In addition, the searching module of the system was divorced from the cataloging module. Henceforth, the searching module would be used exclusively for searches not only in cataloging but also in the forthcoming interlibrary loan and technical processing systems. The Center had nearly completed work on modifying the display of truncated entries in a multiple entry reply. In the future such replies would include symbols to show that the cataloging source was LC, NLM, or the searching library. Also, nearing completion was the addition of a symbol at the end of a library record to indicate that it was the end of the data, and that the next screen contained holdings information, i.e., that data did not continue on the second screen. Still in progress was development of a procedure to store holding symbols separate from bibliographic records. The new method would augment the number of symbols the system could comfortably attach to each record. The Center was also developing programs that would arrange holding symbols in hierarchial patterns listing them first by the institution making the search (if applicable), then by a group of institutions, then by network, and finally by the United States and other nations.

In the spring of 1977, it was reported that OCLC had completed a study of on-line authority files that would provide data to develop the files. Talks were also underway with NLM and LC to find a way to merge NLM's cataloging records with LC's. At this point, the records were incompatible due to differences in such vital areas as the main entry.

Two major projects were under way to increase the usefulness of the data base. The OCLC/Battelle memorial Institute's BASIS system continued to operate in an experimental mode. During the year, OCLC successfully installed the BASIS programs on the Sigma 7. A simulator of the on-line system was similarly installed on the same computer to test new or modified programs on-line without interfering with actual on-line operations. As part of the original agreement with NCEMMH, OCLC was to add to its on-line catalog, bibliographic records of instructional materials for the handicapped. It was reported that more than twenty-eight thousand[10] records were added in the spring. Programs were also formulated to update the NIMIS file, with bibliographic records input into the data base by NCEMMH. No final conclusions could yet be drawn from the experiment, which was to be continued in 1977-1978.

During the year OCLC began to look at possibilities other than the BASIS subject system. The staff attended a demonstration of IBM's Storage and Information Retrieval System (STAIRS) in March 1976 and subsequently tested it at OCLC. Results were encouraging, and IBM suggested to the Center that a proposal to install it be drawn up. By the close of the year a proposal to this effect was presented.

The second project was developing a network supervisor program supported by a grant from the W. K. Kellogg Foundation. By Christmas 1976 over two hundred libraries had agreed to participate in access to other data bases, and OCLC began to make it possible for the libraries to use the non-OCLC data bases. In the spring, staff representatives visited System Development Corporation (SDC) and Lockheed to discuss a linkage. Talks were encouraging, and plans were in the wind to work out the technical difficulties. More meetings with Lockheed and SDC were planned. The major thrust of the activity was the designing and development of the basic specifications for the system. They were then presented to a number of hardware vendors. Out of the eight proposals submitted, the Tandom Computer Corporation, Inc. was chosen to supply the equipment for the project. A more detailed set of specifications was being designed.

All of these activities evolved around the data base and represented the outward signs of a maturing system. Another indication was the increase in direct services rendered to the participants, namely the OCLC-MARC Distribution Service. It allowed participating libraries to receive, through subscription, machine-readable magnetic tapes of the current cataloging records used or input for catalog production during a specified period. The charge in 1976-1977 per tape was $23.00 for handling and delivery and from $.035 to $.001 per record, depending on the number of records to be copied. *OCLC MARC Distribution Service* contained information on the technical documentation of the tapes and their specifications.

The OCLC-MARC Distribution Service pointed the way to the Center's Retrospective OCLC-MARC Project. It offered any participating library the opportunity to recreate in machine-readable form the cataloging records it processed on the on-line system up to December 31, 1976. Both subscribers and nonsubscribers to the OCLC-MARC Distribution Service were free to participate. Charges for this service were the same as those for the Distribution Service. The cut-off date for the first run was extended to include records used through February 26, 1977. Orders for the service were due in Columbus by February 15. It was reported that 253 orders involving 743 institutions were received.[11] By spring the testing of software for the project was nearly completed. Production was slated for the next year. The total number of institutions taking advantage of the service leaped from 147 in the fall to 1,620 in June 1977.[12] In June 1976, OCLC sent out 208,000[13] machine-readable records; exactly one year later it shipped 3.4 million.[14]

In the spring of 1977, these tapes were used in a special way by four libraries as part of an effort to design analytical programs and a tape analysis service for libraries that would be useful for collection development. Three

SUNY libraries (Oneonta, Cortland, and Binghamton) and Cornell University were providing test data and other information needed to evaluate the experiment. The project was financed by a $42,415 grant from OE.

OCLC was maturing in still another way. Its body of bibliographic information was greatly expanded under the two-year Ohio Public Library Retrospective Conversion Project. Supported by a grant from the State Library of Ohio, the massive conversion of the retrospective cataloging of seven major Ohio public libraries and the State Library into machine-readable form was launched in September 1976. Two months earlier, on July 28, the Ohio Public Library Retrospective Conversion Project Advisory Committee met to discuss the intricacies of the project. On September 15, Columbus Public Library began to microfilm its catalog for eventual conversion into machine-readable form. Soon after, the State Library of Ohio became the first participant to have its records converted. By June 1977 over a half-million records[15] were processed. Moreover, the conversion process was completed for three of the eight libraries. Fortunately, most converted records were already in the on-line file; thus, the holdings information was simply added to the records. Only a small percentage of the records were new.

OCLC was involved in another project that would use to advantage its information-rich data base, COMARC project. Although OCLC had assisted the project since its beginning, it was not until early 1977 that it first sent records for the COMARC project to LC. The tapes were produced weekly during the OCLC-MARC Distribution Service runs. As of January 1977, approximately fourteen thousand MARC records were distributed to participants.[16] In the spring of 1978 the project ended.[17]

In addition to educational workshops on quality control and uses of the OCLC/MARC tapes, OCLC sponsored two educational forums. The first, on the forthcoming serials control system, was held in Columbus on March 8, 1977. (The details of the forum are presented in the discussion of the serials system on page 211.) On May 27, 1977, the Center hosted the second forum. One hundred and ten persons traveled to Columbus to hear Larry L. Learn speak on the Center's computer facilities. Thompson M. Little, chairman of the Corporate Committee on Response Time, reported on the activities of the Committee and explained how average response time was calculated. The educational forums served the needs of users by providing the meeting ground for a discussion of problems and concerns related to daily use of the system.

Educating users was also accomplished through self-instruction. *Self-Instructional Introduction to the OCLC Model 100 Terminal* was announced in the December 22 issue of the *OCLC Newsletter*.[18] SOLINET also produced a self-instruction tool. Five lessons on operating the terminal were presented in the kit, which included a manual and five accompanying audiocassettes.

News about OCLC traveled not only by the spoken and written word but also through the visual medium of the videotape. In the winter, it was announced that Ohio Dominican College (ODC) was completing a videotape program on OCLC to educate the public. On February 7, 1977, the film crew from the college arrived in Columbus to produce the 29-minute program entitled "The Electronic Library: Cooperation through Computers." The equipment for the filming and the filming itself was provided by ODC.[19]

During fiscal year 1974-1975, Kent State University produced a series of videotapes about OCLC. These were updated with the production of a new series in 1976-1977. The four programs were entitled "Finding Information in the OCLC System (Parts I and II)," "The OCLC System," and "On-Line Cataloging."

The OCLC staff become a part of the Center's educational endeavors through in-house opportunities for continuing education. Videotape courses on such topics as management and data processing were offered. Plans were being laid to allow staff to attend seminars and to enroll in academic courses.

As had been the custom, OCLC continued to exhibit at ALA's annual conference. That year it set up a booth in Detroit. Moreover, in the course of the year, a steady stream of visitors learned about OCLC by touring its Columbus facility.

HSOCLCUG continued to meet throughout the year to share and exchange information and experiences. Its fall meeting was held on November 4-5 in Cleveland at the Cleveland Health Sciences Library. The main topic was input standards for medical literature. Nearly a month later, on December 2-3, the organization met again in Cleveland for a two-day workshop-seminar on the use of the OCLC system in the health science community. Speakers included personnel from NLM, OCLC, and HSOCLCUG. Seventy-six persons attended the Medical Library Association's (MLA) continuing education course, "OCLC Utilization in Health Science Libraries." Small group discussions on standards were also held.

The second annual meeting of HSOCLCUG was held in Seattle, Washington, on June 15, 1977, in conjunction with MLA's annual gathering. Members established goals for 1977-1978 and heard about the latest developments at NLM and OCLC. The same continuing education course that was offered in December was available in a revised and updated form.

During the year a draft of proposed input standards was prepared by the HSOCLCUG Standards Committee. The creation of a peer review council for health science libraries was also discussed, but no decision was reached. Moreover, the Continuing Education Committee was preparing a draft of a training document to supplement materials produced by OCLC.

HSOCLCUG membership had nearly doubled since spring 1976. By June 1977 there were fifty-four active, twenty-seven associate, and fifty-four individual members. The group elected its officers for 1977-1978 by mail ballot.[20]

The story of MOUG continued with the work of the OCLC Task Force for the Cataloging of Music and Sound Recordings. In December, it recommended a MARC music format to the OCLC Cataloging Advisory Committee, which subsequently approved it in January 1977.

Another accomplishment was the Committee's proposal to establish editing libraries to maintain quality control. As the year closed, six libraries had been selected: Bowling Green State University (for recordings only), Cornell University, Harvard University, University of North Carolina, Oberlin College, and The Ohio State University. Also proposed and accepted was a recommendation for stricter standards in adding bibliographic information to the data base. These recommendations were to be incorporated into a revised version of on-line cataloging manuals slated for publication in the summer of 1977. The group met for the last time as a Task Force in February 1977.

The use of the MARC music format by OCLC participants required more explanation than the Task Force could provide. As a result, discussions were held with the MLA Automation Committee and MDO in Washington, D.C. As a result, MDO issued two documents. "Guidelines for Subfielding Music Uniform Titles" appeared in the May 1977 issue of *Music Cataloging Bulletin* and in the July 1977 issue of *Cataloging Service Bulletin. Music: A MARC Format: Addendum No. 1* was released in August 1977.

Late one evening during the February 1977 MLA national meeting in Nashville, a group of concerned OCLC music users, including members of the inactive Task Force, met informally to discuss the need for a music OCLC users group. Five librarians volunteered to formulate plans for the organization.[21] Together they worked on a newsletter, by-laws, a mailing list of potential members, and plans for the group's first official meeting.

The organization was not in full swing until 1978. The group's first newsletter appeared in October 1977, and its officers were elected at the first annual meeting of MOUG, held in conjunction with MLA's annual meeting in Boston in 1978. It was there that the organization's by-laws were adopted.

The third users group, OCLC/SIS of AALL was founded to serve specific needs of law libraries. Although like HSOCLCUG and MOUG, it was born out of the strong desire by a special group of users to communicate with one another, its early development followed a different path.

In 1975 law librarians, all members of the OCLC family, began to create an informal chain of correspondence among themselves.[22] In Boston, on June 23, 1976, law librarians who were using OCLC gathered for their first informal meeting. Brought to Boston, Massachusetts, for the AALL annual meeting, the twenty to twenty-five people who attended the informal session found much to their amazement that there was, indeed, a strong interest among law librarians (using and not using OCLC) to create an organization of their own.

The 1977 AALL annual meeting was held through June 26-30 in Toronto, Canada. Several months earlier, plans were laid to include on the conference's agenda a time and a place to meet for those interested in forming an OCLC special interest group. A draft of proposed by-laws was also formulated.[23] In addition, signed petitions were circulated to recognize the group as a legal entity of AALL. On June 26, over 150 persons attended an OCLC workshop. Following it, the organizational meeting of OCLC/SIS was called to order by Frederick S. Baum (Yeshiva University).

Baum reported that since a sufficient number of signed petitions had been sent to AALL, the group should receive official status with AALL. The by-laws were approved, and the group elected its first slate of officers.[24] An advisory committee was also elected to assist the newly formed group.[25]

The purpose of OCLC/SIS, as stated in page one of the by-laws, was

> to assist its members in utilizing the capabilities of the OCLC system to the best of their abilities; to communicate their concerns to OCLC and provide input in the policy-making process at OCLC; to represent their interests within AALL; to facilitate the exchange of ideas and information among the members; and to concern itself with all aspects of OCLC as it may affect users.[26]

A unique feature of OCLC/SIS was that membership was open to any AALL member who requested affiliation. As 1977 ended, the organization had sixty-five members. Its founders had anticipated fewer members since less than twenty-five law libraries were using OCLC. OCLC/SIS was officially constituted as a special interest section of AALL a few months later.

This section would be incomplete without mentioning the growth in the number of institutions that used the data base. In the course of the twelve-month period (July 1, 1976-June 30, 1977) OCLC increased its membership by 7 percent as six more Ohio libraries joined.[27] Three new consortia also joined. At the close of its tenth year of activity, OCLC boasted an Ohio membership of ninety institutions.

Equipment

The demands on the system were great. Catalog card production had increased from 39.6 million cards in 1975-1976 to 60.9 million in 1976-1977.[28] The on-line catalog swelled to over 3 million records. The number of MARC II records added to the data base reached a total of 186,362 as of June 1977.[29] The number of installed terminals leaped from 1,219 in July 1976 to 1,670 in June 1977.

The previous chapter left the story of the development of the quadruple processor system fed by seven minicomputers at midpoint with the dual processor system activated in December 1975. Sigmas 903 and 904 had arrived and were awaiting testing. Operation of the quadruple system brightened the year 1976-1977. In November 1976, Sigma 903 was linked to the system. At this point the dual processor became a multiprocessor. Three months later the fourth Sigma 9 was hooked up.

The triple processor system was activated several days ahead of schedule on November 4. Service on the weekends of September 24 and October 1 was halted to enable the staff to move the data base equipment in place. Implementation began on the evening of October 29 with complete shutdown of the system for a week. On the weekend of February 25, the Center added the fourth computer. Running ahead of its schedule by fifteen days, the Center had the new system in full operation on February 28. Installation was accomplished during the system's off-line hours; users sacrificed none of their on-line time. Addition of the fourth computer proved to be a much less complicated procedure than installation of the third. To maximize efficient use of computer power, the Center transferred the on-line system from four to two computers during evening hours. The transfer meant a five-minute interruption of services from 6:00 P.M. to 6:05 P.M., Eastern Standard Time, Monday through Friday. When not devoted to on-line activities the two computers were put to use in off-line duties, including card production and preparation of accession lists. The sixth minicomputer, or telecommunication processor, became operational in the fall.

In the relatively short span of four and one-half years, the Center had greatly expanded its computer power. From August 1971 to January 1975, the Sigma 5 computer was alone. From February to November 1975, it was joined by the first Sigma 9. One month later, a second Sigma 9 was activated; in November 1976, the third one came; and in February, the fourth.

As the Center looked to the future, it was fully aware of the need for more computer power. The major concern of staff was what procedure to adopt when needs exceeded the current capacity of the four Sigmas. Plans were already being made for an OCLC System II to replicate the current system. Initially, it would use only two computers, allowing the system to support another one thousand to twelve hundred[30] terminals. The dual processor could then be expanded into a quadruple one. OCLC II was seen by staff as the beginning of a node in a national library network.

The advent of Sigmas 905 and 906 laid the groundwork for OCLC II. Acquisition of Sigma 905 was approved by the Board of Trustees in April; it was delivered on June 15, 1977. Projected for operation by the following fall, it would not be used for on-line activities but rather for administrative and production jobs. Plans included the weekend transfer of software on the Sigma 7 to the Sigma 905. Sigma 906 did not arrive until fall of the next fiscal year. Plans called for acquiring a seventh Sigma (907) to provide still more power.

In 1976-1977 OCLC installed 509 terminals at 488 institutions. Several years earlier the Center began to replace Spiras terminals in Ohio institutions with Model 100 Display units. By June 30, 1977, the project was accomplished. Another achievement was implementing an automated system for keeping track of terminal installations, histories of services performed on them, spare parts inventory, and rates of failure.

The work begun earlier on development of a new terminal continued. The Center realized that it needed terminals with varying capabilities. One was needed mainly for cataloging. Another terminal, which was less sophisticated, would be useful for technical processing, serials control, and interlibrary loan systems. A third terminal with even fewer capabilities could operate as a public service terminal.

A third way to access the OCLC data base was also being developed. Although the dial-up access through Tymshare's Tymnet communications network had been in use for several years through the FLC experiment, direct dial-up service was not yet functional as an alternative access mode. In 1975-1976 OCLC released *Dial-Up Access to OCLC* (May 1976). About six months later, it was replaced by a revised edition under the same title. By spring of 1977, the Center was formulating a contract for dial-access. One point already agreed upon was that users of the new access mode would be required to participate in the on-line union catalog and shared cataloging system. They could not use it for searching only.

Future equipment needs would be dictated by needs of the users. In the spring of 1977 the Task Force on Printers was created. Composed of OCLC staff members, its purpose was to survey users to determine if there was sufficient interest in developing a printer terminal to warrant work on its design. The printer would be attached to the terminal and would reproduce information from the data base to a paper copy.

In 1976 the Center established an in-house security committee and hired a security consultant to formulate recommendations. Following the report's recommendations, in the fall of 1976, OCLC began to use a computerized security access system. Staff members inserted a badge into a slot on the outside of the Center's doors. Each door was especially equipped with a detection device to allow or deny access. In December 1976, the "Engineering

Report on Computer Center Power System for Ohio College Library Center" was prepared by H. A. Williams and Associates, Inc. and circulated to the directors of the divisions. It provided for an emergency power backup system to prevent the disruption of communications between the Center and the computers, and to protect the system against damage. The plans, as outlined in the document, were approved, and the Center spent the remaining months of the year planning for the new power system.

Finances

At the December 1977 meeting of the membership, William Chait (Dayton and Montgomery County Public Library) presented the OCLC treasurer's report that included a summary of the Center's financial history. One of its main points was that the expansion of the membership outside of Ohio benefited the Center's financial situation. A month before, this very same point was stressed by Kilgour at the Board of Trustee's meeting. He said: "If OCLC had not extended services outside of Ohio, the current first-time-use charge would be $2.70 as opposed to the $1.87 now charged to Ohio libraries."[31] During its first four years, the Center's financial support, including operations and developmental activities, came totally from the Ohio membership and grants. During fiscal year 1971-1972, when OCLC went on-line, it received a large grant (in installments) from the Ohio Board of Regents. Only then did the membership begin to pay for the services and products it received.

Chait reported that in fiscal year 1972-1973, 13 percent[32] of the financial support came from libraries outside Ohio, with the rest supplied by Ohio members and the Ohio Board of Regents. Although the Ohio membership never stopped growing, outside participation grew until out-of-state users far exceeded the Ohio constituency both in numbers and in dollar support. This trend was not expected to change. By fiscal year 1976-1977, Ohio's financial contribution to the total revenue of OCLC made a complete turn around. Instead of the out-of-state participants contributing 13 percent and Ohio members 87 percent, as in 1972-1973, Ohio members were now contributing 13 percent and out-of-state population 87 percent! These figures are even more astonishing when one recalls that from 1968 to 1972 Ohio furnished 100 percent of the Center's operating revenues.

Since its founding in 1967, OCLC had the good fortune of receiving generous grants for research and development. Table T-16, page 196, documents this support. However, were it not for the expanded list of users, OCLC would have been unable to fund its own research and development. Moreover, the cost of the data base storage equipment for OCLC, even if the Center had never gone beyond Ohio, was phenomenal. There was no way that the Ohio members could have funded those purchases alone.

TABLE T-16
OCLC Grant Support from 1968/69 to 1977/78[33]

Fiscal Year	Granting Agency	Total Amount of Grant
1968/69	National Agriculture Library	$ 4,182
	Ohio State Library Board	18,588
1969/70	U.S. Office of Education	90,135
	Council on Library Resources #489	14,113
	National Agriculture Library	1,750
1970/71	U.S. Office of Education	125,000
	Council on Library Resources #526	75,000
1971/72	State of Ohio--Board of Regents Appropriation	390,000
1972/73	State of Ohio--Board of Regents Appropriation	195,000
	Council on Library Resources #558	194,000
1973/74	Federal Library Committee	66,000
1974/75	Council on Library Resources #618	124,250
	Federal Library Committee	21,000
	Council on Library Resources #558	24,000
	Council on Library Resources #526	5,000
1975/76	Council on Library Resources #618	76,250
	The State Library of Ohio	56,000
	U.S. Office of Education	108,875
1976/77	Kellogg Foundation	339,319
	The State Library of Ohio	550,000
1977/78	Council on Library Resources #665	122,000
	The State Library of Ohio	9,000
	TOTAL	$2,609,462

Another point emphasized in the report was the way in which the increasing rate at which OCLC was acquiring property and computer equipment affected its financial stature. "In 1974 OCLC had about $1.5 million in property and computer equipment; in 1977, $11.4 million. Presently there is more than $4 million of additional equipment on order."[34] From 1973 to 1975 equipment purchases were possible only because of financial agreements OCLC negotiated with the equipment vendors. As of June 30, 1975, OCLC had but a meager $0.32 of equity built up for each dollar of long-term debt. The Center was able to increase equity thanks to the decision by the Board of Trustees in July 1975 to increase charges to participants. Exactly two years later the equity had risen to $0.93 for each dollar of long-term debt. The decision to increase charges was the prominent factor that led to the improvement of the Center's financial condition. The *Annual Report 1976/ 1977* announced: "The Center is now in a much more favorable position to negotiate prices and purchase discounts with suppliers than it was in previous years."[35]

The financial status of OCLC is measurable through a number of accounting tests. One is the ratio of current assets to current liabilities. OCLC viewed a ratio of 2 to 1 as acceptable and good. A look at the ups and downs of this ratio over the past decade accentuates the validity of the decision made in 1975-1976 to increase charges. As shown here, the increases helped to bring 'he current ratio to a more favorable 1.63.

TABLE T-17
Ratios of Current Assets to Current Liabilities 1968-1977[36]

Fiscal Year	Current Ratio
1968	1.92
1969	1.81
1970	.97
1971	1.15
1972	1.25
1973	.56
1974	.69
1975	.63
1976	.92
1977	1.63

Fiscal year 1976-1977 was a financial success. Kilgour said that "for the first time in four years the Center enjoys a net working capital position and its financial soundness is clearly improving."[37] In the recent past, OCLC found it necessary to take out a short-term capital loan to see it through the last half of its fiscal year. Happily, as the 1976-1977 year closed, OCLC found it did not need such a loan. In fact, the year terminated with the Center reporting a cash balance of $5,156,818, as of June 30, 1977.

In the spring, as was customary, the Center formulated its budget for the coming year. The "Budget Plan 1977/78" called for expenses of $18,428,000 to earn an equal amount of revenue. In comparison, the previous year's budget figure was $15,074,000. Described as "the most pleasant feature"[38] of the Plan was the small rise in the overall cost of on-line cataloging. The Ohio inclusive first-time-use charge would be increased only 1.0 percent, from $1.92 to $1.94. In addition, the basic charge would be raised only $.02, from $1.11 to $1.13. The only other additional charge was for reclassification, which rose from 55.5¢ to 56.5¢. Also good news was the announcement that charges for producing catalog cards would remain at 3.9¢, the same as in the current year. A major reason for this stability was a change in the procedure for mailing catalog cards to participating libraries. In the course of the year, the Center discontinued shipping cards via the United Parcel Service and instead sent them through the U.S. mail. The switch amounted to a saving of about $100,000 a year. The Plan also called for 317 full-time positions for OCLC at a cost of $5,725,000 (as opposed to $3,742,000 for personnel in 1976-1977). Seventy-six new positions would be created in 1977-1978. Table T-18 compares the budget for 1976-1977 with that for 1977-1978.

TABLE T-18
Budget Plan Comparison (1976/77 and 1977/78)[39]

	1976/77 Budget Plan		1977/78 Budget Plan	
Projected Revenue				
System Usage	$ 6,944,000	46.1%	$ 9,102,000	49.4%
Catalog Card Income	2,274,000	15.1%	2,937,000	15.9%
Terminals	2,503,000	16.6%	2,875,000	15.6%
Telephone Income	2,405,000	16.0%	2,482,000	13.5%
Grant Income	619,000	4.1%	400,000	2.2%
Other Income	329,000	2.2%	632,000	3.4%
TOTAL	$15,074,000	100.1%	$18,428,000	100.0%
Expenses to Generate Projected Revenue				
Personnel	$ 3,742,000	24.8%	$ 5,725,000*	31.1%*
General Operating Expenses	1,590,000	10.5%	1,790,000	9.7%
Computer and Support Equipment Maintenance	229,000	1.5%	360,000	2.0%
Data Processing Supplies and Expense	840,000	5.6%	1,023,000	5.6%
Data Communications and Tymnet	2,546,000	16.9%	2,618,000	14.2%
Terminal Costs	1,953,000	13.0%	1,638,000	8.9%
Physical Facilities Debt Service and Rental	272,000	1.8%	527,000	2.9%
Capital Equipment Debt Service and Rental	1,657,000	11.0%	2,264,000	12.3%
Capital Equipment – Cash Purchase	955,000	6.3%	1,023,000	5.5%
Capitalization	1,290,000	8.6%	1,460,000	7.9%
TOTAL	$15,074,000	100.0%	$18,428,000	100.1%

---

*Includes $259,000 for temporary help of which $240,000 will be expended on the State Library of Ohio Conversion Project. Subtracting the $259,000 from the $5,725,000 produces a 29.7% of personnel costs to be compared with 24.8% for 1976/77.

The overall increase in the budget figures meant that participating libraries would have to be prepared to meet the added expenses. Most institutions projected their coming year's expenses in the fall, although OCLC projected expenses in the spring prior to the coming year. What made it even more difficult for both the Center and the participants to plan for the next year was the fact that some of the charges, mainly those of AT & T, were unpredictable. To assist libraries in planning for the future, on October 19, 1976, the Board of Trustees adopted a resolution suggesting that users include in their own budget projections an increase of 8 percent in payments to the Center for fiscal year 1977-1978.

Organization

The work of the seventeen-member Advisory Committee culminated in the fall 1977 release of the Arthur D. Little report, *A New Governance Structure for OCLC: Principles and Recommendations*. At the same time, long-range plans for the development of OCLC, including its reorganization, were being made by the Center's top management, which spent approximately six months projecting expansion and technical development over the next six years. The four division directors, personnel manager, associate executive director, and the executive director met for four two- and three-day sessions. The first meeting included a management planning consultant. Although future plans had always been a part of the Center's annual budgeting process, the 1977-1978 budget was the first to include plans for six to seven years hence. One Board of Trustees member described it as "a fiscal plan set within a long-range plan."[40] Some of the ideas found in "Budget Plan 1977/78" were incorporated in the Little report.

The long-range plan delineated the Center's purpose, long-range goals, objectives for the next three years and those for another three years following the installation of new technology, and future projects of the Center after the quadruple processor computer system had reached its limits.[41] The future would bring new hardware and new software, incorporating the most sophisticated computer technology available. It would mean designing a new on-line system offering users new services and products. It would require more physical space and eventually a new, more secure building. It would also result in continued growth in the number of users, which would, in turn, force OCLC to adopt a more closely controlled method for adding new participants.

The previous year OCLC had been reorganized into five divisions. The Center's long-range plans would alter this pattern, as illustrated by chart C-2, page 200. Under the umbrella of the executive director's office were five main divisions plus the Personnel Department. Through the transfer of positions from the Computer Facilities and the Research and Development Divisions, the Documentation Department was established within the Library Systems Division. Personnel from the Administration and Finance Division were moved to the Research and Development Division where the Administrative Systems Development Department was created. The Library Systems Division was to be further expanded by addition of the Conversion Projects Department and the OCLC Library. The User Services Division was the newest of the five. In February 1977 the Board of Trustees announced that Mary Ellen

CHART C-2
Organization Chart[42]

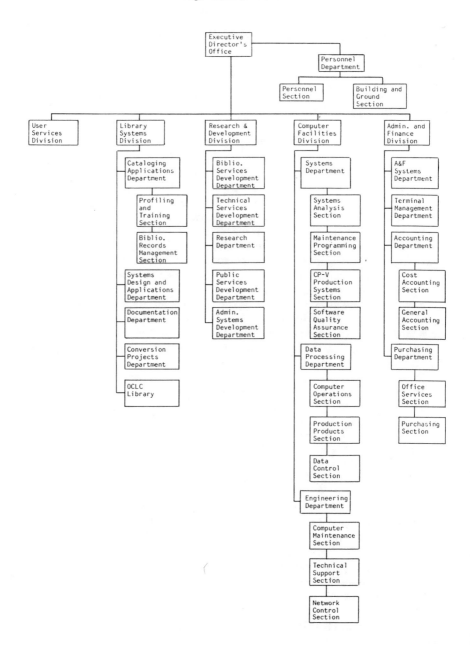

Jacob had accepted the position of the division director and would begin her duties in May. The new division's goals were

> [to] assist participants to make effective use of OCLC processes and products; foster user satisfaction with OCLC processes and products; promote better knowledge and understanding of OCLC processes and products and goals among the library and user community generally; and undertake market research activities related to identifying user needs and wants for OCLC planning and development.[43]

The past efforts to create a library for OCLC led to a major breakthrough following the move of the corporate headquarters to Kinnear Road. Then the OCLC library became a formal part of the Library Systems Division, which was established to house serials and monographs of interest to the professional staff and to serve as a permanent home for most OCLC documents.[44] A second, separately operated library, designated as the documentation library, was established to collect and organize the technical manuals and documentation for the Center's computer hardware and software, together with the many in-house statistical reports.

The new building mentioned in the Center's long-range plan was originally projected for completion by mid-1980. In the spring of 1977, the Center created the Building Site Task Force and the Building Program Task Force to choose a site and develop plans for a new facility. As the year ended, the Building Program Task Force was selecting an architectural firm to create the design.

Until the new building was ready, OCLC made several decisions to accommodate its need for more space. In the fall of 1976, the Library Systems and the Research and Development Divisions moved to 2939 Kenny Road, approximately one and one-half miles from the Kinnear Road facility. On July 19, 1977, the Board of Trustees approved construction of a building at the 1125 Kinnear Road site to house production equipment and associated personnel.

OCLC had many addresses (see plate III, page 202). In August 1967, it began its operations from room 328 of the main library of The Ohio State University Libraries at 1858 Neil Avenue. In October 1968, OCLC offices moved to the University's Research Center in the Research Foundation Building located at 1314 Kinnear Road. In March 1973, the offices were moved to 1550 West Henderson Road, while the computer center remained at 1314 Kinnear Road. On October 1975, the OCLC offices moved to 1125 Kinnear Road. Approximately three months later, all staff and computer equipment were together at 1125 Kinnear Road.

1967-1969
OSU Main Library

1968-1975
OSU Research Center

Plate III. Some of the Sites Occupied by OCLC in Columbus, Ohio
(Courtesy of OCLC)

1973-1975
1550 W. Henderson
Road

1975-1981
1125 Kinnear Road
(5 buildings on 6 acres)

1976-1981
2935-2941 Kenny
Road

Plate III (cont'd)

At the November 5, 1976 annual meeting, Donald J. Sager (Public Library of Columbus and Franklin County), Harold B. Schell (University of Cincinnati), and James L. Wood (Chemical Abstracts Service) were elected to the Board of Trustees. The same day, following the annual meeting, the Board elected as its officers H. Paul Schrank, Jr. (University of Akron), chairman and president; Harold B. Schell, vice-chairman; William Chait (Dayton and Montgomery County Public Library), treasurer; and L. Ronald Frommeyer (Wright State University), secretary.[45]

From an organizational standpoint the OCLC system was complex. Thus, it had to delineate its functions by forming small groups to handle a variety of topics. During 1976-1977, the list included staff committees, task forces, and project teams. Corporate committees on response time, security, physical facilities, personnel, network relations, system design, and the OCLC staff had become a necessity. Task forces on telecommunications, printers, and space allocation were also active.

Major organizational changes began to take shape on July 9, 1976, when the Advisory Council met for the first time to devise a plan to extend the membership beyond Ohio and to reorganize the Center with respect to its role as a participant in the national networking activities. Thus far, each year of the Center's history has been described in the context of the fiscal year, i.e., July 1 to June 30. The following discussion is an exception to the rule. It extends the final date to December 20, 1977, when the Ohio representatives made a landmark decision to adopt the new governance structure for OCLC as recommended by Arthur D. Little, Inc.

At the July 1976 meeting, the Advisory Council agreed to secure the assistance of a consulting firm. In addition, the outline for a proposal to be sent to a dozen firms selected by the Council was formulated. The OCLC staff then prepared a draft request that was sent to the Council for review. The final request for a proposal was sent to the twelve firms in mid-August. The bid deadline was October 1, 1976.

The request posed three vital questions to the consultant. First, what would a national computerized library network look like considering the views and plans of NCLIS, LC, CLR, and other library groups? Such aspects as the physical security of the operations, the availability of the resources to the users, and the economics of scale would also have to be considered. Second, how should OCLC function with regard to a number of network elements, including other computer-based, on-line networks, networks under agreements with OCLC, and the commercial data banks? Third, how should OCLC be organized and governed in its role and mission within the national library network?[46] The bidder was to detail the means, methods, techniques, and manpower needed to answer the questions.

On December 2, 1976, the Advisory Council met to select a firm. Out of the eight firms that submitted proposals, Arthur D. Little, Inc., of Cambridge, Massachusetts was chosen. The Board of Trustees then approved the Council's request that Arthur D. Little undertake the six-month study. The Council would guide and direct it. Based upon the recommendations of the report, the Council would then submit its own recommendations for the governance and organization of OCLC to the Board of Trustees. Pending Board approval, the Council would go to the membership for a vote.

The pioneering spirit of the study made it a likely candidate for grant support. CLR responded in January 1977 with the award of a $122,000 grant.

Network participation was an important part of the story of OCLC's impending new governance structure. To understand the context in which the Arthur D. Little report was written, it is necessary to gain a historical perspective of the involvement of the networks during the previous decade.[47]

In July 1967, the Ohio College Library Center was created "to increase the availability of library resources throughout Ohio to users of Ohio libraries ... [and] to lower the rate of rise of per-unit library costs while increasing availability of library resources."[48] In other words, OCLC was created by and for Ohio academic libraries. Nevertheless, the system was designed to serve as a prototype node in a national network. Within three years of its founding and before the system was operating in an on-line interactive mode, the Center was already negotiating with library consortia outside of Ohio to provide OCLC products and services to their respective member libraries on an experimental basis. In November 1970, PRLC and OCLC signed an agreement "to work together toward the development of a model for an information network using the methods and services developed by OCLC."[49] In 1971, an earlier grant from the OE was extended to cover the expense of an interface with CCLC in Atlanta to demonstrate "that the OCLC system will reduce processing costs in a centralized processing center."[50]

In 1972, NELINET and ULC signed agreements to use the OCLC system to demonstrate its usefulness in other network environments and to determine the feasibility of replicating the system elsewhere.

There was growing concern among some member libraries about possible deleterious effects of expanding participation beyond the state. Therefore, in May 1972, the membership recommended that OCLC investigate the extension of services outside of Ohio on a continuing basis. By the March 1973 membership meeting, the Center had explored various aspects of extended services. Moreover, it had developed a design model of a national communications network, developed model agreements for regions, and drawn up a functional organization chart that incorporated a council of regions. The council would provide a forum for discussion between the Center and its affiliated regions. It would also establish OCLC as the central node in a national network. Based upon the report of these activities, the membership approved the Board recommendation to extend services to library groups outside of Ohio, and further recommended that the Board consider the feasibility of extending services to individual libraries outside of Ohio.

At the same meeting, Kilgour reported that other regional library groups were exerting pressure on the Center to write affiliate agreements with them. Five regional representatives had joined forces and together approached OCLC to discuss terms of affiliation. They were most concerned about the governance structure that provided no representation for affiliated networks and suggested that the Center reorganize into a national corporation with a new, expanded Board of Trustees. However, the concept of a council of regions assuaged, at least for the moment, their apprehensions regarding governance.

Seven library groups, either affiliated or negotiating with OCLC, met with OCLC representatives on May 24, 1973, "to explore the creation and development of a group which represents the interests and concerns of regions which are, or intend to be, connected with on-line interactive bibliographic networks."[51] The group took the name Council of Regions (COR). Immediately, members of COR began to prepare a series of working papers to articulate the Council's purpose, its relationship with OCLC, and most emphatically the need for regional representation within the OCLC structure.

These papers were discussed at a joint meeting of COR and the OCLC Board of Trustees in July 1973. Among other things, COR requested that a COR representative be a nonvoting member of the OCLC Board, that COR members receive minutes of Board meetings, and that COR member regions continue to participate directly in OCLC advisory committee meetings, but in a more formal capacity, with weighted voting privileges to counteract the imbalance in numbers of attendees between Ohio and the regions. COR proposed to schedule its meetings on the day before Board meetings to delineate regional concerns that its representative could then present to the Board.

The Board had no objection to continuing regional participation in OCLC advisory committees and left the matter of committee structure up to Center management. No action was taken on the issue of sending Board meeting minutes to COR representatives until the October meeting, when the Board approved the request, effective retrospectively on July 1, 1973. The issue of COR representation on the Board was more complex. Some Trustees argued that any representative should be a full Board member with voting rights, which would require a change in the charter. The Board agreed that the charter should not be changed until a national network was better defined.

In December 1973, COR formalized its structure and changed its name to Council for Computerized Library Networks (CCLN), in part, because the membership of certain library groups defied geographic regional delimitation. OCLC was a founding member of CCLN; all other founding members were either affiliated with OCLC or were negotiating agreements. CCLN continued the drive for the affiliated networks to have some direct voice in the affairs of OCLC. In February 1974, the OCLC Board agreed to invite networks that had agreements with OCLC to choose from among themselves no more than seven persons to participate in the OCLC Board of Trustees meetings.[52]

At a special meeting in May 1974, the membership approved a change in the purpose clause of the Articles of Incorporation to read "...and provide services and products for the benefit of libraries and library users...," omitting any reference to Ohio libraries and opening the way for individual out-of-state libraries to contract directly for OCLC services. Thus, libraries within a network region might opt to bypass network affiliation to affiliate with OCLC. This did, indeed, happen in a few isolated cases. However, OCLC urged all non-Ohio libraries to participate through an established network, if possible.

In the fall of 1974, staff members from most OCLC affiliated networks began to meet with the director of the OCLC Library Systems Division and occasionally other staff, on an ad hoc basis, usually before advisory committee meetings, to exchange information concerning the use of the OCLC system. The group, called Network Coordinators, comprised those individuals responsible for training libraries within the regional networks. Discussions concentrated on training and system operations, but also dealt with proposed system developments. Sometimes talks involved policy issues, which the coordinators did not have authority to decide but needed to have resolved. That OCLC did not recognize the group as an official body with advisory capacity somewhat frustrated its efforts.

Also, in 1974 the first non-OCLC-affiliated network joined CCLN, and the focus of the group began to drift from strictly OCLC-related matters. Therefore, by late 1975, network directors felt they lacked a mechanism by which to consider together questions of policy relating to OCLC, including issues arising from meetings of Network Coordinators.[53] To fill this void, network directors in December 1975 began to meet regularly with the OCLC director and other OCLC staff just before OCLC Board meetings, as COR/CCLN had done earlier.

In September 1975, the OCLC Board received a request from the director of NELINET to "consider enlarging network representation at Board meetings to accommodate all participating networks."[54] The Board referred the request to its Committee on Governance. However, the Board never acted on the request because the governance issue was already being investigated, along with Board representation.

As documented in chapter 9, in December 1975, the Board empowered the director "to seek competent advice on means for undertaking a study of the advisability of extending membership [as opposed to participation] to libraries outside of the state of Ohio."[55] By July 1976 the Advisory Council was formed.

While network directors, through CCLN and later their own group, pursued network involvement in OCLC policy and governance issues, the OCLC advisory committees continued to welcome attendance by individuals from networks and network libraries. Since advisory committees had no formal representative structure, many Ohio libraries sent several representatives, others sent none, a few network libraries sent one, and most network offices sent one.

Throughout 1974, total attendance at the Advisory Committee on Cataloging averaged seventy-two, with fifty-seven persons from Ohio and fifteen from outside of Ohio. The discrepancy between Ohio and non-Ohio institutions present was not as great: there were thirty-three Ohio institutions represented and thirteen non-Ohio ones. By late 1975, attendance frequently soared to over one hundred. The imbalance between Ohio representatives and network representatives became more acute particularly since the number of out-of-state participants was growing at a far greater rate than the number of Ohio participants.[56]

Therefore, beginning in early 1976, OCLC formalized advisory committee representation in an attempt to reduce the size of meetings and to reduce the imbalance between representatives from Ohio and the networks. Ohio libraries were limited to one representative per meeting, anticipating about thirty-five actual attendees, and networks were limited to no more than two representatives, a maximum of thirty attendees. Network representatives compensated for their few numbers by their strong participation. Their comments and recommendations contributed significantly to the design of new system components and system enhancements. By that time, most networks had their own advisory committees that provided input to and received reports from their network representatives to OCLC advisory committees. Also, most networks agreed to pay travel expenses to OCLC advisory committee meetings, which removed the financial burden from libraries whose staff members were network representatives.

Against this background of network participation, Arthur D. Little completed its study in the summer of 1977 and submitted its preliminary document to the Advisory Council. On September 12 and 13, 1977, the Council met with Arthur D. Little representatives to examine it. On November 7 the final draft of the report was reviewed and accepted by a subcommittee of the Advisory Council. The subcommittee was then directed by the Council to present the Little report to the Board of Trustees and to recommend that it be the foundation for the new governance structure.

On November 8, 1977, the Board of Trustees passed a resolution recommending that the membership adopt the amended Articles of Incorporation creating OCLC, Inc., as well as the proposed Code of Regulations for OCLC, Inc. The passage of both documents was a prerequisite to creating the new structure as outlined in the Little report. In November, Board members traveled around Ohio to explain the new governance structure and its affect on Ohio members. Prior to the annual meeting, all members received a package of documents to review. It contained the Little report, a general description of the proposed new governance, the revised Articles and Code, and guidelines for the creation of the network called OHIONET, to which all of the Ohio libraries would belong.

The governance issue was put on the agenda on December 19 at the annual meeting of the membership. The resolution to change the governance structure of OCLC was adopted by recorded vote of fifty-seven ayes, five nays, and two abstentions. Kilgour described the event as "a step which is a part of an evolutionary process that has been going on for 10 years."[57]

The Little study was an influential document in the destiny of OCLC. It had two objectives: "to derive governance principles, and to provide recommendations for a governance structure, after projecting the shape of the future national library network (NLN) and determining a role for OCLC within that network."[58] It began with a consideration of seven possible types of governance structures: a government agency, a quasi-official government corporation, a for-profit corporation, a user cooperative, a network cooperative, a loosely held not-for-profit corporation, and a tightly held not-for-profit corporation. The first three were quickly ruled out as inconsistent with the philosophy of OCLC. The Little investigators sifted through a great many documents from historical presentations and statistics to the plans of the Library of Congress. OCLC management and staff, librarians, and network representatives were interviewed. The key driving forces behind the development of OCLC and the environment that surrounded it were studied.

In the spring of 1977, Arthur D. Little sponsored a colloquium in Columbus. It was attended by twenty invited participants who were involved in OCLC and the national library networking developments. The firm outlined for them the possible developments for OCLC between then and the mid 1980s. A discussion of the different types of conceivable organizational structures for the Center and its governance followed.

Arthur D. Little succinctly recommended in the final report: "that OCLC establish a governance structure that offers a compromise in character between a 'tightly held, non-profit corporation,' and a 'network cooperative.' "[59] According to Arthur D. Little, it would ensure financial stability, enhance planning, increase market and technological research abilities, provide maximum flexibility to meet changing market needs and technological opportunities, and allow the Center to make intelligent decisions quickly. Moreover, the firm believed that the new OCLC governance structure would foster communications between itself and the participants, create a strong feeling of belonging in those using the system, and challenge OCLC to attain its basic public service objectives in the context of the changing environment. Finally, it would assure continuity.

A closer look at the governance structure, as prescribed by Arthur D. Little, shows how all of the criteria were blended into one unifying system. The new configuration included an expanded Board of Trustees, the creation of a users council, and the membership. Together they were known as OCLC, Inc.[60]

The number of seats on the Board was to be enlarged from nine to fifteen. No member would serve more than two consecutive six-year terms. A third term could be served only after an interim period of at least one year. Members would serve on a rotating term basis. The Board could elect eight of the fifteen members, providing that five were nonlibrarians and three were librarians. One of the fifteen trustees was the executive director of OCLC. The Board would govern OCLC. The Users Council was empowered to elect six trustees. An interim Board of Trustees, composed of the current nine members along with the executive director, was to bridge the old and the new governance structures until the new delegates were named.

The Users Council was established "to give the networks and other current users of OCLC an institutionalized role, particularly in the making of policy decisions that would directly affect their own operations."[61] Membership was open to all networks, systems, and other library cooperatives that directly contracted with OCLC, Inc. for services. The Little report recommended that "the *number of voting members* allocated to each network or directly subscribing organization be proportioned to the square root of the volume of business done with OCLC."[62] A total membership of fifty was suggested.

The creation of OHIONET represented a new avenue of partnership for the Ohio members. It was designed to meet the local needs of Ohio libraries, allowing them to continue to play a role in the Center's governance. The intricacies of the organization's structure and operation were left to the Committee on a Future Ohio Network, founded in the fall of 1977 as a result of the Little recommendations. Bob L. Mowery (Wittenberg University) acted as its chairman, Donald J. Sager (Public Library of Columbus and Franklin County) as secretary. H. Paul Schrank, Jr. (Akron University) and Hyman W. Kritzer (Kent State University) were the other members. All four were on the Interim Board of Trustees. The final shape of OHIONET was formulated and recorded some time later in its first Articles of Incorporation and Code of Regulations.[63]

On December 19, 1977, the OCLC Board of Trustees meeting closed with the passage of the following resolution regarding OHIONET:

> Resolved, That the Ohio College Library Center is prepared to entertain, accept and agree to a support proposal from OHIONET for a funding grant at the level of $300,000, transfer of Ohio allocated terminals, physical space and personnel in connection with

operations at no charge for a term, all subject only to appropriate incorporation of OHIONET and approval by the Internal Revenue Service of the Corporation as a tax exempt entity under Section 501 (c) (3) of the Code.[64]

The same day, at the membership's annual meeting, Mowery presented the following resolution, which was subsequently approved:

WHEREAS the Board of Trustees of the Center have, by its Committee on a Future Ohio Network, studied the desirability of, necessity for, and alternative forms of such a Network; and

WHEREAS said Committee has reported its recommendations to the Membership respecting an Ohio Network: Therefore be it

RESOLVED, That the report and recommendations of the Committee on a Future Ohio Network are approved; and be it

RESOLVED FURTHER, That the Organizational Meeting shall convene upon the adjournment of the Annual Membership Meeting for purposes of organizing and forming an Ohio Network and carrying out such other business as may come before the Meeting; and be it

RESOLVED further, That Paul Schrank is hereby appointed Chairman and Don Sager Secretary of the Organizational Meeting.[65]

After two days of intensive discussions, the membership approved the amended Articles of Incorporation and the Code of Regulations of OCLC, Inc. on December 20, 1977.[66] Note that two basic tenets that were part of the Articles as conceived in 1967 remained intact in the revised version, namely, that OCLC was founded to increase the availability of library resources to users and to reduce the rate of rise of per unit costs in libraries.

ON-LINE SYSTEMS

"OCLC is pleased to announce that the automatic check-in component of the Serials Control subsystem is on-line and ready for use by participating libraries."[67] This announcement appeared in the December 22, 1976 issue of the OCLC *Newsletter*. Prior to its release, the Center had installed the programs for the automatic check-in component of the serials control system. By the beginning of November, four Ohio libraries had successfully tested it: The Ohio University, Kent State University, Case Western Reserve University, and the State Library. On December 9, OCLC hosted a training session for the Ohio member libraries. A second session was also held in December for the out-of-state participants.

Initially, approximately 150 institutions were authorized to use the serials control system, although the number requesting authorization was far greater. Of course, not all of these institutions that received authorization could participate during the year. Additional data would have to be collected and analyzed before the Center flung open the gates to the use of the system. In the fall of

1977, OCLC began to print catalog cards for serials cataloged on-line. It is important to keep in mind that even though in December 1976 the system was announced as ready for use, it was still in its infancy in 1977. Users were added at a controlled rate since the Center foresaw a future of continual refinements and redesigns.

On March 8, OCLC held its third Educational Forum, which was attended by one hundred persons from Ohio and several networks outside the state. The topic was the serials control system. OCLC staff members described the system and the four Ohio libraries involved in the testing shared their experiences.

The Center also generated a number of documents and circulated them to the participants. In August, it distributed through its *Technical Bulletin* No. 11 the revisions to the *Serials Control Subsystem: Users Manual* (December 1975). Further revisions and additions to the *Manual*, including a revision of the serials check-in procedure, were released in *Bulletin* No. 16 (November 30, 1976).

In February 1977, the *Newsletter* announced the availability of a "pocket-sized reference guide to OCLC's Serials Control Subsystem." The twelve-page booklet was entitled "OCLC Serials Control Subsystem: Reference Guide." It summarized the new system and pinpointed the essential information for using the check-in module. Two more publications were added to the literature: *Variable Field Tags for Serials*[68] and *A Serials Workbook: A Problem-Solving Manual for OCLC Serials Catalogers.*[69] It was designed to facilitate the use of Gates' *Serials Cataloging for the Ohio College Library Center System: A Manual* (April 1976). The eighty-three-page *Workbook* was a tool to train serials catalogers in the intricacies of on-line serials cataloging.

The cooperative spirit that created OCLC and enabled the on-line union catalog and shared cataloging system to succeed carried over into educational documentation and training tools. The Medical College of Ohio's *Serials Titles Held in the Raymond H. Mulford Library* was offered to OCLC participants at a cost of six dollars per list. The listing of over three thousand current and ceased (primarily biomedical) serial titles was arranged alphabetically by key title; it included the ISSN and the OCLC control number for each. The titles were an indispensable aid to libraries with collections of biomedical serials contemplating participation in the serials system.

On the national serials scene, OCLC continued its active role in the CONSER project. In June 1976, CONSER became fully operational at the LC. During 1976-1977, OCLC completed the computer programming needed to supply LC with machine-readable tapes of the serial records. Harvard University and the United States Department of Interior were the newest participants. A total of twelve institutions across the nation were involved. As the year ended, a proposal was being formulated for OCLC to assume administration of the project.

Another system scheduled for activation was technical processing. Thanks to CLR's grant awarded the previous year, considerable progress was made in its development. The final detailed specifications were nearly done. Programming of the system was well underway, although the simulated version containing the preorder search and order generation components was not to be available in the near future. The acquisitions survey, distributed at the close of the last fiscal year, was returned by 482 libraries. Data on ordering helped the Center project the order file's initial size and growth. Other data, such as acquisitions salary budgets, the number of titles ordered and received, and the size of the staff would be used later in the final stages of the system's development. The results of the survey were printed and bound as a summary report. A revision of *OCLC Technical Processing System—A Preliminary Outline* (February 1972) was being updated.

The functional specifications of the on-line technical processing system were completed in June 1977. They were a prerequisite to the designing of the computer software. In October 1976, Kilgour appointed four staff members to the Budget Planning Committee for Acquisitions. It undertook a study of services to be offered in the new system and their projected costs. In the spring, the Center prepared a grant extension proposal to CLR to continue the developmental work on the system.

Another system under development was Interlibrary Loan (ILL) Communications. In September, with the assistance of the Advisory Committee on ILL, the Center created *Interlibrary Loan Communications Subsystem: Users Manual* (September 1976). This preliminary document was distributed to several participating libraries for comments. The final specifications were nearly ready, and the test data base to simulate the system was to be ready by spring of 1977. Plans called for testing of the system in August 1977. No pricing schedule had been established, although it was estimated that an ILL transaction would cost a library approximately eighty-six cents.

OUT-OF-STATE COOPERATIVE ACTIVITIES AND NETWORKING

During 1976-1977 OCLC added three new participating consortia: Midwest Region Library Network (MIDLNET), Minnesota Interlibrary Teletype Exchange (MINITEX), and Nebraska Library Commission (NEBASE).[70] Practically every state in the union, except for Alaska and Hawaii, had established contact with the Center. Map M-1 shows the geographic distribution of the Center's networks and services as of March 1980. The participating independent institutions have been omitted.[71]

Out-of-state activities grew in another beneficial direction. The Western Service Center (WSC) at Claremont College in Claremont, California, began full operations. Nearly forty institutions were associated with it by June 30, 1977.

Through the FLECC program with OCLC, the number of federal libraries participating in OCLC grew from seven in January 1974 to over thirty by June 1975. FEDLINK anticipated a membership of more than one hundred institutions by the close of calendar 1977. In 1976-1977, the telecommunications lines leased to FEDLINK were expanded to the Denver region, to the Southwest, and to the New York metropolitan area. The lines running into Washington, D.C. were reconfigured to double the communications load for federal libraries near the Capitol. Talks were under way to expand activities to federal libraries in New England, the Southeast, and Texas.

In the summer of 1976, FEDLINK coordinated an agreement between OCLC and GPO to produce the *Monthly Catalog of Government Publications* from OCLC-MARC tapes. Beginning in July 1976, the Government Printing Office (GPO) produced the *Catalog* on-line via OCLC. The MARC format

MAP M-1. Geographic Areas Served by Regional Networks

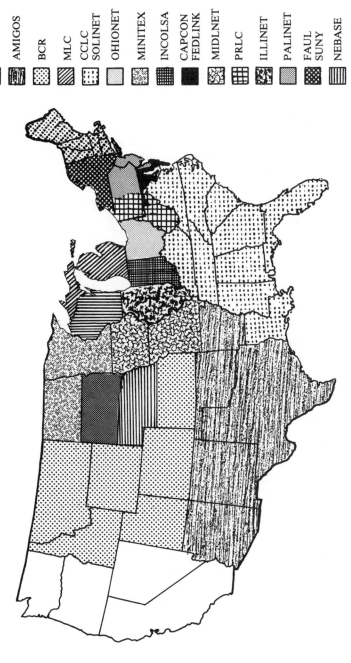

was used along with the *Anglo-American Cataloging Rules*. For GPO the new procedure saved printing time. For nearly nine hundred libraries using OCLC, it provided on-line access to the bibliographic information on government documents before publication in the *Catalog*. At the time of input into the on-line file at OCLC, each document was assigned a unique OCLC number for rapid access to the records. The future plans of FEDLINK included investigating the feasibility of creating a federal data base built upon OCLC records. Another plan dealt with extending the LC-MARC II data base to include the GPO library.

In 1967, Frederick G. Kilgour, working with a small staff in limited quarters in the Main Library on the campus of The Ohio State University, began to sculpt OCLC, the first large-scale computerized library system in America. Drawing upon the faith and trust of the Ohio supporters, he sought and received the financial and spiritual support he needed for OCLC to reach a new and bold level of cooperation.

Relying upon the latest developments in information processing and computer technology, and the administrative and marketing skills of its leader, the Center moved toward fulfilling its dream of a comprehensive library system. That OCLC was held together in the early years by an uncommon faith that was skillfully transformed into a cooperative effort largely contributed to its success. One librarian playfully expressed his feelings this way:

> I pledge allegiance to OCLC
>
> and to the computer for which it stands,
>
> One data base,
>
> Machine-readable,
>
> With cataloging
>
> and holding symbols
>
> For all![72]

Not unnaturally, the original zest for OCLC somewhat waned with time, though the sense of cooperation remained. Kilgour described this change in an article published in June 1979: "As OCLC grew to include those who had never had the opportunity to be believers, the warmth of the earlier spirit dwindled, but the spirit of cooperation continued."[73]

OCLC has a lasting place in the history of librarianship. It not only reached its initial goals but exceeded them, creating new levels of bibliographic sophistication. Moreover, it forced librarianship to abandon the traditional viewpoint of an independent library and to embrace the new idea of a library as part of a network sharing common experiences, resources, and responsibilities for the betterment of all concerned.

Board of Trustees member, Donald J. Sager (Public Library of Columbus and Franklin County) went on record as saying that "an organization that does not look to its future has no future."[74] OCLC always had a vision of tomorrow thanks to the initial leadership of Frederick G. Kilgour. Five years later, on July 10, 1982, OCLC's founder received ALA's highest award, Honorary Life Membership in ALA. The citation read, in part, as follows:

Frederick Kilgour has devoted only slightly less than a half century to library and information service. The most recent third of that career has been dedicated to the establishment and development of OCLC, the single best-known and most successful library automation project—indeed, the most successful library venture with the exception of those initiated by Melvil Dewey.[75]

NOTES

1. Ohio College Library Center, *Newsletter*, 8 June 1977, p. 1.

2. The following served on the Corporate Committee on Response Time: James Barrentine (R & D), Peggy Johnson (Library Systems Division), Don Keates (Computer Facilities Division) and Thompson M. Little (associate executive director), serving as chairman.

3. Ohio College Library Center, "Minutes of the Baord of Trustees Meeting" (Columbus: Ohio College Library Center, 15 February 1977), p. 4.

4. Ohio College Library Center, *Annual Report 1976/1977* (Columbus: Ohio College Library Center, 1977), p. 3.

5. At the tenth annual meeting in November 1976, the representatives elected Patricia L. Lyons (Walsh College) and Janice Strickland (Heidelberg College) to serve on the Council.

6. Ohio College Library Center, "Minutes of Inter-Network Quality Control Council" (Columbus: Ohio College Library Center, 14 December 1977), p. 3.

7. IQCC was subsequently approved by the Board of Trustees. It was, however, abolished in 1982.

8. *On-line Cataloging of Audio-Visual Media and Special Instructional Materials—Preliminary Document, On-line Cataloging of Manuscripts—Preliminary Document, On-line Cataloging of Maps—Preliminary Document, On-line Cataloging of Sound Recordings—Preliminary Document*, and *On-line Cataloging of Music Scores—Preliminary Document*.

9. Op. cit., Ohio College Library Center, *Annual Report 1976/1977*, p. 6.

10. Ohio College Library Center, *Newsletter*, 29 April 1977, p. 3.

11. Ohio College Library Center, "Minutes of the Directors of the Divisions Meeting" (Columbus: Ohio College Library Center, 2 March 1977), p. 3.

12. Op. cit., Ohio College Library Center, *Annual Report 1976/1977*, p. 6.

13. Ibid.

14. Ibid.

15. Ibid., p. 9.

16. Library of Congress, Network Development Office, *COMARC Meeting Report* (Washington, D.C.: Library of Congress, March 1977), p. 3.

17. See chapter 2 for details.

18. *Self-Instructional Introduction to the OCLC Model 100 Terminals* was written by Bonnie Jurgens and published by AMIGOS Bibliographic Council in Richardson, Texas.

19.   OCLC's editor, Philip Schieber, wrote the script. The videotape was produced by Margaret G. Fielders, chairman of the Library Science Department at ODC, and directed by Larry Cepek, director of the College's Audiovisual Center.

20.   The 1977-1978 HSOCLCUG officers were Susan Hill (Cleveland Health Sciences Library), chairperson; Sarah Salley (Medical College of Ohio at Toledo), vice-chairperson/chairperson elect; and James E. Raper, Jr. (Medical Library Center of New York), secretary/treasurer.

21.   Lenore Coral (University of Wisconsin), Karen Hagberg (Eastman School of Music), David Knapp (Oberlin College), Mary Lou Little (Harvard University), and Karl Van Ausdal (SUNY, College at Purchase).

22.   Robert Jacobs (Southern Illinois University) fostered this idea of closer communication and became a coordinator of early activities.

23.   The draft of proposed by-laws was formulated by Frederick S. Baum (Yeshiva University) and assisted by Christian Boissonnas (Cornell University) and Elizabeth W. Matthews (Southern Illinois University).

24.   Christian Boissonnas was elected president. Elizabeth W. Matthews and Jill Brophy (University of California, Los Angeles) were the first vice-president and secretary/treasurer, respectively.

25.   The members of the Advisory Committee included Gayle Edelman (De Paul University), Sonya Sasuta (Columbia University), and Cherylyn Briggs (Yeshiva University).

26.   American Association of Law Libraries, "American Association of Law Libraries, OCLC Special Interest Section Bylaws" (unpublished), p. [1].

27.   Kent State University-Trumbull Campus, Northeastern Ohio Universities College of Medicine, Ohio University-Lancaster Campus, Public Library of Cincinnati and Hamilton County, University of Dayton Law Library, and Westerville Public Library.

28.   Op. cit., Ohio College Library Center, *Annual Report 1976/1977*, p. 1.

29.   Ibid., p. 3.

30.   Ibid., p. 6.

31.   Ohio College Library Center, "Minutes of the Board of Trustees Meeting" (Columbus: Ohio College Library Center, 5 November 1976), p. 2.

32.   Ohio College Library Center, "Minutes of the Members Meeting: Exhibit C (Notes from Bill Chait for *Treasurer's Report* at OCLC Annual Meeting)" (Columbus: Ohio College Library Center, 19-20 December 1977), p. [1].

33.   Ibid., p. 6.

34.   Ohio College Library Center, "Minutes of the Members Meeting" (Columbus: Ohio College Library Center, 19-20 December 1977), p. 8.

35.   Op. cit., Ohio College Library Center, *Annual Report 1976/1977*, p. 13.

36.   Op. cit., Ohio College Library Center, "Minutes of the Members Meeting: Exhibit C," p. 7.

37.   Op. cit., Ohio College Library Center, *Annual Report 1976/1977*, p. 20.

38.   Ohio College Library Center, "Ohio College Library Center: Budget Plan 1977/78" (Columbus: Ohio College Library Center, 5 April 1977), p. 3.

39. Ibid., p. 6.

40. Ohio College Library Center, "Minutes of the Board of Trustees Meeting" (Columbus: Ohio College Library Center, 19 April 1977), p. 4.

41. For details on the long-range plan see appendix 1, Exhibit Q.

42. Op. cit., Ohio College Library Center, "Budget Plan 1977/78," p. 17.

43. Op. cit., Ohio College Library Center, *Annual Report 1976/1977*, p. 16.

44. In March 1977, Ann T. Dodson became the Center's first full-time information specialist and librarian.

45. See appendix 1, Exhibit D, for a complete list of the Board of Trustees members.

46. Ohio College Library Center, "Request for Proposal and Information and Instructions to Bidders" (Columbus: Ohio College Library Center, 12 August 1976), p. 2.

47. The author gratefully acknowledges the generous assistance of Ann Ekstrom (archives and records manager, OCLC) for providing the following information on the involvement of the networks during the previous decade.

48. Frederick G. Kilgour, "Projects of the Ohio College Library Center," *Illinois Libraries* 55 (May 1973): 337.

49. Ohio College Library Center, *Annual Report 1970/1971* (Columbus: Ohio College Library Center, 1971), p. 2.

50. Ibid.

51. Council of Regions, "Minutes of the COR Meeting" (24 May 1973), p. 1.

52. Ohio College Library Center, "Minutes of the Board of Trustees Meeting" (Columbus: Ohio College Library Center, 20 February 1974), p. 2.

53. Memorandum from Robert C. Stewart to Network Directors, December 1975.

54. Ohio College Library Center, "Minutes of the Board of Trustees Meeting" (Columbus: Ohio College Library Center, 16 September 1975), p. 16.

55. Ohic College Library Center, "Minutes of the Board of Trustees Meeting" (Columbus: Ohio College Library Center, 16 December 1975), p. 6.

56. Computer-produced data on cataloging activity indicated that by early 1974, the number of out-of-state libraries participating in the OCLC system equaled the number of Ohio libraries, if the 28 libraries serviced by the processing center CCLC were counted as one. By the end of the 1976-1977 fiscal year there were 110 Ohio libraries participating and 1,178 out-of-state libraries, including processing center libraries and OCLC Western Service Center libraries.

57. Op. cit., Ohio College Library Center, "Minutes of the Members Meeting," p. 5.

58. Arthur D. Little, *A New Governance Structure for OCLC: Principles and Recommendations* (Metuchen, N.J.: The Scarecrow Press, 1978), p. 17.

59. Ibid., p. 81.

60. The acronym no longer stood for the Ohio College Library Center. OCLC had become the nondescript name for the organization.

61. Op. cit., Arthur D. Little, *A New Governance Structure for OCLC*, p. 82.

62. Ibid., p. 83.

63. See appendix 1, Exhibit R, for OHIONET's Articles of Incorporation and Code of Regulations.

64. Ohio College Library Center, "Minutes of the Board of Trustees Meeting" (Columbus: Ohio College Library Center, 19 December 1977), p. 2.

65. Op. cit., Ohio College Library Center, "Minutes of the Members Meeting," p. 13.

66. See appendix 1, Exhibits B and C, for the amended Articles of Incorporation and the Code of Regulations of OCLC, Inc.

67. Ohio College Library Center, *Newsletter*, 22 December 1976, p. 6.

68. *Variable Field Tags for Serials* was compiled by Gretchen Redfield and published by the Bibliographical Center for Research, Denver, Colorado, in 1977.

69. *A Serials Workbook* was written and published by E. Sue Weber of the State University of New York at Stony Brook in 1977.

70. See appendix 1, Exhibit J, for a list of the members of each consortium.

71. Although the map is dated March 1980, the network boundaries remained basically as they were in 1977.

72. Ohio College Library Center, *Newsletter*, 8 December 1977, p. 3. (The librarian was Stephen Pentek, acquisitions librarian, Boston University School of Theology Library.)

73. Frederick G. Kilgour, "OCLC Grows Up," *American Libraries* 10 (June 1979): 363.

74. Ohio College Library Center, "Meeting of the Board of Trustees" (Columbus: Ohio College Library Center, 15 February 1977), p. 6.

75. See appendix 1, Exhibit S, for the full text of the ALA citation.

EPILOGUE
By Philip Schieber

In ten years OCLC had grown from a concept to a nationwide computer network for libraries. In the next five, from 1977 to 1982, it continued to grow, change, and mature.

Numbers told an impressive story. There were two employees and $67,000 in gross revenues in 1967; fifteen years later, in 1982, there were 495 employees and $37.9 million in gross revenues (unaudited). Membership in 1967 totaled 54 Ohio academic libraries; 2,934 academic, research, public, special, law, medical, and other libraries were participating in 1982. One mainframe computer served 54 libraries with one terminal each in 1971, while in 1982 there were 4,490 terminals linked to 6 mainframes. Over 6,000 libraries were using OCLC processes and products in 1982.

The numbers attested to a larger story, that of OCLC having to change and adapt in an environment that was changing even more rapidly. In the five years since Ohio institutions relinquished control of the Ohio College Library Center and sent it on its way as an independent, nonprofit OCLC, Inc., change was concentrated in these areas: governance, computer systems (both centralized and decentralized), finances, facilities, and research. Moreover, in 1979 a change in top management of OCLC also took place. In December 1980, Rowland C. W. Brown, an attorney and business executive, became the second chief executive officer in OCLC's history. And, as the organization prepared to move into a new $25.7 million facility, its name was changed again from OCLC to "OCLC Online Computer Library Center."

GOVERNANCE

The new governance structure for OCLC that was developed by Arthur D. Little, Inc. and recommended to the Ohio Membership by the Board of Trustees had been adopted at the 11th Annual Meeting of the Membership of the Ohio College Library Center in Columbus on December 20, 1977. The January 4, 1978 issue of the *Newsletter* described it as being "designed to make OCLC increasingly effective in attaining its purpose, which is to promote the evolution of library use, of libraries themselves and of librarianship."[1] The *Newsletter* stated that the structure

> combines the benefits of a tightly held not-for-profit corporation and a network cooperative. Libraries participating in organizations contracting with OCLC, Inc. are members of OCLC, Inc. Decision-making powers with regard to replacement of management and approval of policy and budgets reside in a Board of Trustees. The Users Council provides a formal institutional means for participating libraries in networks and other direct contractors of OCLC, Inc. to participate in election of Trustees, and thus, in policy decisions.[2]

The Users Council's formal responsibilities, as set forth in the Code of Regulations of OCLC, included these functions: to elect six of its delegates to the OCLC Board of Trustees; to vote upon the ratification of any and all amendments to the Code of Regulations and Articles of Incorporation; and to "reflect and articulate" the interests of the General Members (users).

In February 1978, fifty-eight persons from OCLC participating networks attended a two-day orientation meeting on the OCLC Users Council in Columbus, where OCLC executives and attorneys explained OCLC's new governance structure and the role that the Users Council would play. In June 1978 the Users Council held its first "official" meeting in which fifty-eight delegates [calculated on the basis of the number of terminals a member (network) has] elected Joseph F. Boykin, Jr. as president. (Boykin was library director, University of North Carolina in Charlotte, and a SOLINET delegate.) The Council also expressed concerns to OCLC about implementation of Anglo-American Cataloging Rules (AACR) II, OCLC's development schedules and priorities, and communication. Meeting again in September 1978, the Users Council elected six persons to the OCLC Board of Trustees: Miriam A. Drake and Russel Shank for six-year terms; Hugh C. Atkinson and Anthony A. Martin for four-year terms; and Glyn T. Evans and D. Kaye Gapen for two-year terms.

The Users Council had a staff of two, a coordinator, and a secretary. Sharon Walbridge became the first Users Council coordinator in March 1979. The coordinator's office facilitates work of the Council, administers policies and programs, and prepares reports for the Council.

Under the broad purpose of reflecting and articulating the concerns of general members (libraries using OCLC), the Users Council began to shape a role for itself within OCLC's governance structure. The concept of a users council was an innovation within the OCLC community. The following excerpt is from an article entitled "The OCLC Users Council" by Joseph F.

Boykin, Jr. and Sharon Walbridge, which appeared in the Winter 1981/Spring 1982 issue of *Resource Sharing & Library Networks*. It illustrates that the success of a users council was not a forgone conclusion:

> One of the fears of the various OCLC participants is that the Users Council is only a facade, or a public relations tool for OCLC. The experience of Council delegates would seem to speak against that fear. To ignore the input of library directors and network directors would be unwise to say the least. At a time when competition from other bibliographic utilities is present, if not mounting, OCLC can hardly afford to ignore the Users Council.[3]

By 1982 the Users Council had found its voice and occupied an important place in the OCLC community in particular and the library community in general. There were eighty-eight delegates to the Users Council in 1982, representing the following types of libraries or organizations: fifty-four delegates from academic libraries; twelve from network; nine, public; five, special; five, federal; two, consortia; and one, state. These delegates met three times a year to hear reports from OCLC management, outside organizations, and from delegates themselves.

The Council created task forces to address a number of concerns of the membership, including: impact of AACR II and authority control; a revised telecommunication pricing algorithm; enforcement of cataloging standards; use of OCLC/MARC Distribution Service tapes; extended use of OCLC subsystems; effects of movement of research libraries to other bibliographic networks; system priorities and needs; effectiveness of the Users Council; and responsible use of the OCLC system.

Presidents of the Users Council have been Joseph F. Boykin, Jr. in 1978-1979 and 1979-1980; Richard Chapin, 1980-1981; and Nancy Marshall, 1981-1982. Boykin and Marshall were subsequently elected to the OCLC Board of Trustees.

The relationship that has developed between the OCLC Users Council and OCLC can be illustrated by a chain of events that probably would not have happened had OCLC users thought of their dealings with OCLC as vendor-customer instead of membership-organization. Because of a variety of problems, mostly resulting from a year-long move of computer equipment from OCLC's Kinnear Road complex to its new facility in Dublin, response time and system availability in late 1981 were considered unacceptable by OCLC and generally considered poor by the thousands of terminal operators who were working with the OCLC system every day.

At the February 1982 Users Council meeting, the delegates adopted a resolution requesting that OCLC regularly communicate progress it had made and actions it was taking to improve system stability. Through the winter and spring of 1982, as performance and stability improved, OCLC introduced an array of reporting mechanisms that gave users throughout the system thorough and up-to-date information about efforts to improve stability and performance. At the May 1982 meeting of the Council, OCLC President Rowland Brown told the delegates: "We took your resolution to heart. We've tried successfully to improve communication about what's happening with the system at OCLC."[4] Included in this communication effort were a more timely log-on message, more informative screen messages, and a more detailed written system performance report. At that same meeting the Users Council passed another resolution, this time commending OCLC for its communication efforts. It was this kind of give-and-take and earnest listening on the part of both the Council and OCLC that perhaps more than anything else fostered a feeling of membership among users of OCLC across the country.

In 1981 OCLC and the Users Council sponsored "Spotlight OCLC," an open-to-the-public annual meeting that drew about 250 persons to the evening event on June 30 as the Annual Conference of ALA was winding down in San Francisco. Speakers included: Miriam A. Drake, chairman of the OCLC Board of Trustees; Rowland C. W. Brown, president of OCLC; Joseph F. Boykin, Jr., substituting for Users Council President Richard Chapin; and Scott Bruntjen, chairman of the Network Directors Group. A question-and-answer period was followed by a social hour. In Philadelphia on July 11, 1982, the second annual "Spotlight OCLC" with a similar program of speakers attracted an audience of over 600 people.

The new governance structure also changed the composition of the Board of Trustees, expanding that body from nine members to fifteen, and specifying that five of the Trustees should be elected from fields such as business, law, finance, government, economics, accounting, computer science, communication technology, or marketing. In October 1978 Ronald L. Wigington, director of research and development, Chemical Abstracts Service, became the first trustee to be elected from a field outside librarianship. Later in 1978, Paul L. Oppenheimer, president of Silent Watchman Corporation, Dr. W. Arthur Cullman, professor of marketing at The Ohio State University, and John B. Deinhardt, president and chief executive officer of Multicon Development, Inc., Multicon Mortgage Services, Inc., Multicon Insurance Agency, Inc., and Multicon International, Inc. were elected to the Board. In June 1979, Lawrence G. Roberts, president and chief executive officer of Telenet Communications Corporation, was elected to the Board.

In the summer of 1977 the Board of Trustees had a long agenda. Purchases of computer hardware, authorizations for construction of a new card production facility at Kinnear Road, policies dealing with remote communication processors, and an agreement with the Royal Library of the Netherlands for the use and dissemination of machine-readable records were just a few of the issues that had to be resolved.

The Board also had to review and revise the report of Arthur D. Little, Inc., entitled "A New Governance Structure for OCLC: Principles and Recommendations." That autumn, Trustees held regional meetings with Ohio library directors to explain the various aspects of the new governance structure that had been developed by Arthur D. Little. In November 1977, the Board recommended to the Membership that it adopt the amended Articles of Incorporation of the Ohio College Library Center and a new Code of Regulations for OCLC, Inc. And finally, the Board said that it would entertain a proposal from OHIONET, a new network being organized for Ohio participants in the OCLC on-line system. On December 20, the same day Ohio members relinquished control of OCLC, they organized OHIONET and approved its Articles of Incorporation and Code of Regulations.

Almost half of the forty-seven resolutions adopted by the OCLC Board of Trustees in 1978 dealt with the new governance structure in one form or another. On March 13, 1978, the Trustees accepted a three hundred thousand dollar support proposal from OHIONET in recognition of Ohio institutions' contributions to OCLC in its four years before on-line operations.

In October 1978 the Trustees authorized OCLC management to enter and complete a construction project for new OCLC facilities. Since 1971 OCLC's operations had continuously outgrown facilities. In 1974 OCLC had launched a building project and approached the threshold of construction, but had to change its plans because the costs of the construction project, after delays, turned out to be too large a debt for OCLC to undertake at the time. In April 1975 OCLC acquired its 1125 Kinnear Road facilities and began moving in that summer. A year later, the first contingents of personnel were already moving to rented office facilities at Kenny and Ackerman Roads, locations that were to become home for about half of OCLC's 360 employees by 1979.

During the five years under discussion, the Board also addressed the following: third-party use of records in the OCLC data base; search for a new chief executive officer; search for a new name and corporate identity for OCLC; and development of new ways for libraries to participate in OCLC.

From November 1979 to January 1980 the Board's Committee on Extended Utilization of Machine-Readable Records held a series of open hearings in New York, San Francisco, Dallas, and Chicago to provide the opportunity for OCLC member libraries, regional networks, and interested people to state their opinions on third-party use of records composing the OCLC data base. Interest in this topic was keen. On January 23, 1980, approximately 250 people showed up for the hearing in Chicago (during the midwinter meeting of the American Library Association) where the Committee received testimony from seven persons. On February 11, the Board, acting on recommendations from the Committee, adopted the policy that OCLC would not place restrictions or limitations on third-party use of records from OCLC's data base provided that such use was for the benefit of participating libraries, networks, and OCLC. This policy, hailed by librarians, affirmed that networks contracting with OCLC and OCLC General Member libraries "owe each other a reciprocal duty of good faith and loyalty, derived from continuing, mutual and cooperative efforts, by which OCLC came to be, is currently maintained, and will continue to grow in the future."[5]

On February 11, 1980, the Board also established a Search Committee for a new chief executive officer of OCLC. Kilgour, sixty-six years old, OCLC's first president and executive director, had indicated to the Board that he would like to step aside from managing OCLC so that he could devote his efforts to innovation. Board Chairman H. Paul Schrank, Jr. was quoted in the *Newsletter* (March 7, 1980) as follows: "The search is being done at Mr. Kilgour's request. For some time he has felt that the heavy responsibilities of day-to-day management have not allowed him to engage in the kind of creative and innovative activities at which he is superb and which brought OCLC into existence."[6]

In June 1980 the Users Council ratified changes to the OCLC Code of Regulations, including amendments that would permit implementation of a succession plan for the chief executive officer of OCLC. The plan, proposed by the Board and subject to ratification by the Users Council, called for creation of an additional seat on the Board, that of Permanent Founder Trustee, and election of Kilgour to that position.

The Board also elected H. Paul Schrank, Jr. to the newly created position of full-time vice-chairman, marketing, of the Board of Trustees of OCLC, where he would be responsible for developing the Board's public, community, and professional relations. Schrank would continue to serve as chairman of the Board until a new chief executive officer joined OCLC.

On October 20 the Board named Rowland C. W. Brown to succeed Kilgour as president of OCLC. A business executive and an attorney, Brown was president and chief executive officer of Buckeye International, Inc., Columbus, Ohio, from 1970 until its acquisition in 1980 by Worthington Industries. Buckeye International manufactures plastic products, steel castings, and precision machine parts for the railroad and automotive industries. The World War II Marine Corps fighter pilot received the A.B. (cum laude) from Harvard University and the J.D. from Harvard Law School. He also attended the Massachusetts Institute of Technology Sloan School of Management. Brown joined OCLC in December 1980, as it was preparing to move its computers and staff to Dublin, Ohio, a Columbus suburb, where OCLC would have a new home, a new name, and a new look.

In June 1979, two-and-a-half years after the Ohio College Library Center had changed its name to OCLC, the Board established an Ad Hoc Committee on the Name of the Corporation. The Committee retained Landor Associates, a firm that specialized in corporate identity programs, to answer the question "What's in a name?" The study would entail an analysis of OCLC's identity requirements to establish how OCLC must be perceived, and by whom, in order to accomplish its intended business objectives. Part of the problem was that an increasing number of people were tired of being asked what the letters "OCLC" stood for. The January 4, 1978 *Newsletter* answered the question "What does the OCLC in OCLC, Inc. stand for?" in a way described by *American Libraries* as Orwellian "newspeak": "The 'OCLC' in OCLC, Inc., the new name replacing the former 'Ohio College Library Center,' does not stand for anything. OCLC, Inc. is not an acronym. OCLC is OCLC."[7]

In April 1980 Landor Associates made a preliminary presentation to the Board, at which time the Board asked the firm to explore developing a meaning for the acronym "OCLC," developing an entirely new name, and also developing combinations of the former and the latter. In April 1981, OCLC became "OCLC Online Computer Library Center." A new logotype was introduced that represented OCLC's "literary tradition in combination with its electronic future."

OCLC historically required that "participants" be libraries that do all their Roman alphabet cataloging on-line. This policy underlined the cooperative nature of the on-line union catalog, which in April 1982 contained over 8.2 million bibliographic records, including 5.9 million records input by participants. By the 1980s, however, there was a growing feeling in the library community that the requirement was too restrictive, especially in light of new subsystems, such as Interlibrary Loan and Acquisitions, that OCLC had introduced. In December 1981 the Board authorized OCLC management to proceed with plans to bring OCLC services to a broader range of libraries.

In February 1982, OCLC President Rowland Brown announced new expanded opportunities for participation in OCLC that would enable any library to use OCLC's noncataloging subsystems whether or not it does its Roman alphabet cataloging on-line via OCLC. Brown said: "We are making it possible for any library in the United States to participate in OCLC in ways that meet their particular needs. The concepts of partial use of the OCLC on-line system by non-member libraries and membership by tapeload strengthen OCLC's status as the national on-line library network."[8]

Under the new requirements for participation, three user categories were defined: *participant, special user,* and *partial user.* A participant is a library that does all its Roman alphabet cataloging on-line or by tapeload. In some cases, a nonprofit, noncataloging organization may be a participant because its participation is deemed to be in the best interests of the general membership and furthers the purpose of increasing availability of library resources. A special user is a library that uses the on-line system but does not qualify as a participant. Examples are some CONSER participants, national libraries, library schools, and experimental users. A partial user is a library that elects not to contribute its Roman alphabet cataloging to the OCLC data base but uses any of OCLC's noncataloging subsystems. A library must apply for partial user status, which OCLC, at its discretion, could grant or deny. On-line system charges for partial users would be higher than for participants.[9]

In 1982 OCLC and regional network affiliates were examining their roles and relationships. Over 99 percent of libraries using OCLC did so through twenty-one regional networks or two OCLC service centers. Regional networks are independent organizations that contract with OCLC to provide services to their member libraries. OCLC participants received ongoing support, training, and in some cases, additional automation services from network affiliates.

The Board authorized OCLC management to make OCLC processes and products available outside the United States in April 1980. OCLC Europe, yet another OCLC service center, opened offices in Birmingham, England, in January 1981 to market OCLC computer services to libraries in Great Britain and Europe.

In 1982 libraries in Australia, Canada, Finland, Mexico, the United Kingdom, West Germany, and the United States were on-line to OCLC's computer facility in Dublin, Ohio. Back in 1974 when the on-line system was operated by the Ohio College Library Center, Kilgour had written in a brochure: "Computerized cooperatives, such as the Ohio College Library Center, can make available to users in individual libraries resources throughout an entire region, nation, or group of nations."[10]

COMPUTER SYSTEMS

From 1977 to 1982 OCLC continued to pursue a vigorous program of development of its computer systems. While OCLC was refining and enhancing what was becoming known as one of the largest on-line computer networks in the United States (with a monthly telecommunication bill approaching five hundred thousand dollars), it was already looking to a future that promised local, decentralized, stand-alone computer systems.

In the 1979-1980 OCLC *Annual Report* Kilgour wrote: "Dramatic changes in the ways of providing information are in store for the years ahead." He described advances in silicon-chip technology that were affecting television, printing, and publishing. He continued: "Production of information in part or in whole of a separate, distinct corpus will invalidate the basic assumption on which library systems have been based since Gutenberg—that each copy of a book is an exact duplicate of every other copy of the same printing. This development will clearly turn libraries toward information servicing and away from dealing in packages of data—namely, books, serials, maps and films."[11]

A counting of computer equipment in OCLC's 1125 Kinnear Road facility in 1981, just before the move of the on-line system to Dublin, Ohio, was to begin, would have revealed the following inventory in the 25,300-square foot computer rooms: 9 mainframe Sigma 9 computers, 46 minicomputers and 140 spindles of disk storage.

A brief history of OCLC's computer architecture begins with the Xerox Sigma 5 computer that ran the on-line system from August 1971 until installation of the first Sigma 9 in February 1975. In December 1975 OCLC added a second Sigma 9, a third in November 1976, a fourth in February 1977, a fifth in December 1979, and a sixth in February 1981.

A Data Base Processor consisting of Tandem computer equipment was activated in October 1978 and was designed to improve reliability and to increase the capacity of the on-line union catalog. A Network Supervisor consisting of Tandem computer equipment was installed in March 1979 and eventually will be used to provide OCLC users with access to non-OCLC data bases. In the summer of 1982 OCLC completed a $2.4 million modem conversion project whereby AT & T modems were replaced with Paradyne modems that would enable OCLC to provide better service to users.

In September 1980 OCLC installed the first Remote Communication Processor (RCP) in the network at SOLINET headquarters in Atlanta, Georgia. The RCP, an OCLC-owned-and-designed Tandem computer, was linked to Dublin by a high-speed 56,000-baud telecommunication line. (Other lines in the OCLC telecommunication network were 2,400 baud.) The *Newsletter* described the purpose of the RCP as follows: "to reduce telecommunication costs eventually; to provide regional networks such as SOLINET with a practical mechanism for linking its regional support system with the OCLC system; and to allow OCLC to experiment with distributing some processing to a remote site."[12]

In 1981 in addition to the six Sigma 9 computers in the on-line system, OCLC had two administrative/development computers (a Sigma 9 and a Tandem processor) and two Sigma 9 systems for production of OCLC/MARC Distribution Service tapes, catalog cards, accessions lists, and acquisitions action forms. Also, OCLC was using an IBM 4331 computer with seven 3302 line printers, two tape drives, and two 65-megabyte disk drives to print cards and other products. A Xerox laser printing system was used for producing internal and external products.

This recitation of computer equipment demonstrates the acute need OCLC had for a large, secure facility to house its on-line system and to adequately safeguard the information that libraries had been using and sharing since 1971. If the OCLC system were down for an hour in 1982, it essentially idled 4,390 workers across the country at OCLC terminals. Libraries' increasing reliance on OCLC's computer technology led OCLC to take steps to ensure availability of the system so that users could depend on it for catalog access, interlibrary loans, acquisitions, and serials control.

With the weather in central Ohio having the capacity to affect the productivity of a terminal operator in California, OCLC developed its own alternative power supplies for the on-line system. OCLC plugged the on-line system into a 500-kilowatt diesel generator for twenty-three days in March 1978 during an electric power crisis in Ohio accompanied by a coal strike. OCLC had purchased the generator for its Kinnear Road facility before the energy crisis began as backup power for the on-line system. Its first test ran longer than originally planned. The generator had been dubbed "NEWT" by OCLC engineers, and its run was described by the *Newsletter* (April 7, 1978): "When providing power for the on-line system, NEWT consumes about 1,200 gallons of fuel oil a day. Every 10 days or 350,000 books cataloged, NEWT needs a lube job and an oil change."[13]

In OCLC's Dublin Center, four 750-kilowatt diesel generators were available for backup power for the computer rooms, emergency lighting, elevators, and heating, ventilating, and air-conditioning motors. An uninterruptible power system would provide up to ten minutes of power in the event of a blackout. If the outage were to continue, the auxiliary power system would take over. Moreover, in the new facility, heat recovered from the computers would be used to heat the rest of the building.

In March 1978 OCLC's new Model 105 terminal, manufactured by Beehive International, started production. The Model 105 had the same capabilities as the OCLC Model 100 terminal. Engineering modifications in the Model 105 were designed to improve reliability and maintainability.

The move of computer equipment from Kinnear Road to OCLC's new center in Dublin was completed on December 7, 1981. In a communication to OCLC staff a few days later OCLC President Brown wrote: "At long last we are all under one roof. With the transfer on December 7 of Computer Support Staff, Telecommunication, Network Operations Center, and the last pieces of computer equipment, we mark the end of a long and arduous task that has few parallels in the data processing industry."[14] Planning for the computer move was under way before ground was broken for the new building in June 1979. The move of OCLC computers and systems actually began in late 1980 while construction was still going on. In the same communication Brown stated: "You have moved a very large integrated computer system while at the same time ensuring operation of that system which is the lifeblood of OCLC, a corporation that employs 480 persons and provides services to over 6,000 libraries and their patrons."[15]

From 1977 to 1982 OCLC introduced major subsystems and additions to the on-line system, including Interlibrary Loan, Acquisitions, and Serials Union Listing. The name authority file of the Library of Congress was added, and a Name-Address file was installed. And in December 1980 OCLC successfully converted the data base to AACR II form.

Some of the enhancements were transparent to users, such as a new multilevel indexing technique that required three consecutive weekends in the fall of 1977 for installation. This enhancement reduced significantly the number of input/output transactions executed within the computer system for derived search key searching and adding records to the on-line catalog, with a result of improved response time for users. Similarly, in April 1978, another user-transparent enhancement was installed to overcome the previous limitation of storing 1,524 institution symbols. Now there was no practical limit to the number of institution symbols that the on-line system could accommodate. In 1980-1981 alone, OCLC installed 265 enhancements and changes (affecting 1,705 pieces of software) to its on-line system. These computer programs were designed and developed at OCLC as part of its ongoing schedule of maintenance and improvement of existing subsystems.

On September 23, 1977, OCLC completed processing of deferred LC-MARC II records ahead of schedule. Since December 1976, when OCLC began using a new matching algorithm to process LC-MARC II records, some ninety thousand previously deferred records as well as incoming records from weekly tapes from LC were added to the on-line catalog. The new program developed by OCLC did not defer records, and it also detected and eliminated duplicate records in the on-line catalog.

On January 15, 1979, OCLC began to test its Interlibrary Loan sub-system, initially in twelve Ohio libraries, and later in thirty-six additional libraries across the country. In April the system was opened to the library community, and users placed approximately 12,000 on-line interlibrary loan requests that first month. In 1980-1981, users transacted over 940,000 interlibrary loans on the system. The one millionth Interlibrary Loan request was conducted by Belk Library at Appalachian State University in Boone, North Carolina, on November 13, 1980, only twenty months after the system became generally available.

In the fall of 1980 the on-line Name Address Directory became available to users. This on-line file contained names, addresses, and other communication and policy information about libraries, publishers, vendors, and other organizations in the information industry. In July 1982 this file also began to support "paperless interlibrary loan policies" by providing interlibrary loan librarians with the opportunity to enter on-line information regarding their loan periods, charges, and other interlibrary-loan-related issues.

In April 1981 OCLC installed its Acquisitions subsystem that included on-line preorder searching and order generation, and made it generally available in July 1981. In its first year of operation, libraries were using the system to order over twenty-two thousand titles a month from vendors and publishers.

In June 1980 OCLC installed software that rearranged the display of holdings symbols in the on-line union catalog. Holdings symbols used to be arranged in the order in which a library joined OCLC's nationwide network. Now, however, a simple request at the terminal showed the institution symbols arranged alphabetically by state, or by regional grouping of states.

The Cataloging subsystem continued to be enhanced. In September 1980 the *Newsletter* reported that OCLC "has increased the payload of its on-line searching capabilities with a group of enhancements that included retrieval by Government Document number, performers and performing groups, variant names and titles, and publication data and record type." In addition, OCLC also raised the ceiling on the number of records that could be retrieved by a derived search key (author, name-title, and title) from 256 records to 1,500. For the first time, Shakespeare's *Hamlet* could be retrieved.[16]

Of the six subsystems called for in the original overall development plan of the Ohio College Library Center, OCLC by 1982 had succeeded in bringing up cataloging, serials control, interlibrary loan, and acquisitions. Subject access and circulation control remained to be done. A major obstacle to development of a subject search capability for OCLC libraries was the problem of how to make it available to a large number of simultaneous users. This was largely a technical problem with no easy solution in sight. In the case of circulation control, however, the problems may have had too many solutions available at a time when libraries began exploring local library systems that might or might not be linked to a large centralized system such as OCLC's.

In December 1979 the Board reaffirmed OCLC's intention to implement an on-line circulation system and directed OCLC staff to develop an original-equipment-manufacturer (OEM) type of arrangement. After review of existing operational circulation systems suitable for integration with current and planned OCLC library processes and products, OCLC entered into negotiations for an OEM agreement with one vendor, but the negotiations fell through. In June 1980 the Board directed OCLC to proceed with in-house development of an on-line circulation system. By the fall of 1981, though, OCLC had reexamined what role it would play in development of circulation control systems, and ultimately, local library systems.

In the 1980-1981 *Annual Report*, Brown wrote: "It is clear that local library systems, individual or clustered, patterned on the same goals and objectives of OCLC's centralized on-line system, are going to play a strategic role in the evolution of library use and librarianship. OCLC took the initial steps this past year to assume a leadership role in developing local systems that ultimately will meet the total automation needs of libraries."[17]

On October 29, 1981, OCLC and the Claremont University Center in Claremont, California, announced the signing of an exclusive licensing agreement whereby OCLC would market the award-winning Claremont Total Library System (TLS), which was designed and developed by the staff of the Libraries of the Claremont Colleges. TLS earned the Honnold Library of the Claremont Colleges the prestigous Cost Reduction and Incentive award funded by the U.S. Steel Foundation and granted by the National Association of College and University Business Officers. It was selected after careful screening of many alternatives because it offered the best combination of operationally tested features and equipment at a price that libraries could afford. TLS would complement OCLC's own Local Library System (LLS) that was being internally developed.

OCLC's direction in local library systems was summarized in the 1980-1981 *Annual Report*:

> OCLC is currently developing an automated local library system utilizing Tandem computers that will eventually have at the local level such desired systems as circulation and an on-line local catalog in addition to access to the OCLC centralized system for cataloging, acquisitions, serials control and interlibrary loan. This system will be particularly adaptable to clustered use, and it will be capable of almost infinite growth.
>
> In addition OCLC has obtained exclusive rights to enhance, market and support the Total Library System now in operation at the Claremont Colleges in California. This highly acclaimed system utilizes Hewlett-Packard computers and broadens OCLC's offerings at the local library level.

Unlike many commercial offerings now available—which are essentially enhanced circulation systems—OCLC, in cooperative development with libraries and networks, is designing total library systems which permit the library to adopt its automation in building-block stages in a cost-effective manner, to cluster with other libraries where appropriate, and to begin with a system which is capable of growing with users' needs without having to make difficult hardware or software changes.[18]

In May 1982 OCLC and Five Colleges, Inc. announced a collaborative agreement whereby OCLC would develop, install, and evaluate an automated local library system that would link the library resources and services of five academic institutions (Amherst, Hampshire, Mount Holyoke, Smith Colleges, and the University of Massachusetts-Amherst). Their libraries, whose combined holdings totaled over 4,495,000 volumes and microforms, were to provide a working environment for OCLC to develop an automated local library system.

FINANCES

From 1977 to 1982 OCLC's revenues grew from $14.9 million to $37.9 million (unaudited). At approximately the same time, from 1978 to 1982, OCLC's first-time-use (for cataloging) costs to libraries went up to 19 percent while the Producer Price Index was projected to increase at approximately 60 percent. Brown wrote in the 1980-1981 *Annual Report*: "OCLC's objective of reducing the rate-of-rise of costs in libraries was continuing to be realized while at the same time it was possible for libraries to share resources more efficiently than ever before and to improve patron services."[19]

In 1979 OCLC embarked on a $38.5 million industrial revenue bond project, including $25.7 million for construction of the new facility in Dublin, Ohio, $8.6 million for refinance of existing debt, and $3.8 million for acquisition of new equipment. The bonds, which yielded 7.5 percent interest, went on the market May 25, 1979, and were totally subscribed to by May 30. Industrial revenue bonds enable businesses to expand their operations to preserve existing jobs or create new ones. The bonds carry a lower rate of interest than conventional loans and enable organizations to obtain more favorable financing than would be available through conventional loans.

In the 1980-1981 *Annual Report* Brown wrote: "The financial well being of OCLC is intertwined with that of the nation's libraries." He continued: "In the next few years the challenge to OCLC will be to provide technologically-supported services, within the resources available to us, that financially-strapped libraries will need more than ever, while at the same time obtaining the funds to accommodate future growth and system improvement and enhancement."[20]

As a not-for-profit corporation, OCLC had only two sources of working capital: operations and borrowed funds. Its pricing covered not only current annual operating expense but also had to provide funds for debt repayment, research and development activity for future growth of services, and adequate funds for future capital asset acquisition.

Grant awards for specific research and development projects provided only a small portion of revenues in the years 1977-1982. In 1981, for example, total operating revenues were $30.6 million, of which grants and contracts totaled $696,031.

OCLC received the following grants from 1977 to 1982. In 1977 the Council on Library Resources provided $122,000 for the Arthur D. Little study of OCLC's governance structure and the role that OCLC might play in the emerging national network. The State Library of Ohio awarded OCLC $9,000 for design of a holdings component that would provide on-line local catalog information; in 1978 the State Library awarded $80,687 for continuation of that project.

In 1978 The State Library of Ohio provided a grant of $394,587 for retrospective conversion of the catalogs of the Cleveland Public Library. Indiana State University awarded OCLC $107,875 for development of a union list of serials. In 1979 OCLC also received a grant of $60,000 from the National Endowment for the Humanities, Carnegie Corporation, and the Council on Library Resources for development of non-Roman alphabet capability for library processes.

In 1979-1980, the National Library of Medicine granted $88,013 to OCLC for modeling and evaluating on-line user behavior. The National Science Foundation awarded two grants: $97,902 to study on-line catalog use in libraries, and $42,321 to study name authority control in an on-line catalog. The Council on Library Resources, Inc. awarded OCLC $8,150 for study of patron access to on-line catalogs. In 1980-1981 it awarded OCLC a grant of $178,999 to support a study of on-line public access systems in a variety of libraries across the country.

RESEARCH

The March 1, 1982 issue of *Library Journal* carried an article entitled "OCLC Is Not a 'Dinosaur,' but Will Set the Pace." Written by Noelle Savage, the article described a Virginia Legislative Study Commission on Library Networking report that maintained that "super networks" like OCLC were becoming obsolete. Savage restated the conclusions of the report as follows: "The technological revolution, the study maintained, has changed the shape of networking irrevocably by opening up new possibilities for libraries and consortia; they no longer need to rely on big utilities."[21]

The article quoted Brown's reply:

Far from being a technological dinosaur, OCLC, on a national level, continues to exercise leadership in preparing libraries for the technological opportunities of the 80's. By combining both a 'top down approach' to the national online union catalog and interlibrary loan system with a 'bottom up approach' to local or clustered library automation using small but powerful software and hardware systems, such as our TLS (Total Library System based on the Claremont College automation system) and Local Library Systems, OCLC belies the concern that we are either victims of inertia or are moving away from the purposes of the constituent libraries for which we came into existence to serve.[22]

One of the things that helped OCLC set the pace in library networking and automation was its research. Although OCLC had a formalized Research and Development Division since 1974, most of that Division's work had been development rather than research. In 1978, OCLC activated a Research Department (that subsequently became the Office of Research in 1981). The August 2, 1978 *Newsletter* said: "OCLC is undertaking mission-oriented research that it hopes will yield information needed by every computerized library network for development."[23]

In 1977 OCLC reported research and development costs of $670,000. By 1981 that figure had increased to $3,094,000. By 1982, OCLC's Office of Research had conducted mission-oriented research in these areas: human/computer interaction; microcomputer applications; electronic document delivery; on-line catalogs; distributed processing; and improved access techniques to information stored in large on-line systems.

In August 1979 the Office of Research published the first in a series of response reports, "Subject Heading Patterns in OCLC Monographic Records," by Edward T. O'Neill and Rao Aluri. By 1982 OCLC had issued seven research reports and six technical reports. In May 1982 it launched a monograph series, "The OCLC Library, Information and Computer Science Series," with publication of *Online Public Access Catalogs: The User Interface* by Charles Hildreth.

In 1980 OCLC attracted national attention in the news media with its CHANNEL 2000 experiment. A prototype personalized information system for use in the home or office, CHANNEL 2000 turned a television set and telephone into a computer terminal. The system, designed and developed by OCLC, was tested in two hundred homes in the Columbus area from October to December 1980. Families used their TV sets to find and check out books from the public library, to look up articles in the world's first electronic encyclopedia, to consult a community calendar of events, or to pay bills through a local electronic banking system. There were also math and reading programs for children. Experience gained from the CHANNEL 2000 test assisted OCLC in its explorations of viewdata systems and other innovative ways of bringing information to people.

FACILITIES

On June 2, 1979, OCLC broke ground for its new $25.7 million Center in Dublin. The 328,000 square foot, four-story structure included a three-story, 44,000 square foot computer room, a cafeteria, auditorium, and a variety of training and conference rooms. The building was designed to accommodate up to 625 staff persons. In February 1981 OCLC staff moved in, and in September, the facility was dedicated.

On the occasion of the dedication, Brown issued the following message to librarians, educators, and the general public:

> With the dedication of OCLC's new center to its public purpose of furthering use of knowledge and information, we feel a deep sense of pride in the progress we have made in our 14-year history, and gratitude to the many people who have contributed to this program.

Plate IV. New OCLC Facility in Dublin, Ohio (Courtesy of OCLC)

OCLC's journey—from its founding in 1967, to inauguration of online library services in 1971, to introduction of an in-home information system in 1980—has been but preparation for the challenges that await us.

It is our hope that this new building in its attractive setting in Dublin will become the Center, for OCLC in its role as researcher, developer, innovator, and communicator throughout the nation and the world, and for people, in their roles as librarians, educators and citizens.[24]

NOTES

1. OCLC, Inc., *Newsletter*, 4 January 1978, p. [4].

2. Ibid., p. 4.

3. Joseph F. Boykin, Jr., and Sharon Walbridge, "The OCLC Users Council," *Resource Sharing and Library Networks* 1 [2/3] (Winter 1981, Spring 1982), pp. 51-65.

4. OCLC Online Computer Library Center, Inc., *Newsletter*, July 1982, p. [2].

5. OCLC, Inc., *Newsletter*, 7 March 1980, p. [2].

6. Ibid.

7. OCLC, Inc., *Newsletter*, 4 January 1978, p. [2].

8. OCLC Online Computer Library Center, Inc., *Newsletter*, March 1982, p. [1].

9. Ibid.

10. Ohio College Library Center, "Computerized Regional Library Resources" (Columbus: Ohio College Library Center, Autumn 1974).

11. OCLC, Inc., *Annual Report 1979/1980* (Columbus: OCLC, Inc., 1980), p. 2.

12. OCLC, Inc., *Newsletter*, 31 October 1980, p. [6].

13. OCLC, Inc., *Newsletter*, 7 April 1978, p. [1].

14. OCLC Online Computer Library Center, Inc., *Newsletter*, January 1982, p. [1].

15. Ibid.

16. OCLC, Inc., *Newsletter*, 26 September 1980, p. [1].

17. OCLC Online Computer Library Center, Inc., *Annual Report 1980/1981* (Columbus: OCLC Online Computer Library Center, Inc., 1981), p. 1.

18. Ibid., p. 7.

19. Ibid., p. 1.

20. Ibid., p. 1.

21. Noelle Savage, "OCLC Is Not a 'Dinosaur,' but Will Set the Pace," *Library Journal* 107 (1 March 1982): 493.

22. Ibid.

23. OCLC, Inc., *Newsletter*, 2 August 1978, p. [2].

24. OCLC Online Computer Library Center, Inc., *Newsletter*, November 1981, p. [4].

CHRONOLOGY OF SIGNIFICANT EVENTS
OCLC Highlights of 1967-1977
By Philip Schieber

1967

July 6, 1967 — Articles of Incorporation signed. OCLC is incorporated as a not-for-profit corporation, chartered in the State of Ohio, by the Ohio College Association.

July 11, 1967 — Frederick G. Kilgour accepts position as director of OCLC.

Fall 1967 — OCLC opens offices in space made available by The Ohio State University Libraries.

October 25, 1967 — First Annual Membership Meeting held at Denison University. Forty-eight Ohio academic libraries paid assessments for membership in OCLC. Developmental program presented: shared cataloging; bibliographic information retrieval; circulation control; serials control; and technical processing.

Board approves OCLC's first budget (1967-1968): $66,428.

December 18, 1967 — First OCLC newsletter issued, under title "OCLC."

1968

June 19, 1968 | Second OCLC *Newsletter* issued.

October 10, 1968 | OCLC's offices are now located in space formerly occupied by The Ohio State University Research Center at 1314 Kinnear Road in Columbus.

November 8, 1968 | Second Annual Membership Meeting held at The Ohio State University.

1969

Spring 1969 | Board approves "Statement of Academic Objective, Economic Goal, and Missions to Achieve These Ends."

Center enters into contract with National Agricultural Library, which provided $4,182 for continuation of research on retrieval of single entries from large bibliographic files.

April 1969 | Center receives matching grant from State Library of Ohio ($18,588) to conduct simulation study of a computer system to operate a computerized regional network for academic libraries.

September 1969 | Simulation study completed.

Fall 1969 | Off-line catalog card production begins, but not for member catalogs.

November 14, 1969 | Third Annual Membership Meeting held at Ohio Wesleyan University.

1970

Winter 1970 | Advisory Cataloging Committee appointed to advise OCLC in design of on-line cataloging system.

January 1, 1970 | U.S. Office of Education awards OCLC $90,135 grant to develop and implement an on-line shared cataloging system.

February 12, 1970 | Board selects Xerox Data Systems Sigma 5 computer for on-line system.

April 1970 | Three member libraries receive cards from off-line catalog card production.

April 30, 1970 | OCLC Advisory Committee meets "to review OCLC's overall plans in general, and shared cataloging plans in particular."

June 1970	Council on Library Resources gives OCLC $14,133 grant for materials, telecommunication, and terminals for on-line system.
June 25, 1970	National Agricultural Library awards OCLC $1,750 grant to investigate retrieval of title-only entries from computerized files of large numbers of bibliographic entries by use of truncated search keys.
July 1970	Off-line catalog card production begins for all Ohio libraries; 440,711 cards are produced during first year at average cost of 6.9¢ a card.
August 1970	Xerox Sigma 5 computer arrives.
September 1970	Board accepts recommendation of Center staff to use Spiras Systems, Inc. Irascope Model LTE terminals for on-line system. (Seventy terminals will be acquired by January 1971.)
November 1970	Pittsburgh Regional Library Center signs first out-of-state agreement with OCLC for off-line, and subsequently, when available, on-line participation in OCLC.
November 13, 1970	Fourth Annual Membership Meeting held at Ohio Northern University.

1971

Spring 1971	Council on Library Resources awards OCLC $75,000 to continue research to develop a computerized regional library system.
March 19, 1971	OCLC *Newsletter* tells libraries how to prepare sites for their cataloging terminals.
June 1971	Author-title, title, and Library of Congress card-number indices are available on-line, although on-line systems not yet ready for membership use.
June 28, 1971	OCLC holds meeting for Ohio librarians in Columbus to teach the basic knowledge required to operate a CRT terminal.
June 30, 1971	U.S. Office of Education extends grant (by $125,000) for development of computerized regional shared cataloging system by OCLC.
July 27, 1971	OCLC *Newsletter* reports that twenty terminals have been shipped to libraries. A telephone workers strike delays start of on-line operations.
July 31, 1971	Eleven terminals installed and operating in libraries. Training system is available 7 A.M. to 7 P.M., Monday through Friday, Eastern Standard Time.

August 26, 1971	On-line cataloging system begins. Ohio University, Athens, Ohio, becomes first library to do OCLC on-line cataloging; 147 titles are cataloged the first day. That night a lightning strike damages OCLC's computer equipment.
October 1, 1971	Advisory Committee on Serials meets at OCLC for the first time.
October 13, 1971	Holdings information for the first time is displayed on a bibliographic record.
October 18, 1971	On-line system starts accepting member input cataloging.
November 12, 1971	Fifth Annual Membership Meeting held at College of Wooster.
November 24, 1971	Advisory Committee on Technical Processing is formed.
December 10, 1971	Ohio Legislature approves subsidy for Ohio Board of Regents to assist OCLC members over a two-year period in implementation of on-line computerized library system. It gives members a two-year period to take advantage of normal attrition of personnel to transfer salary payments to OCLC; total subsidy— $581,587.

1972

January 1972	New England Library Information Network receives grant from Council on Library Resources to test transferability of OCLC's system to other groups of libraries.
January 26, 1972	OCLC control number index becomes available on-line.
May 1972	Philip L. Long is promoted to assistant director of OCLC.
May 17, 1972	Membership instructs Board to proceed to amend Articles of Incorporation to permit nonacademic libraries in Ohio to become members of OCLC.
	Board establishes the Committee on Implementation of *Standards for Input Cataloging*.
November 10, 1972	Sixth Annual Membership Meeting held at The Ohio State University. Membership rejects proposal to expand Board from nine members to thirteen, of which three might be from fields outside librarianship. Membership authorizes Board to explore possibilities of expansion outside Ohio.

December 1972   Council on Library Resources awards OCLC $194,000 grant for continued enhancement of on-line union catalog and shared cataloging system, and development of serials control subsystem.

1973

January 1973   OCLC makes in-bound WATS line available for users.

February 12, 1973   OCLC activates extended search function making it possible to retrieve up to 256 items.

Spring 1973   Federal Library Committee signs contract with OCLC.

                     OCLC and Beehive Medical Electronics, Inc. sign contract for a new terminal, OCLC Model 100 Display.

March 26, 1973   OCLC Membership votes to extend OCLC services to regional library groups outside Ohio.

April 1973   OCLC moves offices to 1550 West Henderson Road in Columbus, Ohio. Computers remain at OSU Research Center.

September 1973   Computer-produced accessions lists become available.

                     Philip L. Long becomes associate director of OCLC.

November 9, 1973   Seventh Annual Membership Meeting held at The Ohio State University.

                     Peer Council is created to implement standards and maintain quality control.

1974

January 1974   Board approves placing order for a second Xerox Sigma 9 computer.

January 14-16, 1974 Board holds a three-day conference to formulate new purposes, goals, and objectives for the organization. "Statement of Purpose, Objectives, Systems, and Plans for Attaining Objectives" is approved.

May 21, 1974   Board approves $2,218,000 budget for 1974-1975; an increase of $614,000 over previous year.

                     Ohio members amend purpose clause in Articles of Incorporation at special meeting in Columbus.

                     On-line hours of operation extended from 7 A.M. to 7 P.M., to 7 A.M. to 8 P.M., Monday through Friday, Eastern Standard Time.

                     Board adopts discount policy for advance payments.

June 1974 — OCLC receives $18,867 grant from State Library of Ohio under LSCA Title III to test public use terminals.

July 1974 — OCLC to purchase two additional Xerox Sigma 9 computers ($4.5 million).

W. Stuart Debenham named assistant executive director of OCLC.

August 20, 1974 — On-line system demonstrated in Sydney, Australia, by F. G. Kilgour.

September 6, 1974 — Northeastern University in Boston, Massachusetts, inputs millionth record into OCLC data base.

October 1974 — OCLC implements screen message to be displayed when system is down. By depressing SEND key, users receive immediate information about status of system without calling the Center.

November 1974 — Librarians from ten foreign countries visit OCLC as part of preconference tour of International Federation of Library Associations.

November 8, 1974 — Eighth Annual Membership Meeting held in Columbus.

OCLC sponsors seminar on "Economics of Libraries" in Columbus.

December 1974 — Center starts charging for profile changes. OCLC reorganizes into five divisions: Executive Director's Office; Library Systems; Research & Development; Computer Facilities; and Administration and Finance.

December 17, 1974 — CONSER Project starts (Council on Library Resources and OCLC sign agreement).

1975

January 1975 — OCLC begins to expand and reorganize data base.

February 1-2, 1975 — New search key structures introduced that are more specific.

February 10, 1975 — Personal author index to on-line union catalog becomes available.

February 18, 1975 — Board approves charges for serials check-in on OCLC system.

February 25, 1975 — First Xerox Sigma 9 computer comes on-line.

March 1975 — On-line system available 100 percent of scheduled time on March 10-21.

Drexel University Graduate School of Library Science is the first library school to become an educational affiliate of OCLC.

March 3, 1975	On-line hours of operation extended from 7 A.M. to 10 P.M., Monday through Friday, Eastern Standard Time.
March 11, 1975	Board approves $10,730,000 budget for 1975-1976.
March 24, 1975	ISBN, ISSN, and CODEN files become available for searching.
April 15, 1975	Board defers implementation of search-key search charges "pending further study and review."
April 16, 1975	Staff from OCLC and Battelle Memorial Institute meet for first time to discuss subject search using BASIS.
April 22, 1975	On-line system demonstrated in Vienna, Austria, by F. G. Kilgour.
May 1, 1975	Second Xerox Sigma 9 computer arrives at OCLC.
May 20, 1975	Board creates Standing Finance Committee.
June 3, 1975	"New" command installed.
June 17, 1975	Board implements charge for search-key searches on public use terminals at rate of 2.2¢ per search with maximum annual charge per terminal of $2,280.
June 19, 1975	State Library of Ohio awards OCLC $56,000 towards purchase of terminals for Ohio libraries.
June 30, 1975	OCLC acquires six-acre tract of land with four buildings at 1125 Kinnear Road in Columbus. Construction and remodeling begin July 7, 1975, with staff scheduled to move in October 1975. Cost of total project is $2.4 million.
July 13, 1975	OCLC begins adding records to data base from Minnesota Union List of Serials; 71,000 serials records are to be added.
July 15, 1975	OCLC announces that it has received $124,250 grant from Council on Library Resources to assist in development of on-line authority files, acquisitions, and OCLC/Battelle subject access project.
	U.S. Office of Education awards OCLC $108,575 for development of computer-based interlibrary loan subsystem.
September 16, 1975	Board announces increase in basic first-time use charge by $0.10 (starting in July 1976) to generate working capital for OCLC.

October 4, 1975	OCLC extends on-line operating hours to Saturdays, 9 A.M. to 5 P.M., Eastern Standard Time, "to compensate libraries for lost time due to the temporary increase in response time during peak hours of system activity."

OCLC *Newsletter* No. 87 describes feathering procedure whereby terminals on groups of two and three telephone lines will be suspended from activity at the same time each day for a period of perhaps one hour between 9 A.M. and 5 P.M., Eastern Standard Time.

October 7, 1975   HSOCLCUG is founded.

November 7, 1975   Ninth Annual Membership Meeting held at The Ohio State University; members tour OCLC's new facilities; OCLC sponsors seminar on "On-Line Retrieval Services from Non-Monographic Data Bases."

Membership amends Code of Regulations to formalize membership of public libraries.

Members direct Board "to study the advisability of extending membership to libraries outside the State of Ohio and report its recommendations to the Membership at the next Annual Meeting."

November 28, 1975   OCLC stops adding terminals to on-line system until acceptable level of response time is achieved.

December 1, 1975   OCLC suspends installations of software until acceptable level of response time is achieved.

December 15, 1975   Dual computer system brought up in OCLC's new computer facility at 1125 Kinnear Road.

Training for serials check-in begins in midmonth for Ohio libraries.

1976

January 12, 1976   OCLC lifts moratorium on installation of new terminals.

System activity soars as dual computer system stabilizes; 514,901 books are cataloged in January 1976, as opposed to 359,970 in November 1975.

January 27, 1976   Seventy persons attend First Educational Forum in Columbus sponsored by OCLC. Topics include OCLC's computer facilities and R & D efforts.

February 14, 1976   On-line system to be available on Saturdays on regular basis, 8 A.M. to 8 P.M., Eastern Standard Time.

February 18, 1976   Boston University School of Theology inputs two millionth bibliographic record into data base.

February 25, 1976   First issue of OCLC's *Technical Bulletin* is produced.

March 16, 1976   Board approves its largest budget to date, $15,074,000 for 1976-1977.

March 27, 1976   New polling procedure installed that allows minicomputer to poll entire chain of terminals with one poll rather than "talking" specifically with each terminal in chain; improves efficiency in telecommunications.

April 13, 1976   OCLC removes poll-all procedure from on-line system because of problems.

May 1976   OCLC reinstalls poll-all procedure.

Center starts employing on-line identification numbers for terminals to facilitate reporting of terminal malfunctions.

May 2, 1976   Second OCLC Educational Forum in Columbus draws seventy-six persons to hear procedures for designing and developing new subsystems.

May 17, 1976   New search capabilities implemented: corporate name index, revised truncated entry display, and retrieval of personal names from added entry fields.

OCLC receives $339,319 grant from W. K. Kellogg Foundation to develop a mechanism to link OCLC's system with other on-line data bases.

May 18, 1976   Board approves establishment of user support centers for participating libraries in regions where there are no networks with which OCLC has an affiliation. The OCLC Western Service Center in Claremont, California, becomes the first such center.

May 22, 1976   Center implements ALL PRODUCE function.

June 7, 1976   Because of increases in response time owing to implementation of new search capabilities, OCLC invokes a moratorium on installation of terminals.

The State Library of Ohio awards OCLC a $550,000 grant to convert to machine-readable form retrospective cataloging at seven major Ohio public libraries and the State Library of Ohio.

July 1976   Thanks to a new maintenance agreement, terminal maintenance charges for fiscal year 1976-1977 are reduced from $47.50 per terminal per month to $39.06, mainly because of improvements in terminal maintenance by OCLC.

Government Printing Office produces its *Monthly Catalog of Government Publications* from OCLC-MARC tapes.

July 6, 1976	OCLC introduces new frequency options (quarterly and semiannual) to its tape production schedule.
July 9, 1976	Advisory Council, formed by Executive Director at request of Board and Membership, meets in Columbus for the first time. Composed of thirteen persons from librarianship, science, and business, the Council's task is to recommend a plan for extending membership outside Ohio and for reorganizing OCLC.
August 30, 1976	OCLC announces it will schedule downtime for implementation of three-computer system. Because of adverse effects on response time, the Center makes personal and corporate name index available only during off-peak hours.
September 7, 1976	Thompson M. Little becomes associate executive director.
September 24, 1976	In anticipation of installation of triple processor, OCLC begins moving data base equipment on weekends. OCLC system is to be down eight days beginning October 29 for implementation of new triple processor.
October 13, 1976	OCLC establishes a Corporate Committee on Response Time to assure an acceptable level of average response time on the OCLC system.
October 25-29, 1976	Participating libraries catalog more books in fewer hours than ever before in anticipation of week-long shutdown of on-line system. Books cataloged in five days: 173,696 in 70.4 hours; compared with 162,638 books in 86 hours the previous week.
October 29, 1976	OCLC shuts down on-line system to implement triple processor system; service to resume at 7 A.M. on November 8.
November 4, 1976	OCLC installs triple processor more quickly than anticipated—the system is brought up four days early, and some users begin cataloging almost immediately even though they had been notified that the system would probably be down until November 8.
November 5, 1976	Tenth Annual Membership Meeting held at The Ohio State University.
November 24, 1976	OCLC implements card production for MARC II formats in addition to books: audiovisual and special instructional materials, manuscripts, maps, music scores, and sound recordings.

December 1976   OCLC begins processing into the data base MARC II records that had earlier been deferred from addition to the data base. Besides enabling OCLC to process deferred records at the same time it processes new weekly LC-MARC II tapes, the new programs also detect and eliminate duplicate records in the on-line catalog.

December 1, 1976   OCLC lifts moratorium on terminal installations in effect since June 7, 1976, based on recommendation of Corporate Committee on Response Time.

Automatic check-in of serials component of serials control subsystem is activated.

Staff from Library Systems and Research and Development Divisions move from 1125 Kinnear Road to rented office space one and one-half miles away at 2939 Kenny Road. Move is due to predicted shortage of office space at Kinnear Road.

1977

January 1977   Council on Library Resources awards OCLC $122,000 grant to study OCLC's governance and organization by the consulting firm of Arthur D. Little, Inc., Cambridge, Massachusetts.

February 1977   Plans for the formal creation of MOUG are laid.

February 25, 1977   OCLC implements quadruple processor system two weeks ahead of target date of March 15. There is no interruption of on-line service.

March 8, 1977   About one hundred people attend Third OCLC Educational Forum on serials control in Columbus.

April 19, 1977   Board approves acquisition of a fifth Sigma 9 for "not-on-line activity" such as production of cards, accessions lists, tapes, and support of administrative activiies and research and development.

Board approves long-range plan for OCLC that includes a program for a new building.

Board adopts $18.4 million budget plan for 1977-1978.

May 27, 1977   SUNY-Potsdam inputs three millionth record into OCLC data base.

June 1977   Plans for the formal creation of OCLC/SIS are laid.

APPENDIX 1

HISTORICAL DOCUMENTS

EXHIBIT E   Ohio College Library Center, 1967-1968 Members

EXHIBIT F   Statement of Academic Objective, Economic Goal, and Missions to Achieve These Ends, April 9, 1969

EXHIBIT G   Fixed and Variable Costs of Catalog Card Production

EXHIBIT H   Memorandum to Representatives of OCLC Members Concerning Faculty Borrowing among OCLC Libraries, December 12, 1968

EXHIBIT I   Participants in Faculty Borrowing among OCLC Libraries, December 1969

EXHIBIT J   OCLC Networks and Their Members

EXHIBIT K   Catalog Record Displayed on a Terminal Screen

EXHIBIT L   Union Catalog Location Symbols

EXHIBIT M   Input Cataloging Work Form

EXHIBIT N   Screen Display in Extended Search

EXHIBIT O   Board of Trustee's Resolution on Behalf of Lewis C. Branscomb, November 10, 1972

Board of Trustee's Resolution on Behalf of Lewis C. Branscomb, June 17, 1975

EXHIBIT P   Statement of Purpose, Objectives, Systems, and Plans for Attaining Objectives, January 16, 1974

EXHIBIT Q   Ohio College Library Center: Long-Range Plan, 1977-1978

EXHIBIT R   Articles of Incorporation of OHIONET, December 20, 1977

Code of Regulations of OHIONET, December 20, 1977

EXHIBIT S   Frederick Gridley Kilgour: ALA Life Membership Award

EXHIBIT A

PRELIMINARY DESCRIPTION OF THE ACTIVITIES OF THE OHIO COLLEGE LIBRARY CENTER

This description of OCLC activities is being prepared in the early months of the Center's infancy. It should therefore be viewed as an interim document whose accuracy will diminish, hopefully, with the passage of time.

The Center was chartered on 6 July, 1967 and consists of member institutions who have paid an assessed fee which the membership itself determines. A nine-man Board of Trustees elected by the membership is responsible for the conduct of the business and affairs of the Center. A Director, who is responsible to the Board of Trustees, heads the Center's operations which are located in the Ohio State University Library, 1858 Neil Avenue, Columbus, Ohio 43210. The Center's activities as defined by the charter, are limited to Ohio colleges and universities, but the systems and designs for operations are including the two probabilities that at some undetermined time in the future other types of libraries will be included in the system and the geographic limitation of Ohio's political boundaries may be removed. However, the 60 odd institutions of higher education in Ohio constitute a more than significantly large population to participate in the initial activation of the Center's operations.

The principal purpose of the Center is to increase resources for the research and educational programs in Ohio colleges and universities, and the staff of the Center will be engaged in two principal types of activity, namely, research and development. Development will proceed in the direction of non-conventional computerized systems, and the first major operation will be a computerized shared cataloging system.

The Center is getting under way at a time when pressure of demand on library facilities dictates a radical departure from classical library operations. The ultimate system toward which any present systems design should point is that of a library which always has all information "on the shelves" and which any user may "take out" any time he wishes wherever he may be. Moreover, the system should have the capability of performing two major library activities, namely, classifying and subject indexing the information within the overall collection for the use of individual users. In short, the library will be personalized. This library system does not lie in the foreseeable future depending as it does upon major technical and intellectual advances. For instance, it will be necessary to have efficient machine translation and efficient mechanical reading before this remarkable library of the future can be worked

Preliminary Description of the Activities of the Ohio College Library Center (Source: Ohio College Library Center, "Minutes of the Members Meeting" (Columbus: Ohio College Library Center, 25 October 1967), Exhibit E.)

toward as a reality. It is, however, likely that a third major library activity, descriptive cataloging, can be mechanized. It is within this frame of reference that the work of OCLC will be undertaken.

Research

Research projects will be designed to examine regularities that exist in academic libraries and their use so that findings will furnish a base for further research and will be applicable in development projects in other groups of libraries as well as the Ohio group.

The first group of studies which the Center is sponsoring will be carried out, it is hoped, by the Center for Documentation and Communication Research at Case Western Reserve University. These studies include: 1) an investigation into duplicate processing among academic libraries; 2) a study of the use of library materials by individuals obtaining such materials outside their own library community; and, 3) a study to identify the heavily used core collections in academic libraries.

Benefits of each of these studies will include serving as a base for further research and for application in the design of OCLC systems, as well as design of other cooperative library systems. For instance, the investigation into duplicate processing will most certainly produce a pattern that will raise questions demanding further research. At the same time, it will yield information that will guide systems design for any library system involving more than one processing activity. At the present time this circumstance exists in various university library systems, and with the development of decentralized computerized systems, it will be important to have the findings of the first study available particularly where multiple processing units have not theretofore existed.

The Center also intends to embark on research that will develop at least some of the information required to design a mechanized system for descriptive cataloging. Research in this direction is already under way at the Yale University Library where two major grant-supported projects are investigating the information which a user has available to him when he approaches a card catalog to obtain materials from a library, and a second project to investigate techniques for efficient organization of large files of self-addressing entries.

The Center will undertake investigation of the feasibility of constructing file entries mechanically from information on title pages of publications. The study will simulate optical reading, but actually the title pages will be keyboarded. Some flagging of information on the title page will be necessary, and it will be an aim of the feasibility study to maintain that flagging at the lowest possible level. Computer trials will be run employing a simple linear table into which title page information will be entered by so-called hashing techniques. A linear arrangement would not be adequate for a huge file, but would be sufficient for a feasibility study.

Development

Development projects will be pointed primarily toward improving accuracy and speed of availability of information to library users. In development of its computer based systems, the Center will attempt to work with other groups engaged in similar activities, but at the present time such cooperative activity is not easy to achieve. Here, the problem is not just sharing computer programs, but also coordinate participation in design of systems and programs.

The first major project which the Center will undertake will be a regional shared cataloging system that will have the capacity to include all academic libraries in Ohio and the flexibility and compatibility that will enable other types of libraries to join later. As principally envisaged, the system would consist of a random access memory attached to a time-sharing computer. The memory would contain the file of bibliographic references to which would be added 1) holding information by individual library, 2) associated call number or numbers, 3) notes pertinent to a particular copy, 4) added entries, and 5) subject headings. The MARC II format will be used for the record and included in the file will be all examples of MARC records that could be made available to the Center. Access to the file will be via a console located in individual libraries, and presumably the console would be of the cathode ray type (CRT) with an associated keyboard. At the present time there is no CRT available that entirely conforms to the specifications required by libraries, but it is the intent of the Center to work with other library groups and manufacturers toward the development of such a library console. Here, the problems are more commercial than technical.

A major objective of the shared cataloging system will be a design that can be used in its entirety by other groups of libraries; moreover, not only will the system be used, but also the data in the system, namely, the huge file of cataloging information. Such sharing and compatibility of system and data is not now known to exist in libraries or in computer applications, but its obviously tremendous advantage incite major effort to achieve such a design. Although a large computer is required to run sophisticated catalog card production programs, relatively small processing will be needed for the on-line operation. Therefore, it appears feasible that a relatively small communications control computer could operate the on-line consoles, huge random access unit, and tapes. Card records from which catalog cards would be produced for individual libraries would be stored on a tape to be subsequently processed by a larger machine. Moreover, this arrangement would be satisfactory to handle a bibliographic information retrieval system when it is added to shared cataloging. Finally, the communications computer could be linked with other communications computers to enlarge the system. Similarly, it could be interfaced with a larger computer when greater processing power will be required, as in the case of a technical processing system. The high potential for designing a system which could be installed in other regions and among other types of libraries, with little or no modification and bringing with it the huge data base needed in other regions, demands that such a system be the type first explored. Moreover, the system would have compatibility, enabling it to be linked with other operational systems: at the same time it has immense flexibility to make possible future expansion of function.

In the case of the shared cataloging system, the principal users that will benefit immediately will be cataloging staff in the participating libraries, and since their activities will be lightened and the flow of books being cataloged increased, the faculty and students will also benefit. In addition, the technique will build a large file of machine readable cataloging information that will continuously and increasingly enhance the economy of cataloging. Essentially, the system will make cataloging information available to the cataloger when and where he needs it. It will, in effect, greatly increase the flow of bibliographic information in the Ohio network.

One recent estimate of the cost of duplicative cataloging in the United States produced limits of between $50-70,000,000. With the activation of its shared cataloging network, OCLC will attain the goal toward which American librarians began to strive in the 1870s, and which has been but imperfectly approached. Only by using modern communications networks and that remarkable information processing machine, the computer, can the goal of shared cataloging be achieved.

In addition to the benefits of computerized coordinated cataloging that have already been discussed, the shared cataloging project will include the production of new book lists for those libraries desiring such lists. The Center will print out on stencils, or for photo-offset reproduction, new titles arranged by subject or author that an individual library had received since the last list had been prepared. The Center will then send the stencils to the library which will duplicate them for dissemination. As the central file grows, union catalog information will accrue to facilitate users obtaining information from libraries outside their immediate library community. The central file will also be used for preparation of bibliographies and will be designed so that it can include within it holding records for serials for individual libraries, as well as acquisitions and in-process records.

Operation of the shared cataloging system will proceed somewhat as follows. In the process of cataloging, a cataloger will request of the file whether or not a record of the title is already in the file. Should the file have the record, it would be put out on the cataloger's console where it would be possible for the cataloger to determine if his library already possessed the book. If the library did not have it, he would then use the descriptive information already present in the record merely by adding his call number to it, the fact that his library possesses the title, and, perhaps, notes added entries or subject headings. These additions would also be added to the central record in the file attached to the computer, and the bibliographic record with his additions would be set aside by the machine for the manufacture of catalog cards which would be done within a day. Cards will be supplied to libraries in packs, each pack being designated to go into a specific catalog of the holding library. Headings on the cards would be placed either at the far left, first indention, or second indention, as desired by the library receiving them. Such headings will be either in upper case or upper and lower case, as the library desires. Cards will be alphabeted within each pack so that they will be ready to be filed manually directly into card catalogs. The pack for the shelf list catalog would, of course, be arranged by call number. The system will produce spine labels and book pockets for libraries needing these products.

At some period of time, it will be possible for each library participating in the system to stop maintaining its card catalog and to rely entirely on the computerized catalog. Indeed, a new library starting after the bibliographic information retrieval project has been activated would not need to have any card catalog, but could rely on the computerized version. Determination as to when continuation of the card catalog will cease will depend on a decision in each individual library, and not on the system.

At the present time the Center is investigating the possibility of activating some sections of computerized systems prior to the initiation of the shared cataloging system which it is hoped will be under way in 1970. Before then it may be that some libraries will start batch processing to produce catalog cards and accession lists, but at the moment this project is tentative.

The second major project which the Center will activate is a bibliographic information retrieval system with the user employing a console and approaching the data from the viewpoint of subject, rather than by specific item. The principal requirement here is the development of an arrangement to increase the amount of subject indexing for books. Academic libraries employ somewhere in the vicinity of 1.5 subject headings per title, which is woefully inadequate. It may be necesary to increase this subject heading work ten-fold or certainly five-fold.

Although the cataloger will be the principal direct beneficiary of the shared cataloging system with the library user being the indirect beneficiary, it will be the library user who will profit directly from the bibliographic information retrieval system. This system will make it possible for the user to locate cataloging information with great speed and accuracy from the subject point of view. A coordinate subject heading technique will be employed whereby references which the user seeks will be swiftly retrieved from the central computerized file and displayed sequentially on the console. The system will also have the capability of reporting to the user the number of references on subjects classed close to the subject he has selected. The Lockheed Missiles and Space Laboratory has already developed such a system called DIALOG while the SDC has recently announced its ORBIT (On-line Retrieval of Bibliographic Text). The Center hopes to incorporate into its retrieval store machine readable indexing produced elsewhere such as MEDLARS, Chemical Titles, and the NASA file.

Subsequent to the shared cataloging and bibliographic information retrieval projects will come projects involving acquisition activities, serials, and circulation. It is expected that acquisitions and serials will be included in the same file as other bibliographic references, whereas files of circulation records will be kept uniquely by library. Nevertheless, in the maintenance of circulation records, all libraries will use and share the same computer programs.

This description of projects has emphasized computerization at the processing and retrieval level, but it is also expected that the Center will develop programs which will computerize the supervision of processes to some extend and will furnish management information to executive librarians. These two types of development will of course be for unique application in individual libraries, even though the central system produces the information. In particular, management information would be available only to the library concerned. These segments of the regional system will begin operation in perhaps five years.

The Center does not plan to engage in development of equipment, but it will plan to use new devices as soon as they are available.

EXHIBIT B

ARTICLES OF
INCORPORATION OF
THE OHIO COLLEGE LIBRARY CENTER
July 5, 1967

The undersigned, a majority of whom are citizens of the United States, desiring to form a corporation, not for profit, under the General Corporation Act of Ohio, do hereby certify:

FIRST. The name of said corporation shall be The Ohio College Library Center.

SECOND. The place in this State where the principal office of the corporation is to be located is Columbus, Franklin County.

THIRD. The purpose or purposes for which this corporation is formed are to establish, maintain and operate a computerized, regional library center to serve the academic libraries of Ohio (both state and private) and designed so as to become a part of any national electronic network for bibliographical communication; to develop, maintain and operate a shared cataloging program based upon a central computer store; to create, maintain and operate a computerized central catalog (inventory) of books and journals in the participating libraries; and to do such research and development related to the above as are necessary to accomplish and to extend the concept.

FOURTH. No part of the earnings, dues or receipts of this corporation shall inure to the benefit of or be distributed to its members, trustees, officers or other private persons, except only that the corporation shall be authorized and empowered to pay reasonable compensation for services rendered and expenses incurred and to make payments or distributions in furtherance of the purposes set forth in Article Third hereof.

FIFTH. Upon any dissolution of the corporation, the Board of Trustees, after paying or making provision for the payments of all the liabilities of the corporation, shall adopt such plan of dissolution and distribution of the remaining assets as to them shall seem just and fair and consistent with the purposes hereof.

SIXTH. The following persons shall serve said corporation *as trustees* until the first annual meeting or other meeting called to elect trustees:

Original Articles of Incorporation (July 5, 1967) and Amended Articles of Incorporation (January 16, 1973 and December 20, 1977). Courtesy of OCLC.

A. Blair Knapp, President, Denison University, Granville, Ohio

Paul L. O'Connor, S.J., President, Xavier University, Cincinnati, Ohio

Phillip R. Shriver, President, Miami University, Oxford, Ohio

Emerson Shuck, Vice President, Ohio Wesleyan University, Delaware, Ohio

John Kamerick, Vice President, Kent State University, Kent, Ohio

Lewis C. Branscomb, Director of Library, The Ohio State University, Columbus, Ohio

A. Robert Rogers, Director of Library, Bowling Green State University, Bowling Green, Ohio

Robert F. Cayton, Librarian, Marietta College, Marietta, Ohio

Robert Mowery, Director of Library, Wittenberg University, Springfield, Ohio

IN WITNESS WHEREOF, we have hereunto subscribed our name, this 5th day of July, 1967.

_____
A. Blair Knapp

_____
Paul L. O'Connor, S.J.

_____
Phillip R. Shriver

_____
Emerson Shuck

_____
John Kamerick

_____
Gordon B. Carson

_____
Lewis C. Branscomb

_____
A. Robert Rogers

_____
Robert F. Cayton

_____
Bob Mowery

INCORPORATORS

AMENDED
ARTICLES OF
INCORPORATION OF
THE OHIO COLLEGE LIBRARY CENTER
January 16, 1973

FIRST   The name of said corporation shall be The Ohio College Library Center.

SECOND   The place in this state where the principal office of the corporation is to be located is Columbus, Franklin County.

THIRD   The purposes for which the corporation is formed are to establish, maintain and operate a computerized, regional library center to serve the libraries of Ohio (both state and private) and designed so as to become a part of any national electronic network for bibliographical communication; to develop, maintain and operate a shared cataloging program based upon a central computer store; to create, maintain and operate a computerized central catalog (inventory) of books and journals in the participating libraries; and to do such research and development related to the above as are necessary to accomplish and to extend the concept. The term libraries of Ohio (both state and private) shall be and hereby is defined as those libraries within the State of Ohio operated exclusively for educational and scientific purposes as shall at all times hereafter qualify as exempt organization or organizations under Section 501 (c) (3) of the Internal Revenue Code of 1954 (or the corresponding provision of any future United States Internal Revenue Law).

FOURTH   No part of the earnings, dues or receipts of this corporation shall inure to the benefit of or be distributed to its members, trustees, officers or other private persons, except only that the corporation shall be authorized and empowered to pay reasonable compensation for services rendered and expenses incurred and to make payments or distributions in furtherance of the purposes set forth in Article Third hereof.

FIFTH   Upon the dissolution of the corporation, the Board of Trustees shall, after paying or making provision for the payment of all of the liabilities of the corporation, dispose of all of the assets of the corporation exclusively for the purposes of the corporation in such manner, or to such organization or organizations organized and operated exclusively for charitable, educational, religious, or scientific purposes as shall at the time qualify as an exempt organization or organizations under Section 501 (c) (3) of the Internal Revenue Code of 1954 (or the corresponding provision of any future United States Internal Revenue Law), as the Board of Trustees shall determine. Any of such assets not so disposed of shall be disposed of by the Court of Common Pleas of the county in which the principal office of the corporation is then located, exclusively for such purposes or to such organization or organizations, as said Court shall determine, which are organized and operated exclusively for such purposes.

SIXTH   These Amended Articles of Incorporation supersede and take the place of the existing original Articles of Incorporation.

AMENDED ARTICLES OF INCORPORATION OF OCLC, INC.
December 20, 1977

FIRST   The name of said Corporation shall be OCLC, Inc.

SECOND   The place in this State where the principal office of the Corporation is to be located is Clinton Township, Franklin County.

THIRD   The purpose or purposes for which this Corporation is formed are to establish, maintain and operate a computerized library network and to promote the evolution of library use, of libraries themselves, and of librarianship, and to provide processes and products for the benefit of library users and libraries, including such objectives as increasing availability of library resources to individual library patrons and reducing rate of rise of library per-unit costs, all for the fundamental public purpose of furthering ease of access to and use of the ever-expanding body of worldwide scientific, literary and educational knowledge and information.

FOURTH   The affairs of the Corporation shall be managed by the Board of Trustees. The qualifications of the Trustees, together with their terms of office, manner of election, removal, change of number, filling of vacancies and of newly-created trusteeships, powers, duties and liabilities, shall, except as otherwise provided in these Articles, or by the laws of the State of Ohio, be as prescribed by the Code of Regulations.

FIFTH   There shall be three classes of members of the Corporation and they shall be General Members, Users Council Members and Trustee Members. The voting powers of each class of members shall be only as defined in the Code of Regulations.

SIXTH   There shall be a Users Council which shall be that body as defined in the Code of Regulations.

SEVENTH   The Articles of Incorporation may be amended at any business meeting of the Trustee Members called for that purpose provided that written notice of the proposed amendment(s) has been sent to the Trustee Members at least ten (10) days prior to said meeting. A two-thirds (⅔) vote of all of the authorized number of Trustee Members of the Corporation is required for approval, and the proposed amendment(s) must be ratified by a majority vote of Members of the Users Council present at a meeting called for that purpose.

EIGHTH   The duration of this Corporation shall be perpetual.

NINTH   No part of the earnings, dues or receipts of this Corporation shall inure to the benefit of or be distributed to its members, trustees, officers or other private persons, except only that the Corporation shall be authorized and empowered to pay reasonable compensation for services rendered and expenses incurred and to make payments or distributions in furtherance of the purposes set forth in Article Third hereof. No substantial part of the activities of the corporation shall be the carrying on of propaganda, or otherwise attempting to influence legislation, and the corporation shall not participate in, or intervene in (including the publishing or distribution of statements) any political campaign on behalf of any candidate for public office. Notwithstanding any other provision of these articles, the corporation shall not carry on any other activities not permitted to be carried on (a) by a corporation exempt from Federal income tax under section 501 (c) (3) of the Internal Revenue Code of 1954 (or the corresponding provision of any future United States Internal Revenue Law) or (b) by a corporation, contributions to which are deductible under section 170 (c) (2) of the Internal Revenue Code of 1954 (or the corresponding provision of any future United States Internal Revenue Law).

TENTH   Upon the dissolution of the Corporation, the Board of Trustees shall, after paying or making provision for the payment of all of the liabilities of the Corporation, dispose of all of the assets of the Corporation exclusively for the purposes of the Corporation in such manner, or to such organization or organizations as are described in Section 170 (c) (1) or (2) of the Internal Revenue Code of 1954 (or the corresponding provision of any future United States Internal Revenue Code), as the Board of Trustees shall determine. Any of such assets not so disposed of shall be disposed of by the Court of Common Pleas of the county in which the principal office of the Corporation is then located, exclusively for such purposes or to such organization or organizations, as said Court shall determine, which are organized and operated exclusively for such purposes.

ELEVENTH   These Articles supersede all prior Articles or Amended Articles.

IN WITNESS WHEREOF, said H. Paul Schrank, Jr., Chairman and President, and Donald J. Sager, Secretary, of The Ohio College Library Center, acting for and on behalf of said corporation, have hereunto subscribed their names this 20th day of December, 1977

H. Paul Schrank, Jr., Chairman and President

Donald J. Sager, Secretary

EXHIBIT C

CODE OF REGULATIONS OF
THE OHIO COLLEGE LIBRARY CENTER
July 1967

ARTICLE I

Definitions

As used in this Code of Regulations, the word "Center" means this corporation, that is to say, The Ohio College Library Center and the word "Trustees" and the terms "Board of Trustees" and "Board," unless the context otherwise indicates, mean the trustees of said corporation provided for by law.

ARTICLE II

Members

Section 1.
The Members of the Center shall consist of all of the subscribing colleges and universities of Ohio, both public and private represented for all purposes herein by such natural person as each college and university shall designate from time to time.

Section 2.
The costs and expenses of the Center shall be distributed among the Members and be borne as dues or fees in such manner and in such amounts as shall be determined by Membership vote, subject to official institutional approval.

ARTICLE III

Voting Rights

At any meeting of the Members of the Center each Member of the Center shall be entitled to one vote on each matter properly submitted to the Members for their vote, consent, waiver, release, or other action.

ARTICLE IV

Meetings of Members

Section 1.
The annual meeting of the Members of the Center for the transaction of such business as may properly come before it shall be held each year in such place, at such day and time as may be designated by the Board.

Original Code of Regulations (July 1967) and Amended Code of Regulations (November 7, 1975 and December 20, 1977) Courtesy of OCLC.

Exhibit C—Code of Regulations, July 1967 / 261

Section 2.

A special meeting of the Members of the Center may be called at any time by the Chairman, or Board of Trustees, or by ten or more Members of the Center to be held at such time and place as may be designated in the notice of the meeting.

Section 3.

Meetings of the Members of the Center may be held either within or without this state.

Section 4.

At any meeting of the Members of the Center twenty (20) Members shall constitute a quorum, but a majority of the Members present, whether or not a quorum is present, may adjourn any meeting from time to time. A majority of the Members present and voting at any meeting shall decide any question brought before such meeting, unless the question is one upon which by express provision of law a larger or different vote is required.

ARTICLE V

Board of Trustees

Section 1.

There shall be nine (9) members of the Board of Trustees who shall be elected from the designated representatives of the Membership of the Center. Members of the Board of Trustees shall hold staggered three-year terms. Initially, three Trustees shall hold three-year terms, three shall hold two-year terms, and three shall hold one-year terms. Each Trustee shall hold office until his successor has been duly elected and qualified. Any vacancy upon the Board of Trustees shall be filled by action of the Board.

Section 2.

Except as otherwise provided by law, the Articles of Incorporation, or this Code of Regulations, the corporate authority, property and affairs of the Center shall be exercised, controlled and conducted by the Board of Trustees, which shall have authority to make, prescribe and enforce all needful rules and regulations for the conduct of the business and affairs of the Center and the management and control of its property.

Section 3.

A regular meeting of the Board of Trustees shall be held annually in such place and immediately after the annual meeting of Members of the Center, and other regular meetings may be held at such time and place as may be determined by resolution of the Board of Trustees.

Section 4.

A special meeting of the Board of Trustees may be called at any time by the Chairman, the Vice Chairman or the Secretary, or three or more of the Directors, to be held at such time and place as may be designated in the notice of the meeting.

Section 5.
At any meeting of the Board of Trustees five (5) Trustees shall constitute a quorum, but a lesser number may adjourn any meeting from time to time until a quorum is present, and the meeting may be held as adjourned without further notice. A majority of the Trustees present and voting at any meeting when a quorum is present shall decide any question brought before such meeting, unless the question is one upon which by express provision of law a larger or different vote is required.

ARTICLE VI

Officers

Section 1.
The officers of the Center shall consist of a Chairman, a Vice Chairman, a Secretary, and a Treasurer, who shall be elected by the Board of Trustees annually at the meeting of said Board following the annual meeting of Members of the Center. The officers so elected shall serve for a term of one (1) year and until their successors are elected and qualified. Officers may succeed themselves, with a maximum of three years' service for the Chairman and Vice Chairman.

Section 2.
There shall be an Executive Director of the Center who shall be chosen by the Board of Trustees and shall serve during the pleasure of the Board.

Section 3.
The Chairman, Vice Chairman, Secretary and Treasurer of the Center shall have such powers and duties as are normally incident to such offices.

Section 4.
The Executive Director shall have, subject to the direction of the Board of Trustees and, the Chairman, direct administrative supervision over and immediate executive authority with respect to the conduct of the business and affairs of the Center.

ARTICLE VII

Committees

The Board of Trustees may create such committees as to it seem necessary and desirable.

ARTICLE VIII

Negotiable Instruments, Contracts, etc.

Section 1.
All checks, drafts, bills of exchange, notes or other instruments or orders for the payment of money shall be signed in the name of the Center or, if made

Exhibit C — Code of Regulations, July 1967 / 263

payable to the Center, may be endorsed for deposit to the credit of the Center, by such officer or officers, person or persons, as the Board of Trustees may from time to time designate by resolution.

Section 2.
The Board of Trustees may authorize any officer or officers, agent or agents, in the name of and on behalf of the Center, to enter into or execute and deliver any and all deeds, bonds, mortgages, contracts, and other obligations or instruments, and such authority may be general or confined to specific instances.

ARTICLE IX

Amendments

This Code of Regulations may be amended, revised or repealed, and a new Code of Regulations may be adopted, at any annual or special meeting of the Members of the Center by the affirmative vote of two-thirds (⅔) of the Members present, providing notice of such amendment, revision or repeal shall have been given in the notice of the meeting.

CODE OF REGULATIONS OF
THE OHIO COLLEGE LIBRARY CENTER
Revised November 7, 1975

ARTICLE I

Definitions

As used in this Code of Regulations, the word "Center" means this corporation, that is to say, The Ohio College Library Center and the word "Trustees" and the terms "Board of Trustees" and "Board," unless the context otherwise indicates, means the trustees of said corporation provided for by law.

ARTICLE II

Members

The members of the Center shall consist of all of the subscribing colleges and universities of Ohio, both public and private, and all subscribing non-academic libraries of Ohio, both public and private, serving educational, scientific or charitable purposes, represented for all purposes herein by such natural person as each college, university, and library shall designate from time to time.

ARTICLE III

Voting Rights

At any meeting of the Members of the Center each Member of the Center shall be entitled to one vote on each matter properly submitted to the Members for their vote, consent, waiver, release, or other action.

ARTICLE IV

Meetings of Members

Section 1.

The annual meeting of the Members of the Center for the transaction of such business as may properly come before it shall be held each year in such place, at such day and time as may be designated by the Board.

Section 2.

A special meeting of the Members of the Center may be called at any time by the Chairman and President, or Board of Trustees, or by ten or more Members of the Center to be held at such time and place as may be designated in the notice of the meeting.

Exhibit C — Code of Regulations, Revised November 7, 1975 / 265

Section 3.

Meetings of the Members of the Center may be held either within or without this state.

Section 4.

At any meeting of the Members of the Center twenty (20) Members shall constitute a quorum, but a majority of the Members present, whether or not a quorum is present, may adjourn any meeting from time to time. A majority of the Members present and voting at any meeting shall decide any question brought before such meeting, unless the question is one upon which by express provision of law a larger or different vote is required.

ARTICLE V

Board of Trustees

Section 1.

There shall be nine (9) members of the Board of Trustees who shall be elected from the designated representatives of the Membership of the Center. Members of the Board of Trustees shall hold staggered three-year terms. Initially, three Trustees shall hold three-year terms, three shall hold two-year terms, and three shall hold one-year terms. Each Trustee shall hold office until his successor has been duly elected and qualified. Any vacancy upon the Board of Trustees shall be filled by action of the Board.

Section 2.

Except as otherwise provided by law, the Articles of Incorporation, or this Code of Regulations, the corporate authority, property and affairs of the Center shall be exercised, controlled and conducted by the Board of Trustees, which shall have authority to make, prescribe and enforce all needful rules and regulations for the conduct of the business and affairs of the Center and the management and control of its property.

Section 3.

A regular meeting of the Board of Trustees shall be held annually in such place and immediately after the annual meeting of Members of the Center, and other regular meetings may be held at such time and place as may be determined by resolution of the Board of Trustees.

Section 4.

A special meeting of the Board of Trustees may be called at any time by the Chairman and President, the Vice Chairman or the Secretary, or three or more of the Directors, to be held at such time and place as may be designated in the notice of the meeting.

Section 5.

At any meeting of the Board of Trustees five (5) Trustees shall constitute a quorum, but a lesser number may adjourn any meeting from time to time until a quorum is present, and the meeting may be held as adjourned without further notice. A majority of the Trustees present and voting at any meeting when a quorum is present shall decide any question brought before such meeting, unless the question is one upon which by express provision of law a larger or different vote is required.

ARTICLE VI

Officers

Section 1.

The officers of the Center shall consist of a Chairman and President, a Vice Chairman, a Secretary, and a Treasurer, who shall be elected by the Board of Trustees annually at the meeting of said Board following the annual meeting of the Members of the Center. The officers so elected shall serve for a term of one (1) year and until their successors are elected and qualified. Officers may succeed themselves, with a maximum of three years' service for the Chairman and President and Vice Chairman.

Section 2.

There shall be an Executive Director of the Center who shall be chosen by the Board of Trustees and shall serve during the pleasure of the Board.

Section 3.

The Chairman and President, Vice Chairman, Secretary and Treasurer of the Center shall have such powers and duties as are normally incident to such offices.

Section 4.

The Executive Director shall have, subject to the direction of the Board of Trustees and, the Chairman and President, direct administrative supervision over the immediate executive authority with respect to the conduct of the business and affairs of the Center.

ARTICLE VII

Committees

The Board of Trustees may create such committees as to it seem necessary and desirable.

Exhibit C—Code of Regulations, Revised November 7, 1975 / 267

ARTICLE VIII

Negotiable Instruments, Contracts, etc.

Section 1.

All checks, drafts, bills of exchange, notes or other instruments or orders for the payment of money shall be signed in the name of the Center or, if made payable to the Center, may be endorsed for deposit to the credit of the Center, by such officer or officers, person or persons, as the Board of Trustees may from time to time designate by resolution.

Section 2.

The Board of Trustees may authorize any officer or officers, agent or agents, in the name of and on behalf of the Center, to enter into or execute and deliver any and all deeds, bonds, mortgages, contracts, and other obligations or instruments, such authority may be general or confined to specific instances.

ARTICLE IX

Amendments

This Code of Regulations may be amended, revised or repealed, and a new Code of Regulations may be adopted, at any annual or special meeting of the Members of the Center by the affirmative vote of two-thirds (⅔) of the Members present, providing notice of such amendment, revision or repeal shall have been given in the notice of the meeting.

CODE OF REGULATIONS OF OCLC, INC.
December 20, 1977

ARTICLE I

NAME AND LOCATION OF CORPORATION

The name of this Corporation is OCLC, INC. Its principal office will be located in Franklin County, Ohio.

ARTICLE II

DEFINITIONS

As used in this Code of Regulations, the word "Corporation" means this Corporation, that is to say, OCLC, INC., and the word "Trustees" and the terms "Board of Trustees" and "Board," unless the context otherwise indicates, means the Trustees of said Corporation provided for by law and by the Articles of Incorporation.

ARTICLE III

PURPOSE

The purpose or purposes for which this Corporation is formed are to establish, maintain and operate a computerized library network and to promote the evolution of library use, of libraries themselves and of librarianship, and to provide processes and products for the benefit of library users and libraries, including such objectives as increasing availability of library resources to individual library patrons and reducing the rate of rise of library per-unit costs, all for the fundamental public purpose of furthering ease of access to and use of the ever-expanding body of worldwide scientific, literary and educational knowledge and information.

ARTICLE IV

GENERAL MEMBERS

A. *Definition.* The General Members of the Corporation shall consist of libraries, public or private, academic or non-academic, which participate in the OCLC system.

B. *Voting Rights.* The voting rights of the General Members shall be limited to the right to vote for the selection of delegates to the Users Council provided in Article V E(2), under rules determined by the Users Council.

C. *Committees.* Persons from General Members are eligible for appointment by the Board of Trustees and by the Users Council to serve on the respective committees thereof.

Exhibit C—Code of Regulations, December 20, 1977 / 269

ARTICLE V

USERS COUNCIL AND USERS COUNCIL MEMBERS

A. *Purpose*. The Users Council will serve to reflect and articulate the various interests of General Members. The Users Council shall be empowered to elect six Trustees of the Board of Trustees.

B. *Membership*. The Users Council Members shall be those entities which contract with the Corporation and provide under their contract at least one percent (1%) of the number of the total computer terminals, or their equivalent, on the OCLC system participating in the processes of the Corporation, as reflected by the business records of the Corporation, on a date certain, thirty (30) days prior to the annual meeting of the Users Council each year.

In addition, such General Members who are not otherwise represented by a Users Council Member, and who contract with the Corporation through a given single service center of the Corporation, or its equivalent, and provide under their contracts, taken together, at least one percent (1%) of the total computer terminals, or their equivalent, on the OCLC system participating in the processes of the Corporation, as reflected by the business records of the Corporation on a date certain, thirty (30) days prior to the annual meeting of the Users Council each year, shall together constitute a single Users Council Member.

C. *Voting Rights*. The number of votes (V) to which a Users Council Member shall be entitled, from time to time, shall be equal to the square root of its number of computer terminals (N), or their equivalent, set forth upon the business records of the Corporation as provided in paragraph B of this Article, multiplied by that factor derived by a formula designed to establish and ascertain the total number of delegates to and votes in the whole Users Council ranging from fifty (50) to one hundred (100) as the total number of General Members increases from one thousand (1,000) to three thousand (3,000), as follows:

$$V = N \times \frac{50 + \dfrac{G - 1000}{40}}{T}$$

where V = the number of votes to which a Users Council Member shall be entitled, and

N = the square root of the total number of terminals possessed by the General members of a Users Council Member, and

G = the total number of General Members, and

T = the sum of the square roots of the number of computer terminals calculated for each Users Council Member.

This calculation of the respective voting rights of each Users Council Member shall be performed annually at the same time as eligibility for Users Council Membership is determined, as set forth in paragraph B of this Article.

In the event that the number of votes calculated by the above formula is a fraction less than one-half (½), the number of votes to which a Member shall be entitled shall be rounded off to the next lowest whole number, and if the fraction is one-half (½) or more, said number of votes shall be rounded off to the next highest whole number. The number of votes shall in no event be less than one (1).

D. *Meetings.*

(1) *Place of Meetings.* Meetings of the Users Council Members shall be held at any suitable place convenient to them as may be designated by the Users Council.

(2) *Time of Meetings.* The Users Council shall hold an annual meeting, regular meetings and special meetings as shall be determined by the Users Council.

(3) *Notice of Meetings.* At least ten (10) days in advance thereof, the Secretary of the Users Council shall mail to its Members notice of any meeting.

(4) *Quorum.* The presence at any meeting of fifty percent (50%) of the delegates to the users Council shall constitute a quorum and matters properly before the Users Council shall be decided by majority vote.

(5) *Adjourned Meetings.* If any meeting of the Users Council cannot transact business because a quorum is not present, the delegates present may adjourn the meeting to a time not less than forty-eight (48) hours from the time the original meeting was called.

E. *Representation by Delegates.*

(1) *Qualifications.* The Users Council Members shall be represented on the Users Council by delegates. The delegates may be members of the governing boards of the Users Council Members, or members of governing boards of constituent General Members thereof, or librarians of a constituent General Member. No more than one administrative officer or other employee of a Users Council Member is eligible to be chosen as a delegate. All delegates must be authorized to act on behalf of the Users Council Member.

(2) *Selection.* The delegates of each Users Council Member shall be nominated and elected, removed and replaced by those General Members of the Corporation that comprise the participants of that Users Council Member. In the case of a single entity Users Council Member, the process of designation of delegates will be by selection and appointment, and removal by simple revocation of authority. In the absence of requirements of the Users Council to the contrary, each Users Council Member shall promulgate rules through which said nomination, election, selection, appointment, removal and replacement shall be accomplished so long as the rules do not conflict with the Articles of Incorporation or Code of Regulations of the Corporation.

(3) *Number of Delegates.* The number and distribution of delegates among each Member of the users Council shall be the same as the number of votes to which the Members of the Users Council are entitled. Voting by alternate delegates and/or by proxy shall be permitted, subject to rules promulgated by the Users Council for those purposes.

(4) *Voting Rights.* At any meeting of the Users Council, each delegate shall be entitled to vote in person or by proxy on each matter properly

Exhibit C—Code of Regulations, December 20, 1977 / 271

submitted to the Users Council for vote, consent, waiver, release or other action.

(5) *Costs.* Costs and expenses of the Users Council and expenses of delegates shall be paid by the Corporation upon such total budgeted amounts as are determined by the Board of Trustees.

F. *Committees.*

The Users Council shall create such committees as it deems necessary or desirable to carry out its purposes. It shall appoint thereto persons serving as delegates on the Users Council, and may appoint other persons -

(1) From a General Member which, though participating in the selection of delegates, does not have a person serving as a delegate to the Users Council, or

(2) From a General Member not eligible for participating in the selection of delegates as defined in Article V E(2) of the Code of Regulations.

G. *Officers.*

The Users Council shall create such offices and elect such officers to conduct the business of the Users Council as to it shall seem appropriate.

ARTICLE VI

TRUSTEE MEMBERS

A. *Definition.* The Trustee Members of the Corporation are defined as the members of the Board of Trustees.

B. *Voting Rights.* At any meeting of the Trustee Members, each Trustee Member shall be entitled to one vote on each matter properly submitted to them for their vote, consent, waiver, release or other action.

C. *Powers of Trustee Members.* The Trustee Members shall vote upon election and removal of Trustees, amendments to the Articles and Code of Regulations, as hereinafter provided, and shall have and may exercise all other membership powers and rights not expressly granted or reserved to the other classes of members by the Articles or this Code of Regulations.

D. *Meetings.* The Trustee Members shall hold an annual meeting and shall hold such other meetings as may be necessary.

(1) The time and place of meetings shall be as determined from time to time by resolution of the Trustee Members.

(2) The quorum for such meetings and the vote and procedures shall be the same as set forth respecting Trustees in Article VII, Section H(5), except as otherwise provided in the Articles of Incorporation or this Code of Regulations.

(3) Notice of meetings shall be provided in writing at least ten (10) days prior to the date thereof.

ARTICLE VII

BOARD OF TRUSTEES

A. *Number.* The Board of Trustees shall be comprised of fifteen (15) members.

B. *Qualifications.* Nine Trustees, hereinafter referred to as "Nine," shall be persons from varying disciplines and community interests. Five of these nine Trustees shall be selected from among categories such as the following: an executive officer of a large corporation; an individual experienced in banking and finance; an individual with background or present service in government, national, state or local; an economist; an accountant with experience in taxation and business enterprise; an attorney with experience in corporation law; an individual with experience in electronic computer science or industry; an individual with experience in communications technology; an individual with marketing and distribution knowledge; and other individuals with comparable knowledge and experience.

Three Trustees of the "Nine" shall be members of the library profession.

One Trustee of the "Nine" shall be the Executive Director of the Corporation and shall serve upon the Board of Trustees by reason of his office, equal in status to all other Trustees for all purposes, including voting and determination of quorum.

Six Trustees, hereinafter referred to as "Six," shall be elected by the Users Council, as provided herein, and shall be persons serving as delegates to the Users Council when elected.

No more than two Trustees shall be administrative officers or other employees of a Users Council Member.

C. *Election and Term of Office.*

(1) *Initial Terms.* Eight of the "Nine" shall be elected by a majority vote of the interim Trustees following the adoption of this Code of Regulations. The then serving Executive Director shall be the ninth Trustee. Three Trustees, chosen from among the interim Trustees, shall serve as initial members of the "Nine," from the library profession.

The respective terms of the "Nine" shall commence as of the election and shall be as follows: Three Trustees elected by the interim Trustees shall each have two-year terms; three shall each have four-year terms; two of the Trustees elected by the interim Trustees shall each have six-year terms. The two six-year terms and one four-year term shall be filled by the three Trustees chosen from among the interim Trustees.

The "Six" shall be elected by a majority vote of the Users Council at the first meeting called for that purpose, at which time their terms of office shall commence. The respective terms of office of the initial "Six" shall be as follows: Two shall each have two-year terms; two shall each have four-year terms; two shall each have six-year terms.

(2) *Terms of Successors.* Except for the Executive Director, who shall serve upon the Board of Trustees by reason of and during the term of his office, the successors to each of the "Nine" shall be elected to six-year terms by a majority of the Trustee members.

The successors to each of the "Six" shall be elected to six-year terms by a majority vote of the Users Council.

Exhibit C—Code of Regulations, December 20, 1977 / 273

Each Trustee shall hold office until his/her successor has been qualified, elected and has commenced his/her term.

(3) *Limitation on Consecutive Terms.* Trustees may not serve more than two consecutive six-year terms.

(4) *Nomination and Election.* Nominations for and election of the "Nine" shall take place at the annual meeting of the Trustee Members.

Nominations for and election of the "Six" shall take place at the annual meeting of the Users Council except when the Users Council may be filling unexpired terms.

D.   *Governing Powers.* The Board of Trustees shall have all the powers and duties necessary or appropriate for the administration of the affairs of this Corporation and may do all such acts and things as are not reserved or prohibited by law or by the Articles of Incorporation or by this Code of Regulations.

E.   *Vacancies.* The Board of Trustees, by majority vote, shall appoint a successor to fill the unexpired term of a Trustee. An appointee to the term of the "Six" Trustees shall serve only until the Users Council meets and elects a successor to fill the unexpired term.

F.   *Removal of Trustees.* At any annual or special meeting duly called, any one or more of the Board of Trustees may be removed for cause by a vote of two-thirds (⅔'s) of the Trustee Members.

G.   *Compensation.* Compensation as determined by the Board of Trustees, may be paid to Trustees for their services in their capacity as Trustees. Trustees may be reimbursed for actual expenses incurred by them in the performance of their duties, as approved by a majority of the Board of Trustees.

H.   *Meetings.*

(1) *Annual Meeting.* The Board of Trustees shall meet annually as determined by the Board of Trustees, after the annual meetings of the Trustee Members, to conduct such business of the Corporation as may come before it.

(2) *Regular Meetings.* Regular meetings of the Board of Trustees may be held at such time and place as shall be determined, from time to time, by resolution of the Board of Trustees. Notice of regular meetings of the Board of Trustees shall be given by the Secretary to each Trustee, personally, or by mail, telephone or telegraph, at least ten (10) days prior to the day named for such meeting.

(3) *Special Meetings.* A special meeting of the Board of Trustees may be called at any time by the Chairman, the Vice Chairman, or three or more of the Trustees, to be held at such time and place as may be designated in the notice of the meeting. The Secretary shall give such notice to each Trustee personally, or by mail, telephone or telegraph, at least three (3) days prior to the day named for such meeting.

(4) *Location.* Any meetings may be held at such place or places as the Board of Trustees may determine.

(5) *Quorum.* At all meetings of the Board of Trustees, a majority of the Trustees shall constitute a quorum for the transaction of business, and the acts of the majority of the Trustees present at a meeting at which a quorum

is present shall be the acts of the Board of Trustees, except where a larger number is required by law, the Articles of Incorporation, or this Code of Regulations. If, at any meeting of the Board of Trustees, there is less than a quorum present, the majority of those present may adjourn the meeting from time to time. At any such adjourned meeting, any business which might have been transacted at the meeting as originally called may be transacted without further notice.

I.　*Interim Board of Trustees.* Trustees serving the Corporation on the date of the adoption of the Articles of Incorporation and Code of Regulations of the Corporation, plus the Executive Director then serving the Corporation shall become the Interim Board of Trustees of the Corporation. Interim Board shall select five (5) of the initial "Nine" and designate three Interim Trustees to the initial "Nine," as provided for in Article VII C(1). These initial Trustees shall take their respective places on the Board when they are selected and designated. The Executive Director shall have taken his place under Article VII C(1).

The Users Council will elect the initial "Six" as provided in Article VII C(1) and these Trustees shall take their respective places on the Board when they are elected.

The full complement of the initial fifteen (15) member Board shall be achieved as soon as is reasonable and feasible. Interim Trustees will serve unfilled positions on the initial fifteen (15) member Board until individual initial successors have been selected, designated or elected.

J.　*Committees.* The Board of Trustees may create such committees as it deems necessary and desirable.

ARTICLE VIII

OFFICERS

A.　*Powers and Terms.* The officers of the Corporation shall consist of a Chairman of the Board of Trustees, a Vice Chairman of the Board of Trustees, a Secretary and a Treasurer.

The Chairman and Vice Chairman shall be elected by the Board of Trustees annually at the meeting of said Board following the election of successor Trustees. They shall serve for a term of one (1) year and until their successors are elected and qualified and may succeed themselves, with a maximum of three (3) consecutive years' service.

The Secretary and Treasurer shall have such terms and succession as determined by the Board of Trustees upon their appointment.

The Board of Trustees may appoint an Assistant Secretary, an Assistant Treasurer, and such other officers as in their judgment may be necessary.

The Chairman, Vice Chairman, Secretary and Treasurer of the Corporation shall have such powers and duties as are normally incident to such offices.

There shall also be an Executive Director, who shall have the powers conferred upon a President pursuant to Chapter 1702.01 *et. seq.,* Ohio Revised Code, who shall be chosen by the Board of Trustees and shall serve during the pleasure of the Board.

Exhibit C—Code of Regulations, December 20, 1977 / 275

The Executive Director shall have, subject to the direction of the Board of Trustees, direct administrative supervision over the immediate executive authority with respect to the conduct of the business and affairs of the Corporation.

B. *Removal.* Upon an affirmative vote of a majority of the Board of Trustees, any officer may be removed for cause after notice, and his/her successor shall be elected at any regular meeting of the Board, or at any special meeting called for that purpose. The Secretary shall notify the officer sought to be removed within three (3) days of this meeting by telephone, mail, or in person.

ARTICLE IX

NEGOTIABLE INSTRUMENTS, CONTRACTS, ETC.

A. All checks, drafts, bills of exchange, notes or other instruments or orders for the payment of money shall be signed in the name of the Corporation or, if made payable to the Corporation, may be endorsed for deposit to the credit of the Corporation, by such officer or officers, person or persons, as the Board of Trustees may from time to time designate by resolution.

B. The Board of Trustees may authorize any officer or officers, agent or agents, in the name of and on behalf of the Corporation, to enter into or execute and deliver any and all deeds, bonds, mortgages, contracts, and other obligations or instruments, such authority may be general or confined to specific instances.

ARTICLE X

AMENDMENTS

Except as otherwise required by law, this Code of Regulations may be amended by the Trustee Members at any meeting called for that purpose, provided that written notice of the proposed amendment shall have been given at least ten (10) days prior to such meeting. Such amendment shall require an affirmative vote of two-thirds of all of the authorized number of Trustee Members of the Corporation at a duly constituted meeting, and must be ratified by a majority vote of Members of the Users Council present at a meeting called for that purpose.

EXHIBIT D

BOARD OF TRUSTEES
October 25, 1967

	Term
Lewis C. Branscomb (Vice-Chairman) Director of Libraries Ohio State University	Two Years
Robert F. Cayton (Secretary) Librarian Marietta College	Three Years
Joseph M. Denham Associate Professor of Chemistry Hiram College	Three Years
Arthur T. Hamlin University Librarian University of Cincinnati	Two Years
John Kamerick Vice President of Academic Affairs Kent State University	Two Years
A. Blair Knapp (Chairman) President Denison University	One Year
Bob Mowery (Treasurer) Director of Libraries Wittenberg University	One Year
A. Robert Rogers Director of Libraries Bowling Green State University	Three Years
Phillip R. Shriver President Miami University	One Year

A. Blair Knapp passed away May 14, 1968 and was replaced on the Board by:
Robert W. Morse, President, Case Western Reserve University
(Elected by Trustees by mail vote to fill unexpired one-year term June 1968)

John J. Kamerick resigned effective August 31, 1968 and his two-year term was filled by:
Eileen Thornton, Oberlin College (Effective November 8, 1968)

BOARD OF TRUSTEES
November 8, 1968

BOARD OF TRUSTEES
November 14, 1969

BOARD OF TRUSTEES
November 13, 1970

BOARD OF TRUSTEES
November 12, 1971

BOARD OF TRUSTEES
November 10, 1972

The title of Chairman of the Board of Trustees was changed to Chairman and President at the Annual Meeting of the Members March 26, 1973.

BOARD OF TRUSTEES
November 9, 1973

	Term
Patrick Barkey Director of Libraries University of Toledo	Two Years
Robert F. Cayton Librarian Marietta College	One Year
James V. Jones (Chairman and President) Director of Libraries Case Western Reserve University	One Year
Thompson M. Little (Secretary) Director of Libraries Ohio University	Three Years
Patricia L. Lyons Librarian Walsh College	Three Years
Lewis C. Naylor Director of Libraries Toledo-Lucas County Public Library	Three Years
Richard J. Owen (Treasurer) Librarian Heidelberg College	Two Years
H. Paul Schrank, Jr. (Vice-Chairman) University Librarian University of Akron	Two Years
Phillip R. Shriver President Miami University	One Year

Patrick Barkey resigned from the Board July 1, 1974 and his two-year term was filled by:
> L. Ronald Frommeyer, Director of Libraries, Wright State University (Effective July 2, 1974)

BOARD OF TRUSTEES
November 8, 1974

BOARD OF TRUSTEES
November 7, 1975

	Term
William Chait Director of Libraries Dayton-Montgomery County Public Library	Two Years
L. Ronald Frommeyer (Secretary) Director of Libraries Wright State University	Three Years
James V. Jones Director of Libraries Case Western Reserve University	Two Years
Thompson M. Little (Vice-Chairman) Director of Libraries Ohio University	One Year
Patricia L. Lyons Librarian Walsh College	One Year
Lewis C. Naylor Director of Libraries Toledo-Lucas County Public Library	One Year
Richard J. Owen (Treasurer) Librarian Heidelberg College	Three Years
H. Paul Schrank, Jr. (Chairman and President) University Librarian University of Akron	Three Years
Joseph F. Shubert State Librarian of Ohio State Library of Ohio	Two Years

---

Thompson M. Little resigned from the Board effective July 27, 1976 and his one-year term was filled by:
> Hal B. Schell, Vice Provost for University Libraries, University of Cincinnati (Effective July 28, 1976)

BOARD OF TRUSTEES
November 5, 1976

BOARD OF TRUSTEES
(Interim Board)
December 20, 1977

Effective May 8, 1978, the following three interim Board members became permanent Board members:

William Chait	Six-year term
Hal B. Schell	Four-year term
H. Paul Schrank, Jr.	Six-year term

Effective March 13, 1978, the Executive Director's title was changed to President and Executive Director.

EXHIBIT E

OHIO COLLEGE LIBRARY CENTER
1967-1968 Members

Antioch College
Ashland College
Athenaeum of Ohio
Bluffton College
Borromeo Seminary of Ohio
Bowling Green State University
Capital University
Case Western Reserve University
Cedarville College
Central State University
Cleveland State University
College of Mt. St. Joseph on the
    Ohio
College of Wooster
Cuyahoga Community College
Defiance College
Denison University
Edgecliff College
Findlay College
Heidelberg College
Hiram College
John Carroll University
Kent State University
Kenyon College
Lake Erie College
Malone College
Marietta College
Miami University

Mount Union College
Muskingum College
Oberlin College
Ohio College of Applied Science
Ohio Dominican College
Ohio Northern University
Ohio State University
Ohio University
Ohio Wesleyan University
Otterbein College
Pontifical College of Josephinum
Rio Grande College
Sinclair College
St. John College of Cleveland
University of Akron
University of Cincinnati
University of Dayton
University of Toledo
Ursuline College for Women
Walsh College
Western College for Women
Wilberforce University
Wilmington College
Wittenberg University
Wright State University
Xavier University
Youngstown State University

EXHIBIT F

STATEMENT OF
ACADEMIC OBJECTIVE,
ECONOMIC GOAL, AND
MISSIONS TO ACHIEVE THESE ENDS
April 9, 1969

::::: the ohio college library center
:: . : 1858 neil ave. – columbus ohio – 43210

9 April, 1969

STATEMENT OF ACADEMIC OBJECTIVE, ECONOMIC GOAL, AND
MISSIONS TO ACHIEVE THESE ENDS.

The principal academic objective of the Ohio College Library Center is to
increase availability of library resources for use in educational and research
programs of Ohio colleges and universities. The principal economic goal of the
Center is to lower the rate of rise of per-student library costs, while increasing
availability of library resources.

The Ohio College Library Center is a not-for-profit corporation, chartered by the State of Ohio. Its members are Ohio colleges and universities
which pay to the Center an assessment that is based on the number of titles
which each institution's library added to its collection in the previous academic
year. Each member institution appoints a representative, and representatives
elect from their group nine trustees whose responsibility and authority are
comparable to those functions which college and university trustees possess.

Activities of the Center are research, development, implementation, and
operation of computerized systems designed to achieve the Center's objectives
and goals. As yet, no computerized library network of the size of OCLC is in
operation, although smaller projects are partially operational. Therefore,
extensive research and development is required before implementation can be
undertaken. However, five major subsystems have been designed.

Statement of Academic Objective, Economic Goal, and Missions to Achieve These Ends
(April 9, 1969), Courtesy of OCLC.

First to be implemented will be a shared cataloging system based on a central computerized catalog. This system will speed cataloging and reduce cataloging costs in member libraries; 1) by taking advantage of cataloging performed elsewhere and thereby eliminating duplicate effort, and 2) by employment of labor saving machines. In addition, this project will produce at no extra cost a central union catalog whereby each member institution can rapidly determine by author and title location of materials in Ohio. Moreover, the communication system can be employed for rapid requests of materials from other institutions.

The second project will be a remote catalog access and circulation control system which will enable student and faculty members outside the library to determine local institution holdings, as well as those in the state. Access will be by author and title. The system will also make it possible for a user to determine the exact location of the item he needs and whether or not it is immediately available for him before he leaves the building in which he is working or studying. The mechanized circulation control will also cut library costs.

The third system will be a bibliographic information retrieval project whereby instructors and students at remote terminals can search holdings from the subject point of view. Again, large amounts of user time will be saved thereby.

The fourth project is a serials control system that will be designed to facilitate library control of serials holdings.

The fifth project will be a major technical processing system that will computerize most of library processing. One of its major products will be addition to the central catalog of materials in process so that a user can determine existence and location of a specific book in a library system before complete entry in the catalog has been accomplished.

In effect, these systems furnish the advantages of computers to faculty members, students, and the library. They take advantage of existence of materials in other institutions and of effort accomplished in other institutions without increasing costs to such institutions. Of equal importance, the system is based on labor-saving machines which will make it possible to bring exponentially rising library per-student costs into a linear relationship with costs in the general economy before it will be possible to bring rising per-student costs in other areas of college and universities into a linear relationship.

EXHIBIT G

FIXED AND VARIABLE COSTS OF CATALOG CARD PRODUCTION

Fixed Costs	**Variable Costs**
Card punch	Keypunching
Print train	Proofing and corrections
Printer attendants	6 computer runs
Card stock	Sort for file-listing
Ribbons	407 listings
MARC tapes	Pull selections
Slitter	Sort pulled selections
Overhead of 0.5¢ per catalog card	Slitting of cards
	Mailing
	Accounting
	Printing

Fixed and Variable Costs of Catalog Card Production. Source: Ohio College Library Center, *Manual for OCLC Catalog Card Production*, revised and enlarged by Judith Hopkins (Columbus: Ohio College Library Center, 1971), p. 37.

EXHIBIT H

MEMORANDUM TO REPRESENTATIVES OF OCLC MEMBERS CONCERNING FACULTY BORROWING AMONG OCLC LIBRARIES
December 12, 1968

the ohio college library center
1314 kinnear rd. — columbus ohio — 43212

12 December, 1968

MEMORANDUM

To: Representatives of OCLC Members

From: Frederick G. Kilgour, Director   *F. G. K.*

Subject: Faculty Borrowing Among OCLC Libraries

Some time ago, the Dayton and Miami Valley Consortium adopted a set of rules which permitted faculty members of their institutions to borrow directly from each other. Last April, the eleven state universities which comprise the Inter-University Council adopted the same set of rules among themselves, and in October voted to extend the direct borrowing privilege to faculty members of all OCLC member institutions. Enclosed is an IULC news release announcing the new policy.

At the 8 November 1968 meeting of OCLC, the representatives present voted unanimously to support the principle that faculty members of OCLC institutions have borrowing privileges in all OCLC libraries. I was asked to invite each institution formally to accept the rules adopted by the Dayton and Miami

---

Memorandum to Representatives of OCLC Members Concerning Faculty Borrowing among OCLC Libraries (December 12, 1968), Courtesy of OCLC.

Valley Consortium and the IULC. Antioch College, the University of Cincinnati, Ohio Dominican College, and Otterbein College have already indicated their acceptance.

These rules for faculty borrowing are: A Faculty member at any participating institution may, upon presentation of an identification card or letter, borrow circulating materials from the library of any other participating institution. The following conditions will apply:

    a.   the student circulation policies and loan periods of the lending library will be followed.

    b.   all borrowed materials are subject to recall at request of the lending library.

    c.   limitations may be placed on borrowing materials in demand at the lending library.

    d.   no renewals should be expected.

    e.   materials borrowed may be returned either to the lending library or to the home campus.

    f.   overdue notices will be sent to the home library of the borrower, where ultimate responsibility rests for return or replacement of materials borrowed.

    g.   journals will not be loaned.

Please let me know if your library will accept the above rules for faculty borrowing among OCLC institutions.

cc: IULC Members.

Exhibit I—Participants in Faculty Borrowing, December 1969 / 293

EXHIBIT I

PARTICIPANTS IN
FACULTY BORROWING AMONG
OCLC LIBRARIES
December 1969

As of December 1969 all of the institutions listed below agreed to participate in direct faculty lending between libraries.

Antioch College	Mary Manse College
Ashland College	Miami University
Athenaeum of Ohio	Mt. St. Joseph on the Ohio
Bluffton College	Mount Union College
Borromeo Seminary of Ohio	Muskingum College
Bowling Green State University	Oberlin College
Capital University	Ohio Dominican
Cedarville College	Ohio Northern University
Central State University	Ohio State University
Cleveland State University	Ohio University
College of Steubenville	Otterbein College
College of Wooster	Pontifical College Josephinum
Cuyahoga Community College	Rio Grande College
Defiance College	Sinclair College
Denison University	University of Akron
Dyke College	University of Cincinnati
Findlay College	University of Dayton
Hebrew Union	University of Toledo
Heidelberg College	Western College for Women
Hiram College	Wilberforce
John Carroll University	Wilmington College
Kent State University	Wittenberg University
Kenyon College	Wright State University
Lake Erie College	Xavier University
Malone College	Youngstown State University

Participants in Faculty Borrowing among OCLC Libraries (1969), Courtesy of OCLC.

EXHIBIT J

OCLC NETWORKS
AND THEIR MEMBERS

CCLC (1971-1972)

Alabama
Miles College
Oakwood College
Stillman College
Talladega College
Tuskegee Institute

Florida
Florida Memorial College

Georgia
Clark College
Morris Brown College

Louisiana
Dillard University

Mississippi
Mary Holmes College
Rust College
Tougaloo College

North Carolina
Bennett College

South Carolina
Claflin College

Tennesee
Lemoyne-Owen College

Texas
Bishop College
Paul Quinn College

Virginia
Virginia Union University

PRLC
(Membership as of January 1975)

Pennsylvania
Allegheny College
Altoona Area Public Library
B. F. Jones Memorial Library
Cambria County Library System
Carlow College
Carnegie Library of Pittsburgh
Chatham College
Citizen's Library
Clarion State College
Erie Metropolitan Library
Indiana University of Pennsylvania
Monessen Public Library
New Castle Public Library
Pittsburgh Theological Seminary
Point Park College
Robert Morris College
Slippery Rock State College
University of Pittsburgh
Warren Library Association
Westminster College

FAUL (1971-1972)

New York
Cornell University
Rochester University
State University of New York
    at Binghamton
State University of New York
    at Buffalo
Syracuse University

OCLC Networks and Their Members (Information provided by OCLC or the consortia).
NOTE: In general, the institutions listed under each consortium represent the membership at the time of signing the initial agreement with OCLC. Not all institutions were, however, able to provide the list of the initial membership. In such instances, the earliest list available was used.
An institution may appear under more than one network because the networks were in flux. Therefore, the reader should consult the lists with discretion.

NELINET (1971-1972)

Connecticut
Connecticut College
University of Connecticut
Wesleyan University
Yale University

Massachusetts
Boston University
Colby College
Curry College
Hampshire College
Massachusetts State Library
M.I.T.
Newton College of the Sacred
    Heart
Northeastern University
Tufts University
Wellesley College
Worchester Polytechnic Institute

New Hampshire
Colby Junior College
Dartmouth College
Franklin Pierce College
New England College
Notre Dame College
Plymouth State College
St. Anselm's College
University of New Hampshire

New York
Five Associated University
    Libraries
New York State Library

Rhode Island
Brown University
Bryant College of Business
    Administration
Rhode Island College
Rhode Island Junior College
University of Rhode Island
U.S. Naval War College

Vermont
University of Vermont

NELINET (cont'd)

Washington, D.C.
The Consortium of Universities
    of Washington, D.C.

PALINET (1974-1975)

Delaware
University of Delaware

New Jersey
Princeton University Library

Maryland
Johns Hopkins University
University of Maryland, Baltimore
    County

Pennsylvania
Allentown Public Library
Bethlehem Public Library
Bryn Mawr College Library
Bucks County Free Library
Chester County Library and
    District Center
Community College of Philadelphia
Dauphin County Library System
Dickinson College
Drexel University
East Stroudsburg State College
Franklin & Marshall College
Free Library of Philadelphia
Gettysburg College
Haverford College
James V. Brown Library
King's College
Kutztown State College
Lancaster County Library
Lincoln University
Lock Haven State College
Lycoming College
Millersville State College
Montgomery County Community
    College
Montgomery County-Norristown
    Public Library
PALINET Center

PALINET (cont'd)

Pennsylvania (cont'd)
Reading Public Library
Shippensburg State College
State Library of Pennsylvania
St. Charles Borromeo Seminary
    Library
St. Joseph's College
Temple University
Thomas Jefferson University
University of Pennsylvania
West Chester State College
Widener College
Wilson College

IUC (1973-1974)

New Mexico
Eastern New Mexico University
New Mexico State University
University of New Mexico

Texas
Austin College
Baylor College of Dentistry
Baylor University
Bishop College
Dallas Baptist College
East Texas State University
North Texas State University
Southern Methodist University
Texas Christian University
Texas Tech University
Texas Woman's University
University of Dallas
University of Texas at Arlington
The University of Texas at Austin
The University of Texas at Dallas
The University of Texas Health
    Science Center at Dallas

HECC (1974-1975)

Missouri
St. Louis Public Library
Washington University

HECC (cont'd)

Missouri (cont'd)
Washington University School
    of Medicine Library
Webster College

IRRC (1974-1975)

Illinois
Chicago Public Library
Illinois State Library
Southern Illinois University
University of Illinois

SOLINET (1974-1975)

Alabama
Auburn University
Jacksonville State University
Troy State University
University of Alabama
University of Alabama in
    Birmingham
University of Alabama in
    Huntsville
University of South Alabama

Florida
Brevard Community
Broward Community College
Central Florida Community College
Florida A & M University
Florida Atlantic University
Florida International University
Florida Junior College
Florida Technological University
Florida State University
Indian River Community College
Lake-Sumter Community College
Manatee Junior College
Miami-Dade Junior College
North Florida Junior College
Okaloosa-Walton Junior College
Palm Beach Junior College
Polk Community College
Seminole Junior College
State Library of Florida

SOLINET (cont'd)

Florida (cont'd)
Tallahassee Community College
University of Florida
University of Miami
University of North Florida
University of South Florida
University of West Florida
Valencia Community College

Georgia
Abraham Baldwin Agricultural
    College
Augusta College
Columbia Theological Seminary
Emory University
Fort Valley State College
Georgia College
Georgia Institute of Technology
Georgia Southern College
Georgia Southwestern College
Georgia State University
Kennesaw Junior College
Macon Junior College
Medical College of Georgia
Middle Georgia College
North Georgia College
University of Georgia
Valdosta State College
West Georgia College

Kentucky
Asbury Theological Seminary
Kentuckiana Metroversity, Inc.
Northern Kentucky State College
Southern Baptist Theological
    Seminary
University of Kentucky
University of Louisville

Louisiana
Louisiana State University
Loyola University
McNeese State University
New Orleans Public Library
Tulane University
University of Southwestern
    Louisiana

SOLINET (cont'd)

Mississippi
Mississippi State University

North Carolina
Appalachian State University
Davidson College
East Carolina University
Elizabeth City State University
Fayetteville State University
North Carolina A & T
    University
North Carolina School of Fine
    Arts
North Carolina State Library
North Carolina State University
Southeastern Baptist Theological
    Seminary
University of North Carolina
University of North Carolina
    at Asheville
University of North Carolina
    at Charlotte
University of North Carolina
    at Greensboro
University of North Carolina
    at Wilmington
Wake Forest University
Western Carolina University
Winston-Salem State University

South Carolina
Clemson University
College of Charleston
South Carolina State College
University of South Carolina
Winthrop College

Tennessee
Austin Peay State University
Joint University Libraries
Middle Tennessee State
    University
Southern Missionary College
University of the South
University of Tennessee
University of Tennessee at
    Martin

SOLINET (cont'd)

Virginia
College of William & Mary
University of Virginia
Virginia Commonwealth
    University
Virginia State Library
Washington & Lee University

SUNY (1974-1975)

New York
SUNY Agricultural & Technical
    College at Delhi
SUNY Agricultural & Technical
    College at Farmingdale
SUNY Agricultural & Technical
    College at Morrisville
SUNY, at Albany
SUNY, at Stony Brook
SUNY, Central Administration
SUNY, College at Brockport
SUNY, College at Buffalo
SUNY, College at Cortland
SUNY, College at Genesco
SUNY, College at New Platz
SUNY, College at Old Westbury
SUNY, College at Oneonta
SUNY, College at Oswego
SUNY, College at Plattsburgh
SUNY, College at Potsdam
SUNY, College at Purchase
SUNY, College at Utica/Rome
SUNY, College of Ceramics
SUNY, College of Fedonia
SUNY, Downstate Medical Center
SUNY, Upstate Medical Center
CUNY, Brooklyn College
CUNY, City College of New York
CUNY, Graduate School & Uni-
    versity Library Center
CUNY, Hunter College
CUNY, Lehman College
CUNY, Queens College
CUNY, York College
Adelphi University
Alfred University

SUNY (cont'd)

New York (cont'd)
Buffalo & Erie County Public
    Library
Canisius College
Capital District Library Council
Four County Public Library System
Hamilton College
Hobart & William Smith College
Hofstra University
Ithaca (South Central) College
Maritime College
Nassau Community College
New York State Library
New York University
Nioga Library System
Onondago Library System
Rensselaer Polytechnic Institute
Rochester Public Library
Rockland Community College
Russell Sage College
St. Lawrence University
Sarah Lawrence College
Southeastern Library Resources
    Council
Southern Adirondack Library
    System
Southern Tier Library System
U.S. Department of Defense
U.S. Military Academy at West
    Point
Upper Hudson Library Federation
Yeshiva University

AMIGOS (1974-1975)

Arkansas
Arkansas Library Commission
Arkansas Polytechnic College
Henderson State College
Hendrix College
Little Rock Public Library
Ouachita Baptist University
University of Arkansas at
    Little Rock
University of Arkansas at
    Pine Bluff

AMIGOS (cont'd)

Arkansas (cont'd)
University of Arkansas Medical
  Center
University of Central Arkansas

Arizona
Arizona State University
Northern Arizona University
Tucson Public Library
University of Arizona

New Mexico
Eastern New Mexico University
New Mexico State University
University of New Mexico

Oklahoma
Oklahoma Department of Libraries
Oklahoma State University

Texas
Abilene Christian College
Abilene Public Library
Austin College
Austin Public Library
Baylor College of Dentistry
Baylor University
Bishop College
Dallas Baptist College
Dallas Public Library
East Texas State University
El Paso Community College
El Paso Public Library
Fort Worth Public Library
Hardin-Simmons University
Irving Public Library
Lamar University
Lubbock City-County Library
McMurry College
North Texas State University
Southern Methodist University
Southwest Texas State University
Texas A & I University
Texas A & M University
Texas Christian University
Texas Southern University
Texas State Library
Texas Tech University

AMIGOS (cont'd)

Texas (cont'd)
Texas Woman's University
University of Dallas
University of Houston
University of Houston, Victoria
  Center
University of Texas at Arlington
University of Texas at Austin
University of Texas at Dallas
University of Texas at El Paso
University of Texas Health Science
  Center
University of Texas at Permian
  Basin
University of Texas at San Antonio
Waco-McLennan County Library

BCR (1975-1976)

Colorado
Bibliographical Center for Research
  Rocky Mountain Region, Inc.
University of Denver

Iowa
Maharishi International University

Kansas
Kansas City Public Library
Kansas State Library
University of Kansas State Libraries

Nebraska
Boys Town Center for the Study
  of Youth Development

Utah
University of Utah

CAPCON (1975-1976)

Washington, D.C.
The American University
The Catholic University of America
Georgetown University
Howard University

INCOLSA (1975-1976)

Indiana
Ball State University
De Pauw University
Earlham College
Evansville-Vanderburgh County
Public Library
INCOLSA Processing Center
(formerly known as
Crawfordsville Processing
Center)
Indiana State Library
Indiana State University
Indiana University
Indiana University School of
Medicine
Indiana University — Purdue University (Indianapolis)
Lake County Public Library
Marion College
Morrisson-Reeves Public Library
Purdue University
University of Evansville
University of Notre Dame
Vigo County Public Library

MLC (1975-1976)

Michigan
Adrian College
Albion College
Alma College
Andrew University
Aquinas College
Bay De Noc Community College
Calvin College
Central Michigan University
Detroit Associated Libraries
Eastern Michigan University
Ferris State College
Flint Public Library
Grand Rapids Public Library
Grand Valley State College
Hillsdale College
Hope College
Jackson Community College
Jackson County Library
John Wesley College

MLC (cont'd)

Michigan (cont'd)
Kalamazoo College
Kalamazoo Valley Community
College
Kellogg Community College
Lake Superior State College
Lansing Community College
Lawrence Institute of Technology
Madonna College
Marygrove College
Mercy College of Detroit
Michigan State Library
Michigan State University
Michigan Technology University
Monroe County Library System
Nazareth College
Northern Michigan University
Oakland Community College
Oakland University
Olivet College
St. Mary's College
Schoolcraft Community College
Siena Heights College
Spring Arbor College
Suomi College
University of Detroit
University of Michigan
Wayne County Community College
Wayne State University
Western Michigan University
West Shore Community College
Willard Library System

WLC (1975-1976)

Wisconsin
University of Wisconsin at
Eau Claire
University of Wisconsin at
Green Bay
University of Wisconsin at
Madison
University of Wisconsin at
Milwaukee
University of Wisconsin at
Parkside

WLC (cont'd)

Wisconsin (cont'd)
University of Wisconsin at
Stout
University of Wisconsin at
Whitewater

MIDLNET (1976-1977)

Iowa
Iowa State University
University of Northern Iowa

Missouri
Missouri Processing Center
Northeast Missouri State University
University of Missouri

Washington
Washington University
Washington University School of
Medicine

MINITEX (1976-1977)

Minnesota
Augsburg College
Bemidji State University
Bethel College
Carleton College
College of St. Benedict
College of St. Catherine
College of St. Scholastica
College of St. Teresa
College of St. Thomas
Concordia College
Gustavus Adolphus College
Hamline University
James J. Hill Reference Library

MINITEX (cont'd)

Minnesota (cont'd)
Mankato State University
Southwest State University
St. Cloud State University
St. John's University
St. Mary's College
St. Olaf College
Tri-College University Libraries
(Concordia College, Moorehead
State University, and North
Dakota State University)
University of Minnesota (Duluth)
University of Minnesota
(Minneapolis Campus)
University of Minnesota (Morris)
University of Minnesota
(St. Paul Campus)
University of Minnesota Law
Library
Winona State University

North Dakota
North Dakota State Library
University of North Dakota

NEBASE (1976-1977)

Nebraska
Chadron State College
Concordia Teachers College
Doane College
Hastings College
Kearney State College
Nebraska Library Commission
Nebraska Wesleyan University
Union College
University of Nebraska-Lincoln
Wayne State College

EXHIBIT K

CATALOG RECORD
DISPLAYED ON A TERMINAL
SCREEN

```
Type: a Bib lvl: m Lang: eng
Form:    Int lvl:    ISBN: 0262070367
Card no: 78-113725 OCLC no: 132366 Cat'g source: LC ₽
₽
▷ 1 050 0    HV1437.N4 ‡b G63 ₽
▷ 2 082      362/.9746/8 ₽


▷ 3 100 10   Goldenberg, I. Ira, ‡d 1936- ₽
▷ 4 245 1    Build me a mountain; ‡b youth, poverty, and the creation of
settings ‡c [by] I. Ira Goldenberg. ₽
▷ 5 260 0    Cambridge, ‡b MIT Press ‡c [1971] ₽


▷ 6 300      xiv, 498 p. ‡b illus. ‡c 24 cm. ₽
▷ 7 504      Bibliography: p. 487-493. ₽
▷ 8 650  0   Social work with youth ‡z New Haven. ₽
▷ 9 650  0   Socially handicapped ‡z New Haven. ₽
▷10 650  0   Economic assistance, Domestic ‡z New Haven. ₽
 ₽
▷11 090      ‡b  ₽
▷12 049 _ _  ₽
 ₽
OUN KSU WSU CSU MIA AKR ANC YNG CLC DRB TEU FSK
```

Catalog Record Displayed on a Terminal Screen. Source: Ohio College Library Center, *On-Line Cataloging* (Columbus: The Ohio State University Libraries, Office of Educational Services, 1973, Third printing 1978), p. 31.

Exhibit L — Union Catalog Location Symbols / 303

EXHIBIT L

UNION CATALOG
LOCATION SYMBOLS

Newsletter 39 contained a list of location symbols for each OCLC Member Library. These symbols appear at the bottom of a record displayed on the terminal screen to record the libraries holding the material described by the record.

Location symbols are now being shown for non-OCLC members that are making use of the system as well as for OCLC Members. A complete list of these symbols and institutions follows:

AKL	University of Akron Law Library, Akron, Ohio
AKR	University of Akron, Akron, Ohio
ANC	Antioch College, Yellow Springs, Ohio
ASC	Ashland College, Ashland, Ohio
ATO	Athenaeum of Ohio, Cincinnati, Ohio
BEN	Bennett College, Greensboro, North Carolina
BGU	Bowling Green State University, Bowling Green, Ohio
BIS	Bishop College, Dallas, Texas
BLC	Bluffton College, Bluffton, Ohio
CAU	Capital University, Columbus, Ohio
CDC	Cedarville College, Cedarville, Ohio
CFC	Claflin College, Orangeburg, South Carolina
CIN	University of Cincinnati, Cincinnati, Ohio
CLC	Clark College, Atlanta, Georgia
CMJ	College of Mount St. Joseph, Mount St. Joseph, Ohio
CNC	Central State College, Wilberforce, Ohio
CRC	Carlow College, Pittsburgh, Pennsylvania
CSU	Cleveland State University, Cleveland, Ohio
CVT	Center for Vocational and Technical Education, Columbus, Ohio
CWR	Case Western Reserve University, Cleveland, Ohio
DAY	University of Dayton, Dayton, Ohio
DEF	Defiance College, Defiance, Ohio
DIL	Dillard University, New Orleans, Louisiana
DNU	Denison University, Granville, Ohio
DRB	Dartmouth College, Hanover, New Hampshire
DXU	Drexel University, Philadelphia, Pennsylvania
FIN	Findlay College, Findlay, Ohio
FMC	Florida Memorial College, Miami, Florida
HEI	Heidelberg College, Tiffin, Ohio
HUC	Hebrew Union College, Cincinnati, Ohio

Union Catalog Location Symbols for OCLC Participants. Source: Ohio College Library Center, *Newsletter*, 17 March 1972, pp. [1]-2.

KEN	Kenyon College, Gambier, Ohio
KSU	Kent State University, Kent, Ohio
LEC	Lake Erie College, Painesville, Ohio
LOC	Lemoyne-Owen College, Memphis, Tennessee
MAL	Malone College, Canton, Ohio
MBC	Morris Brown College, Atlanta, Georgia
MHC	Mary Holmes College, West Point, Mississippi
MIA	Miami University, Oxford, Ohio
MLC	Miles College, Birmingham, Alabama
MOC	Morris College, Sumter, South Carolina
MRC	Marietta College, Marietta, Ohio
MSC	Muskingum College, New Concord, Ohio
OAK	Oakwood College, Huntsville, Alabama
OBE	Oberlin College, Oberlin, Ohio
ODC	Ohio Dominican College, Columbus, Ohio
ONU	Ohio Northern University, Ada, Ohio
OSU	Ohio State University, Columbus, Ohio
OTC	Otterbein College, Westerville, Ohio
OUN	Ohio University, Athens, Ohio
OWU	Ohio Wesleyan University, Delaware, Ohio
PAU	University of Pennsylvania, Philadelphia, Pennsylvania
PCJ	Pontifical College Josephinum, Worthington, Ohio
PIT	University of Pittsburgh, Pittsburgh, Pennsylvania
PQC	Paul Quinn College, Waco, Texas
PTP	Point Park College, Pittsburgh, Pennsylvania
RGC	Rio Grande College, Rio Grande, Ohio
ROB	Robert Morris College, Coraopolis, Pennsylvania
RUS	Rust College, Holly Springs, Mississippi
SCM	Stillman College, Tuscaloosa, Alabama
SIN	Sinclair Community College, Dayton, Ohio
STU	College of Steubenville, Steubenville, Ohio
TAL	Talladega College, Talladega, Alabama
TEU	Temple University, Philadelphia, Pennsylvania
TGC	Tougaloo College, Tougaloo, Mississippi
TOL	University of Toledo, Toledo, Ohio
TUS	Tuskegee Institute, Tuskegee, Alabama
URB	Urbana College, Urbana, Ohio
UTS	United Theological Seminary, Dayton, Ohio
VUU	Virginia Union University, Richmond, Virginia
WAL	Walsh College, Canton, Ohio
WBU	Wilberforce University, Wilberforce, Ohio
WCW	Western College for Women, Oxford, Ohio
WIT	Wittenberg University, Springfield, Ohio
WMC	Wilmington College, Wilmington, Ohio
WOO	College of Wooster, Wooster, Ohio
WSC	Wright State University, Celina, Ohio
WSP	Wright State University, Piqua, Ohio
WSU	Wright State University, Dayton, Ohio
XAV	Xavier University, Cincinnati, Ohio
YNG	Youngstown State University, Youngstown, Ohio

EXHIBIT M

INPUT CATALOGING
WORK FORM

Type: Int lvl: Lang:

Form: Bib lvl: ISBN:

Card no: ℙ

ℙ

▷ 1 041 _   ‡b ℙ

ℙ

▷ 2 1__ __   ‡d ℙ

▷ 3 24_ _   ‡b ‡c ℙ

▷ 4 250   ℙ

▷ 5 260 _   ‡b ‡c ℙ

ℙ

▷ 6 300   ‡b ‡c ℙ

▷ 7 4__ __   ‡d ℙ

▷ 8 5__ _   ℙ

▷ 9 6__ __   ℙ

▷10 7__ __   ‡d ℙ

▷11 8__ __   ℙ

ℙ

▷12 09C   ‡b ℙ

▷13 049 __   ℙ

▷14 590   ℙ 2a

_____

Input Cataloging Work Form. Source: Ohio College Library Center, *On-Line Cataloging* (Columbus: The Ohio State University Libraries, Office of Educational Services, 1973, Third printing 1978), p. 49.

EXHIBIT N

SCREEN DISPLAY
IN EXTENDED SEARCH

(1)   [First Message]

    us,pro/DISPLAY REC'D/SEND

(2)   [First Response]

    US,PRO produces more than fifty entries.
    Do you wish to continue this search?

(3)   [Second Message]

    yes/SEND

(4)   [Second Response]

    1   (US) 102

    2   (US E) 4

    3   (US F) 6

    4   (US GE) 21

    5   (US LIBRARY OF CONGRESS) 3

    6   U.S. Model Cities Administration. Program guide; model neighbor-
    hoods in demonstration cities. Title I of the Demonstration cities and
    metropolitan development act of 1966. 1968

    7   (US NAT) 11

    8   (US O) 7

    9   (US P) 6

    10   (US T) 3

    11   U.S. Water Resources Council. Special Task Force. Procedures for
    evaluation of water and related land resource projects; findings and
    recommendations, 1971

    12   U.S. 92d Congress, 1st session, 1971. Senate. Proposed Equal
    employment opportunities enforcement act of 1971: S. 2515, S,
    2617, and H.R. 1746; bill texts, section-by-section analyses, changes
    in existing law, comparison of bills introduced. 1971

Screen Display in Extended Search. Source: Ohio College Library Center, *On-Line Catalog-ing* (Columbus: The Ohio State University Libraries, Office of Educational Services, 1973, Third printing 1978), p. 35.

(5) [Third Message]

2/DISPLAY REC'D/SEND

(6) [Third Response]

1 U.S. Electoral Commission, 1877. Proceedings of the Electoral Commission and of the two houses of Congress in joint meeting relative to the count of electoral votes cast December 6, 1876 for the Presidential term commencing March 4, 1877. 1970

2 U.S. Environmental Science Services Administration. Research Laboratories. Office of Programs. Programs and resources. 1970

3 U.S. Environmental Science Services Administration. Research Laboratories. Office of Programs. Programs, resources, and management information. 1968

4 U.S. Equal Employment Opportunity Commission. Promise versus performance; the status of equal employment opportunity in the nation's gas and electric utilities, November 1971. 1972

EXHIBIT O

BOARD OF TRUSTEE'S
RESOLUTION ON BEHALF OF
LEWIS C. BRANSCOMB
November 10, 1972

WHEREAS, Lewis C. Branscomb, presently Professor of Thurber Studies and formerly Director of Libraries, The Ohio State University, has been a long-time proponent of library cooperation on both state and national levels; and,

WHEREAS, Mr. Branscomb was a member of the Ohio College Association Committee of Implementation which established the Ohio College Library Center; and,

WHEREAS, Mr. Branscomb has been a member of the Board of Trustees of the Center from its inception on October 25, 1967 through November 10, 1972; and,

WHEREAS, Mr. Branscomb, while on the Board of the Center, served as Chairman and as Vice Chairman for a total of five years; and,

WHEREAS, Mr. Branscomb has given unstintingly of his time and wise counsel; therefore,

BE IT, AND IT IS HEREBY RESOLVED that the Board of Trustees and the Director of the Center express their deep appreciation to Lewis C. Branscomb for his excellent leadership and other contributions to the programs of the Center; and,

BE IT, AND IT IS HEREBY FURTHER RESOLVED that the text of this resolution be spread upon the minutes of the Board of Trustees' meeting of November 10, 1972 (II), and that copies of this resolution be transmitted by the Secretary of the Center to Mr. Branscomb and to the President of The Ohio State University.

Board of Trustee's Resolution on Behalf of Lewis C. Branscomb. Source: Ohio College Library Center, "Minutes of the Board of Trustees Meeting" (Columbus: Ohio College Library Center, 10 November 1972), pp. 2-3.

BOARD OF TRUSTEE'S RESOLUTION ON BEHALF OF LEWIS C. BRANSCOMB
June 17, 1975

WHEREAS, Lewis C. Branscomb was a member of the Ohio College Association's Committee of Implementation that established the Ohio College Library Center in 1967; and,

WHEREAS, Dr. Branscomb has been representative from the Ohio State University to the Ohio College Library Center from 1967 to 1975; and,

WHEREAS, Dr. Branscomb served on the Board of Trustees of the Center from its first meeting in 1967 to 1972; and,

WHEREAS, Dr. Branscomb while on the Board of Trustees served as Chairman and Vice-Chairman for five years; therefore,

BE IT, AND IT IS HEREBY RESOLVED, that the Board of Trustees and the Executive Director of the Center express their deep gratitude to Lewis C. Branscomb for his excellent leadership, guidance, advice, and counsel to the establishment and development of the Center; and,

BE IT, AND IT IS HEREBY FURTHER RESOLVED, that the text of this resolution be spread upon the minutes of the Board of Trustees' meeting of June 17, 1975 and that copies of this resolution be transmitted by the Secretary of the Center to Dr. Branscomb and to the President of the Ohio State University.

Board of Trustee's Resolution on Behalf of Lewis C. Branscomb. Source: Ohio College Library Center, "Minutes of the Board of Trustees Meeting" (Columbus: Ohio College Library Center, 17 June 1975), p. 10.

EXHIBIT P

STATEMENT OF PURPOSE, OBJECTIVES, SYSTEMS, AND PLANS FOR ATTAINING OBJECTIVES
January 16, 1974

::::: the ohio college library center
:: : 1550 w. henderson rd. – columbus ohio – 43220

16 January 1974

STATEMENT OF PURPOSE, OBJECTIVES, SYSTEMS, AND PLANS FOR ATTAINING OBJECTIVES

PURPOSE
The purpose of the Ohio College Library Center is to enable libraries to break away from passive service functions and to participate actively in furnishing information and services to individual users and libraries when and where they need it.

OBJECTIVES

1. To increase location information and availability of participating library resources to users;

2. To furnish users and libraries with information when and where they need it;

3. To enable libraries to give personalized service;

4. To lower the rate of rise of per-unit costs;

5. To provide management information; and

6. To create and make available new and improved library operational procedures.

SUBSYSTEMS

1. *On-Line Union Catalog and Shared Cataloging*
   The principal subsystem modules are: 1) an on-line union catalog; 2) on-line catalogs of individual libraries; 3) catalog cards in final form arranged for filing in specific catalogs in specific institutions; 4) index by author-title; 5) index by title; 6) index by Library of Congress card number; 7) index by author; and 8) index by subject.

2. *On-Line Serials Union Catalog and Serials Control*
   The principal modules of this subsystem will be: 1) an on-line serials union catalog; 2) serials catalogs for individual libraries; 3) an on-line catalog of truncated entries containing holdings for specific titles; 4) automatic claim notices; and 5) binding notices.

3. *Acquisitions*
   The modules of this subsystem will be: 1) production of purchase orders; 2) an on-line, outstanding order file for each individual library; 3) maintenance of commitment registers and other financial records; and 4) production of claiming notices.

4. *Interlibrary Loan Communications*
   This subsystem will be a message communication procedure enabling users to determine the availability of a work in another library and to request it on interlibrary loan.

5. *Remote Catalog Access for Users*
   This subsystem will provide remote catalog access for users via telephone or from terminals by: 1) author; 2) author-title; 3) title; 4) subject; and 5) call number.

6. *Circulation Control*
   This subsystem will provide modules to: 1) enable users to arrange to obtain works via telephone or terminal; 2) charge works; 3) maintain on-line charge records; 4) issue overdue notices automatically; and 5) maintain on-line files of disqualified borrowers.

PLANS

1. *Research and Development*
   1) The Center will continue research and development.
   2) Research and development will be supported by income from participating libraries.
   3) Since grant funds largely support the present level of research and development, the Center will bring additional participating libraries into the system to obtain the income necessary to replace grant funds.
   4) The Center will continue to seek grant funds for support of research and development.

2. *Extension of Services Outside of Ohio*
   Extension of services will give firm financial support to continued research and development, will lower the cost of the use of the system for each individual library, and will also lower the cost within each individual

library; therefore, whenever feasible, the Center will continue to extend services outside of Ohio.

3. *Retrospective Conversion*

Whenever feasible, the Center will schedule and accept retrospective conversion of catalogs of individual institutions.

4. *Scheduling of Implementation*

To avoid peaks of demand for capital and for research and development, and to insure optimum utilization of equipment, the Center will maintain close control of scheduling of the implementation of plans.

EXHIBIT Q

OHIO COLLEGE LIBRARY CENTER:
Long-Range Plan
1977-1978

Long-Range Goals

OCLC's long-range goals are:

1. To increase availability of library resources to library patrons;
2. To lower the rate of rise of library per-unit costs;
3. To furnish patrons and library staff with information when and where they need it;
4. To enable patrons to receive personalized service; and
5. To provide management information.

Objectives for the Next Three Years

OCLC's objectives for the next three years are:

1. To require every library on the system to participate in the union catalog and shared cataloging function;
2. To encourage each institution on the system to participate also in the acquisitions function;
3. To make available the serials control function to participating libraries;
4. To make available the interlibrary loan function to participating libraries; and
5. To schedule and balance growth of the system to arrive at integrated achievement of objectives.

Objectives to Be Achieved after Installation of New Technology Three Years Hence

OCLC's additional objectives for the period following installation of new technology supplementing Sigma equipment on-line are:

6. To make available a public service function to participating libraries; and
7. To make available a circulation control function to participating libraries.

Ohio College Library Center: Long-Range Plan (excerpt). Source: Ohio College Library Center, "Ohio College Library Center: Budget Plan 1977/78" (Columbus: Ohio College Library Center, 5 April 1977), pp. 10-11.

Schedule Necessitated by Anticipated Saturation of
Quadruple Processor Computer System

To provide for meeting objectives after saturation of the quadruple processor computer system, OCLC will immediately undertake the following projects:

1. Installation of a second multiple processor computer system in the present machine building by first implementing a dual processor (possibly to be increased to a triple processor and finally a quadruple processor) as required to attain Objectives 1 through 4;

2. Design a new on-line system employing new computer technology with processing power ten times greater than that of the Sigma equipment, but employing essentially the present programs that will be operational approximately three years after the decision to undertake the project to make possible attaining Objectives 6 and 7;

3. Produce a program for a new building to be completed in time to house the new on-line system described in the preceding paragraph to also make possible attainment of Objectives 6 and 7; and

4. Design an entirely new on-line system employing processors still more powerful than those called for in 2 in this Schedule and new programs to be operational approximately six years after undertaking the project.

EXHIBIT R

ARTICLES OF INCORPORATION
OF OHIONET
December 20, 1977

The undersigned incorporator, desiring to form a Corporation, not-for-profit, under Ohio Revised Code Section 1702.01, *et. seq.*, hereby certify:

FIRST   The name of said Corporation shall be OHIONET.

SECOND   The place in this state where the principal office of the Corporation is to be located is Clinton Township, Franklin County.

THIRD   The purposes for which this Corporation is formed are exclusively scientific, literary, and educational, within the meaning of Internal Revenue Code Section 501 (c) (3), or any corresponding/equivalent provisions of any future Internal Revenue Code, and include the following: To create and maintain a library network in Ohio, consisting of and supported by its Members as defined herein, which network will: Facilitate the availability and sharing of bibliographic and other library information and resources, to and among its Members and the citizens of Ohio; encourage and facilitate the institution of cost-effective operational practices and procedures by its Members, by means of statewide library cooperation; strive for and participate in the development of a national library network for the same ends.

FOURTH   The Corporation shall be governed by a Board of nine (9) Trustees. The initial Trustees shall be:

H. Paul Schrank, Jr.
University Librarian
The University of Akron
Akron, OH 44325

Hal B. Schell, Vice Provost
  for University Libraries
University of Cincinnati
Cincinnati, OH 45221

Donald J. Sager, Director
Columbus & Franklin County
  Public Library
28 S. Hamilton Road
Columbus, OH 43213

William Chait, Director
Dayton & Montgomery County
  Public Library
215 E. Third Street
Dayton, OH 45402

Articles of Incorporation and Code of Regulations for OHIONET (December 20, 1977), Courtesy of OHIONET

James V. Jones, Director
University Libraries
Case Western Reserve University
11161 East Boulevard
Cleveland, OH 44106

James W. Fry
Deputy Assistant State Librarian for Technical Services
65 S. Front Street
Columbus, OH 43215

Robert Cayton, Director
Dawes Memorial Library
Marietta College
Marietta, OH 45750

Hannah McCauley
Director of the Ohio University
at Lancaster Library
1570 Granville Pike
Lancaster, OH 43130

William J. Studer
Director of Libraries
The Ohio State University
1858 Neil Avenue Mall
Columbus, OH 43210

Their terms and succession shall be as set forth in the Code of Regulations.

FIFTH The Corporation shall consist of General Members and Voting Members, the qualifications, rights and obligations of which shall be as set forth in the Code of Regulations.

SIXTH No part of the earnings, dues or receipts of this Corporation shall inure to the benefit of or be distributed to its Members, Trustees, officers or other private persons, except only that the corporation shall be authorized and empowered to pay reasonable compensation for services rendered and expenses incurred and to make payments or distributions in furtherance of the purposes set forth in Article Third hereof. No substantial part of the activities of the corporation shall be the carrying on of propaganda, or otherwise attempting to influence legislation, and the corporation shall not participate in, or intervene in (including the publishing or distribution of statements) any political campaign on behalf of any candidate for public office. Notwithstanding any other provision of these articles, the corporation shall not carry on any other activities not permitted to be carried on (a) by a corporation exempt from Federal income tax under section 501 (c) (3) of the Internal Revenue Code of 1954 (or the corresponding provision of any future United States Internal Revenue Law) or (b) by a corporation, contributions to which are deductible under section 170 (c) (2) of the Internal Revenue Code of 1954 (or the corresponding provision of any future United States Internal Revenue Law).

SEVENTH Upon the dissolution of the Corporation, the Board of Trustees shall, after paying or making provision for the payment of all of the liabilities of the Corporation, dispose of all of the assets of the Corporation exclusively for the purposes of the Corporation in such manner, or to such organization or organizations as are described in Section 170 (c) (1) or (2) of the Internal Revenue Code of 1954 (or the corresponding provision of any future United States Internal Revenue Code), as the Board of Trustees shall determine. Any of such assets not so disposed of shall be disposed of by the Court of Common Pleas of the county in which the principal office of the Corporation is then located, exclusively for such purposes or to such organization or organizations, as said Court shall determine, which are organized and operated exclusively for such purposes.

EIGHTH   The life of the Corporation shall be perpetual.

NINTH   These Articles may be amended by a majority vote of the Voting Members of the corporation at a meeting called for that purpose.

IN WITNESS WHEREOF, the undersigned has hereby subscribed his name this 20th day of December, 1977.

HUNTINGTON CARLILE

CODE OF REGULATIONS
OF OHIONET
December 20, 1977

ARTICLE I

DEFINITIONS

As used in this Code of Regulations, the word "Network" means this Corporation, that is, OHIONET, and the word "Trustees" and the terms "Board of Trustees" and "Board" shall mean, unless the context otherwise indicates, the Trustees of the Network provided for by law and by the Articles of the Network.

ARTICLE II

MEMBERSHIP

There shall be two classes of Members of the Network; General Members and Voting Members.

General Members shall be libraries of Ohio, whether public or private, academic or non-academic, participating in the OCLC system.

Voting Members shall be those General Members which serve exclusively educational, scientific, or literary purposes, and are that type of organization described in Internal Revenue Code Section 170 (c) (1) or (2), or any corresponding equivalent provision of any future Internal Revenue Code. Each Voting Member shall select its own designated representative, who shall be authorized to act on behalf of the Voting Member.

ARTICLE III

MEMBERSHIP VOTING RIGHTS

At any meeting of the Voting Members of the Network, each Voting Member shall be entitled to one vote on each matter properly submitted to the Voting Members for their vote, consent, waiver, release or other action.

ARTICLE IV

MEMBERSHIP MEETINGS

The annual meeting of the Voting Members of the Network for the transaction of such business as may properly come before it shall be held each year in such place, at such day and time as may be designated by the Board.

A special meeting of the Voting Members of the Network may be called at any time by the Chairman, Vice Chairman, or three members of the Board of Trustees, or by ten or more Voting Members of the Network, to be held at such time and place as may be designated in the notice of the meeting.

Meetings of the Voting Members of the Network may be held either within or without this State.

At any meeting of the Voting Members of the Network, a majority of the Voting Members shall constitute a quorum, but the Voting Members present, whether or not a quorum, may adjourn any meeting from time to time. A majority of the Voting Members present and voting at any meeting shall decide any question brought before such meeting, unless the question is one upon which by express provision of law, the Articles or this Code of Regulations, a larger or different vote is required.

Notice of all annual meetings shall be given in writing to each Voting Member by the Secretary of the Network, at least ten (10) days before the date thereof; notice of any special meeting shall be so given at least three (3) days prior to the date thereof.

ARTICLE V

BOARD OF TRUSTEES

A. *Interim Trustees.* The initial Trustees designated in the Articles of Incorporation shall serve as interim Trustees from the effective date thereof until the selection of their successors.

B. *Qualifications and Election of Successors to Interim Trustees.* The successors to the interim Trustees shall, at the first meeting of the Voting Members of the Network, be elected from the designated representatives of the Voting Membership of the Network. They shall hold staggered three-year terms. Initially, three Trustees shall hold three-year terms, three shall hold two-year terms, and three shall hold one-year terms.

Thereafter, at the annual meeting of the Voting Members, the Trustees shall be elected by the Voting Members to three year terms. Each Trustee shall hold office until his successor has been duly elected and qualified. Any vacancy upon the Board of Trustees shall be filled by action of the Board.

C. *Powers of the Trustees.* Except as otherwise provided by law, the Articles of Incorporation, or this Code of Regulations, the Corporate authority, property and affairs of the network shall be exercised, controlled and conducted by the Board of Trustees, who shall have authority and power to manage the property, business and affairs of the Corporation, including but not limited to the power to borrow money; acquire grants or gifts; enter into contracts on behalf of the Members; purchase, sell, mortgage, lease or otherwise acquire or dispose of property, real or personal.

D. *Meetings.* A regular meeting of the Board of Trustees shall be held annually in such place and immediately after the annual meeting of Voting Members of the Network, and other regular meetings may be held at such time and place, as may be determined by resolution of the Board of Trustees. Notice of regular meetings of the Board of Trustees shall be given by the Secretary to each Trustee, personally or by mail, telephone or telegraph, at least ten (10) days prior to the day named for such meeting.

A special meeting of the Board of Trustees may be called at any time by the Chairman or the Vice Chairman or three or more of the Trustees to be held at such time and place as may be designated in the notice of the meeting, notice of which shall be given as above at least three (3) days prior to the date thereof.

At any meeting of the Board of Trustees, five (5) Trustees shall constitute a quorum, but a lesser number may adjourn any meeting from time to time until a quorum is present, and the meeting may be held as adjourned without further notice. A majority of the Trustees present and voting at any meeting when a quorum is present shall decide any question brought before such meeting, unless the question is one upon which by express provision of law a larger or different vote is required.

E. *Removal of Trustees.* A member of the Board of Trustees may be removed for cause by either a two-thirds (⅔) vote of the Trustees or by a two-thirds (⅔) vote of the Voting Members.

ARTICLE VI

OFFICERS

The officers of the Network shall consist of a Chairman of the Board of Trustees, a Vice Chairman, Secretary, and a Treasurer.

The Chairman and Vice Chairman shall be elected by the Board of Trustees annually at the meeting of said Board following the annual meeting of the Members of the Network. They shall serve for a term of one (1) year, and until their successors are elected and qualified, and may succeed themselves, with a maximum of three (3) consecutive years' service.

A. The Secretary and Treasurer shall have such terms and succession as determined by the Board of Trustees upon their appointment.

B. The Chairman, Vice Chairman, Secretary and Treasurer of the Network shall have such powers and duties as are normally incident to such offices.

C. There shall be an Executive Director of the Network who shall be chosen by the Board of Trustees and shall serve at the pleasure of the Board.

D. The Executive Director shall have, subject to the direction of the Board of Trustees and the Chairman, direct administrative supervision over the conduct of the business and affairs of the Network.

E. All officers are subject to removal action of the Board.

ARTICLE VII

COMMITTEES

The Board of Trustees may create such committees as it deems necessary and desirable.

ARTICLE VIII

NEGOTIABLE INSTRUMENTS, CONTRACTS, ETC.

A. All checks, drafts, bills of exchange, notes or other instruments or orders for the payment of money shall be signed in the name of the Network or, if made payable to the Network, may be endorsed for deposit to the credit of the Network, by such officer or officers, person or persons, as the Board of Trustees may from time to time designate by resolution.

B. The Board of Trustees may authorize any officer or officers, agent or agents, in the name of and on behalf of the Network, to enter into or execute and deliver any and all deeds, bonds, mortgages, contracts, and other obligations or instruments, such authority may be general or confined to specific instances.

ARTICLE IX

AMENDMENTS

This Code of Regulations may be amended at any annual or special meeting of the Voting Members of the Network by the affirmative vote of a majority of the Voting Members of the Network, providing notice of such amendment shall have been given in the notice of the meeting.

EXHIBIT S

FREDERICK GRIDLEY KILGOUR:
ALA Life Membership Award
By S. Michael Malinconico, New York Public Library

The following statement was prepared for the occasion of the presentation of an honorary life membership in the American Library Association to Frederick G. Kilgour. Kilgour was a founding member and president of the Information Sciences and Automation Division — a predecessor of LITA — and editor of its journal, the Journal of Library Automation, *for its first six volumes. He is, of course, most known to the world as the founder of OCLC and developer of the world's first large-scale online library network.*

There are those who on seeing an indistinct shape on the distant horizon create for us soaring visions never before thought or imagined. Sculptures fashioned of light. Elegant, refulgent, seductive, yet insubstantial. There are others who, inspired by the same shimmering distant apparitions, fashion lenses so that their precise measure may be taken and their distance reckoned. The object and the way clearly perceived, it is these latter who confidently point the way to rich new discoveries. It is only when the phenomena are close at hand and readily experienced that we come to comprehend the full import of what these intrepid guides had foretold prior to setting out on the arduous journey of exploration.

Two decades ago, Frederick Kilgour and many of his contemporaries discerned in vague outline the potential that electronic computing and telecommunications technologies held for the practice of librarianship. Some of Fred's contemporaries boldly sketched the outlines of monumental murals that were executed only on the insubstantial canvas of the imagination. Others made pen-and-ink sketches of the shadows of what they beheld to a scale diminished by timidity. Fred carefully avoided the snares that lay at both extremes; maintaining at all times a remarkable sense of proportion between innovation and practicality, he came to know the medium he sought to work with such intimacy that he neither over — nor underestimated it.

Fred's ability to gaze forward in the direction in which technology was developing was rendered particularly acute by many years of gazing backward over the history of science. He thus noted far in advance of his colleagues the rate at which the indistinct phenomenon was growing, and the rapidity with which it was moving toward us. While others fixed their attention on the dazzling corona of the bright object that appeared on the horizon, Fred instead looked deeply into its core and there discovered a potent source of energy that libraries would need to learn to exploit if they were to remain economically viable.

Frederick Kilgour has devoted only slightly less than a half-century to library and information service. The most recent third of that career has been dedicated to the establishment and development of OCLC, the single best-known and most successful library automation project—indeed, the most successful library venture with the exception of those initiated by Melvil Dewey. OCLC was not simply an idea which sprang full grown at the end of the 1960s, nor a fortuitous confluence of events. Rather, it represents the continuous refinement of ideas Fred Kilgour had begun developing as early as 1961 when he helped found the Columbia, Harvard, Yale Medical Libraries Computerization Project, and later in 1965 when he was appointed Yale's associate librarian for Research and Development.

In 1967, Fred Kilgour was named executive director of the newly formed Ohio College Library Center. OCLC afforded Fred the opportunity to execute, on a scale limited by scarcely more than his ability, ideas he had been promoting for nearly a decade. The means were at hand to verify empirically the acuity of his vision. The realization matched the conception with a precision few had been prepared to grant. An entire profession was transformed in the bargain.

OCLC is, of course, Fred's most dazzling achievement; all the more so as it demonstrated his ability to master and direct three enormously powerful forces: computer technology, communications technology, and the potent intellectual energies of youthful engineers anxious to test the limits of their abilities. He dominated and shaped these forces without diminishing them. OCLC thus became the vehicle that revealed the scope and depth of Fred Kilgour's abilities; in addition to exhibiting his technical perspicacity, the success of OCLC served to demonstrate an entrepreneurial flair and executive ability which is found only rarely in librarianship.

There is no doubt that the profession that Frederick Gridley Kilgour has served and graced so long has been profoundly altered by his efforts. It is with a deep sense of gratitude and in recognition of those efforts that the American Library Association confers upon him honorary life membership, its highest award.

APPENDIX 2

GLOSSARY OF TERMS*

access time The time interval between the instant data are called for from the storage unit and the instant data are delivered (read time). The time interval between the instant data are requested to be stored and the instant at which storage is completed (write time).

algorithm A set of well-defined rules for solving a problem in a finite number of steps.

alphanumeric A general term for alphabetic letters (A through Z), numerical digits (0 through 9), and special characters (-, /, *, $, (,), +, etc.) which are machine-processable.

application programs The programs normally written by the using organization, that enable the computer to produce useful work. For example, inventory control, attendance accounting, linear programming, medical accounting.

applications programming The preparation of programs for application to specific problems in order to find solutions.

automatic Pertaining to a process or device that, under specified conditions, functions without intervention by a human operator.

automatic error correction A technique for detecting and correcting errors that occur in data transmission or occur within the system itself.

---

*Donald D. Spencer, Excerpts from *Computer Dictionary for Everyone*. Copyright © 1977, 1979 Camelot Publishing Company, Inc. Reprinted with the permission of Charles Scribner's Sons.

auxiliary storage A storage that supplements the primary internal storage of a computer. Same as *secondary storage.*

available time (1) The time that a computer is available for use.

bank A unit of internal storage.

batch A group of records or programs that is considered as a single unit for processing on a computer.

batch processing A technique by which programs that are to be executed are coded and collected together into groups for processing in groups or batches. The user gives his job to a computer center, it is put in a batch of programs, processed and data returned. The user has no direct access to the machine.

baud A unit for expressing the speed of transmitting data over distances. One baud is one bit per second.

bit A binary digit; a digit (1 or 0) in the representation of a number in binary notation.

bug A term used to denote a mistake in a computer program or system, or a malfunction in a computer hardware component. Hence debugging—removing mistakes and correcting malfunctions. See *malfunction.*

byte (1) A grouping of adjacent binary digits operated on by the computer as a unit. The most common size byte contains eight binary digits. (2) A group of binary digits used to encode a single character.

carriage A control mechanism for a typewriter or printer that automatically feeds, skips, spaces, or ejects paper forms.

cassette See *magnetic tape cassette.*

catalog An ordered compilation of item descriptions and sufficient information to afford access to the items.

cathode ray tube An electronic tube with a screen upon which information may be displayed. Abbreviated CRT.

central processing unit The component of a computer system with the circuitry to control the interpretation and execution of instructions. Abbreviated CPU. Synonymous with *central processor* and *main frame.*

central processor See *central processing unit.*

chadded paper Perforated tape with the chad completely removed.

character   Any symbol, digit, letter, or punctuation mark stored or processed by computing equipment.

classify   To arrange into classes of information according to a system or method.

code   (1) A set of rules outlining the way in which data may be represented. (2) Rules used to convert data from one representation to another. (3) To write a program or routine. (4) Same as *encode*.

coding   (1) The writing of a list of instructions which will cause a computer to perform specified operations. (2) An ordered list or lists of the successive instructions which will cause a computer to perform a particular process.

collate   To merge two (or more) sequenced data sets to produce a resulting data set which reflects the sequencing of the original sets.

command   (1) A control signal. (2) Loosely, a mathematical or logic operator. (3) Loosely, a computer instruction. See *operation code*.

computer   A device designed to execute a sequence of mathematical or logical operations automatically, that is without human intervention. Used for the high-speed processing of large volumes of data.

computer-assisted instruction (CAI)   The use of the computer to augment the individual instruction process by providing the student with programmed sequences of instruction under computer control. The manner of sequencing and progressing through the materials permits students to progress at their own rate. CAI is responsive to the individual needs of the individual student.

computer network   A complex consisting of two or more interconnected computers.

computer system   The physical equipment and instructions; i.e., hardware and software, used as a unit to process data. It includes the central processing unit (CPU), its operating system, and peripheral equipment and programs under its control.

computer utility   A service that provides computational ability. A time-shared computer system. Programs as well as data may be made available to the user. The user also may have his own programs immediately available in the central processing unit, may have them on call at the computer utility, or he may load them by transmitting them to the computer prior to using them. Certain data and programs are shared by all users of the service; other data and programs because of proprietary nature, have restricted access. Computer utilities are generally accessed by means of data communication subsystems.

conditioning The improvement of the data transmission properties of a voiceband transmission line by correction of the amplitude and phase characteristics of the line amplifiers.

configuration An assembly of machines, devices, or systems that work together.

console The part of a computer system that enables human operators to communicate with a computer.

conversational mode A mode of operation that implies a "dialog" between a computer and its user, in which the computer program examines the input supplied by the user and formulates questions or comments which are directed back and to the user.

conversion (1) The process of changing information from one form of representation to another; such as, from the language of one type of computer to that of another or from punch cards to magnetic disk. (2) The process of changing from one data processing method to another, or from one type of equipment to another. (3) The process of changing a number written in one base to the base of another numeral system.

data A formalized representation of facts or concepts suitable for communication, interpretation, or processing by people or by automatic means.

data base A data base is the collection of all data used and produced by a computer program. In large systems, data base analysis is usually concerned with large quantities of data stored in disk and tape files. Smaller personal computer systems are more frequently concerned with data base allocations of available memory locations between program and data storage areas.

data communications The movement of encoded information by means of electrical transmission systems.

data processing (1) One or more operations performed on data to achieve a desired objective. (2) The functions of a computer center. (3) A term used in reference to operations performed by data processing equipment.

data set A device which permits the transmission of data over communication lines by changing the form of the data at one end so that it can be carried over the lines; another data set at the other end changes the data back to its original form so that it is acceptable to the machine (computer, etc.) at that end. Same as *modem*.

debug To detect, locate, and remove all mistakes in a computer program and any malfunctions in the computing system itself.

dial-up In data communications, the use of a dial or push-button telephone to initiate a station-to-station telephone call.

diode An electronic device used to permit current flow in one direction and to inhibit current flow in the opposite direction.

direct access Pertaining to the process of obtaining data from or placing data into storage where the time required for such access is independent of the location of the data most recently obtained or placed in storage. Also called *random access*.

disk pack A set of detachable magnetic disks. Example: A disk pack might consist of eleven disks, 35.56 cm (14 inches) in diameter, mounted on a central spindle. The pack would weight about 4.536 kgs (10 pounds) and hold some 29 million characters of data.

disk storage See *magnetic disk*.

display unit A device which provides a visual representation of data. See *cathode ray tube*.

documentation The preparation of documents, during systems analysis and subsequent programming, that describe such things as the system, the programs prepared, and the changes made at later dates.

downtime The length of time a computer system is inoperative due to a malfunction.

electronic data processing Data processing performed largely by electronic equipment.

electrostatic printer A high-speed line printer. Report page images are magnetized on paper, and then the magnetized paper is passed through an ink fog. The ink adheres to the magnetized spots. Later, the ink is baked into the paper producing the final output sheets.

encode To translate information into a code.

executive A master program that controls the execution of other programs. Often used synonymously with *monitor, supervisory system*, and *operating system*.

feasibility study Concerned with a definition of the data processing problem, together with alternative solutions, a recommended course of action, and a working plan for designing and installing the system.

field A group of related characters treated as a unit—e.g., a group of adjacent card columns used to represent an hourly wage rate. An item in a record.

FIFO An acronym for First In-First Out.

file A collection of related records treated as a unit.

file maintenance The updating of a file to reflect the effects of nonperiodic changes by adding, altering, or deleting data; e.g., the addition of new programs to a program library on magnetic disks.

fixed-length record A record that always contains the same number of characters. Contrast with *variable-length record.*

fixed word length Pertaining to a machine word or operand that always has the same number of bits, bytes, or characters. Contrast with *variable word length.*

format The arrangement of data.

general-purpose computer A computer that is designed to solve a wide class of problems. The majority of digital computers are of this type. Contrast with special-purpose computer.

hardware Physical equipment such as electronic, magnetic, and mechanical devices. Contrast with *software.*

hierarchy (1) Order in which the arithmetic operations, within a formula, or statement, will be executed. (2) Arrangement into a graded series.

illegal character A character or combination of bits which is not accepted as a valid or known representation by the computer.

illegal operation A process which the computer cannot perform.

index (1) A symbol or number used to identify a particular quantity in an array of similar quantities; for example, X(5) is the fifth item in an array of X's. (2) A table of references, held in storage in some sequence, which may be addressed to obtain the addresses of other items of data; e.g., items in a file.

information Meaningful and useful facts that are extracted from data fed to a computer. The meaning assigned to data by known conventions.

information networks The interconnection of a geographically dispersed group of libraries and information centers, through telecommunications, for the purpose of sharing their total information resources among more people.

information processing The totality of operations performed by a computer; the handling of data according to rules of procedure to accomplish operations such as classifying, sorting, calculating, and recording. Same as *data processing.*

input The introduction of data from an external storage medium into a computer's internal storage unit.

key (1) The field or fields which identify a record. (2) The field which determines the position of a record in a sorted sequence. (3) A lever on a manually operated machine, such as a typewriter, teletypewriter, or keypunch.

keyboard A group of marked levers operated manually for recording characters.

keypunching The process by which original, or source data is recorded in punch cards. The operator reads source documents and, by depressing keys on a keypunch machine, converts source document information into punched holes.

large scale integration (LSI) An integrated circuit that contains a large number of transistors and other circuitry on a single chip. LSI chips are small; however, they are slower operating than bipolar logic, such as transistor-transistor logic (TTL). LSI chips are used in microprocessors, microcomputers and other larger machines. See *metallic oxide semiconductor.*

leased line Generally refers to a private full-period data communication line.

length As related to a computer word—the number of characters, bytes, or bits in a computer word. A variable word is made up of several characters ending with a special end character. A fixed word is composed of the same number of bits, bytes, or characters in each word. See *fixed word length* and *variable word length.*

library automation Application of computers and other technology to library operations and services.

line printer An output peripheral device which prints data one line at a time.

line printing The printing of an entire line of characters as a unit.

LSI An acronym for *Large Scale Integration.*

machine-readable information Information recorded on any medium in such a way that it can be sensed or read by a machine.

magnetic disk A peripheral storage device in which data is recorded on magnetizable disk surfaces.

magnetic storage Utilizing the magnetic properties of materials to store data on such devices and media as disks, tapes, cards, drums, cores, and films.

magnetic tape A plastic tape having a magnetic surface for storing data in a code of magnetized spots. Data may be represented on tape using a six- or eight-bit coding structure.

magnetic tape cassette A magnetic tape storage device. A cassette consists of a magnetic tape housed in a plastic container.

magnetic tape drive   A device that moves tape past a head.

main frame   Same as *central processing unit.*

malfunction   A failure in the operation of the central processing unit or peripheral device.

mathematical model   A group of mathematical expressions which represents a process, a system, or the operation of a device. See *simulation.*

message   A group of characters having meaning as a whole and always handled as a group.

message switching   The switching technique of receiving a message, storing it until the proper outgoing circuit and station are available and then retransmitting it toward its destination. Computers are often used to perform the switching function.

message switching center   A center in which messages are routed according to information contained within the messages themselves.

metallic oxide semiconductor   A process that is used in making LSI (large scale integration) chips. MOS chips are smaller; however, slower operating than bipolar logic, such as TTL (transistor-transistor logic).

modem   An acronym for MOdulator-DEModulator. A device that provides the appropriate interface between a communications link and a data processing machine or system by serving as a modulator and/or demodulator. Same as *data set.*

monitor   A control program. See *operating system.*

MOS   An acronym for *Metallic Oxide Semiconductor.*

MOS/LSI   See *metallic oxide semiconductor* and *large scale integration.*

multiplex   To interleave or simultaneously transmit two or more messages over a single channel or other communications facility.

multiplexer   A device that makes it possible to transmit two or more messages simultaneously over a single channel or other transmission facility.

multiplexor channel   A special type of input/output channel that can transmit data between a computer and a number of simultaneously operating peripheral devices.

network   The interconnection of a number of points by data communication facilities. See *computer network.*

off-line   A term describing equipment, devices, or persons not in direct communication with the central processing unit of a computer. Equipment which are not connected to the computer. Contrast with *on-line*.

on-line   A term describing equipment, devices, and persons that are in direct communication with the central processing unit of a computer. Equipment which is physically connected to the computer. Contrast with *off-line*.

on-line problem solving   A teleprocessing application in which a number of users at remote terminals can concurrently use a computing system in solving problems on-line. Often, in this type of application, a dialogue or conversation is carried on between a user at a remote terminal and a program within the central computer system.

on-line processing   Data processing involving direct entry of data into the computer or direct transmission of output from the computer.

on-line storage   Storage under control of the central processing unit.

operating system   An organized collection of software that controls the overall operations of a computer. The operating system does many basic operations which were performed by hardware in older machines, or which are common to many programs. It is available to the computer at all times either being held in internal storage or on an auxiliary storage device.

operation code   The instruction code used to specify the operations a computer is to perform. For example, in "ADD 100 TO 400," "ADD" is the operation code.

operations research   A mathematical science devoted to carrying out complicated operations with the maximum possible efficiency. Among the common scientific techniques in operations research are the following: linear programming, probability theory, information theory, game theory, monte carlo method, and queuing theory.

output   (1) Data transferred from a computer's internal storage unit to some storage or output device. (2) The final result of data processing; data that has been processed by the computer. Contrast with *input*.

polling   In data communications, scanning the networks of terminals or sensors by the computer, asking one after the other if it has any data to submit.

printer   See *electrostatic printer* and *line printer*.

processing   The computer manipulation of data in solving a problem. See *data processing*.

processor A device or system capable of performing operations upon data; e.g., central processing unit (hardware) or compiler (software). A compiler is sometimes referred to as a language processor.

program (1) A set of sequenced instructions to cause a computer to perform particular operations. (2) A plan to achieve a problem solution. (3) To design, write, and test one or more routines. (4) Loosely, a routine.

programming The process of translating a problem from its physical environment to a language that a computer can understand and obey. The process of planning the procedure for solving a problem. This may involve among other things the analysis of the problem, preparation of a flowchart, coding of the problem, establishing input/output formats, establishing testing and checkout procedures, allocation of storage, preparation of documentation, and supervision of the running of the program on a computer.

punched card A cardboard card used in data processing operations in which tiny rectangular holes at hundreds of individual locations denote numerical values, and alphanumeric codes.

quality control A technique for evaluating the quality of a product being processed by checking it against a predetermined standard, and taking the proper corrective action if the quality falls below the standard.

random access See *direct access.*

record A collection of related items of data treated as a unit.

remote terminal A device for communicating with computers from sites which are physically separated from the computer, and often distant enough so that communications facilities such as telephone lines are used rather than direct cables. See *terminal.*

response time The time it takes the computer system to react to a give input. It is the interval between an event and the system's response to the event.

search To examine a set of items for those that have a desired property.

search key Data to be compared to specified parts of each item for the purpose of conducting a search.

second generation Computers belonging to the second era of technological development of computers when the transistor replaced the vacuum tube. These were prominent from 1959 to 1964, and were displaced by computers using integrated circuitry.

secondary storage See *auxiliary storage.*

simulation   To represent the functioning of one system by another; that is, to represent a physical system by the execution of a computer program, or to represent a biological system by a mathematical model. See *mathematical model.*

software   A set of programs, procedures, routines, and documents associated with the operation of a computer system. Software is the name given to the programs that cause a computer to carry out particular operations. The software for a computer system may be classified as *application programs* and *systems programs.* Contrast with *hardware.*

standard   (1) A guide used to establish uniform practices and common techniques. (2) A yardstick (meterstick!) used to measure performance of the computer system function.

storage   Descriptive of a device or medium that can accept data, hold them, and deliver them on demand at a later time. The term is preferred to memory. Synonymous with memory.

storage capacity   The number of items of data which a storage device is capable of containing. Frequently defined in terms of computer words, bytes, or characters.

storage device   A device used for storing data within a computer system; e.g., integrated circuit storage, magnetic disk unit, magnetic tape unit, magnetic drum unit, floppy disk, tape cassette, etc.

subsystem   Systems subordinate to the main system.

supervisory system   See *operating system.*

symbol   (1) A letter, numeral or mark which represents a numeral, operation or relation. (2) An element of the computer's character set.

synchronous transmission   The transmission technique that presents data in a continuous flow of pulses. Once synchronization has been established by a special synchronizing pulse, the pattern of pulses received in a given time period is recorded.

system   An organized grouping of people, methods, machines, and materials collected together to accomplish a set of specific objectives. See *computer system.*

systems programs   Computer programs that provide a particular service to the user; for example, compilers, assemblers, operating systems, sort-merge programs, emulators, linkage editor programs, graphic support programs, and mathematical programs.

telecommunications   The transfer of data from one place to another over communication lines. See *data communications.*

Telpak   A service offered by communications common carriers for the leasing of wide band channels between two or more points.

temporary storage   In programming, storage locations reserved for intermediate results.

terminal   (1) An input/output peripheral device which is on-line to the computer, but which is in a remote location: another room, another city, or another country. (2) A point at which information can enter or leave a communication network.

third generation   Computers which use integrated circuitry and miniaturization of components to replace transistors, reduce costs, work faster, and increase reliability. The third generation of computers began in 1964.

time sharing   A method of operation in which a computer facility is shared by several users for different purposes at (apparently) the same time. Although the computer actually services each user in sequence, the high speed of the computer makes it appear that the users are all handled simultaneously.

transistor   A semiconductor device for controlling the flow of current between two terminals, the emitter and the collector, by means of variations in the current flow between a third terminal, the base, and one of the other two. It was developed by Bell Telephone Laboratories.

truncate   To drop digits of a number of terms of a series, thus lessening precision; for example, 3.14159 truncates the series for π, which could conceivably be extended indefinitely.

update   To incorporate into a master file the changes required to reflect transactions or other events.

user   Anyone who utilizes a computer for problem solving or data manipulation.

utility   See *computer utility*.

utility routines   Software used to perform some frequently required process in the operation of a computer system; e.g., sorting, trigonometric functions, etc.

variable-length record   Pertaining to a file in which the records are not uniform in length. Contrast with *fixed-length record*.

variable word length   Pertaining to a machine word or operand that may consist of a variable number of bits, bytes, or characters. Contrast with *fixed word length*.

verify (1) To determine whether a data processing operation has been accomplished accurately; e.g., to check the results of keypunching. (2) To check data validity.

Wide Area Telephone Service A service provided by telephone companies that permits a customer by use of an access line to make data communications in a specific zone on a dial basis for a flat monthly charge.

APPENDIX 3

ACRONYMS

AACR	*Anglo-American Cataloging Rules*
AALL	American Association of Law Libraries
ALA	American Library Association
ANSI	American National Standards Institute
ARL	Association of Research Libraries
ASCII	American Standard Code for Information Interchange, Department of Commerce
ASIS	American Society for Information Science
AT & T	American Telephone and Telegraph Company
BALLOTS	Bibliographic Automation of Large Library Operations Using Time-Shared Systems
BCR	Bibliographical Center for Research
BSDP	Bibliographic Service Development Program (CLR)
CAPCON	Consortium of Universities of the Washington Metropolitan Area
CCLC	Cooperative College Library Center
CCLN	Council on Computerized Library Networks
CIP	Cataloging in Publication
CLR	Council on Library Resources, Inc.

COMARC	CO-operative MAchine-Readable Cataloging Project (LC)
COMCAT	Florida Computer Output Microform Union Catalog
CONSER	Co-operative CONversion of SERials Project (LC)
COR	Council of Regions
CPU	Central processing unit
CRT	Cathode ray tube terminal
CUNY	City University of New York
EDUCOM	Interuniversity Communications Council
ETS	Educational Testing Service
FAUL	Five Associated University Libraries
FEDLINK	Federal Library and Information Network
FLC	Federal Library Committee
FLECC	Federal Libraries' Experiment in Cooperative Cataloging
GPO	Government Printing Office
HECC	Higher Education Coordinating Council of Metropolitan St. Louis
HSOCLCUG	Health Science OCLC Users Group
IFLA	International Federation of Library Associations
ILL	Interlibrary Loan
INCOLSA	Indiana Cooperative Library Services Authority
IQCC	Inter-Network Quality Control Council
IRRC	Illinois Research and Reference Center Libraries
ISAD	Information Science and Automation Division (ALA)
ISBD	International Standard Bibliographic Description
ISBN	International Standard Book Number
ISDS	International Serials Data System
ISO	Information Systems Office (LC)
ISSN	International Standard Serial Number
IUC	Interuniversity Council of the North Texas Area
IULC	Inter-University Library Council
JOLA	*Journal of Library Automation*
LASIE	Library Automation Systems Information Exchange

LC	Library of Congress
MAMOS	Maryland Michigan Operation System
MARBI	Committee on Representation in Machine-readable Form on Bibliographic Information
MARC	Machine-readable cataloging
MDO	MARC Development Office (LC)
MIC	Mechanized Information Center data base at The Ohio State University
MIDLNET	Midwest Region Library Network
MINITEX	Minnesota Interlibrary Teletype Exchange
MLA	Medical Library Association
MLA	Music Library Association
MLC	Michigan Library Consortium
MOUG	Music OCLC Users Group
MUDG	MARC Users Discussion Group
MULS	Minnesota Union List of Serials
NAC	Network Advisory Committee
NAG	Network Advisory Group
NCEMMH	National Center for Educational Media and Materials for the Handicapped
NCLIS	National Commission on Libraries and Information Science
NDO	Network Development Office (LC)
NEBASE	Nebraska Library Commission
NEBHE	New England Board of Higher Education
NEH	National Endowment for the Humanities
NELINET	New England Library Information Network
NFAIS	National Federation of Abstracting and Indexing Services
NIMIS	National Instructional Materials Information System
NLM	National Library of Medicine
NLN	National Library Network
NSF	National Science Foundation
NTAG	Network Technical Architecture Group

NUC	*National Union Catalog* (LC)
OCA	Ohio College Association
OE	U.S. Office of Education
OLA	Ohio Library Association
PALINET	Pennsylvania Area Library Network
PRLC	Pittsburgh Regional Library Center
RECON	REtrospective CONversion Pilot Project (LC)
RLG	Research Libraries Group
RML	Regional Medical Library program
RTSD/RSAD/ISAD	Resources and Technical Services Division/Reference and Adult Services Division/Information Science and Automation Division (ALA)
SCERT	Comress Systems and Computers Evaluation and Review Technique
SCONUL	Standing Conference of National and University Libraries
SDC	System Development Corporation
SDI	Selective dissemination of information
SIS	OCLC/Special Interest Section of the American Association of Law Libraries (AALL)
SOLINET	Southeastern Library Network
SPIRES	Stanford Public Information Retrieval System
STAIRS	Storage and Information Retrieval System (IBM)
SUNY	State University of New York
ULC	Union Library Catalog of Pennsylvania
UNESCO	United Nations Educational, Scientific, and Cultural Organization
WLC	Wisconsin Library Consortium
WLN	Washington Library Network
WSC	Western Service Center
YBS	Yale Bibliographic System

APPENDIX 4

BIBLIOGRAPHIC NOTE

Research on this book began in 1972. At that time no comprehensive bibliography on OCLC was available. The first unannotated bibliography appeared in June 1974. Written by Nancy F. Rubenstein of Heidelberg College in Tiffin, Ohio, it was entitled "The Ohio College Library Center: A Partial Bibliography." The seven-page list of approximately one hundred citations was divided into three broad subjects, and contained professional journal articles, books (including excerpts), reports, conference and seminar proceedings, as well as OCLC user documents.

Three years later, in 1977, Ann Marie Allison and Ann G. Allan of Kent State University, in Kent, Ohio, prepared another unannotated bibliography with nearly double the number of listings as Rubenstein's. Their "OCLC: A Bibliography" was compiled as a reading list in conjunction with a series of workshops entitled "The Effective Use of OCLC," held at Kent State University.

In June of 1978, OCLC published its first "Bibliography of OCLC User Documents" containing 130 items. Although lacking annotations, it proved to be invaluable. For the first time, OCLC users had access to a complete listing of the Center's materials specifically designed for them. The availability of each document was indicated on the list.

Approximately one year later, OCLC published a second unannotated bibliography under the title "OCLC: A Bibliography" (May 1979). It was prepared by Kim M. Schmidt of OCLC's User Services Division. The majority of the citations were the work of Allison and Allan. The nearly two hundred entries contained articles from professional journals, research papers, books (including excerpts), OCLC training materials produced by agencies and institutions other than OCLC, and newsletters and bulletins of the network and users groups. All documents produced by OCLC were purposely omitted.

Several months later, in September 1979, the first *annotated* bibliography appeared in print. *A Bibliographic Guide to OCLC* was written by Pal V. Rao of Eastern Illinois University, Charleston, Illinois, and was published by the ERIC Document Reproduction Service (Document Number ED 181 906). The work, covering a ten-year period, 1969-1979, was arranged alphabetically by author. Although the citations covered a wide range of sources, the work's value was diminished by its brevity; it consisted approximately of only thirty-five entries.

A major bibliographic breakthrough occurred still in 1979, with the publication of the annotated bibliography *OCLC: A National Library Network* by Ann Marie Allison and Ann G. Allan. Published by Enslow Publishers of Short Hills, New Jersey, it was more extensive than its ancestors, presenting a bibliographic panorama of major primary and secondary source materials "by or about OCLC through 1977." Materials were categorized under four broad subject headings: history and philosophy, application and implementation, manuals and instructional materials, and technical documentation. Included were professional journal articles, entire books as well as excerpts, conference proceedings, reports, newsletters, OCLC documents, bibliographies, lists, studies, papers, proposals, dissertations, and theses.

The purpose of a bibliography for this volume would be to list the most relevant sources. Practically every item in *OCLC: A National Library Network* is relevant and has been consulted by the author. Listing them here would be tantamount to repeating the entire bibliography. Therefore the reader is referred to the work by Allison and Allan.

The following overview of the main sources used in collecting data for this book may be helpful. List A gives two examples of sources listed in *OCLC: A National Library Network*. List B refers to those sources that are *not* included in that volume.

List A

OCLC *Annual Report* (1967-1977)

The *Annual Report* highlighted the major events of each year.

OCLC *Newsletter* (1967-1977)

The *Newsletter* completed many of the details on the Center's evolution. Each issue was not just filled with news, it conveyed a sense of what OCLC was trying to accomplish and how the system was perceived by the users.

List B

OCLC minutes from
Board of Trustees meetings (1967-1977)
Membership meetings (1967-1977)
Directors of the Divisions meetings (1974-1977)
Committee meetings (1967-1977)

Together all these sources provided an invaluable diary of core materials, revealing OCLC's development.

Miscellaneous documents, reports, and unpublished materials from OCLC archival files

OCLC informational and promotional brochures and booklets for public distribution

OCLC memoranda from Frederick G. Kilgour, Philip Long, Judith Hopkins, Ann Ekstrom, and others

OCLC correspondence between its staff and a wide range of people representing a cross section of libraries and other institutions

OCLC grant proposals

OCLC grant reports

These materials were used to complete many of the details of the story.

Personal interviews and personal correspondence

The author conducted a number of informal interviews with many of the personalities in OCLC. She exchanged many letters with a broad range of people who in various ways played a part in OCLC's history. Those contacted included past and present heads of the various divisions at OCLC, key administrators of the networks, past and present officers of the users groups, individuals active in the national networking activities, and many others connected with OCLC on various levels. These personal contacts were invaluable. They supplied information that could not be located elsewhere, clarified facts and issues, and on a few occasions revealed to the writer new data that might otherwise have been unintentionally omitted.

There are still a few other sources of information that should be a part of any bibliography on OCLC. They are as follows:

Davis, Jinnie Y. "Individuals, Information, and Structure in the Establishment of OCLC: A Study of Innovation Decision Making." Unpublished Ph.D. dissertation, Indiana University (Bloomington, Indiana), 1980.

Maruskin, Albert F. *OCLC: Its Governance, Function, Financing, and Technology* (New York: Marcel Dekker), 1980.

Timmons, Sarah S. "Shared Cataloging by Computer in Ohio: Studies of Four Participating Libraries." Unpublished Master's research paper, Kent State University (Kent, Ohio), 1974.

The Timmons paper investigated the impact of the OCLC on-line shared cataloging system on four charter member Ohio academic libraries (Wittenberg University, Oberlin College, Wright State University, and Cedarville College) during the early days of on-line activities. Emphasis was placed on experiences during the fiscal year 1972-1973. Seen from a historical point of view, it records those early impressions of and experiences with OCLC.

The Davis study, in the words of the author, "investigates the conditions under which the [Ohio] librarians decided to select an innovative alternative that established the first cooperative, on-line bibliographic data base in the world." Its purpose was to answer the question "Under what conditions of the variables of individuals, information, and structure does a decision-making group make an innovation decision..."

Maruskin's work is a critical analysis of the growth and development of OCLC. The concepts of resource sharing and library cooperation underscore the discussion of OCLC with regard to its network governance structure, major subsystems, financial growth, and use of modern technology to process information.

There is no doubt that as studies on OCLC proliferate in the future, the bibliographies too will grow.

RÉSUMÉS

RÉSUMÉ

Le "Ohio College Library Center (OCLC)" a été créé en 1967 comme corporation à but non-lucratif et dont la charte a été accordée par l'Etat de l'Ohio. Le but principal, comme il a été conçu par ses fondateurs, devait être une réduction dans la hausse des coûts du fonctionnement des bibliothèques et une augmentation des ressources mises à la disposition des usagers. La structure du système a été basée sur le développement de plusieurs sous-systèmes, y compris un catalogue collectif en direct et des systèmes de catalogage partagé, de contrôle des périodiques, de prêts entre bibliothèques et autres services techniques. Le rêve des concepteurs était le développement et la mise en marche d'un système global. Les objectifs du Centre, tels qu'énumérés dans les Statuts d'Incorporation, étaient d'établir, de maintenir et de faire fonctionner un centre régional automatisé d'information documentaire qui desservirait les bibliothèques de l'enseignement supérieur de l'Ohio — tant des institutions privées que d'état — et conçu de telle façon qu'il puisse devenir partie intégrante de tout réseau national automatisé de renseignements bibliographiques.

L'histoire de la première décennie de l'OCLC a pris naissance dans la coopération. Avant même la création du Centre, l'Ohio a connu un siècle de coopération entre les bibliothèques universitaires qui remontent à 1867, l'année même de la création de l' "Ohio College Association (OCA)". Pendant cette période, l'idée d'une coopération entre bibliothèques de l'enseignement supérieur à l'échelle de l'état s'est répandue petit à petit.

Après plusieurs essais infructueux et, peu s'en est fallu, l'abandon total du projet, l'Ohio College Library Center a émergé sur la scène des réseaux automatisés nationaux. En dix ans, il a connu un tel succès qu'il est devenu le premier grand système automatisé du pays.

Sous l'habile direction de son premier directeur exécutif, Frederick G. Kilgour, le Centre a pris un essor prodigieux. En 1967-1968, le budget de l'OCLC était de l'ordre de $66,428; dix ans plus tard, cette somme s'élevait à $15,074,000. Le Centre, qui en 1967 comptait au départ 54 bibliothèques d'enseignement supérieur, est devenu un réseau national. En 1977, plus de 2,100 bibliothèques de cinquante états, plus le District of Columbia, utilisaient l'OCLC et des projets étaient déjà en cours afin d'étendre son service à l'étranger. Pendant la première année de fonctionnement en ligne (1971-1972), le Centre a reproduit plus de 3.4 millions de fiches; en 1976-1977, 60.9 millions. A la fin de la première décennie, la base de données du Centre contenait plus de 3 millions de notices.

De 1967 à 1977, le développement de l'OCLC a demandé la participation de bibliothécaires, administrateurs de bibliothèques, formateurs, informaticiens et avocats aussi bien que des experts dans les domaines de l'automatisation des bibliothèques et des réseaux. Plusieurs organismes ont aussi contribué à son évolution, dont l'Ohio College Association, Library of Congress (Bibliothèque du Congrès), Council on Library Resources Inc., U.S. Office of Education (Bureau de l'Education des Etats-Unis), Ohio Board of

Regents* et la Fondation W.K. Kellogg. Chacun a été impliqué dans l'histoire du Centre.

Les années 1967-1977 ont été remplies d'activités de toutes sortes et sur plusieurs fronts à la fois, ce qui a permis de modeler et d'adapter le système aux besoins de ses usagers. La base de données prit de nouvelles proportions à mesure que, d'année en année, les usagers se fiaient davantage sur le système pour les besoins quotidiens. La capacité du système en ordinateurs a quadruplé et on y a même ajouté des minis ordinateurs. La recherche et le développement a mené à de nouvelles fonctions et de meilleurs rendements, ouvrant aussi la route à de nouvelles perspectives en bibliothéconomie.

L'histoire de l'OCLC est une histoire haute en couleur et remplied'émotions. On a vécu un véritable suspense quand, en 1971, la question s'est posée à savoir si l'Ohio Board of Regents consentirait à aider les bibliothèques de l'Ohio à faire face aux coûts des premières années du système. La joie régnait le 26 août 1971 quand l'Université de l'Ohio à Athens a été la première bibliothèque à cataloguer les livres en ligne directe avec l'OCLC. Les membres ont ressenti une vive émotion le 6 septembre 1974 quand l'Université Northeastern à Boston a entré dans la base de données de l'OCLC la millionième notice.

Par contre, on a vécu une grosse déception en 1974 quand le Centre s'est lancé dans un projet de construction d'un bâtiment et que, au moment de démarrer, on a dû y renoncer. Les coûts de construction étaient en effet montés en flèche bien au-dessus des possibilités de l'OCLC. Les usagers ont souffert en novembre 1975 quand le délai de la réponse du système s'est détérioré, nécessitant un moratoire sur l'installation des terminaux jusqu'au moment où un délai acceptable a été atteint.

L'histoire prend fin d'une façon assez dramatique avec la création d'une structure nouvelle de direction à l'OCLC, laissant prévoir un nouveau stade de développement. A travers toute son histoire, on retrouve, en filigrane, le thème de la coopération. A peine âgé de dix ans, l'OCLC s'est révélé un véritable pionnier et un modèle dans le domaine des services et des réseaux bibliographiques en ligne.

---

*L'organisme gouvernemental qui régit les universités d'état de l'Ohio.

ZUSAMMENFASSUNG

Das Ohio-College—Bibliothekszentrum wurde 1967 als gemeinnützige, im Staate Ohio priviligierte Aktiengesellschaft gegründet. Sein von den Gründern erdachtes Hauptziel war die Steigerung der Betriebskosten für Bibliotheken zu vermindern und die Verfügbarkeit der Bücherschätze für die Bibliotheksbenützer zu vermehren. Die Struktur des Systems gründete sich auf die Entwicklung mehrerer Untersysteme, darunter das On-line-Gesamtverzeichnis und das Katalogsystem für Mitglieder, Kontrolle der periodischen Zeitschriften, das Leihsystem zu Bibliotheken und technische Bearbeitungsmethoden. Der Traum der Konstrukteure war ein allgemeines Bibliothekswesen zu entwickeln und einzusetzen. Der Zweck des Zentrums, den man in den Satzungen von 1967 festsetzte, war "ein mit Rechenautomaten versorgtes regionales Bibliothekszentrum zu gründen, instandzuhalten und zu führen, um die akademischen Bibliotheken in Ohio, staatlich sowie privat, zu bedienen. Es soll so geplant sein, daβ es ein Teil irgendeines das ganze Land umfassenden Komputerverbindungsnetzes für bibliographische Auskunft werden könnte."

Die Geschichte des ersten Jahrzehnts im Leben des OCLC besteht auf Zusammenarbeit. Vor der Schöpfung des Zentrums erlebten die akademischen Bibliotheken in Ohio ein Jahrhundert der Zusammenarbeit, die bis zum Jahr 1867 zurückreichte, das Jahr, worin die Ohio-College-Vereinigung (OCA) gegründet wurde. Während dieser Zeit gewann der Begriff der Zusammenarbeit unter allen Colleges und Universitäten im Staat Momentum. Nach einigen Fehlschlägen und fast völliger Aufgabe des Plans erschien das Ohio-Bibliothekszentrum auf dem Feld des Verbindungsnetzes und der Automation des Landes. In einem Jahrzehnt wurde es das erste erfolgreiche, groβangelegte, rechnergeführte Bibliothekszentrum im Lande.

Unter der tüchtigen Leitung des ersten Direktors, Frederick G. Kilgour, wuchs das Zentrum sprunghaft. Im Jahre 1967-68 hatte das OCLC ein Budget mit $66.428,-. Zehn Jahre später war die Summe $15.074.000,-. Aus einer Mitgliedschaft von 54 Bibliotheken in Colleges und Universitäten in Ohio im Jahre 1967 entfaltete sich ein das ganze Land umfassendes System. Im Jahre 1977 diente das OCLC mehr als 2.100 Bibliotheken in fünfzig Staaten des Landes und im District of Columbia. Man hatte schon vor, den Dienst auch nach fremden Ländern auszudehnen. Im ersten Jahre der gekoppelten Betriebsweise (1971-72) stellte das Zentrum mehr als 3,4 Millionen Karteikatalogkarten her. Im Jahre 1976-77 stellte es 60,9 Millionen Karten her. Bis zum Ende des ersten Jahrzehnts speicherte das Zentrum über drei Millionen Verzeichnisdokumente.

An der Geschichte der OCLC-Entwicklung zwischen 1967 und 1977 beteiligten sich Bibliothekare, Bibliotheksdirektoren, Pädagogen, Fachleute in den Rechnen- und Rechtswissenschaften und Fachleute auf den Gebieten von Bibliotheksautomation und Netztechnik. Viele Organisationen und Gruppen waren am Werden beteiligt, darunter die Ohio-College-Vereinigung (OCA), die US-Kongreβbibliothek (LC), die Beratungstelle für Bibliotheksbestand

(Council on Library Resources), das US-Büro für Bildungswesen (U.S. Office of Education), der Ohio-Bildungsvorstand (Ohio Board of Regents) und die W. K. Kellogg Stiftung. Jedes Glied hat zu der Geschichte des Zentrums einen Beitrag geleistet.

An allen Seiten entfaltete sich in den Jahren zwischen 1967 und 1977 große Aktivität, die das System nach den Bedürfnissen der Benützer gestaltete. Die Datenbank wuchs Jahr für Jahr in Größe an, als die Benützer immermehr für ihre tägliche Beschäftigung auf das System angewiesen wurden. Die Leistung des Rechensystems vermehrte sich vom Programmablauf eines Rechners zu einem durch Minikomputer unterstützten Vierechnerzentrum. Forschung und Entwicklung führten zu neuen Tätigkeiten und Betriebsverfeinerung und bahnten den Weg zu neuen Perspektiven im Bibliotheksgebrauch.

Die Geschichte des OCLC ist lebhaft und emotionell. Spannung brachte die Frage, ob der Ohio-Bildungsvorstand mithelfen würde, die Unkosten des Zentrums in den ersten Jahren zu tragen. Man freute sich, als am 26. August 1971 das On-line-System entstand und die Ohio Universität zu Athens, Ohio, die erste Bibliothek wurde, die den On-line-Katalog anwendete. Freudig erregt war die Mitgliedschaft, als am 6. September 1974 die Northeastern Universität zu Boston den millionsten Datensatz in die OCLC-Datenbank einführte. Eine der Enttäuschungen kam 1974 während eines Bauprogramms. Man war fast dabei die Baugrube auszuheben, als die Pläne zusammenbrachen, weil die Baukosten weit über die Geldmittel des OCLC emporschossen. Es tat den Benützern weh, als sich die Ansprechzeit verlängerte und im November 1975 so unglaublich lang wurde, daß ein Moratorium in der Installierung von Komputerstationen nötig war, bis man die erwünschte Ansprechzeit erreichte.

Die Geschichte des OCLC kommt mit der Erzeugung einer neuen Verwaltungsstruktur des OCLC zu einem dramatischen Ende, aber eine neue Entwicklungsstufe winkt aus der Zukunft. Ein überall beherrschendes Thema ist die Zusammenarbeit, die wie ein silberner Faden durch alles führt. Im zarten Alter von zehn Jahren hat sich das OCLC als wahrer Pionier und Pfadfinder in der On-line-Netzwerk- und der bibliographischen Interbibliothek-Aktivität bewährt.

SÍNTESIS

El "Ohio College Library Center" (OCLC) fue fundado en 1967 como una corporación sin propósitos lucrativos, auspiciada por el estado de Ohio. Su meta principal, según fue concebida por sus iniciadores, era reducir el aumento del costo en el funcionamiento de las bibliotecas y aumentar el acceso a los recursos bibliotecarios para las personas que las usan. La estructura del sistema fue basada en el desarrollo de un número de subsistemas incluyendo el "online union catalog" y compartiendo el sistema "cataloging," el control de las series, los préstamos entre las bibliotecas y los sistemas técnicos de procesar. El sueño de sus diseñadores era desarrollar e implementar un sistema de bibliotecas completo. El propósito del Centro, según se asentó en los Artículos de Incorporación de 1967, era "para establecer, mantener y operar un centro regional de bibliotecas controlado por computadoras electrónicas, para servir a las bibliotecas académicas en Ohio (ambas, del estado y particulares) y diseñado en forma tal que llegue a ser parte de cualquier red electrónica nacional para información bibliográfica."

La historia de la primera década de OCLC tiene sus raíces en la cooperación. Antes del nacimiento de este Centro, Ohio disfrutó de un siglo de la cooperación de las bibliotecas académicas desde el año de 1867, en el cual "Ohio College Association" (OCA) (la Asociación de Universidades de Ohio) fue fundada. Durante este período, la idea de establecer un cooperativismo entre todas las Universidades de Ohio ganó ímpetu, y después de varios intentos malogrados y casi un abandono total del proyecto, el "Ohio College Library Center" emergió en la red nacional de bibliotecas y en el panorama de la automatización. En una década creció lo suficiente para llegar a ser el primer sistema de bibliotecas controlado por computadoras electrónicas en gran escala, que tuvo éxito en la nación.

Bajo la capaz dirección de su primer Director Ejecutivo, Frederick G. Kilgour, el centro creció a pasos agigantados. Entre los años de 1967 y 1968, OCLC funcionó con un presupuesto de $66,428 dólares. Diez años más tarde esa cifra fue de $15,074,000 dólares. De una asociación de 54 bibliotecas universitarias en 1967, evolucionó hasta llegar a ser un sistema nacional. En 1977 OCLC era usado por más de 2,100 bibliotecas en cincuenta estados y en el Distrito de Colombia. Más planes se seguían haciendo para extender sus servicios a naciones extranjeras. Durante el primer año de actividades "on-line" (1971-1972), el Centro produjo más de 3.4 millones de tarjetas con información (catalog cards). Durante 1976-1977, produjo 60.9 millones. Hacia el final de la primera década la información básica (data base) del Centro, "memorizó" más de tres millones de listas descriptivas e información en general para tener acceso fácil a ellas (catalog records).

La historia del desarrollo de OCLC de 1967 a 1977 incluye bibliotecarios, administradores de bibliotecas, educadores, expertos jurídicos y expertos en la ciencia de computadoras, y pioneros en el campo de automatización y redes de bibliotecas. Muchas organizaciones y grupos fueron también parte de esta fascinante aventura, incluyendo Ohio College Association (la Asociación de

Universidades de Ohio), Library of Congress (la Biblioteca del Congreso), Council on Library Resources, Inc. (la Corporación del Consejo en Recursos Bibliotecarios), U.S. Office of Education (la Dirección de Educación de los Estados Unidos), Ohio Board of Regents (la Junta de Regentes de Ohio), y W. K. Kellogg Foundation (la Fundación W. K. Kellogg). Cada grupo contribuye a la formación de la historia del Centro.

Los años comprendidos entre 1967 y 1977 fueron muy activos en diversos aspectos para llegar a moldear el sistema de acuerdo a las necesidades de quienes lo usaban. La "data base" aumentaba cada año porque quienes usaban el sistema llegaron a depender más y más de él para usarlo en sus actividades diarias. La fuerza de la computadora se aumentó de la operación de una computadora a un sistema de cuatro computadoras asistidos por minicomputadoras. Las investigaciones y el desarrollo condujeron a nuevos funcionamientos y a operaciones que se mejoraron y abrieron el camino a nuevos horizontes para el servicio que pueden rendir las bibliotecas.

La historia de OCLC es una historia pintoresca y llena de emociones. Hubo suspenso en 1971 cuando no se sabía si la Junta de Regentes de Ohio (Ohio Board of Regents) ayudaría a las bibliotecas de Ohio a devengar el costo del sistema en los años iniciales. Inmensa alegría fue experimentada el 26 de agosto de 1971, cuando el sistema "on-line" comenzó y la Universidad de Ohio en Athens, Ohio, llegó a ser la primera biblioteca que uso "on-line cataloging" por medio de OCLC. Se generó excitación entre los miembros del sistema cuando el 6 de septiembre de 1974, "Northeastern University" en Boston introdujo los datos que registraron el millón en la información basica de OCLC (OCLC data base). Una de las desilusiones ocurrió en 1974, cuando el centro puso en marcha un proyecto de construcción y estuvo a punto de iniciarse. Sin embargo, tales planes se derrumbaron cuando el costo de la contrucción aumentó considerablemente, al punto de ser considerablemente mayor que los recursos monetarios de los que OCLC podía disponer. Quienes usaban el sistema experimentaron dolor cuando el tiempo que empleaban las computadoras en responder empeoró y llegó a su cumbre en noviembre de 1975, al punto de que se necesitó un "moratorium" en la instalación de terminales hasta que un tiempo más aceptable de reacción fuera logrado.

La historia termina con una nota dramatica al crearse una nueva estructura para la operación de OCLC, con la cual empieza una nueva etapa de desarrollo. El tema penetrante que corre como un hilo de plata a través de su historia, es la cooperación. A la tierna edad de los 10 años, OCLC ha probado ser una verdadera pionera y una marcadora del paso en "online" y en las actividades bibliográficas de la red de bibliotecas.

РЕЗЮМЕ

Библиотечный Центр Огайо Колледжа (О-СИ-Л-СИ) был основан в 1967 году как не коммерческое общество учреждённое штатом Огайо. Его главной целью, как было задумано его основателями, являлось уменьшение наростания эксплуатационных расходов библиотек и увеличение доступности библиотечных ресурсов потребителям библиотек. Построение системы было основано на развитии ряда под-систем, включая "работающий" в темпе поступления информаций сводный каталог и систему совместной каталогизации, контроль продолжающихся изданий, МБО и систему библиотечной обработки. Мечтою его организаторов было развитие и осуществление исчерпывающей библиотечной системы. Назначением Центра, как указано в Уставах Оформления Общества от 1967 года, являлось "основание, поддержка и управление компьютеризованным областным библиотечным центром для обслуживания академических библиотек в Огайо (штатных и частных) и проектированным так, чтобы стать частью любой государственной электронной системы для библиографической информации"

История перваго десятилетия О-СИ-Л-СИ основана на сотрудничестве. До основания Центра Огайо имело успех в сотрудничестве академических библиотек в течении целого столетия, начиная с 1867 года, то есть года основания Общества Огайо Колледжа (О-СИ-А). В течении этого промежутка времени идея сотрудничества Огайо колледжей и университетов в штатном масштабе имела большой подъём и после нескольких неудачных попыток и почти что окончательного отказа продолжать проект, Библиотечный Центр Охайо Колледжа появился на сцене государственной библиотечной информационной системы и автоматизации. За одно десятилетие он вырос и стал первой удачной государственной автоматизированной библиотечной системой в широком масштабе.

Под умелым управлением его первого административнаго директора Фредерика Г. Килгоура Центр быстро рос. С 1967 по 1968-ой год О-СИ-Л-СИ работало с бюджетом в §66.428. Десять лет спустя эта цифра дошла до §15.074.000. Из членства 54-х колледжских и университетских библиотек в Огайо в 1967 году Центр развился в общенациональную систему. В 1977 году более 2.100 библиотек в 50-ти штатах и округе

Колумбия пользовалось О-СИ-Л-СИ. Подготовлялись планы к обслуживанию иностранных библиотек. За первый год действия системы работающей в темпе поступления информаций (1971-1972) Центр произвёл более 3.4 миллионов каталожных карточек. За 1976-1977 он произвёл 60.9 миллионов. В конце первого десятилетия База Данных Центра хранила более трёх миллионов каталожных записей.

История развития О-СИ-Л-СИ с 1967 по 1977 год включала библиотекарей, библиотечных администраторов, педагогов, специалистов по компьютерной науке и праву, и руководителей в области библиотечной автоматизации и системы работающей в темпе поступления информаций. Много организаций и групп также было воткано в гобелен истории, включая Общество Огайо Колледжа, Библиотеку Конгресса, Совет Библиотечных Ресурсов (официально зарегистрированный), Министерство Народнаго Просвещения С.Ш.А., Совет Членов Правления Огайо и Фонд В.К.Келлога. Все эти внесли свой вклад в историю Центра.

Годы с 1967 по 1977 были полны лихорадочной деятельностью на различных фронтах, которые сформовали систему соответствующую нуждам потребителей. База Данных ежегодно увеличивалась в размере, так как потребители в своей ежедневной деятельности стали всё более и более зависеть от системы. Объём памяти компьютера был увеличен с эксплуатации одной машины на эксплуатацию четырёх-машинной системы при помощи вычислительных мини-машин. Исследования и усовершенствования вели к новым действиям и улучшенной эксплуатации, прокладывая путь к новым перспективам библиотечнаго обслуживания.

История О-СИ-Л-СИ яркая и преисполненная Эмоции. Тревога поднялась в 1971 году, когда возник вопрос поможет-ли Совет Членов Правления Огайо библиотекам в Огайо нести расходы по системе в начальные годы. Радость была велика, когда 26-го августа 1971 года система работающая в темпе поступления информации начала работать и Огайо университет в Афинах, Огайо - стал первой библиотекой выполняющей каталогизацию через систему О-СИ-Л-СИ. Волнение было вызвано среди членства, когда 6-го сентября 1974 года Северовосточный Университет в Бостоне закончил введение перваго миллиона записей в Базу Данных О-СИ-Л-СИ. Одно из разочарований случилось в 1974 году, когда Центр предпринял строительный прект и уже готов был его начать. Планы эти крушились так как стоимость строительства поднялась выше средств О-СИ-Л-СИ. Потребители были огорчены ухудшением Времени Ответа, которое достигло максимума в ноябре 1975 года, что и повлекло за собой мораторий по установке терминалов до тех пор, пока не будет опять достигнуто приемлемое Время Ответа.

История заканчивается драматически - созданием новой структуры управления для О-СИ-Л-СИ, обещающей новую фазу развития. Сотрудничество, пробегающее белой нитью по всей его истории, является его всеобхватывающей темой. В юном десятилетнем возрасте О-СИ-Л-СИ показало себя настоящим пионером-новатором в системе работающей в темпе поступления информаций и деятельности библиографической библиотечной информационной системы.

摘　要

　　俄亥俄大學圖書館中心，是一個經俄亥俄州特許，於一九六七年創辦的非營利社團。它的創辦宗旨，正如它的發起人所設想：以用來減低圖書館的管理費用，並增進人們對圖書資料的應用。此圖書館中心系統，是由一些補助系統的發展而形成，這些補助系統包括：電腦處理資料的聯合編目、和共享編目系統、定期刊物控制、各圖書館間的借貸、以及技術性程序的系統。當初那些設計此中心者的夢想是：要發展其為一個包羅萬象的圖書館系統。該中心成立之目的，正如它在一九六七年社團組織條款中所說：「為了建立、維持、及啓用一個電腦化的區域性圖書館中心，以便服務各俄亥俄州的公私立大學圖書館，並將其設計為全國性書目資料之電子網的一部份」。

　　該中心最初十年的歷史，全是基於「共同合作」。早在一八六七年，該中心誕生前，也即是俄亥俄大學協會成立時，俄亥俄州就享受了一百年大學圖書館合作的益處。這一百年間，俄亥俄大學間的合作構想，有擴展之形勢。人們經過數次的失敗嘗試，於幾乎放棄此計劃之際，該中心却以全國性圖書館，和自動化之形態出現。十年內，它成長為全美國第一個既成功，且大規模的電腦化圖書館系統。

　　該中心在第一任首席主管賓得瑞克起國先生的英明領導下，進步神速。它在一九六七年至一九六八年的年預算是六萬六千四百二十美元。十年後的年預算是一千五百七萬四千美元。一九六七年，它由一個擁有五十四個俄亥俄大學圖書館的會員額，而變為全國性的系統。到了一九七七年，美國的五十州和哥倫比亞特轄區內，共有兩千一百以上的圖書館，使用該中心。該中心且擬定許多計劃，要擴展其服務到外國。從一九七一年到一九七二年的第一年間，該中心因使用電腦處理資料的結果，總計印出三百多萬目錄卡片，而一九七六年至一九七七年間，所印出的目錄卡片，共有六千九十萬。十年中，該中心電腦資料的存根儲存了三百多萬的目錄。

一九七六年至一九七七年間，該中心的發展過程中，是由一些圖書館員、圖書館行政人員、教育家、電腦科學和法律專家，以及圖書館自動化及組織界的首腦人物，參加工作，還有許多組織及團體，通力促成此中心，它們包括：俄亥俄大學協會、國會圖書館、圖書館資料委員會公司、美國教育部、俄亥俄高等教育司、和克利樂基金會。它們對該中心的成立，都奉獻了一己的力量。

　　一九六七年到一九七七年間，該中心為應客戶們的需要，在電腦系統的各方面，從事多項活動，電腦資料的存根數，因為用戶們愈來愈依賴該系統的每日工作，而逐年增加。電腦能力是：自一個電腦的應用，而增至四個電腦，致以迷你電腦的運用。由於研究及發展的結果，該中心導至新功能，改進經理方式，並對圖書館服務有了新的展望。

　　論及該中心成立之經過，可謂「憂喜參半」：一九七一年，曾為了是否讓高等教育司，負擔俄亥俄各圖書館最初幾年參加此系統不足之款，遲遲未決的問題而憂慮；一九七一年八月二十六日，當電腦處理資料系統啟用之日，俄亥俄州亞丹市的俄亥俄大學，率先藉該中心，從事電腦資料處理系統編目，此舉令人不勝喜悅；一九七四年九月六日，會員中也發生了一件無比興奮的事，波士頓的東北大學，向該中心輸入了第一百萬的電腦資料存根，但同年曾發生了一件令人氣餒的事；當該中心將破土興建一座建築物之際，却因建築費用高漲，而未如願進行原有的計劃；一九七五年十一月，用戶們感到電腦系統反應時間太慢的不方便，暫緩裝置更多的電腦終端機，以期反應時間快到令人滿意為止。

　　由該中心十年來發展的情形看來，我們可以發現，它是因新管理制度的產生，導致發展的新階段，而達到戲劇性的成就，實際上這部發展史，即是「共同合作」史。這短短的十年間，該中心在電腦資料處理，及圖書目錄編製業中，成為道地的開路先鋒。

現在OCLCとして知られている機関は、1967年に「オハイオ大学図書館センター」(Ohio College Library Center) という名称でオハイオ州法による財団法人として発足した。創立者の眼目は図書館運営費を下げると同時に、図書館利用者の資料使用率を上げるという点にあった。システムはオンライン総合目録、共同目録整理作業、逐次刊行物の整理、相互貸借、並びに整理技術を含む多数のサブシステムから成立している。一大総括的な図書館組織をつくるというわけである。1967年のセンター設立條項は、「コンピューター化した地域図書館センターをつくり、それを維持し、経営することによって、オハイオ州内の公私学術図書館に奉仕し、かつ、文献情報の全国ネットワークの一部となる」とうたっている。

OCLCの初期の仕事は協力の一語につきる。オハイオ州には、1867年以来オハイオ大学協会が存在し、大学図書館間の協力体制があった。州全体の協力というアイデアは、危く放棄されかけたこともあったが、遂に実現、十年後には全国でも一の図書館システムとなった。

初代のセンター長、フレデリック・キルゴアの任期中センターは飛躍的に発展。予算は66,428弗から十年後には15,074,000弗となった。メンバーの数はオハイオ州内の54校から、1977年には全国50州にまたがる2,100館と伸び、外国への拡張も計画された。オンライン活動を始めた1971-72年度、センターは3百40万目録カードを作製、1976-77年度には6千90万と増大した。データベースの目録数は、10年間で、3百万となった。

1967年から1977年までの期間には、センターは、図書館員、図書館管理者、図書館学者、コンピューター専門家、法律家、図書館機械化とネットワーク関係の指導者などを容し、また、オハイオ大学協会、

議会図書館、図書館資料審議会、教育方、オハイオ教育理事会、ケロッグ財団などの団体やグループが多数関係するところとなった。

当初の10年間に、活動も多方面にわたり、利用者の要求に応じてシステムも発展した。また利用者の増加に伴い、データベースも年々増大、コンピューターも最初の一つから四つになり、マイクロ・コンピューターも加えられた。研究開発の結果、新分野開拓、改革が盛んに行われた。

OCLCの了史は次の様に感動にみちたものである。当初の1971年には、オハイオ州教育委員会が経費を補助するか否かでもめた。その年の8月、アテネ市のオハイオ大学がOCLCの第一の参加校としてオンライン活動を開始し、1974年の9月6日には、ボストン市のノースイースタン大学が市百万番目の目録記録を入力するという記録をつくった。反対に失望の場面もあり、その一つは、1974年にセンターの新館建築計画がコスト高のために成立しなかったことである。また反応秒数がだんだん長くなり、1975年11月にはその頂点に達して、そのために新しい端末機の配布を制限しなければならないという状態も起った。

INDEX